D0723901

Armenian Karin/Erzerum

Կարինէ

Սար օր Հայքի

պարունակատ Հայապատ

սիրբրէ

All Good Wishes,

Richard G. Hovannisian

The UCLA conference series, "Historic Armenian Cities and Provinces,"
has been organized to convey the historical, political, cultural, religious,
and economic legacy of a people rooted on the Armenian Plateau
for more than three millennia.

Also by Richard G. Hovannisian

Armenia on the Road to Independence
The Republic of Armenia (4 volumes)
The Armenian Image in History and Literature
The Armenian People from Ancient to Modern Times (2 volumes)
Enlightenment and Diaspora: The Armenian and Jewish Cases
The Armenian Genocide in Perspective
The Armenian Genocide: History, Politics, Ethics
Remembrance and Denial: The Case of the Armenian Genocide
Islam's Understanding of Itself
Ethics in Islam
Poetry and Mysticism in Islam: The Heritage of Rumi
"The Thousand and One Nights" in Arabic Literature and Society
The Persian Presence in Islam
Religion and Culture in Medieval Islam
Armenian Van/Vaspurakan
Armenian Baghesh/Bitlis and Taron/Mush
Armenian Tsopk/Kharpert
*Looking Backward, Moving Forward: Confronting
the Armenian Genocide*

UCLA ARMENIAN HISTORY AND CULTURE SERIES
Historic Armenian Cities and Provinces, 4

Armenian Karin/Erzerum

Edited by

Richard G. Hovannisian

MAZDA PUBLISHERS, Inc. ◆ Costa Mesa, California ◆ 2003

Mazda Publishers, Inc.
Academic publishers since 1980
P.O. Box 2603
Costa Mesa, California 92628 U.S.A.
www.mazdapub.com

Copyright © 2003 by Richard G. Hovannisian.
All rights reserved. No parts of this publication may be
reproduced or transmitted by any form or by any means without
written permission from the publisher except in the case of brief
quotations embodied in critical articles and reviews.

Library of Congress Cataloging-in-Publication Data

Armenian Karin/Erzerum/ edited by Richard G. Hovannisian.
p. cm.—(UCLA Armenian History and Culture Series. Historic
Armenian Cities and Provinces: 4)
Includes bibliographical references and index.
ISBN: 1-56859-151-9
(pbk., alk. paper)

1. Erzerum İli (Turkey)—History. 2. Armenians—Turkey—Erzerum İli—
History. 3. Armenians—Turkey—Karin. 4. Armenia—History
I. Hovannisian, Richard G. II. Series.
DS51.E8A76 2003
956.6'2—dc21
2003059677

CONTENTS

LIST OF MAPS AND ILLUSTRATIONS

MAPS

ILLUSTRATIONS

Sources of Illustrations*

Armenian Architecture: A Documented Photo-Archival Collection on Microfiche for the Study of Armenian Architecture. Armenian Educational Council. V.L. Parsegian, Director. Vol. 6. Zug, Switzerland: Inter Documentation Co., 1980.

Bachmann, Walter. *Kirchen und Moscheen in Armenien und Kurdistan.* Leipzig: J.C. Hinrichs, 1913.

Curzon, Robert. *Armenia: A Year at Erzeroom and on the Frontiers of Russia, Turkey, and Persia.* London: John Murray, 1854.

Edwards, Robert W. "Medieval Architecture in the Oltu-Penek Valley: A Preliminary Report on the Marchlands of Northeast Turkey," *Dumbarton Oaks Papers* 39 (Washington, DC: Dumbarton Oaks, 1985): 15-37.

Eprikian, Sukias. *Patkerazard bnashkharhik bararan.* Vol. 2. Venice: Mekhitarist Press, 1907.

Hoffmeister, Eduard von. *Durch Armenien: Eine Wanderung und der Zug Xenophons bis zum Schwarzen Meere.* Leipzig and Berlin, B.G. Teubner, 1911.

Kévorkian, Raymond H. and Paul B. Paboudjian. *Les Arméniens dans l'Empire ottoman à la veille du Génocide.* Paris: Éditions d'Art et d'Histoire ARHIS, 1992.

Kosian, Hakob. *Bardzr Hayk: Teghagrutiun, patmutiun ev sovorutiunner.* 2 vols. Vienna: Mekhitarist Press, 1925-1926.

Kotcholosian Hovannisian, Vartiter. *Dzitogh Dashti Karno.* Beirut: Hamazkayin Press, 1972.

Lynch, H.F.B. *Armenia: Travels and Studies.* Vol. 2. London and New York: Longmans, Green, and Co., 1901.

Manjikian, Hagop [Hakob] et al. *Hushamatian Hay Heghapokhakan Dashnaktsutian: Albom-Atlas.* Vol. 1. Los Angeles: ARF Western America Central Committee, 1992.

Pietschmann, Victor. *Durch kurdische Berge und armenische Städte: Tagebuch der österreichischen Armenienexpedition 1914.* Vienna: Adolf Luser Verlag, 1940.

Sinclair, T.A. *Eastern Turkey: An Architectural and Archaeological Survey.* Vol. 2. London: Pindar Press, 1989.

Tarbassian, Hratch A. *Erzurum (Garin): Its Armenian History and Traditions.* [New York]: Garin Compatriotic Union of the United States, 1975.

---

* The sources of photographs and drawings in the chapters that include illustrations are as follows (in chapter order):

Richard G. Hovannisian: Nearly all of the sources listed above.
Christina Maranci: *Armenian Architecture,* except for two taken by the author and the one of the tomb tower in Erzerum.
Rubina Peroomian: Manjikian and Tarbassian.
Pamela N. Young: Tarbassian and several supplied by the author.
Gia Aivazian: The UCLA W.L. Sachtleben Collection.
Vartiter Kotcholosian Hovannisian: Kosian, Tarbassian, and her *Dzitogh Dashti Karno.*
Isabel Kaprielian-Churchill: *Armenian Architecture.*

CONTRIBUTORS

GIA AIVAZIAN is Librarian for Armenian and Greek at the Young Research Library and a Ph.D. candidate in Armenian literature at UCLA. She has played an important role in the development of the university's extensive Armenian library collection and in the modernization of the cataloging and bibliographic control of Armenian materials. She has mounted many exhibits related to Armenian history and culture and has lectured, given conference papers, and written feature articles on Armenian literature, folklore, and women, and is preparing an annotated bibliography of Armenian folk literature. In 1991 the National Library of Armenia awarded her the Hakob Meghapart Medal for Achievement in Armenian Bibliography and Librarianship.

DAVID STEPHEN CALONNE is the author of *William Saroyan: My Real Work Is Being*, and *The Colossus of Armenia: G.I. Gurdjieff and Henry Miller*; as well as essays in scholarly and literary journals. He has taught at the University of Texas at Austin, University of Michigan-Ann Arbor, Wayne State University, and Eastern Michigan University, and has lectured in various university and community forums in the United States and in Europe.

NINA G. GARSOIAN is Professor Emerita of History and the first holder of the Gevork Avedissian Chair in Armenian History and Civilization at Columbia University. For two years, she also served as the Dean of Graduate Studies at Princeton University. She has written and translated many works on Armenian history and culture, including *The Paulician Heresy*; *Armenia between Byzantium and the Sasanians*; *Church and Culture in Early Medieval Armenia*; *The Epic Histories Attributed to P'awstos Buzand*; and *The Book of a Thousand Judgements: A Sasanian Law-Book*. She is the recipient of numerous awards and honors, including a festschrift edited by Jean-Pierre Mahé and Robert W. Thomson, *From Byzantium to Iran: Armenian Studies in Honour of Nina G. Garsoïan*.

ROBERT H. HEWSEN is Professor Emeritus of History at Rowan University, New Jersey, and has taught Armenian history at several universities in the United States and Europe. He is the co-founder of the Society for the Study of Caucasia and is a contributor to the *Journal of the Society for Armenian Studies, Revue des études arménnienes*, and other scholarly journals. A specialist in the historical geography of Armenia, he has prepared several maps for the *Tübingen Atlas of the Middle East*, translated with critical commentary the *Ashkharhatsoyts*, an early geography that he attributes to Anania of Shirak, and *Armenia: A Historical Atlas*, a major reference work.

RICHARD G. HOVANNISIAN is Holder of the Armenian Educational Foundation Chair in Modern Armenian History at UCLA and editor of this series. His publications include *Armenia on the Road to Independence*, the four-volume *Republic of Armenia*, four volumes on the Armenian Genocide, and ten other volumes and sixty research articles relating to Armenian history and culture and to Caucasian, Middle Eastern, and Islamic studies. A Guggenheim Fellow, he was elected Academician of the National Academy of Sciences of Armenia in 1990 and has been awarded honorary doctoral degrees by Erevan State University and Artsakh State University, medals by the Republic of Armenia and the Nagorno-Karabagh Republic, and encyclicals and medals by the Holy See of Echmiadzin and the Holy See of the Great House of Cilicia.

VARTITER KOTCHOLOSIAN HOVANNISIAN is an M.D. in the Department of Internal Medicine, Southern California Permanente Medical Group. She has conducted research on modern Armenian history in archives in many countries and is the author of a historical-ethnographic study and memorial volume on the one-time Armenian village of Dzitogh in the plain of Karin, *Dzitogh Dashti Karno*. She has been a health-care volunteer in Armenia since 1988 and is a contributor to the periodic press on contemporary issues relating to Armenia and the Armenian people.

ISABEL KAPRIELIAN-CHURCHILL is Professor of Modern Armenian and Immigration History at California State University, Fresno. Her work focuses on Armenian diasporan history, especially the history of Armenians in Canada and the United States, for which she has received research grants from the Heritage Canada and the Social Sciences and Humanities Research Council of Canada. Her most recent study, *Like Our Mountains: A History of Armenians in Canada*, is to be published by McGill-Queen's University Press.

DICKRAN KOUYMJIAN is Holder of the Haig and Isabel Berberian Chair in Armenian Studies and Director of the Armenian Studies Program at California State University, Fresno. He has also taught at the Haigazian College and the American University in Beirut, the American University of Cairo, and at the Institut nationale des langues et civilisations orientales in Paris. He is the author of numerous studies in Armenian history, art history, and literature, the most recent being *Album of Armenian Paleography* and an edited volume of essays on Movses Khorenatsi.

CHRISTINA MARANCI is Assistant Professor of Medieval Art at the University of Wisconsin-Milwaukee. Her research focuses on medieval Armenia and cross-cultural relations with the Byzantine, Sasanian, and Islamic worlds, as well as problems of historiography. Her book, *Medieval Armenian Architecture: Constructions of Race and Nation*, examines the role of Austrian art historian Josef Strzygowski in shaping the study of the field. In more recent publications, she has explored the cultural appropriation of Byzantine ideas into Armenian architecture and sculpture, and, in the realm of illuminated manuscripts, is pursuing a study of art and performance in the illustrated Armenian *Alexander Romance*.

ASHOT A. MELKONYAN is Director of the Institute of History of the Armenian National Academy of Sciences. He is the author of numerous studies and articles on the history and demography of Western Armenia and Javakhk (Akhalkalak) and on the Armenian Question and the Armenian Genocide. His publications include (titles translated) *Erzerum: The Armenian Population of Erzerum during the First Third of the Nineteenth Century*; *Javakhk: Historical Survey*; *History of Armenia*; *Archbishop Karapet Bagratuni*; and *Javakhk in the First Quarter of the Nineteenth Century*. He has participated in numerous international conferences and is the recipient of scholarly awards and prizes.

SIMON PAYASLIAN is Kaloosdian/Mugar Professor of Modern Armenian History and Armenian Genocide Studies at Clark University. He is the author of *The Armenian Genocide, 1915-1923: A Handbook for Students and Teachers*; *International Political Economy: Conflict and Cooperation in the Global System* (co-author), and *U.S. Foreign Economic and Military Aid: The Reagan and Bush Administrations*, as well as articles and chapters on the United Nations, international law and human rights, peace studies, the Kurdish Question, and U.S. foreign policy. He is preparing a study on U.S. policy relating to the Armenian Question and Genocide.

RUBINA PEROOMIAN is Research Associate at the University of California, Los Angeles. She has taught Armenian Studies courses at UCLA, Glendale Community College, and the University of La Verne. Her publications include *Literary Responses to Catastrophe: A Comparison of the Armenian and the Jewish Experience,* and, in the Armenian language, *Armenia in the Context of Relations between the Armenian Revolutionary Federation and the Bolsheviks, 1917-1921* (also in Russian), three secondary-school textbooks titled *The Armenian Question,* and several research articles on the Armenian Genocide and diasporan literature. She has been awarded an encyclical and medal for her educational work by the Holy See of the Great House of Cilicia.

JAMES REID is Acting Director of the Speros Basil Vryonis Center for the Study of Hellenism. He is author of *Safavid Mind, Society, and Culture,* and *Crisis of the Ottoman Empire: Prelude to Collapse, 1829-1878,* which considers the reasons for the Ottoman military collapse and emergence of a genocidal mentality among the Ottoman ruling elite. He has also published articles and chapters on the Ottoman Empire, the Armenian Genocide, Iran, and Kurdistan and is currently working on his next book *Archilocus' Shield,* based on personal narratives from the Armenian massacres of the 1890s, the Greco-Turkish war of 1897, the Macedonian conflict and Balkan wars, and World War I and the Armenian Genocide.

ROBERT W. THOMSON is Calouste Gulbenkian Professor Emeritus of Armenian Studies at Oxford University. He was the first Mashtots Professor of Armenian at Harvard University and has served as

Director of Dumbarton Oaks Research Library and Collection, Washington, D.C. His research centers on classical and medieval Armenian literature within the wider field of Eastern Christian Studies. He has edited many texts in Armenian and Syriac and has translated with introduction and commentary a number of Armenian historians, including Agatangeghos, Eghishe, Movses Khorenatsi, Sebeos, Ghazar Parpetsi, Tovma Artsruni, and Vardan Areveltsi. His latest work is a study of the Lawcode *(Datastanagirk)* of Mkhitar Gosh. In 1995 he was elected a Fellow of the British Academy.

PAMELA YOUNG is a Regional Policy Officer for the Middle East, Eastern Europe, and the Commonwealth of Independent States at Oxfam GB, a development, relief, and campaigning organization in the United Kingdom dedicated to working with others to overcome poverty and suffering throughout the world. Her dissertation is titled "Knowledge, Nation and the Curriculum: Ottoman Armenian Education, 1853-1915," and her interests include educational policy, school reform, inclusive education, and human rights.

PREFACE

Armenian Karin/Erzerum is based on the papers delivered in the fourth in the series of international conferences held at UCLA on *Historic Armenian Cities and Provinces*. The series began in the spring of 1997 with Armenian Van/Vaspurakan, followed by Baghesh/Bitlis and Taron/Mush, Tsopk/Kharpert, Karin/Erzerum, Sebastia/Sivas, Tigranakert/Diarbekir and Edessa/Urfa, Cilicia, Kars and Ani, and sequential conferences on the Armenian Communities of Constantinople, the Black Sea-Pontus Region, Smyrna/Izmir, and Caesarea/Kesaria. The proceedings of each of these conferences are being edited and published as individual volumes.

The challenge of bringing consistency in style and format to a variety of essays in different disciplines is formidable, requiring of the editor great patience and much attention to detail both in form and in content. The views expressed by the individual contributors, however, are their own.

In this series, *Historic Armenian Cities and Provinces*, a simplified system of transliteration is utilized to make the words and titles recognizable for persons who have some fluency in Armenian but who would find it difficult to comprehend scholarly scientific transliteration systems with diacritical marks (for example, *c'*, representing *ts* as in the English word "lo<u>ts</u>" or the Armenian word "ha<u>ts</u>," meaning bread). Except for chapters in which the authors have expressed a definite preference, the transliteration of the Armenian letter *vo* in the initial position is rendered as *vo* rather than *o,* thus "vordi" rather than "ordi", and the silent letter *he* in the end position is not transliterated rather than being rendered as *y*, thus "Karno" rather than "Karnoy." The drawback of this adaptation is that it does not allow for a precise conversion from the Latin alphabet back to the original Armenian script, as, for example, the transliterated character "e" may stand for any one of three Armenian letters. In the citation of works that use a scientific system and diacritical marks, however, the form as it appears on the given title page has been retained. The transliteration of identical Armenian words may vary slightly depending on the orthography used in the original. Hence, the word for "history" or "story" may appear as *patmutiun* when taken from works published in traditional Armenian orthography or as *patmutyun* when transliterated from the reformed orthography that was adopted in Soviet Armenia and used throughout the former Soviet Union.

In this modified transliteration system, Eastern Armenian phonetic values are used in the citations, but exceptions have been made in the text in the case of the more familiar Western Armenian forms of place names and personal names, as in Agn rather than Akn and Nubar rather than Nupar. Most Western Armenian forms have been retained in the chapters by Young and Kaprielian-Churchill except when the reference is to a person of Eastern Armenian origin. Turkish names and terms are usually given in the style commonly used before the Turkish alphabet reform of 1928; thus, Erzinjan rather than Erzincan and *pasha* rather than *paşa*. Foreign-language terms such as *vilayet* or *millet* are italicized only the first time they appear in any given chapter. In certain instances, the editor has not required absolute consistency when discrepancies seem to exist in the information given or data cited by different authors.

As with the foregoing volumes, Dr. Simon Payaslian and Dr. Vartiter Kotcholosian Hovannisian have collaborated closely with the editor at each stage in the painstaking process of moving the manuscript toward publication. Dr. Robert H. Hewsen drafted the maps for the volume, Miss Ani Sarkissian helped to prepare the index, and Mr. Armen Aroyan supplied the color photograph of the citadel of Erzerum on the front cover and the plain of Karin/Erzerum on the back cover. To make the descriptions in the text all the more vivid, the editor has selected a large number of related photographs. It is hoped that *Armenian Karin/Erzerum* will offer a rewarding glimpse into the history, geography, demography, economy, culture, and daily life of the strategic region of Upper Armenia—Bardzr Hayk.

❧ 1 ❧

ARMENIAN KARIN/ERZERUM
AND BARDZR HAYK/UPPER ARMENIA

Richard G. Hovannisian

Bardzr Hayk—Upper Armenia—is the heartland of the Armenian Plateau extending from the western reaches of the Euphrates River to the peaks of Artsakh/Karabagh in the east and from the Pontus Mountains in the north to the Taurus Mountains in the south. The political, military, and economic importance of Bardzr Hayk has been attested since antiquity, as possession of this vital core has been the key to dominion over the entire plateau. It is not by chance that powerful empires have vied for this coveted prize from pre-Christian times down to the twentieth century. Here, too, the Armenian nobility defended their domains and engaged in acts of extraordinary valor to resist and rebel against oppressive foreign regimes. Despite frequent warfare, invasion, and occupation, these native leaders were able to prevail for a thousand years until the fourth century A.D. when for the first time Greater Armenia (Mets Hayk) was partitioned between the Roman/Byzantine and Persian empires. Thereafter, the Armenians demonstrated their resourcefulness in the maintenance of a distinct cultural-religious identity and as much autonomy as conditions would allow. The noble *nakharar* House of the Mamikonians distinguished itself on the battlefield in challenging alien overlords against overwhelming odds, just as the House of the Bagratuni distinguished itself through its flexibility and diplomacy to win concessions from those same overlords. In the unending parade of Persian, Roman, Byzantine, Arab, Seljuk, Turkmen, Mongol, and Ottoman armies, Bardzr Hayk preserved its essentially Armenian character down to the modern era.

At the pinnacle of Bardzr Hayk lies Karin, now Erzurum, a fortress city that has been a military bastion since Roman times and, in the modern period, was the eastern bulwark of the Ottoman Empire against Persian and Russian encroachments. The citadel perched above the city was surrounded by the fortress with its double walls, between which government buildings, markets, workshops, inns, and homes were located, and outside of which were the expanding suburbs. As the most important link on the caravan route between the Black Sea and Persia, Karin became an emporium of trade and a major merchant center. Armenians predominated in the marketplace and acted both as proprietors and as agents for foreign firms. Roads radiated in all directions from the city, beginning from one of its four main gates leading southeastward toward Kars and Tabriz, northeastward toward Georgia, northwestward toward Baberd/Baiburt and Trebizond on the Black Sea, and westward toward Erznka/ Erzinjan and Constantinople/Istanbul. Karin is surrounded by mountain ranges, from where the Euphrates (Eprat), Tigris, Araxes (Eraskh), and Chorokh rivers and many large and small tributaries take their source, giving it the name "breast of the land" (*kurtske erkri*). It is a water wonderland, with invigorating air, gurgling brooks, clear, gushing streams, and treacherous currents, and many hot springs noted for their medicinal qualities. Lying just north of the city is the fertile plain of Karin (*Karno dasht*), criss-crossed by streams and tributaries of the upper arm of the Euphrates River and dotted with large and small villages. At the turn of the twentieth century, there were still nearly 50 wholly or partially Armenian-inhabited such settlements in the plain.

At more than 6,000 feet in elevation, Karin is snow-covered for nearly half the year, but the fertile soil allows for rapid growth of the wheat and assorted other grains. And as the terrain slopes downward toward Erznka in the west and toward the plains of Tortum and Sper/Ispir in the north, the climate becomes more temperate and the land gives way to colorful fields and orchards, which supply the markets of Karin with apricots, peaches, plums, cherries, mulberries, melons, and all sorts of greens. Draft animals and long- and short-horned livestock abound in the region—horses, oxen, water buffalos, mules, donkeys, cows, sheep, goats. In districts with little arable land, such as Kghi to the southwest of Karin, alpine pastures sustained large flocks, providing the Armenian villagers with most of their needs as well as wool and hides for home manufactures and for sale or exchange.

Called by the Arabs Arzan ar-Rum, from which the name Arzrum, Erzrum, or Erzerum is derived, Armenian Karin, together with the rest of Bardzr Hayk, was incorporated into the Ottoman Empire in first quarter of the sixteenth century. Governed as an enormous province or *pashalik* and then as an *eyalet*, the region was transformed into the *vilayet* of Erzerum in the administrative reforms of the nineteenth century. The vilayet, taking in most of historic Bardzr Hayk and certain peripheral territories, was divided into the *sanjak*s (counties) of Erzerum at the center, Erzinjan to the west, and Bayazit to the east. The vilayet stretched for some 300 miles, from the Euphrates River near Kemakh to the Alashkert plain and the border of the province of Kars, the latter being lost to the Russian Empire in 1878.

The great upheavals that accompanied the decline of the Ottoman Empire in the eighteenth and nineteenth centuries produced decisive changes in the demographic and socioeconomic complexion of the Turkish Armenian provinces. In Erzerum, the government's population policies, the growing insecurity of life and property, and the coerced religious conversion or flight of a sizable part of the native population all contributed to the Armenians becoming a minority both in the city and province, with the exception of certain districts such as Khnus and Kghi. Mass exodus from the city and plain of Erzerum occurred following the withdrawal of the Russian armies that had occupied the area in 1828-29 and again in 1877-78 as well as in the wake of the massacres of 1894-96. Many of the menfolk also set out as *bandukht*s, laborer-sojourners, because of the economic hardships in the countryside, seeking to save up enough money in distant cities and lands to assist their families or to return and gain their economic independence. There was widespread sojourning among the Armenian Catholic villages of the Khodorchur (Khotorjur) valley in historic Tayk to the northeast, the mountainous villages of Kghi in the southwest, and the Alashkert plain bordering upon the Russian Empire in the east. Many young men from the plain of Karin itself set out for the Caucasus and other parts of Russia to seek their fortunes or to escape from the insecure conditions

4 *Richard G. Hovannisian*

in the Ottoman Empire.

The Armenian quarters of Karin/Erzerum were concentrated in the northern part of the city at the approaches to the plain. Here were the Armenian prelacy and the Cathedral of Surb Astvatsatsin (Holy Mother of God), the highly-regarded Sana-sarian Academy, and several elementary and middle schools operated by the Armenian Apostolic Church, the smaller Armenian Catholic and Protestant communities, and foreign religious orders. Far from Western Europe and cosmopolitan Constantinople, Armenian Karin was nonetheless receptive to intellectual and political currents that were channeled through students returning from abroad and through the rising ferment in the Russian Empire. Small circles of intellectuals were drawn to the concepts of the opposition, often socialist, movements of Europe, with their emphasis on political, social, and economic reforms and human rights. One of the first clandestine groups advocating Armenian self-defense appeared in Karin. In the prevailing atmosphere of fear and fatalism, however, such groups were unable to mobilize the population at large or to prevent the approaching maelstrom from engulfing the whole of Bardzr Hayk, along with nearly all other Armenian-populated areas of the empire.

The massacres during the Hamidian regime were followed by a brief spurt of optimism prompted by the Young Turk revolution in 1908 and the restoration of the liberal constitution that Sultan Abdul-Hamid II (1876-1908/09) had suspended thirty years earlier. And in a new externally-imposed reform measure in February 1914 the Ottoman government reluctantly agreed to the reconfiguration of the six Turkish Armenian provinces and Trebizond into two extensive de facto Armenian provinces under European supervision, with Erzerum designated as the capital of one of these inspectorates. But all such optimism was dashed by the extreme wing of the Young Turk party, which seized power at the beginning of 1913 and then in the autumn of 1914 led the Ottoman Empire into World War I as an ally of Imperial Germany. That conflagration provided the opportunity to impose the death warrant on Armenian Karin and all of Bardzr Hayk. By the time the Allied Powers defeated the German and Ottoman empires at the end of 1918, Armenian Karin was no more.

5

Old Erzerum Panorma

"Erzeroom from the British Consulate," Engraving

Erzerum from the British Consulate, Photograph

Old Erzerum

City Quarter

Traditional Homes

A City Stream

The Citadel

Chifte Minare

Surb Astvatsatsin Cathedral, Drawing

Surb Astvatsatsin Cathedral

16

The Sanasarian School

Armenian Catholic Church

Armenian Catholic Prelacy

Armenian Protestant Church

Prelate Smbat Saatetian, Martyred in 1915

Catholic Bishop Hovsep Melkisetian, Deported in 1915

Bayazit

Basen (Passin)

Sper (Ispir)

Tortum: Landscape and Fortress

Khodorchur District Village and Villagers

Baiburt: Fortress and Street Scene

Terjan

Kghi

Karin and Bardzr Hayk in Perspective

Fifteen contributors to this volume provide a multidisciplinary view of Armenian Karin and Bardzr Hayk from the early Armenian dynastic periods down to the *Aghet*—The Calamity of 1915.

As in previous volumes in this series, Robert Hewsen offers a general historical overview of the region and its Armenian population in the ancient, medieval, and Ottoman periods. He notes that although Bardzr Hayk had a certain geographical unity and was included in the realms of successive Armenian dynasts, it was nonetheless made up of several distinct administrative units and was formed into a single political entity only in the fourth century A.D. Like most other authors, he ascribes the founding of the citadel-fortress of Karin to the Roman/Byzantine emperor Theodosius II in the fifth century.

Nina Garsoïan challenges the widely accepted date for the founding of Karin. She believes that the fragmentary evidence on which many scholars have credited that feat to Theodosius II is not supported by the facts. She builds a case to sustain the thesis that it was actually the emperor's grandfather, Theodosius I, who constructed the fortress, which he named Theodosiopolis in his own honor and for his glory shortly after the first partition of Greater Armenia between Persia and Rome in the latter part of the fourth century. This thesis is supported by a reexamination of Armenian, Greek, and Latin sources, some of which, it is argued, have been misleading, if not simply mistaken. A careful reading of several key passages points directly to Theodosius I.

Robert Thomson compares the ways in which Armenian writers viewed and explained the calamities that befell their people. Aristakes of Lastivert (Lastiverttsi), who bore witness to the terrible Seljuk destruction of the proud, non-walled mercantile city of Artsn in the eleventh century, followed the established tradition that ascribed such woes to God, who, as in the Bible, rained punishment on the sinful population but who was prepared to show mercy once the wayward people had repented. Matthew of Edessa (Urhayetsi), on the other hand, interprets such calamities as the inevitable fulfillment of prophecy, above and beyond individual or collective behavior. Their differing approaches aside, the medieval Armenian writers have preserved useful information about the political, military, social, and religious developments of their time.

Christina Maranci surveys the architectural heritage of the Erzerum region, particularly in the northeastern district of Tayk, where there was an active interchange between several ethno-religious groups, including Armenian monophysites, Armenian Chalcedonians (Orthodox), Byzantines, Georgians, and Seljuk Turks. After examining the style, decorations, and epigraphy of the churches of Banak, Ishkhan, Oshk, Khakhu, Varzahan, the Olan cloister near Pernek, and Seljuk tomb towers in the city of Erzerum, she concludes: "Rather than an insular and narrowly circumscribed tradition, the monuments offer a more complicated picture of Armenian architecture, in which architectural production was informed not only by internal forces but also by the process of cultural exchange."

Dickran Kouymjian measures the decline and revival of Erzerum between the sixteenth and eighteenth centuries based on the number of extant Armenian manuscripts and colophons and on Ottoman *defters* or registers of the period. Because of the incessant Ottoman-Persian warfare, Erzerum had become virtually deserted by the sixteenth century. A gradual revival began toward the end of that century and continued into the next, as evidenced by the significant growth in population and increase in the number of manuscripts produced, from only four in the sixteenth century to thirty-two in the seventeenth and forty-five in the eighteenth century. Contemporary travel accounts of both Muslim and Christian European writers give valuable, colorful descriptions of the city and its inhabitants.

Ashot Melkonyan maintains that, despite the oppressive conditions under which the Armenians had to endure from generation to generation, Bardzr Hayk retained its Armenian character until modern times. The seventeenth-century chronicler Hakob Karnetsi who traveled throughout the region attests to the beauty and wealth of the land and the preponderance of the Armenian towns and villages. The goal of successive sultans to dilute the Armenian element was gradually achieved through the movement of many Kurdish tribes from the south and the forced conversion of scores of Armenian villages in the northern districts, where the population came to be known as "kes-kes" (half and half),

Muslim yet still Armenian, or crypto-Christian. Nevertheless, even at the beginning of the nineteenth century there were nearly 400,000 Armenians living in more than 900 sites throughout the province. The massive emigration and bloodshed that ensued, however, reduced the Armenian population to barely 150,000 in fewer than 400 sites by the turn of the next century. The conclusion reached is that "Erzerum, like the rest of Western Armenia, was ethnically cleansed over a long period through the intentional policies of forced conversion, assimilation, massacre, and expulsion."

James Reid discusses the abuses, graft, and corruption within the Ottoman army in the second half of the nineteenth century, especially during the Crimean War (1853-56) and the Russo-Turkish War (1877-78). Using the accounts and memoirs of British military advisers, diplomatic agents, and correspondents, of a Maltese-Armenian family in British service, and of Turkish officials and army commanders, he links the deprivation of the men under arms with their exploitation and cruel treatment of the local population, especially the Armenian villagers. "If Ottoman generals starved, beat, and flogged Muslim soldiers and denied them the basic necessities of life and occasionally drove them into battle at the tip of their sabers, how could one expect non-Muslim peasants to receive better treatment?"

Rubina Peroomian maintains that despite the various reform edicts and promises of equality in the nineteenth century the excesses in Ottoman Armenia continued unabated, driving the population to despair. The progressive aspects of the Armenian "National Constitution," which was confirmed in 1863 by Sultan Abdul-Aziz (1861-76), had little bearing on everyday life in the Armenian provinces. The feelings of frustration and abandonment led some local Armenian intellectuals to romantic notions of popular self-defense. Karin gave birth to the earliest of clandestine circles that became precursors of Armenian political parties. But the Armenian revolutionaries faced insurmountable obstacles, including the non-preparedness of most Armenian villagers and the caution and conservatism of the urban elite. Still, their legacy and the hopes associated with their movement are preserved in the oft-sung refrain, "A Call Sounded from the Armenian Mountains of Erzerum."

Pamela Young surveys the educational scene in Armenian
Karin during the latter half of the nineteenth and first years of
the twentieth century. She shows that Karin/Erzerum was not
isolated from the intellectual currents that penetrated the Ottoman
Empire and that the interaction of Western ideas and Armenian
traditions spurred national consciousness. The spread of popular
education was evidenced through the rapid growth in the number
of schools both in the city and countryside. In Karin, aside from
the schools of the Armenian Church, the Armenian Catholic and
Protestant denominations, and the foreign missionaries, the
Sanasarian *Varzharan* or Academy functioned as an institution
of higher learning that drew students from all over Ottoman
Armenia. The curriculum, administration, and far-reaching impact
of the school are presented in the discussion.

Gia Aivazian has discovered valuable diaries and photographs
of an eyewitness to the mayhem that gripped the marketplace and
Armenian quarters of Erzerum in October 1895. Housed in
Special Collections of the UCLA Research Library, the papers
of William L. Sachtleben constitute an additional source relating
to the massacres of the Armenian population in the Ottoman
Empire in 1894-96, generally regarded as the onset of the contin-
uum that would culminate in the genocide of 1915. The questions
surrounding Sachtleben's mission in Erzerum in 1895 are
shrouded in a certain sense of mystery and pose a puzzle, which
is eventually pieced together into a fascinating picture through
careful study and comparison of the diaries and photographs in
the Sachtleben collection with unattributed reports and illustrations that appeared in the London *Times* and other journals.

Vartiter Kotcholosian Hovannisian focuses on the plain of
Karin. Using the village of Dzitogh as an example and drawing
upon the memoirs of the last generation of Armenians to be born
in the plain, she offers a glimpse of daily life: dwellings, household, social order, customs, occupations, cooperative labor, the
summer *yaila* meadowland, religious practices and pilgrimages,
and educational and political activities. She has also prepared a
composite sketch map of the villages of the plain. Each village
had a distinct character and a particular view of every other
village, as reflected in song and sayings. Dzitogh was a proud
and sometimes defiant village, putting up a successful defense

during the massacres that bloodied and darkened Karin and many of its villages in October 1895 and once again in 1904. But neither Dzitogh nor any other Armenian-inhabited city, town, or village of Erzerum province could withstand the genocidal policies of the Young Turk regime during World War I.

Isabel Kaprielian-Churchill demonstrates the importance of village associations of immigrants in assisting newcomers to adjust to life in North America and their role in supporting and sustaining schools in their home villages. Concentrating on the district of Kghi, she explains the causes of emigration and the establishment, structure, activities, and contributions of the village societies, namely those of Kghi-Kasaba, Darman (Temran), Khoups, Osnag, and Astghapert. While the sojourning bandukhts assisted one another in acclimating to their new surroundings, they clustered around their compatriotic societies to cope with their loneliness and to assist and enlighten their native villages. The result in Kghi by the early part of the twentieth century was a virtual "explosion" in schooling and literacy, which unfortunately also deepened the suspicions and antagonism of the Turkish authorities.

Simon Payaslian recounts the death of Armenian Karin. The seizure of power by the chauvinist wing of the Young Turk party and its carrying the Ottoman Empire into World War I as an ally of Germany placed the Armenians living on both sides of the Russo-Turkish border in extreme jeopardy. The posturing of the Armenian leaders failed to ameliorate the situation and when Minister of War Enver Pasha thrust an entire army into the jaws of death in blizzard conditions between Erzerum and Sarikamish, the price for his failure was to fall first and foremost on the Armenian population of the empire. In the province of Erzerum, the mass arrests and localized massacres in the spring of 1915 were followed by the organized mass deportations and killings in June and July. German and American consular officials reported that the brutal operations were clearly intended to achieve the "complete extermination" of the Armenian people. By the time that the Russian army occupied Erzerum in February 1916, the Armenians from Bayazit and Alashkert in the east to Erzinjan and Kemakh in the west and from Sper and Khodorchur in the north to Khnus and Kghi in the south had vanished.

Richard Hovannisian reviews the contest for Erzerum between 1914 and 1921. The Russian military occupation of the region in 1916 and the liberal policies of the Russian Provisional Government after the "democratic" revolution in March 1917 evoked renewed hope among Armenian refugees and political leaders alike. But the Bolshevik revolution in November 1917, which initiated the Russian civil war and accelerated the abandonment of the Caucasus front, soon resulted in Turkish recapture of Erzerum and invasion of the Russian Armenian provinces. The Allied victory over the Ottoman Empire in October 1918 presented the possibility for the small Armenian republic that had been formed around Erevan in Russian Armenia in May 1918 to expand westward into Erzerum and the other Turkish Armenian provinces. This study assesses the postwar policies and actions of the Allied Powers, the United States of America, the Armenian government and delegation at the Paris Peace Conference, the sultan's government in Constantinople, the opposition Turkish Nationalist movement in Anatolia, and Soviet Russia. For all parties concerned, possession of Erzerum was regarded as the key to security and success.

David Calonne focuses on the place of Erzerum in the works of American-Armenian writer William Saroyan. Although Saroyan's family originated in Bitlis, it had stayed in Erzerum for a time while en route to the United States. Saroyan often invokes the name of Erzerum in his short stories, novels, plays, and autobiographical pieces. He is enthusiastic about Erzerum, which appears in various forms and contexts. The Pulitzer Prize winner was increasingly drawn to his roots in Bitlis, Erzerum, and other cities of historic Armenia, which he visited in 1964 while he was in his fifties and when few other Armenians had ventured back to the lost ancestral lands. Lively excerpts of his monologues and dialogues are included to show how William Saroyan related to Erzerum.

The chapters that follow offer a multidisciplinary collage of the history and culture of Upper Armenia—the bosom of Greater Armenia. It is hoped that this volume will provide the reader with a deeper understanding and appreciation of the unbroken Armenian presence in Karin-Bardzr Hayk down through the ages until that defining moment when everything suddenly stopped.

❁ 2 ❁

SUMMIT OF THE EARTH:
THE HISTORICAL GEOGRAPHY OF BARDZR HAYK

Robert H. Hewsen

The northwestern part of Greater Armenia was historically known as Bardzr Hayk (Upper Armenia) or as Karin Ashkharh (Country of Karin). The area consists of a series of well-defined plains extending from east to west, bounded by the Pontus Mountains on the north and the Central Armenian Mountains on the south. It is watered by the upper arm of the Euphrates (Eprat) River, now the Kara Su, whose source is only a few miles northeast of the city of Erzerum. The Upper Euphrates flows westward through several plains and the narrow gorges that separate them before turning southward to join its lower arm, the Aratsani or Murat Su, in the region of Kharpert and on to Mesopotamia and the Persian Gulf. The Araxes River, too, begins near Erzerum and flows eastward several hundred miles to the Caspian Sea. Ancient historians and geographers called this region of Bardzr Hayk, with its broad meadows and well-watered pasture lands, the "bosom of the earth."[1]

Although this part of Armenia, the later Erzerum *vilayet*—has a definite geographic unity and was possibly the location of a proto-Armenian principality of a group known as the Hayasa, its firm political unity is not attested by any source prior to the end of the fourth century A.D. when it became identified as Upper

---

[1] Hratch A. Tarbassian, *Erzurum (Garin): Its Armenian History and Traditions*, trans. Nigol Schahgaldian ([New York]: Garin Compatriotic Union of the United States, 1975), p. 14.

Armenia.[2] All together, medieval Upper Armenia covered some 23,860 square kilometers (slightly more than 9,200 square miles).[3] In the late Ottoman period during the 1870s, much of Upper Armenia was incorporated in the large vilayet of Erzerum. In 1890, Vital Cuinet showed the land usage of the vilayet to be as follows: arable, 25,500 square kilometers (9,840 square miles); orchards, vineyards, gardens, 15,860 square kilometers (6,120 square miles); forests, pasture lands, and mountains, 35,360 square kilometers (13,650 square miles). The plains were noted for their hot springs, twenty-seven of which were being exploited for their saltwater at the end of the nineteenth century. The entire province was rich in livestock, and some tobacco was grown in the *sanjak*s (counties) of Erzerum and Erzinjan.[4] The high elevation makes the climate severe, with the temperature in December averaging 8 to 35 degrees Fahrenheit (or -13 to 2 centigrade). Blizzards are frequent, and snow lies on the ground for some five months of the year.

Ancient Karin

In the 380s A.D., sovereignty over Armenia was disputed between two brothers, Arshak and Khosrov, both of the Arshakuni/Arsacid royal house. The dispute was taken advantage of by Emperor Theodosius I of Rome and his counterpart, Shah Shapur III of Sasanid Persia, to arrange the partition of Armenia between the two princes in 387. One brother became King Arshak III in Western Armenia under Roman tutelage, and the other became King Khosrov IV in the east under Persian overlordship. The partition was uneven, as Arshak's kingdom consisted only of the northwestern sector of the country, with the lion's share

---

[2] Suren T. Eremyan, *Hayastane est "Ashkharhatsoyts"-i* [Armenia According to the "Ashkharhatsoyts"] (Erevan: Armenian Academy of Sciences, 1963), p. 116.

[3] Nicholas[Nikoghayos] Adontz, *Armeniia v epokhu Iustiniana* (St. Petersburg, 1908), trans. and comm. Nina G. Garsoïan, *Armenia in the Period of Justinian* (Lisbon: Calouste Gulbenkian Foundation, 1970), pp. 39-53, citations hereafter are to the English translation.

[4] Vital Cuinet, *La Turquie d'Asie: Géographie administrative, statistique, descriptive et raisonnée de chaque province de l'Asie-Mineure*, vol. 2 (Paris: E. Leroux, 1892), p. 133.

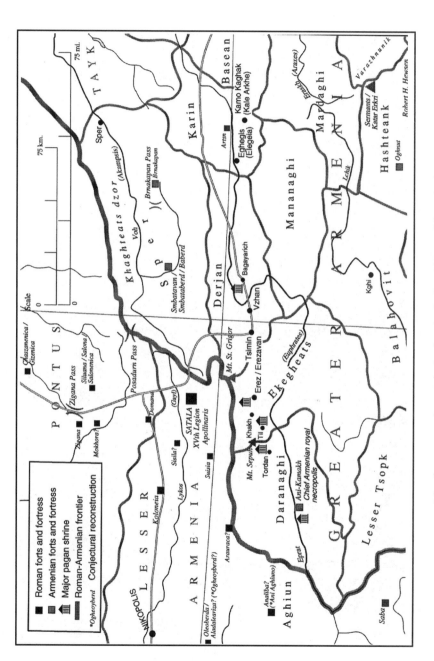

Northwestern Armenia in the Arshakuni/Arsacid Period

going to Khosrov.[5]

Arshak died in 390, and, whether he had heirs or not, the Romans simply annexed his kingdom and turned it into a province. It was the kingdom of Arshak III and its succeeding Roman/Byzantine province that gave the first prolonged unity to this region. Until the reign of Arshak, this part of Armenia consisted of nine districts grouped into six political units: one royal land, one principality, three temple-states, and one district owned by the Romans which had been a part of Lesser Armenia. These six political units were as follows:[6]

1. The royal land of Karin (Greek: Karinitis).[7] This district was distinguished by its great swamp, the habitat of countless birds, as well as by its numerous mineral springs, especially the one at Eghegis, where the Roman emperor Trajan held his durbar after invading Armenia in 115 and where he announced his short-lived annexation of Armenia as a Roman province. Also lying in the Karin royal land was the town of Artsn, famed as a mercantile center in the Middle Ages and destroyed by the Seljuk Turks in 1049. Adjoining Karin on the northeast was the small and seldom mentioned district of Shataghagomk (Shatagh Stables) or Shaghgomk, which was probably a division of Karin itself and whose name suggests a possible connection with the Sala or Salua people of the pre-Armenian period.[8]

[5] Pavstos Buzandatsi, *Patmutiun Hayots* [History of Armenia], 4th ed. (Venice: Mekhitarist Press, 1933), trans. and comm. Nina G. Garsoïan, *The Epic Histories Attributed to P'awstos Buzand (Buzandaran Patmut'iwnk')* (Cambridge, MA: Harvard University Press, 1989), VI.1, pp. 233-34; Cyril Toumanoff, *Studies in Christian Caucasian History* (Washington, DC: Georgetown University Press, 1963), pp. 151, 363.

[6] Adontz, *Armenia*, pp. 39-53; Eremyan, *Hayastane*, p. 116; Robert H. Hewsen, *The Geography of Ananias of Širak (Ašxarhac'oyc'): The Long and Short Recensions* (Wiesbaden: Ludwig Reichert, 1992), pp. 59-59a, 150-53.

[7] Toumanoff, *Christian Caucasian History*, pp. 212, 215; Igor M. Diakonoff, *The Pre-History of the Armenian People*, trans. Lori Jennings (Delmar, NY: Caravan Books, 1984). Movses Khorenatsi, *Patmutiun Hayots*, trans. and comm. Robert W. Thomson, as Moses of Khoren, *History of the Armenians* (Cambridge, MA: Harvard University Press, 1978), p. 142, says of Slak, the ancestor of the Sghnuni (Sała) clan, that it is not certain "whether he descended from Hayk or from those who were in the country before him," thus indicating a certain foreignness about the family that suggested to Khorenatsi a pre-Armenian origin.

[8] Thomas A. Sinclair, *Eastern Turkey: An Architectural and Archaeological*

2. Northwest of Karin lay the principality of Sper (Greek and Roman: Sysperitis).⁹ This was an ancestral domain of the illustrious Bagratuni clan, who expanded to control most of Armenia and who around 885 A.D. restored the Armenian monarchy, dormant since the fifth century. The home base of the Bagratunis was the fortress of Smbatavan or Smbataberd, which may be the present town of Baiburt (Armenian: Baberd or Papert), located on the Chorokh River and still noted for its large castle. Alternatively, the Bagratuni center may have been at Sper, which had its own castle and nearby gold mines that were famed as early as the first century B.C.¹⁰ In the northern part of this principality was the land of a non-Armenian people called the Khaldians, the memory of whom was preserved in the alternative name for the valley of Sper: Khaghto Dzor (Khaldian Valley).¹¹

3. South of Sper and west of Karin was the temple-state of Derjan (Greek: Derxene), centered at the village of Bagayarich, where the great Temple of Mihr, one of the most important shrines of pagan Armenia, was located.¹² The shrine was situated along the main road through northern Armenia and was well known to the Romans, who called it the Temple of Baris or Lucus Basaro (Grove of Basarus),¹³ an indication that the temple

Survey, vol. 2 (London: Pindar Press, 1989), p. 217.

⁹ Strabo, *Geography* (Loeb Classical Library), 11.14.9 and 11.14.12; Eremyan, *Hayastane*, p. 81; Hewsen, *Geography of Ananias*, p. 152n10.

¹⁰ Toumanoff, *Christian Caucasian History*, p. 202; idem, "Armenia and Georgia," in *The Cambridge Medieval History*, vol. 4, pt. 1: *The Byzantine Empire: Byzantium and Its Neighbors* (Cambridge: Cambridge University Press, 1966), pp. 612ff; Strabo, *Geography*, 11.14. 9.

¹¹ Eremyan, *Hayastane*, p. 55.

¹² Adontz, *Armenia*, p. 43; Eremyan, *Hayastane*, pp. 49, 116; Hewsen, *Geography of Ananias*, p. 152n9. Strabo, *Geography*, 11.14.5, has Xerxene for Derxene. A temple-state usually was a large autonomous district that belonged entirely to a major pagan shrine. Besides great holdings in land, the shrine owned all the villages in its territory, with thousands of peasants and vast herds of horses, cattle, sheep, and goats. The temple was protected by its own military force and was staffed by a host of priests and priestesses, musicians, singers and dancers of both sexes, and a corps of sacred prostitutes. The crowds of pilgrims that flocked to the temple at the festival of its patron deity added greatly to the income of the temple-state, which must have been a dynamic and influential participant in the life of the kingdom.

¹³ Adontz, *Armenia*, p. 132*, Peutinger Table XCV. Strabo, *Geography*, 1.14.14, states that the temple lay along the road to Ecbatana. This road through northern

contained a grove of sacred trees, the rustling of whose leaves would have been used in divination as they were at a similar grove at the Temple of the Sun and the Moon at Armavir.[14] There were other places of note in this temple state: Vzhan (Greek: Sana; Bazanis or Bizana), which in the time of the emperor Leo (457-74) was renamed Leontopolis, and Derjan (Terjan), which in Ottoman times became Mamakhatun. South of Derjan and Karin spread the valley of Mananaghi.[15] As the district did not have a prince, it could have belonged either to Karin or to the Derjan temple state, from which it was more accessible.

4. To the west of Derjan lay the clearly defined plain of Ekegheats (Greek and Roman: Akilisene), sometimes called the Anaitis district or Anaetica. This was the territory of the temple state of the goddess Anahit, the "Golden Mother" of pagan Armenia, another shrine well-known to the Romans.[16] It was centered at the town of Erez or Erezavan, later known as Erznka (Erzinga; Turkish: Erzinjan/Erzincan). Within walking distance of Erez and still within Ekegheats was a secondary shrine, the temple of the goddess Nana at the village of Til. Farther away in the mountains and less accessible was the temple of the god Barshamina at the village of Tordan, where a Christian church was later erected and where King Trdat/Tiridates, the first Christian king of Armenia, and his queen, Ashkhen, were buried.[17] There were other notable places in Ekegheats, including the town of Tsimin (Greek: Tsumina), which the emperor Justinian had

---

Armenia to Media would certainly have passed through Derjan, where the temple of Bagayarich was located.

[14] James R. Russell, *Zoroastrianism in Armenia* (Cambridge, MA: Harvard University Press, 1987), p. 52.

[15] Adontz, *Armenia*, pp. 39-42, 116-17; Eremyan, *Hayastane*, pp. 64-65; Hewsen, *Geography of Ananias*, p. 152n8.

[16] Adontz, *Armenia*, pp. 40-42, 200-02; Eremyan, *Hayastane*, 50; Hewsen, *Geography of Ananias*, p. 152n7; Pliny (the Elder), *Natural History* (Loeb Classical Library), V.24.20. Strabo, *Geography*, 11.14.16, gives a description of the cult of Anaitis.

[17] Russell, *Zoroastrianism*, pp. 174, 235-53, 339. When I visited Tordan in 1999, the village headman pointed to a table-like stone structure in a corner of the ruined church and said: "A king and queen are buried there."

renamed Justinianopolis.[18] Near Erznka was the royal village of Hakh, where King Pap (367-74) had a palace and where he is said to have had the supreme patriarch, Catholicos Nerses the Great (353-73), poisoned.[19]

5. East of Ekegheats was the valley of Daranaghi, which comprised the temple state of Ani-Kamakh with its shrine to the god Aramazd.[20] This temple was of special significance to the Armenians, for here at the fortified center of Kamakh, also known as Ani, lay the tombs of the Armenian kings, a most curious fact given that the kings ruled from their capitals far to the east and that when they died their bodies would have to have been transported by caisson, dragged along rough, unpaved roads over mountains and plains to reach the final resting place. This fact may be posed as evidence that the first Armenian kingdom came into being in this part of Armenia and that Ani-Kamakh, a most ancient site, may have been the original Armenian capital.

Daranaghi was unknown to Greek and Roman authors, and it is conceivable that this entire complex of four temples, Erez, Til, Tordan, and Ani-Kamakh, all belonged to the one temple-state centered at the shrine of Anahit at Erez and that Daranaghi was originally a division of Ekegheats. The origin of these five Armenian deities with major shrines in Upper Armenia highlights the diversity and eclecticism of Armenian paganism: Aramazd, Mihr, and Anahit were of Persian origin; Nana was the Sumerian and Babylonian moon-goddess Inanna; and Barshamina, the Babylonian sun-god Ba'al Shamash (Lord-God the Sun).[21] South of Ekegheats and Daranaghi stretched the mountainous district of Mzur or Mndzur, a remote, little known part of Armenia, now the region of Dersim, which did not have a princely family and therefore probably belonged to either Ekegheats or Daranaghi.[22]

6. Finally, to the west of Daranaghi, at the point where the Upper Euphrates turns sharply southward lay the little valley

---

[18] Adontz, *Armenia*, pp. 116-17.

[19] Pavstos Buzand, *Hayots Patmutiun*, V.xxiv, pp. 203-05.

[20] On Aramazd, see Russell, *Zoroastrianism*, pp. 153-75.

[21] Ibid., pp. 27, 171, 174, 339.

[22] Adontz, *Armenia*, pp. 39-40; Eremyan, *Hayastane*, p. 72; Hewsen, *Geography of Ananias*, p. 152n6.

of Aghiun[23] or Ariuts. It appears to have belonged directly to the Roman Empire, for the Greek geographer Ptolemy, writing in the mid-second century A.D., mentions a district in Lesser Armenia called Aitoulane,[24] which, given the similarity between the letters *lambda* and *tau* in Greek script, may well be an error for Ailouane, that is, the district of Aghiun. That this district belonged to Rome is demonstrated by the fact that its chief fortress, variously called Analiba,[25] Analibla,[26] and Analibna,[27] was located on the Roman side of the frontier. The Soviet Armenian scholar Stepan Eremyan cleverly interpreted this place-name to be a Greek rendering of the Armenian Ani-Aghiuno or Ani of Aghiun, probably so called to distinguish it from Ani in Daranaghi, a short distance to the east.[28] The importance and longevity of this fortress—it stood for hundreds of years—would have been due precisely to its having been erected on the frontier between the kingdom of Armenia and the Roman/Byzantine Empire.

These districts combined formed the kingdom of Arshak III. There seems to have been no prior lasting unification of these lands. Once annexed by the Romans in 390, however, the territory was organized as a proper province, and a fortress was built to protect it from Persian aggression.[29] The fortress was Theodosiopolis, named in honor of Emperor Theodosius II (408-50), who is generally thought to have founded the stronghold in connection with Byzantine-Persian conflicts of 421-22 or 441.[30] To the Armenians, this fortress-city would be known either as Teodupaulis[31] or Karno Kaghak (City of Karin), from which the

---

[23] Adontz, *Armenia*, pp. 47-48; Eremyan, *Hayastane*, p. 33; Hewsen, *Geography of Ananias*, pp. 252-53n5.

[24] Claudius Ptolemy, *Geography*, trans. Edward L. Stevenson (New York: New York Public Library, 1932; repr., 1991), V.12 and map 3 (Asia tabula tertia).

[25] Adontz, *Armenia*, p. 129*, Peutinger Table XCVII.

[26] Catholic Church, Councils, *Sacrorum Conciliorum Nova et Amplissima Collectio*, ed. Giovan Domenico Mansi et al., 54 vols. (Florence-Venice: A Zatta, 1759-1798; new ed., Paris: H. Welter, 1901-1927), vol. 11, p. 645.

[27] Ptolemy, *Geography*, 5.6.20.

[28] Eremyan, *Hayastane*, p. 33.

[29] Hewsen, *Geography of Ananias*, p. 150.

[30] Adontz, *Armenia*, pp. 14-15, 19-22, 115-24. For a differing view regarding the founding of Theodosiopolis, see the chapter in this volume by Nina G. Garsoïan.

[31] Moses of Khoren, *History*, III.59, pp. 331-32.

Arabs would call it Kalikala.[32] Earlier, the site had been that of a mere village whose name was rendered in Greek as Kale Arkhe. From the time of its founding, Karin-Theodosiopolis-Arzrum-Erzerum, located on the most practicable road from Asia Minor to Persia, became the largest city in western Armenia and remains so to the present, now in eastern Turkey. The fortress was restored and strengthened by the emperor Anastasius (491-518), who attempted unsuccessfully to replace the name of Theodosius with his own. Later, Emperor Justinian I (527-65) also took pains to restore the fortress, demonstrating once more its importance to the imperial defenses in the east.[33]

As a province, the former kingdom of Arshak III was originally named Armenia Interior or Inner Armenia, probably because its territory lay within the traditional area of the kingdom of Armenia, but in the time of Justinian it was enlarged by additional territories and renamed Greater Armenia,[34] as if to suggest that by possessing this territory the Roman/Byzantine Empire owned the whole country. In the seventh-century Armenian geographical text known as the *Ashkharhatsoyts*, this unified territory is called Bardzr Hayk, and there is no question that for the author the word *bardzr* means "high." This name was given to the region, he explains, because of its high elevation. In Classical Armenian *bardzr* does, of course, mean "high," but it also has a secondary meaning of "great."[35] Thus, while Bardzr Hayk does mean Upper Armenia, it conceivably might also mean Greater Armenia and simply be a translation of *Armenia Magna* or *Armenia Maior,* the Roman/Byzantine name for the region.[36]

---

[32] Hakob A. Manandian, *The Trade and Cities of Armenia in Relation to Ancient World Trade*, trans. Nina G. Garsoïan (Lisbon: Calouste Gulbenkian Foundation, 1965), p. 133.

[33] Procopius, *Buildings*, III.v.3-12.

[34] Adontz, *Armenia*, p. 39.

[35] See Gabriel Avetikian, Khachatur Siurmelian, and Mkrtich Avgerian, *Nor bargirk haykazian lezvi* [New Dictionary of the Armenian Language], 2 vols. (Venice: Mekhitarist Press, 1836-1837; new ed., Erevan: Erevan State University, 1979-1981), vol. 1, p. 462, where the word is glossed as Greek "hypselos" and Latin, "altus, elatus, excelsus, sublimes." Matthias Bedrossian [Matatia Petrosian], *New Dictionary, Armenian-English* (Beirut: Librairie du Liban, 1985), p. 96, offers "eminent" and "great" as secondary meanings of the classical word.

[36] Adontz, *Armenia*, p. 39.

The reason that the Armenians called the Byzantine province Bardzr Hayk rather than Mets Hayk may be easy to explain. Mets Hayk or Greater Armenia meant the entire territory of the old Armenian kingdom. If Bardzr Hayk also meant Greater Armenia even if only in the lesser, Byzantine sense, the use of the synonym *bardzr* for *mets* would have avoided confusion between the two areas, one the land of Greater Armenia, long a major kingdom in Western Asia, and the other, the short-lived Byzantine province of the same name. Later, as a result of the reforms of the emperor Maurice (591 A.D. or shortly thereafter), the Byzantine province was reorganized and called Second Armenia, a name retained until the Arab invasions a half century later.[37]

Medieval Karin

The history of this part of Armenia, like that of the rest of the country, was turbulent. With the fall of the Persian Sasanian Empire to the Arab armies in the 640s, the fortress-city of Theodosiopolis/Kalikala became a major bastion between the Byzantine and Arab empires. The city was often taken and destroyed. The Arabs initially captured Theodosiopolis in 653, the Byzantines regained it in 686, the Arabs again in 700, the Byzantines in 754, the Arabs briefly yet again, and finally the Byzantines in 949-79, when the fortress became the capital of the new Byzantine theme (military province) of Theodosiopolis. Briefly held by the Tayk branch of the Bagratuni dynasty, it was reacquired by Byzantium in 1000 and refortified in 1018-19.

Later, after the Seljuk destruction of the nearby unwalled city of Artsn in 1049 and the flight of its surviving population to Theodosiopolis, the latter city came to be called Arzan ar-Rum—Arzan of the Romans—probably to distinguish it from Arzan, another important city with a similar name in southern

[37] For Maurice's changes, see George of Cyprus, *Descripto orbis Romani*, ed. Heinrich Gelzer (Leipzig: Teubner, 1890), pp. 174-75; Joseph Laurent, *L'Arménie entre Byzance et l'Islam depuis la conquête arabe jusqu'en 886* (Paris: Fontemoing, 1919; new ed., Lisbon: Librairie Bertrand, 1980), p. 304; Paul Goubert, *Byzance avant l'Islam* (Paris: A. et J. Picard, 1951), pp. 290-301. For the local history of Theodosiopolis/Erzerum, see Sinclair, *Eastern Turkey*, chapter 5, pp. 185-292.

43

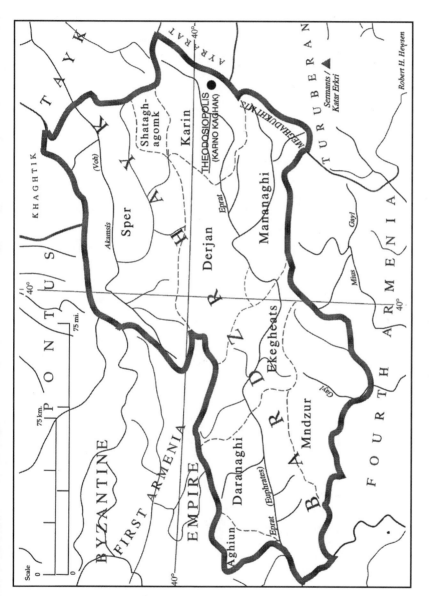

Bardzr Hayk (Upper Armenia) According to the *Ashkharhatsoyts*

Armenia.[38] It is from the Arabic Arzan ar-Rum that the name Erzerum has evolved.

With the coming of the Seljuk Turks, who captured the city in 1080, most of Upper Armenia passed to vassal Turkmen emirs (Saltukids), who remained in control until ousted by the Seljuk sultan in around 1202. The western part of Upper Armenia was ruled by another vassal Turkmen dynasty, the Mangujakids, who eventually set up separate emirates at Erzinjan, Divrig, and Shabin-Karahisar. Overrun by the Mongols in the thirteenth century, Upper Armenia remained part of the Mongol Ilkhanid successor state until its disintegration in the fourteenth century. In about 1374 much of Upper Armenia passed to the Kara Koyunlu (Black Sheep) Turkmen clans and then in 1468 to their rivals of the Ak Koyunlu (White Sheep) federation. Turkmen rule was briefly interrupted by the invasions and occupation of Timur (Tamerlane) and his heirs between 1397 and 1408. Later fought over by the Safavid Persians and the Ottoman Turks, the Erzerum region passed to the Ottomans during the reign of Sultan Selim (1512-20). When Sultan Suleiman marched through the area on a campaign in 1534, he made most of western Armenia into the large *pashalik* or military governorship of Erzerum. It was at this time that the fortress city was rebuilt as the administrative center and a great military base, which it has remained ever since. Despite the Turkish occupation of the major towns and cities of Upper Armenia, the countryside continued to be preponderantly Armenian until the early nineteenth century.[39]

Ottoman Erzerum

For a long time, Upper Armenia formed part of the large Erzerum pashalik under its *beylerbey*. A fascinating picture of the pashalik is provided by the Armenian cleric Hakob Karnetsi, who has left a detailed description of the military province as it

---

[38] Laurent, *L'Arménie entre Byzance et l'Islam*, pp. 87-88n83.
[39] Sinclair, *Eastern Turkey*, pp. 281-91; *Encyclopaedia of Islam*, new ed., vol. 8 (Leiden: Brill, 1998), p. 1001, s.v. "Saltuk Oghulları"; John E. Woods, *The Aqquyunlu: Clan, Confederation, Empire* (Salt Lake City: University of Utah Press, 1999).

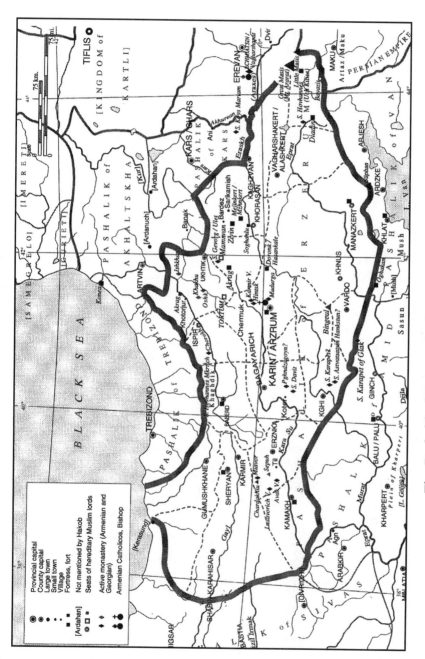

The *Pashalik* of Erzerum in the Seventeenth Century

was in the seventeenth century, when its population was still overwhelmingly Armenian.[40] Lying as it did along the much-traveled caravan route between Tabriz and Trebizond and on the main roads eastward to Kars and westward to Erzinjan, the city of Erzerum frequently appeared in the travel accounts of merchants, ambassadors, and explorers who passed that way. In 1865 the eastern pashaliks of the Ottoman Empire were grouped into one large *eyalet* (governor-generalship). Ten years later, however, this unwieldy administrative unit was broken up into the six vilayets (civil provinces) of Erzerum, Van, Hakkari, Bitlis, Khozat (Dersim), and Kars-Childir—the last being lost to the Russians in 1878 and Khozat being attached to the vilayet of Mamuret ul-Aziz (Kharpert) in 1888.[41] The only important change made in the administration of the Erzerum vilayet was the reduction of the *sanjak* of Baiburt to a *kaza* (district) of the Erzinjan sanjak in 1888. Other minor changes included the transfer of the kazas of Shiran and Kelkit in the Erzerum sanjak to the Trebizond vilayet that same year, and the transfer of the the kaza of Kuzijan (Khuzuchan) from Mamuret ul-Aziz to Erzerum in 1892-93. These civil provinces were retained until after World War I when the Kemalist government broke the vilayets into smaller, more manageable units called *ils*, usually based on the former sanjaks.

The vilayet of Erzerum encompassed an area of some 76,720 square kilometers (29,920 square miles) and was divided into three sanjaks and nineteen kazas: Erzerum sanjak with the kazas of Erzerum, Ova, Kghi, Terjan, Khnus, Tortum, Keskin, and Passin (Basen); Erzinjan sanjak with the kazas of Erzinjan, Refayie (Refayet), Kuruchai, Kemakh, Baiburt, and Ispir (Sper); and Bayazit (Bayazed) sanjak with the kazas of Bayazit, Diadin, Karakilise, Alashkert (Alashgerd), and Antab. The kazas of the province were subdivided into more than 150 village clusters or cantons known as *nahiyes*. Because of these administrative divisions, there was virtually no town that was not an administrative

---

[40] Hakovb Karnetsi [Jacob of Karin] "Erzeroum ou topographie de la Haute Arménie," trans. F. Macler, *Journal Asiatique* (March-April 1919): 153-237.

[41] Mesrob K. Krikorian, *Armenians in the Service of the Ottoman Empire, 1860-1908* (London: Routledge and Kegan Paul, 1977), p. 39.

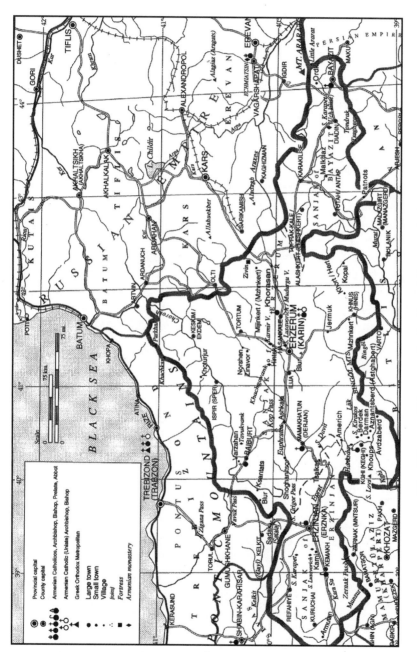

The *Vilayet* of Erzerum in the Late Nineteenth Century

center of one kind or another.[42] The Erzerum vilayet, together
with the remaining five Armenian vilayets, was defended by the
IV Army Corps, headquartered at Erzinjan and composed of some
36,000 troops of all services, with the Eighth Infantry Division
posted at Erzerum. The troops were supplemented by a regiment
of four gendarme battalions numbering about 1,200 men, slightly
more than half of whom were mounted.[43]

Under Ottoman rule, Erzerum long flourished as the most
important way station for traders transporting goods between
Persia and Constantinople via the Black Sea and as a bastion of
Ottoman defenses in the east. As a result of the shift in trade
routes brought about by the Age of Exploration, however, the
city began to decline. Taken by the Russians in 1829 and 1878,
Erzerum was returned each time to the Ottomans, prompting
large numbers of Armenians to abandon the city and surrounding
villages to follow the tsarist armies into the Russian Empire.
Thus, even today the Erzerum dialect is widely spoken in the
northernmost districts of the Armenian republic as well as in the
Akhalkalak (Javakheti; Javakhk) and Akhaltskha (Akhaltsikh)
districts of southern Georgia.[44]

Population

As with most of the other vilayets of the Ottoman Empire, population statistics for Erzerum are contradictory, both in sheer

---

[42] Cuinet, *La Turquie d'Asie*, pp. 132-34, 138; Krikorian, *Armenians*, p. 40;
T.Kh. Hakobyan, St.T. Melik-Bakhshyan, H.Kh. Barseghyan, *Hayastani ev harakits
shrjanneri teghanunneri bararan* [Toponymical Dictionary of Armenia and
Neighboring Regions], 5 vols. (Erevan: Erevan State University, 1986-2001), vol.
2, pp. 365-67. Raymond H. Kévorkian and Paul B. Papoudjian, *Les Arméniens dans
l'Empire ottoman à la veille du Génocide* (Paris: Editions d'Art et et d'Histoire
ARHIS, 1992), pp. 417, 452, 457, maps, shows more than 375 villages in the
Erzerum vilayet inhabited entirely or partly by Armenians. See also Sukias Eprikian,
Patkerazard bnashkharhik bararan [Illustrated Topographical Dictionary], 2 vols.
(Venice: Mekhitarist Press, 1902-1907), vol. 2, pp. 299-325.
[43] Cuinet, *La Turquie d'Asie*, p. 136.
[44] Tarbassian, *Erzurum*, pp. 68-69, 226; Hakob Adjarian, *Classification des
dialects arméniens* (Paris: H. Champion, 1909), pp. 44-47. According to Tarbassian,
14,000 Armenians who left Erzerum in 1829 settled in the Akhalkalak and
Akhaltsikh districts.

numbers and in the relative proportions of the several ethno-religious groups. Ormanian's figures appear moderate and reasonable, although this does not necessarily make them precise. McCarthy's figures, while "corrected" to compensate for the undercounting of women, do not appear to be corrected enough. The following statistics are those found in the major sources:

Vital Cuinet (circa 1890)[45]

Muslim	500,782
Armenian Apostolic	120,273
Armenian Catholic	12,022
Armenian Protestant	2,672
Greek Orthodox	3,725
Yabanji [Aliens]	4,986
Ejnebi [Foreigners]	1,220
Copt	16
Jew	6
TOTAL	645,702

Maghakia Ormanian
(Armenians in Eight Dioceses of Erzerum Vilayet, 1910)[46]

Armenian Apostolic	190,000
Armenian Catholic	9,500
Armenian Protestant	3,900
TOTAL	203,400

Armenian Patriarchate (1912)[47]

Armenian	215,000
Zaza and Other	30,000
Turk	240,000

---

[45] Cuinet, *La Turquie d'Asie*, pp. 137-38. The Armenian Patriarchate's statistics for 1882 show 280,000 Armenians in the province of Erzerum. See Patriarcat de Constantinople, *Population arménienne de la Turquie avant la guerre: Statistiques établies par le Patriarcat Arménien de Constantinople* (Paris: H. Turabian, 1920), Annex A, p. 9, and *Réponse au mémoire de la Sublime-Porte en date du 12 février 1919* (Constantinople, 1919), Annex C, p. 43.

[46] Malachia [Maghakia] Ormanian, *The Church of Armenia* (London: Mowbray, 1910; New York: St. Vartan Press, 1955), Appendix II, pp. 205-06.

[47] *Population arménienne de la Turquie avant la guerre*, Annex B, p. 10.

Kizilbash (Shiite Muslim)	25,000
Nomadic Kurd	40,000
Sedentary Kurd	35,000
Persian	13,000
Laz	10,000
Circassian	7,000
Greek and Other Christian	12,000
Yezidi	3,000
TOTAL	630,000

Ottoman Census (1914)[48]

Muslim	673,297
Armenian Apostolic	125,657
Armenian Catholic	8,720
Greek Orthodox	4,859
Greek Catholic	5
Protestant	2,241
Roman Catholic (Latin)	1
Syrian Orthodox	88
Chaldean (Assyrian Catholic)	13
Yezidi	618
Jew	10
Gypsy	29
TOTAL	815,432

Justin McCarthy (for 1911-12)[49]

Muslim	804,388
Syrian Nestorian and Chaldean	121
Armenian	163,218
Jew	10
Greek	5,811
Other	648
TOTAL	974,196

---

[48] Kemal H. Karpat, *Ottoman Population, 1830-1914: Demographic and Social Characteristics* (Madison: University of Wisconsin Press, 1985), pp. 188-89.

[49] Justin McCarthy, *Muslims and Minorities: The Population of Ottoman Anatolia and the End of the Empire* (New York: New York University Press, 1983), pp. 53-58.

Large numbers of Kurds were still tribal-based confederations, of which two were semi-autonomous. They had settled in the province, along with Greeks and Persians, who were found only in the towns. According to McCarthy, the annual birthrate for the vilayet of Erzerum was 49 per thousand, the death rate 35 per thousand, the net gain being 14 per thousand per year, about average for Anatolia. Life expectancy at birth was estimated at thirty years. The population density for the vilayet of Erzerum is given as about 18 per square kilometer, and the proportion of Armenians to the total population is placed at 16.75 percent.[50] McCarthy's figures for the Armenian population, as well as its proportion of the total, appear to be underestimated.

Ecclesiastical Organization

An archbishop resided in Karin/Erzerum since its foundation, and there were bishops at Erzinjan, Baiburt, Hasankale, and Bayazit and prelates at Kghi and Kemakh. The vilayet was divided into eight dioceses of the Armenian Apostolic Church, with an archbishop residing in the provincial capital. The archdiocese of Karin or Garin had 90 parishes, 89 churches, and about 75,000 adherents. There were bishops at Erzinjan (Erznka/Erzinga), with 37 parishes, 44 churches, 25,000 adherents; Baiburt (Baberd), with 30 parishes, 31 churches, 17,000 adherents; Terjan (Derjan), 38 parishes, 33 churches, 15,000 adherents; Hasankale (Basen), 30 parishes, 19 churches, 10,000 adherents; and Bayazit (Bagrevand), 50 parishes, 33 churches, 14,000 adherents; and Kghi (Khortsian), 56 parishes, 51 churches, 24,000 adherents. An abbot served as prelate at Kemakh (Kamakh), 19 parishes, 21 churches, 10,000 adherents.[51]

Based on Ormanian's figures, it is clear that many Armenian parishes, probably consisting of isolated villages, were without churches and perhaps even without priests. The diocese of Erzerum was an important one, and its acquisition could lead to further advancement. Three patriarchs of Constantinople—Harutiun Vehapetian (1874-84), Maghakia Ormanian (1896-1908),

---

[50] Ibid., pp. 41, 43.
[51] Ormanian, *Church of Armenia*, Appendix II, pp. 205-06.

and Zaven Ter-Eghiayan (Der Yeghiayan, 1913-22)—had previously served as prelate of Karin. Despite Karin's prestige as a diocese, the Apostolic Armenians possessed only one church in Erzerum itself, the Cathedral of Surb Astvatsatsin, constructed in 1838, along with a small but very old chapel said to have been built in 629. In addition, there were a number of smaller shrines in the city: Surb Toros, Surb Sahak and Surb Hovsep, Surb Minas, Surb Varvara, Surb Nshan, Surb Pargevatu, and Nahatakats Tapan.[52]

Jesuit missionaries had been active in Erzerum from 1685,[53] and from 1815 to 1915 the city was the seat of an Armenian Catholic archbishop (reduced to a bishop in 1890) whose jurisdiction encompassed the entire province. According to Bishop Jean (Hovhannes) Naslian, this was the most important and best organized Roman Catholic diocese in Armenia. The chief Catholic communities were to be found in the thirteen exclusively Armenian Catholic villages in the Khodorchur (Khotorjur) valley: Khodorchur, Kerman, Sunints, Keghud, Areki, Gakhmekhud, Veri-Moghrgoyd, Vari-Moghrgoyd, Garmerik, Kisag, Jijabagh, Khentadzor, and Veri-Khentadzor.[54] The Armenian Catholics had a single church in Erzerum, also called Surb Astvatsatsin. Erected in 1840 and serving as their cathedral, it was located in the so-called Frank Quarter, where the small European and American communities resided.[55] There was also a small but very beautiful Orthodox church, the seat of a Greek metropolitan. The American Board of Commissioners for Foreign Missions had established a mission station in Erzerum as early as 1839.[56] By 1847 it had a fine, American-style Protestant church equipped with an elaborate wooden bell-tower.

---

[52] Tarbassian, *Erzurum*, pp. 35-36, 39-41.

[53] Charles A. Frazee, *Catholics and Sultans: The Church and the Ottoman Empire, 1453-1923* (London and New York: Cambridge University Press, 1983), p. 180.

[54] Jean Naslian, *Les mémoires de Mgr. Jean Naslian, Évêque de Trébizonde*, 2 vols. (Vienna: Mekhitarist Press, 1951), vol. 1, p. 147.

[55] Tarbassian, *Erzurum*, p. 36.

[56] Ibid., pp. 37-38; H.F.B. Lynch, *Armenia: Travels and Studies*, vol. 2 (London and New York: Longmans, Green, 1901), p. 217.

The City of Karin

Karin or Erzerum lay in a fertile plain surrounded by high mountains at an elevation of more than 2,000 meters or 6,500 feet and covering about 10 square kilometers (4 square miles). Divided into numerous quarters, it had more than 7,200 houses in the latter part of the nineteenth century.[57] Ottoman from the sixteenth century, Erzerum was not only the vilayet capital but also the center of the entire defensive system protecting the eastern provinces from a Russian invasion and hence shielding much of Asiatic Turkey. Despite its strength, however, the city fell to the Russians in 1829, 1878, and again in 1916—an indication of how enervated the Ottoman Empire had become.[58] Erzerum was also the main intermediary point along the Black Sea to Persia route (Trebizond to Tabriz) established by the Genoese in the Mongol period. As late as the 1890s, some 30,000 to 40,000 camels laden with goods still passed through the city in large caravans, about two-thirds of the trade being of English manufacture. A British commercial agent was in residence in the city by 1690, and steamers began carrying this trade on the Black Sea in 1836, replacing the sailing vessels of old. The trade with Persia accounted for the relatively large number of Persians residing in Erzerum, where until the latter part of the nineteenth century they had their own quarter. The principal industries in the city were the manufacture of arms and armaments and the tanning of hides.

The population of Karin varied greatly in the nineteenth century, due largely to the emigration of more than 10,000 Armenians when the Russian army departed in 1829. It is reported that only 120 Armenian families—1,000 to 2,000 persons—remained in Erzerum thereafter. The Armenians gradually became a minority both in the city and in the province. The total population of the city in 1835 was estimated at 15,000, whereas by 1890 it had grown to about 40,000, not counting the military garrison of 5,000 to 6,000 men. Described by Lynch as a somber, unattrac-

---

[57] Cuinet, *La Turquie d'Asie*, p. 183.

[58] Sinclair, *Eastern Turkey*, pp. 187, 192; Richard G. Hovannisian, *Armenia on the Road to Independence, 1918* (Berkeley and Los Angeles: University of California Press, 1967), pp. 64-66; Naslian, *Les mémoires*, pp. 160-61.

tive place with solidly built stone houses with few trees, Erzerum has the advantage of being extremely well watered. The walls, built by the Romans when they founded the city, were torn down in the mid-nineteenth century, and new ones, fronted with ditches and pierced by four main gates, were erected between 1855 and 1877. These ramparts embraced an area of 7.75 square kilometers or 3 square miles, but the town itself occupied only a third of this area.[59]

The location of Erzerum close to the main Anatolian fault line resulted in its being struck by severe earthquakes, explaining why so few monuments of earlier eras survive. An earthquake in 1859 destroyed or damaged some 4,500 houses, toppled nine minarets, and seriously damaged much of the earlier walls.[60] The city, however, still contained many mosques, including the Ulu Jami or Great Mosque, probably a former church, the Chifte Minare, located in a central court close to the fortress, and the Lala Pasha Mosque, as well as the palace of the *vali* or civil governor and that of the military governor.

The Armenian schools of Karin included, above all, the Sanasarian *Varzharan* or Academy, equipped with a library and a museum. Founded in 1881 by an Armenian philanthropist, it was essentially a teacher-training institution. In addition, there were six boys' schools and one girls' school operated by the Armenian Church, one Catholic school staffed by four French priests, a "collège" (more of a preparatory school) of the Armenian Catholic Mekhitarist order of Venice, a girls' school of the Armenian Sisters of the Immaculate Conception, and one boys' school and one girls' school maintained by the Protestant community. The Kavafian school established in 1905 broke with tradition by teaching elementary grades with boys and girls under the same roof. The Muslims had numerous religious schools (*medreses*) but only one modern school—though a good one—located in a new building which served as both high school (*rushdiye*) and lycée (*idadiye*), the only such Muslim institution in the province. There were also fifteen monasteries (*tekkes*) of Muslim dervish orders, thirteen inns (*khans*), 225 fountains, and

[59] Lynch, *Armenia*, pp. 206-10.
[60] Ibid., pp. 210-11.

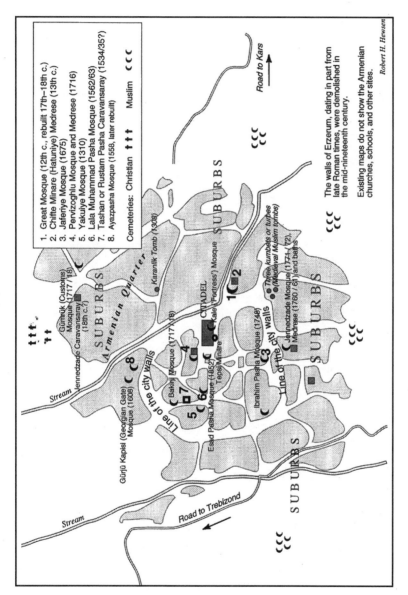

The City of Erzerum in the Late Nineteenth Century

Inset legend:

1. Great Mosque (12th c., rebuilt 17th–18th c.)
2. Chifte Minare (Hatuniye) Medrese (13th c.)
3. Jaferiye Mosque (1675)
4. Pervizoghlu Mosque and Medrese (1716)
5. Yakuîye Mosque (1310)
6. Lala Muhammad Pasha Mosque (1562/63)
7. Tashan or Rustam Pasha Caravansaray (1534/35?)
8. Ayazpasha Mosque (1558, later rebuilt)

Cemeteries: Christian ✝ ✝ ✝   Muslim ☾ ☾ ☾

The walls of Erzerum, dating in part from late Roman times, were demolished in the mid-nineteenth century.

Existing maps do not show the Armenian churches, schools, and other sites.

Robert H. Hewsen

Road to Kars

Road to Trebizond

Stream

Stream

SUBURBS

Armenian Quarter

Karanlîk Tomb (1308)

Gümrük (Customs) Mosque (1717/18)
Mennedzade Caravansaray (18th c.?)

CITADEL
(Kale, 'Fortress') Mosque

Three kumbets or turbes (Medieval Muslim tombs)

Jennedzade Mosque (1724/?), Medrese (1760/6?) and baths

Line of the city walls

Esad Pasha Mosque
Tepsi Minare

Bakirji Mosque (1717/18)

Ibrahim Pasha Mosque (1748)

Gürjü Kapisi (Georgian Gate) Mosque (1608)

a small public garden. As the largest city in the eastern provinces, Erzerum was the residence of British, French, German,
Persian, and Russian consuls or diplomatic agents.[61]

After the Young Turk revolution in 1908, Armenians were
freer to develop their culture with less interference from the
authorities, and the city began to progress. The first regular local
Armenian newspaper, *Harach* [Forward], was published that year,
the first cinema opened, and dramatic performances by touring
companies from Constantinople and Transcaucasia became common. The choral masters Armenak Shahmuratian and Grigor
Siuni formed choruses on their visits, and musical groups were
organized, especially the military band of the Sanasarian school
and the string orchestra of the Armenian Catholic lycée.[62] Notable descendants of Armenian Karin who contributed immeas-
urably to the intellectual and academic life of Tiflis and Erevan
include the renowned historian Hakob Manandian, philologists
Stepan Malkhasiants, Manuk Abeghian, and Hovhannes Ghana-
lanian, geologist Hovhannes Ter-Karapetian, and actors Arus
Voskanian, Ruzanna Vardanian, and Vanik Vardanian. Among
the native heroes of the Armenian resistance movement were
Khachatur Kerektsian, Ashot Tatul, Armen Garo (Garegin Pasdermajian), Keri (Arshak Gavafian), Garegin Karnetsi (Ghroyan),
and Aram Erkanian.[63]

Towns

Erzinjan (Erznka)

Erzinjan (now Erzincan), located about 175 kilometers (120
miles) west of Erzerum, was the second largest city in the
vilayet, with a population in 1914 of some 25,000, of whom
about half were Armenian. The city was surrounded by numerous
villages, of which about 30 were entirely or partly Armenian
(among them Akhorjiugh, Degeneg, Ergan, Garmri, Gharadigin,

[61] Tarbassian, *Erzurum*, pp. 99-114; Lynch, *Armenia*, pp. 213-18; Cuinet, *La Turquie d'Asie*, pp. 184-85.
[62] Tarbassian, *Erzurum*, pp. 83-87, 228-29.
[63] Ibid., pp. 167-80.

Giulija, Harabedi, Hromakrag, Khndzorig, Mahmudtsig, Megh-
utsig, Merteghi, Metsakrag, Mtnni, Ptarij, Srbihan, Veri-Chiftlik,
and Vari-Chiftlik) with some 40 churches, and about 60 such
villages in the sanjak as a whole. The total population of the
Armenian villages was some 45,000 people or an average of
slightly more than 700 inhabitants per village. Erzinjan was an
important center of trade and was noted for its textiles and dried
fruit. It was also the base for a large, permanent military garrison.[64]

Baiburt (Baberd/Papert)

According to Henry Tozer, Baiburt was a relatively small place,
with about 2,000 households, of which 300 were Christian. It was
nonetheless an important commercial center on the main road
from Erzerum to Trebizond, renowned for the fine quality of its
fruit, vegetables, and grain. There were silver mines in its vicinity, and its hilltop was still crowned by a long, rambling fortress.
On the road to Trebizond at the village of Varzahan were the
ruins of three magnificent medieval Armenian churches that were
vandalized by the Kurds in the nineteenth century.[65] In the kaza
there were 29 partially or wholly Armenian-inhabited villages
with about 40 Armenian Apostolic churches and several monasteries.[66]

Hinis (Khnus) and Kghi (Keghi)

The town of Hinis (Armenian: Khnis or Khnus), capital of the
kaza of that name, lay in the center of a broad, fertile, well-
watered plain, which had once formed the ancient principality of

---

[64] Tarbassian, *Erzurum*, p. 30; Cuinet, *La Turquie d'Asie*, pp. 211-13; Eprikian, *Bnashkharhik bararan*, vol. 1, p. 632. For details, see the memorial volume of Galust Siurmenian, *Erznka* (Cairo: Sahak-Mesrop, 1947).

[65] See also Henry Fanshawe Tozer, *Turkish Armenia and Eastern Asia Minor* (London: Longmans, Green, 1881), pp. 423-27; Cuinet, *La Turquie d'Asie*, p. 151; Eprikian, *Bnashkharhik bararan*, vol. 1, pp. 337-38; Naslian, *Les mémoires*, p. 163. For details on the Baiburt district, see Sargis Voskerchyan, *Mer Bayburde* [Our Baiburt] (Erevan: Haypethrat, 1956).

[66] Kévorkian and Papoudjian, *Les Arméniens dans l'Empire ottoman*, pp. 439-42.

Varazhnunik and was noted for its fine wheat, barley, and pasturage and for its excellent butter and cheese. Eprikian cited 24 Christian or predominantly Christian villages in the kaza, which had 15 churches and 7 mosques.[67]

Located in a seemingly remote valley, the town of Kghi was connected by a trade route linking Erzerum with Mush, Bitlis, and Kharpert. Because of close contact with the American mission station at Kharpert, it possessed its own schools and many of its inhabitants eventually made their way to America. The narrow valley in which the town was set and its thick forests made the area unsuitable for agriculture, but the local people managed to develop a large export of medicinal herbs, fruit, charcoal, and cattle. The district was heavily Christian, the kaza having 38 churches and 17 mosques. Here, near Astghberd (Astghapert), were located the Monastery of Surb Kirakos and one of several mountains in Armenia called Surb Loys (Holy Light).[68]

The Rural Areas

In the vicinity of Erzerum were large tracts of marshland along the uppermost reaches of the Euphrates, known in ancient times as Tsovn Karno (Sea of Karin), and in later periods as Lake Shamik or Shamp to the Armenians and as Saz or Sazlek to the Turks. Here an extraordinary variety of wading birds—some say as many as 170 species (storks, cranes, herons, egrets, ibises, and so forth)—were to be observed, the birds being hunted for food and their eggs forming an important element in the local diet.[69] In the 1890s, however, the depredations of the Kurds had created a state of lawlessness and insecurity that was making rural life impossible even for the Muslim villagers, while the Christians were departing in large numbers every year. By 1909, there were fewer than 50 Armenian-inhabited villages remaining in the kaza

---

[67] Eprikian, *Bnashkharhik bararan*, vol. 2, pp. 185-86; Tarbassian, *Erzurum*, p. 27.

[68] Tarbassian, *Erzurum*, pp. 28-29; Eprikian, *Bnashkharhik bararan*, vol. 2, pp. 355-63.

[69] Lynch, *Armenia*, p. 209; Tarbassian, *Erzurum*, p. 24.

of Erzerum. Some 32 monasteries still functioned—however feebly—in the vilayet at the turn of the twentieth century. Among these, three of the most important were in the immediate vicinity of the provincial capital:

1. Surb Lusavorich (Holy Enlightener) was about one and a half hour's walk from the city at the village of Mudurga. Built like a fortress, it was a pilgrimage site and possessed considerable lands and great herds of cattle and flocks of sheep.

2. Khachkavank (Monastery of the Cross) was located at Khachkavank village about 5 miles north of the city. Said to date from 639, it was surrounded by massive walls.

3. Karmir Vank (Red Monastery), known in Western Armenian pronunciation as Garmra Surp Asdvadzadzna Vank (Red Monastery of the Holy Mother of God) was located near the village of Hintsk (Hindzk) about five hours' walk from the city. The monastery church, destroyed in an earthquake in 1770 and rebuilt in 1800, was an especially magnificent structure. It was a popular pilgrimage site and a great resort for Armenians escaping the summer heat. The monastery was a center of education and maintained its own orphanage, hospital, and leprosarium.[70]

There were also several monasteries still functioning near Erzinjan and in the surrounding mountains: Surb Lusavorich, Avag Vank, Til, and Tordan. The most important monastery in the vilayet, however, was that of Surb Hovhannes Mkrtich (Saint John the Baptist), far to the east near Bayazit. Known to the Muslims as Uch Kilise (Three Churches), this monastery marked the spot on the Aratsani (Lower Euphrates) River where Saint Gregory had baptized the royal family and court at the time of the conversion of Armenia to Christianity in the early fourth century.[71]

Karin during the Genocide

As the largest city in Turkish Armenia, Erzerum became a focal point of resistance activity after the failure of the sultan to fulfill his pledges to implement reforms to safeguard the lives and

---

[70] Tarbassian, *Erzurum*, pp. 42-46.

[71] Robert H. Hewsen, *Armenia: A Historical Atlas* (Chicago: University of Chicago Press, 2001), map 165; Tozer, *Turkish Armenia*, pp. 392-94.

properties of the Armenian population. Bloody repressions began in 1890, and in 1895 the province was subjected to the same atrocities that befell all the rest of Turkish Armenia. The massacres and plunder began at Trebizond on October 8, reached Erzinjan on October 21 (260 killed in the town and some 850 in the surrounding villages), the Baiburt villages and then the town itself starting on October 27, and Erzerum on October 30 (several hundred slain and the bazaar completely sacked).[72]

In the Genocide of 1915, the entire Armenian population of the vilayet of Erzerum—Apostolic, Catholic, and Protestant—was deported, the men slain and the women and children sent on to die en route to the Syrian desert. Convoys left from Erzinjan, Kghi, and Baiburt at about the same time. On May 19 the Armenians of Khnus were deported and soon after massacred. In May and June, the Armenian villages in the Erzerum plain were cleared, with few of the deportees even getting beyond Kemakh. The city dwellers were sent off in several convoys between June 16 and July 28, when Bishop Smbat Saatetian left the city, only to be murdered near Erzinjan. In Baiburt, Bishop Anania Hazarapetian was hanged. The German consul at Erzerum, seeing what was happening, informed his ambassador in Constantinople but was instructed to stay out of Ottoman internal affairs. The Ottoman governor directing these deportations was Tahsin Bey, who had formerly been governor of Van and who was noted for his devotion to the Young Turk leadership in Constantinople.[73] When the Russian army occupied Erzerum on February 16, 1916, after the Turks had plundered and abandoned the city, scarcely a hundred Armenians were found alive out of an Armenian population of some 20,000. It is estimated that as much as 90 percent of the Armenian population of the province perished.

---

[72] Christopher J. Walker, *Armenia: The Survival of a Nation* (London: Croom, Helm, 1980), pp. 156-59.

[73] On the deportations and massacres in Erzerum, see Great Britain, Parliament, *The Treatment of Armenians in the Ottoman Empire, 1915-16: Documents Presented to Viscount Grey of Fallodon by Viscount Bryce*, Miscellaneous no. 31, 1916, comp. and ed. Arnold J. Toynbee (London: Sir Joseph Causton and Sons, 1916), pp. 221-56; Tarbassian, *Erzurum*, pp. 231-44; Walker, *Armenia*, pp. 214-15; Naslian, *Les mémoires*, pp. 148-69. See also the chapter by Simon Payaslian in this volume.

Erzerum Today

The vilayet of Erzerum, though occasionally altered in size by the addition or subtraction of one district or another, generally corresponded to the historic Armenian land of Bardzr Hayk. During the Kemalist period after the establishment of the Republic of Turkey, the province was broken down into smaller administrative units called *il*s. Upper Armenia as a unit of any kind thus no longer exists. The city of Erzerum remains a major military center, and with about a quarter of a million inhabitants is one of the few cities in eastern Anatolia where the Turkish element is preponderant. The railroad reached Erzerum in 1939, bus lines connect it to other towns and cities in all directions, industrial enterprises have been established, and there are now several good hotels. Atatürk University was founded there in 1950. Erzinjan, destroyed yet again by earthquake in 1939, has been moved to a new site off the Anatolian fault and is now a modern town of broad, regular streets and wide plazas.

Having visited this part of historic Armenia in 1998 and again the following year, I was struck by the extraordinary beauty of its landscape. Though for some reason, Erzerum itself has tended to impress travelers in a negative way since at least the nineteenth century and the city has often been described as harsh and unattractive, the region in which it is located is wonderful to view. Bounded by mountains on the north and south which repeatedly close in to separate one level expanse from another, its natural division into several plains is easily seen. The broad, shallow waters of the Euphrates surge westwards through colorful canyons and pasture lands, and, at the end of the day, seem to lead one directly toward the sunset. Everywhere, this Bosom of the Earth, this Upper Armenia, continually impresses one with its unforgettable grandeur.

❋ 3 ❋

THE FOUNDATION OF
THEODOSIOPOLIS—KARIN

Nina G. Garsoïan

The importance of the great Byzantine fortress of Theodosiopolis (Armenian: Karin; now Erzurum) has never been questioned. Refortified by the emperor Justinian in the sixth century, it was to be for centuries the northern anchor point of the imperial defenses in the east and the seat of its chief military official, the *magister militum per Armeniam, Pontem Polemoniacum et Gentes*, whose authority stretched from the Pontic lands bordering the Black Sea to the southern semi-autonomous Satrapies lying along the eastern Euphrates or Arsanias River (Armenian: Aratsani; now Murat Su).[1] The outstanding strategic position of Theodosiopolis was maintained after its capture by the Arabs in the seventh century, as the conquerors turned it against its Byzantine former masters, while preserving its essentially military rather than urban character. Thereafter, Theodosiopolis was to be one of the main points of contention between the empire and the caliphate, briefly captured and destroyed by the emperor Constantine V in 751-52, rebuilt by the Muslims, yet once again retaken by Byzantium in the tenth century and held by the empire, despite continuous warfare and its grant for his lifetime to

---

[1] The creation of the office of *magister militum per Armeniam, Pontem Polemoniacum et Gentes* by Justinian is recorded in *Codex Justinianus,* I.xxix.5, in his *Corpus Juris Civitis,* vol. 2. Procopius calls the *magister militum* "the general of the two Armenias." See Procopius, *Buildings,* III.v.12, in *Works* (Loeb Classical Library), ed. and trans. H.B. Dewing and Glanville Downey, 7 vols. (Cambridge, MA: Harvard University Press, and London: William Heinemann, 1914-1940), vol. 7, p. 204/05.

the Bagratid prince David of Tayk/Tao, until its sack by the Seljuk Turks in 1083.[2] But if there is a consensus among the contemporary sources, and consequently among modern historians, as to the continuous military importance of Theodosiopolis, the same cannot be said for the date of its foundation, either by the emperor Theodosius I the Great, late in the fourth century, or by his grandson Theodosius II the Younger, in the first half of the fifth century. The disagreements can be traced back directly to the contradictions and lack of precision in most of the sources.

As far as can be judged from the scant information that has survived, the district of Karin (*gavarn Karnoy*) had probably achieved the status of a royal domain before the end of the fourth century under the Armenian Arshakuni/Arsacid kings, since the court transferred there for the pompous celebration of the marriage of the two young sons of King Pap after their father's death:

> The *sparapet* and commander-in-chief Manuēl went with the Aršakuni queen and her two children, Aršak [Arshak] and Vałaršak [Vagharshak], to the district of Karin, together with the entire Armenian army, the highest nobility and the *naxarar*s and all the *tanuter*s went with them. The *sparapet* Manuēl gave his daughter Vandanduxt in marriage to the young Aršak Aršakuni and thus made him his son-in-law. He also arranged a marriage for his brother Vałaršak, giving him and the daughter to the Bagratuni *aspet* from the district of Sper. . . . The marriages were celebrated with great splendor, and the entire land of Armenia rejoiced, jubilated and was transported with joy.[3]

Despite the importance of the region, no city seems, however, to have existed there at the time. The earliest relevant source, the fifth-century *Buzandaran Patmutiunk*, which is well informed as

---

[2] *The Cambridge Medieval History*, vol. 4: *The Byzantine Empire*, 2d ed., ed. Joan M. Hussey (Cambridge: Cambridge University Press, 1966), pp. 74, 703.

[3] Pavstos Biuzandatsi, *Patmutiun Hayots* [History of Armenia], 4th ed. (Venice: Mekhitarist Press, 1933), V.xliv, p. 258, cited hereafter as BP = *The Epic Histories Attributed to P'awstos Buzand (Buzandaran Patmut'iwnk')*, ed. and comm. Nina G. Garsoïan (Cambridge, MA: Harvard University Press, 1989), p. 228, cited hereafter as BP–G.

to the situation in the fourth century, refers to Karin as a "district" (*gavar*) or a plain" (*dasht*) but never as a "city" (*kaghak*).[4] Similarly, a near contemporary, Ghazar (Łazar) Parpetsi, speaks of the "lake" or "sea" of Karin (*Tsovn Karnoy*).[5] In a passage describing the origin of Bishop Khad, parallel to that of the *Buzandaran*, Movses Khorenatsi gives it as being "from the meadows of Karin" (*i margats Karnoy*).[6] Even the seventh-century Armenian Geography, known as the *Ashkharhatsoyts*, which combines several periods in its presentation of an idealized Armenia, still hesitates in its identification of Karin. It begins with the statement: "Greater Armenia has fifteen districts [*gavars*] around it: first the country [*ashkharh*] of Upper Armenia, that is, the city [*kaghak*] of Karin." But it then goes on to recall that "the country of Upper Armenia has nine districts," which were Daranaghi, Aghiun, Mzur, Ekegheats, Mananaghi, Derjan, Sper, Shaghgomk (Shatgom), and Karin. None of these can be identified in any sense as a "city."[7]

The most that can be gathered from the sources is that a village, usually nameless but called "Fair Beginning" (*Kale Arkhe*) by the seventh-century Armenian Chalcedonian work, *Narratio de rebus Armeniae* (of which only a Greek translation has survived), had existed in the region.[8] The association of this

---

[4] BP, IV.xii; V.xxxvii, pp. 114, 245 = BP-G, pp. 134, 219.

[5] Ghazar Parpetsi, *Patmutiun Hayots*, ed. Galust Ter-Mkrtchian and Stepan Malkhasiants (Tiflis: Or. N. Aghanian, 1904), II.lxxxi, p.148, cited hereafter GhP = *The History of Łazar Pʿarpecʿi*, trans. and comm. Robert W. Thomson (Atlanta: Scholars Press, 1991), p. 207, cited hereafter as ŁP-T.

[6] Movses Khorenatsi, *Patmutiun Hayots*, ed. Manuk Abeghian and Set Harutiunian (Tiflis: Mnatsakan Martirosiants, 1913; repr. with additional collations by Ashot B. Sargsyan, Erevan: Armenian Academy of Sciences, 1991), III.xx, p. 279, cited hereafter as MKh = Moses Khorenatsʿi, *History of the Armenians*, trans. and comm. Robert W. Thomson (Cambridge, MA, and London: Harvard University Press, 1978), p. 274 and n6, cited hereafter as MKh-T.

[7] *Géographie de [Ps.] Moïse de Corène*, trans. Arsène Soukry (Venice: Mekhitarist Press, 1881), pp. 29/39-40 = Robert H. Hewsen, *The Geography of Ananias of Širak (Ašxarhacʿoyc')* (Wiesbaden: Reichert, 1992), pp. 59-59A, 150-53. The minor discrepancy between the long and short recensions of the *Geography* does not bear on the status of Karin as a "district."

[8] Gérard Garitte, *La Narratio de rebus Armeniae* (Louvain: L. Durbecq, 1952), p. 27, cited hereafter as *Narratio* = "La Narratio de rebus Armeniae," trans. Jean-Pierre Mahé, *Revue des études arméniennes*, n.s., 25 (1994-95): 430, cited hereafter

village with a church dedicated to the Mother of God by Saint Bartholomew is late and dubious,[9] but there is little reason to question its location on the site of the later Karin-Theodosiopolis, as the accounts referring to it mention the presence there of springs of "pleasant waters,"[10] whose existence near the site of the city of Karin is well known to later Armenian sources.[11] The association of the early village with these springs provides additional proof of its location at the site of the later city and not, as has occasionally been suggested without supporting evidence, at the Arsacid necropolis of Ani-Kamakh.[12] That site had been totally destroyed by the Persians in the 360s, so that the royal tombs had to be moved to the village of Aghtsk, in the district of Aragatsotn.[13] Ani-Kamakh lay well to the west of Theodosiopolis, which the Greek historian Procopius placed hard by the boundaries of Persarmenia after the fourth-century partition of Greater Armenia.[14]

Thus, up to the end of the fourth century the district of Karin

---

as "Narratio"-Mahé.

[9] On the "Letter to Sahak Arcruni [Artsruni]" attributed to Movses Khorenatsi and the tradition of the mission to Armenia of Saint Bartholomew, see *Narratio*, pp. 66-67, and Michel Van Esbroeck, "La naissance du culte de saint Barthélémy en Arménie," *Revue des études arméniennes,* n.s., 17 (1983): 171-95. However, the presence of a church dedicated to the Mother of God is attested by both Procopius, *Buildings,* III.iv.12, pp.198/99, and the *Narratio* §6-7, p. 27 = "Narratio"-Mahé, p. 430.

[10] *Narratio* § 9, p. 27 = "Narratio"-Mahé, p. 430; MKh, III.Iix, p. 339 = MKh-T, p. 332.

[11] See Sebeos, *Patmutiun Sebeosi* [The History of Sebeos], ed. Gevorg V. Abgaryan (Erevan: Armenian Academy of Sciences, 1979), xvii, p. 89 = *Histoire d'Héraclius, par l'évêque Sébeos,* trans. Frédéric Macler (Paris: Imp. Nationale; E. Leroux, 1904), vii, p. 33, and Stephen of Taron (Asoghik), *Patmutiun tiezerakan* [Universal History], 2d ed. (St. Petersburg, 1885), II.i, pp. 71-72, where, however, he is repeating the account of Movses Khorenatsi (see the preceding note) = *Histoire universelle par Etienne Açoch'ig de Daron,* pt. 1, trans. Édouard Dulaurier (Paris: Leroux, 1883), p. 105. Cf. *Narratio,* pp. 69-70.

[12] William M. Ramsay, *The Historical Geography of Asia Minor* (London: John Murray, 1890), pp. 305, 326, 448; A.H.M. Jones, *The Cities of the Eastern Roman Provinces,* 2d ed. (Oxford: Clarendon Press, 1971), pp. 224-25, 445n15.

[13] BP, IV.xxiv, pp. 150-51= BP-G, pp. 157-58, and on Aghtsk and Ani, pp. 437, 442.

[14] Procopius, *The Persian War,* I.x.18, in *Works,* vol.1, pp. 82/83; idem, vol. 7, *Buildings,* III.i.1, pp. 178/79.

had unquestionably formed a part of the Arshakuni/Arsacid kingdom of Greater Armenia, but with the partition of the kingdom between Byzantium and Persia around 387 A.D., it passed into the area under Byzantine domination and a fortress, named Theodosiopolis in honor of its founder, was erected on the site of the former village.[15] Most scholars, basing themselves on a passage in Procopius' *Buildings* in which he gives the date early in the reign of "Theodosius, son of Arcadius [Theodosius II, 408-50], who was still quite a boy"[16] and on Movses Khorenatsi's description of the foundation of the city by Theodosius II's general Anatolius "by royal command,"[17] attribute this foundation to the younger Theodosius and not to his grandfather.[18] Only a few have opted for the earlier Emperor Theodosius I.[19] Nevertheless, the evidence for the attribution of the foundation of the city to Theodosius II does not withstand close analysis.

The passage in the *History* of Movses Khorenatsi insists that both the first tower of the new city and the city itself had been named Teodos, "in honor of Theodosius" [*i pativ Teodosi*], so that his name "might be rendered immortal by the name of the city," but the author does not specify to which Theodosius he is referring.[20] To be sure, the context of his chapter deals with the

---

[15] On the disputed date of the partition of Armenia, see Nina G. Garsoïan, *Eupsychia: Mélanges offerts à Hélène Ahrweiler* (Paris: Publications de la Sorbonne, 1998): 239 and n1.

[16] Procopius, *Buildings*, III.i.11, pp. 180/81.

[17] MKh, III.liix, pp. 338-39 = MKh-T, pp. 331-32.

[18] Nicholas Adontz, *Armenia in the Period of Justinian,* trans. and comm. Nina G. Garsoïan (Lisbon: Calouste Gulbenkian Foundation, 1970), p. 115; Hakob A. Manandian, *The Trade and Cities of Armenia in Relation to Ancient World Trade,* trans. Nina G. Garsoïan (Lisbon: Livraria Bertrand, 1965), p. 88, who adds "II" after Theodosius in the passage of Procopius cited above in note 17; Thomson, MKh-T, p. 331n1; *Narratio*, pp. 65-70, for a discussion and further bibliography, which, however, omits the work of Karl Güterbock (see next note); Roger C. Blockley, "The Division of Armenia between the Romans and the Persians at the End of the Fourth Century," *Historia* 36:2 (1987): 233-34.

[19] Karl Güterbock, *Römisch-Armenien und die römischen Satrapien im vierten bis sechsten Jahrhundert* (Königsberg: Hartung, 1900), p. 14; Michel Van Esbroeck, "La postérité littéraire des villes fortifiées par Théodose," in *From Byzantium to Iran: Studies in Honour of Nina G. Garsoïan,* ed. Jean-Pierre Mahé and Robert W. Thomson (Atlanta: Scholars Press, 1997), pp. 363-64.

[20] MKh, III.lix, p. 339 = MKh-T, p. 332.

journey of Mashtots to Constantinople, which would indeed place
it during the reign of Theodosius II and of the Greek Patriarch
Atticus (405-25), as attested in Koriun's *Life of Mashtots*,[21] but
this context is highly suspect. In it Khorenatsi speaks of a journey by the Armenian Patriarch Sahak the Great to "the western
regions of our land to the Greek part,"[22] for which there is no
evidence nor for the placing of Mashtots "in charge of the western region" or for the series of letters to and from Saint Sahak
which accompany this account.[23] The Vardan who is said to have
accompanied Mashtots to Constantinople is not mentioned by
Koriun in his meticulous account of his master's journey. The
general Anatolius, who assisted Mashtots on the way to Constantinople, is a well-known figure, master of the army in the East
from 433 to about 446, and the stages of his life can be documented from other sources,[24] but aside from Khorenatsi and the
sources depending on his account, such as Asoghik, no one
attributes the building of Theodosiopolis to Anatolius, nor is
there any reason for thinking that the general's duties took him
to Armenia. Mashtots met with him in Asia Minor. Both Ghazar
Parpetsi and Eghishe seem to be confused as to his activities,
which they consider nefarious, and neither associates him with
the foundation of a new fortress.[25] Khorenatsi gives an elaborate
description of the city as a major stronghold:

At the foot of the pretty mountain . . . he [Anatolius] founded

---

[21] Koriun, *Vark Mashtotsi* [Life of Mashtots], ed. Manuk Abeghian (Erevan:
Haypethrat, 1941; photoreproduction and trans., Delmar, NY: Caravan Books,
1985), xvi, pp. 64, 66 = trans. pp. 38-39.

[22] MKh, III.lvii, p. 333 = MKH-T, p. 327 and n1.

[23] MKh-T, p. 328n4; MKh, III.lviii, p. 337 = MKh-T, pp. 330-31 and notes 2-3;
cf. *Narratio*, p. 66.

[24] John R. Martindale, *The Prosopography of the Later Roman Empire*, vol. 2
(Cambridge: Cambridge University Press, 1980), "Fl. Anatolius 10," pp. 84-85. The
attribution of the founding of Theodosiopolis to Anatolius by Martindale is taken
directly from the account of Khorenatsi, III.lix.

[25] Koriun, *Vark*, xvi, p. 64 = trans. p 38; GhP, II.xli, p. 74 = ŁP-T, p. 118;
Eghishe, *Vasn Vardanay ev Hayots Paterazmin*, ed. Ervand Ter-Minasian (Erevan:
Haypethrat, 1957), iii, p. 73 = Ełishe, *History of Vardan and the Armenian War*,
trans. Robert W. Thomson (Cambridge, MA, and London: Harvard University Press,
1982), p. 124.

the city. Surrounding it with a deep ditch, he set forth the foundations of the wall at a great depth; above he built very high and fearsome towers, . . . Beyond this he built jutting towers like ships' prows and passages with hollow compartments facing the mountain. He did the same on the northern side facing the plain; but to the east and west he erected circular towers. In the center of the city on an elevated spot, he built numerous storehouses. . . . And he brought in additional water to many places through underground conduits. He filled the city with arms and a garrison and named it Theodosiopolis that [the emperor's] name might be rendered immortal by the name of the city.[26]

This description, however, does not coincide with the inadequate defenses of the new foundation even after its reinforcement by an insufficiently high surrounding wall under the emperor Anastasius (491-518), stressed by Procopius:

When Theodosius, the Emperor of the Romans, took over the dominion of Arsaces [Arshak] . . . he built on one of the hills a fort which was easy for assailants to capture and he named it Theodosiopolis. This city Cabades [Kavadh I, 488-531], who was then King of Persia, captured in passing when he was marching on Amida. The Roman Emperor Anastasius not much later built a city there, enclosing within the circuit-wall the hill on which stood the fortress of Theodosius. . . . This wall of Theodosiopolis was of adequate extent, but it did not rise to a height proportionate to its thickness. In fact it attained a height of only about thirty feet and for this reason it had proved to be very easy for an enemy to capture by assault, particularly by the Persians. In other ways too it was vulnerable; for it was protected neither by outworks nor by a moat. Indeed, there was actually a certain elevation which came very close to the city and overtopped the circuit-wall.[27]

Far from depicting the original modest foundation, the description of Khorenatsi is much more reminiscent of Procopius' account of the subsequent major strengthening of the defenses by Emperor Justinian (527-65):

---

[26] MKh, III.lix, p. 339 = MKh-T, p. 332.
[27] Procopius, *Buildings,* III.v.5-9, pp. 200/01- 202/03.

The emperor Justinian took the following measures to meet the situation. First of all he dug a very deep ditch all around, making it very like the ravines between lofty mountains. Next he sliced off the elevated ground [near the city], so transforming it as to make a series of impassable cliffs and gulches affording no outlet. And in order that the wall might be exceptionally high and altogether impregnable, . . . he made the embrasures quite narrow, just wide enough for the defenders to be able to shoot from them, and by adding courses of stones he built thereon a storey like a gallery all round, and then cleverly added other embrasures above them; and surrounding the wall with outworks on all sides he made it much like the circuit wall of Daras, fashioning each tower as a strong fortress. Here he stationed troops and the general of the two Armenias, and thus made the Armenians thenceforth too strong to be afraid of the attacks of the Persians.[28]

Khorenatsi's account is clearly colored by elements taken from a later period than the one he is purportedly describing, but Procopius' data are equally unsatisfactory as to the date for the first establishment of a fortified city.[29] Most scholars have taken his information mentioning the reign of Theodosius II as referring to the first appearance of the city of Theodosiopolis.[30] This, however, is not the case. The event that the historian is explicitly placing in the reign of the younger Theodosius is not the foundation of the new city, which he does not mention at this point, but the partition of Greater Armenia between Byzantium and Persia about which he gives a garbled and inaccurate account:

Two sons were born to a certain Arsaces, King of Armenia, Tigranes and Arsaces by name. When the king was about to reach the end of his life . . . he made both of the boys his successors in the kingdom . . . but leaving to Tigranes a four-fold portion . . . his son Arsaces, resentful and angry because his portion proved inferior, laid the matter before the Roman Emperor. . . . At that time Theodosius, son of Arcadius, who was still quite a boy, was ruling over the Romans. And

---

[28] Ibid., III.v.9-12, pp. 202/03, 204/05; idem, *The Persian War,* I.x.19, vol. 1, pp. 82-83.

[29] Procopius, *Buildings,* III.i.11, pp. 180/81.

[30] Ibid., III.i.1, pp. 178/79.

Tigranes, fearing the vengeance of the Emperor, placed himself in the power of the Persians and handed over his kingdom to them. . . . Arsaces meanwhile . . . resigned his own kingship in favour of the Emperor Theodosius. . . . And for a time the territory of the Armenians was fought over by the Romans and the Persians, but at length they reached an agreement that the Persians should hold the portion of Tigranes and the Romans that of Arsaces.[31]

In addition to his other errors, Procopius is mistaken as to the date of the partition, which unquestionably took place under Theodosius I, late in the fourth century, and under no circumstance in the fifth century. Here then, he may be confusing anachronistically two emperors of the same name, but whatever the case, this passage may not be taken as evidence for the date of the foundation of Theodosiopolis. On all other occasions in which he speaks of the building of the fortress or city, which he clearly associates with this division, Procopius does not specify the Theodosius to whom he is referring.[32]

In the face of Khorenatsi's inaccuracies and Procopius' confusions and apparent contradictions, one more source, insufficiently appreciated by scholars, fortunately supplies the desired chronological precision. The *Narratio de rebus Armeniae,* which explicitly differentiates "the Great" (*o megas*) Theodosius[33] from "the Lesser" or "the Younger" (*o mikros*) Theodosius,[34] unmistakably attributes the foundation of Theodosiopolis to the former:

> Then the kings of Armenia were Khosrov, Tiran, Arshak, Varazdat, Pap, Arshak.
> In the days of the latter, Armenia was divided. At that time was built Theodosiopolis which was formerly a village called Kale Arxe. . . .
> Having considered it and its water, Theodosius the Great appreciated them and founded there a notable city whose name he changed to Theodosiopolis. And the lord of Greater Armenia

---

[31] Ibid., III.i.8-13, pp. 180/81-182/83.

[32] Procopius, *The Persian War*, I.x.17; II.ii.35, pp. 82/83, 200/01, and *Buildings,* III.v.l-2, 5, pp. 200/01-202/03.

[33] *Narratio* §5, 9, pp. 27-28 = "Narratio"-Mahé, p. 430.

[34] Ibid., §31, p. 30 = p. 432.

was subject to him, whereas Khosrov, king of Armenia, was in
the region of Armenia ruled by Shapor, king of Persia.[35]

None of the hesitations, anachronisms, and contradictions of
the other sources are found in this account. The fortress was
built directly on the new border at the moment when it was set
by the division of the former Arshakuni/Arsacid kingdom of
Greater Armenia, as was noted by Procopius,[36] for the purpose
of serving as a stronghold to protect the recently acquired imperial territory from attacks coming from the Persian side. Such a
precaution was manifestly more logical immediately after the
partition of the country than after an interval of two generations,
as would have been the case had it been founded by Theodosius
II. Insufficiently fortified at first, Theodosiopolis would require
further strengthening, under Anastasius I and especially by Justinian in the sixth century, before it achieved its intended purpose
of serving as the bulwark securing the imperial defenses against
the Persians. Its foundation, however, was the work of Theodosius I at the time when the Byzantine frontier moved eastward
across the Euphrates River at the end of the fourth century as a
result of the agreement with Persia which partitioned Greater
Armenia and spelled the end to the Arshakuni kingdom.

---

[35] Ibid., §3-4, 9, pp. 27-28 = p. 430.
[36] See above note 15.

❁ 4 ❁

ARISTAKES OF LASTIVERT
AND ARMENIAN REACTIONS TO INVASION

Robert W. Thomson

For some time I have been interested in the ways in which early and medieval Armenian writers—especially the historians—tried to explain the varied fortunes of their country. The geographical position of Armenia inevitably brought many other peoples into contact with that country, sometimes reasonably peacefully, sometimes violently, and sometimes catastrophically. When Armenian writers described their situation, and particularly the impact of newcomers on the scene, how did they explain these events? What kind of imagery did they employ to clarify things for their readers, and into what sort of framework did they set the Armenian situation?

As Karin/Erzerum is the focal point, let us look at the local historian Aristakes, who came from Lastivert, a village in the environs of Artsn, which was a town about 20 miles north of Karin across the Upper Euphrates River. In his *History*, Aristakes Lastiverttsi describes the two major blows that befell Armenia in the mid-eleventh century: from the west the expansion of Byzantium, which swallowed up the small medieval Armenian kingdoms, and from the east the conquests of the Seljuk Turks.[1]

---

[1] There are numerous editions of the text, but the only critical edition is that by Karen Yuzbashyan [Iuzbashian], *Patmutiun Aristakisi Lastiverttsvoy* (Erevan: Armenian Academy of Sciences, 1963), cited hereafter as Aristakes, *History*. An English rendering by Robert Bedrosian, without commentary, is available on the internet. This has the advantage of giving the full text with all the biblical passages identified. The only printed translations are in modern Armenian, Russian, and French. The translation of Marius Canard and Haig Berbérian, *Recit des malheurs de la nation arménienne* (Brussels: Editions de Byzantion, 1973), was published in the series Bibliothéque de Byzantion and contains an extensive historical commentary. On the

It is not my intention to present a narrative of these events, which have been described in some detail in various general works on the history of that period.[2] Nonetheless, a brief extract describing the Turkish attack into the province of Basean (Basen) on the upper Araxes River will illustrate Aristakes' style and set the scene for the following discussion of his approach to history:

> In that same year [1044] the gate of heavenly anger was opened on our land. Many troops set out from Turkestan; their horses were as swift as eagles and their hooves as hard as stone. Their bows were drawn, and their arrows were sharpened. They were firmly belted and had laced their boots.[3] Descending on the province of Vaspurakan, they attacked the Christians like ravening wolves insatiable for food. They reached the province of Basean, as far as the great estate of Vagharshavan. They ravaged and ruined twenty-four provinces by sword, fire, and captivity. This history is pitiful and worthy of many laments and tears. They sprang like lions, and like lion cubs they mercilessly scattered the corpses of many as carrion for the beasts and birds of the air.[4] In this attack they wished to reach the city of Karin. But He who set the boundary of the sea, saying: "Thus far you will come and no further will you encroach, but here your waves will break,"[5] the same cast a dense darkness before them, halting them in their course. This He did in his ineffable wisdom so that we might be chastised through fear of them, while they might

---

other hand, this translation omits several of the long rhetorical passages that the translators presumably thought unworthy of a historian's perusal.

[2] See Nina Garsoïan, "The Byzantine Annexation of the Armenian Kingdoms in the Eleventh Century," and Robert Bedrosian, "Armenia during the Seljuk and Mongol Periods," both in Richard G. Hovannisian, ed., *The Armenian People from Ancient to Modern Times*, vol. 1 (New York: St. Martin's Press, 1997), chaps. 8 and 10. In addition to the bibliographies attached to those chapters, see Claude Cahen, *Pre-Ottoman Turkey* (London: Sidgwick and Jackson, 1968); Speros Vryonis, Jr., *The Decline of Medieval Hellenism in Asia Minor and the Process of Islamization from the Eleventh through the Fifteenth Century* (Berkeley, Los Angeles, and London: University of California Press, 1971); *L'Arménie et Byzance: Histoire et Culture,* ed. Nina Garsoïan (Paris: Publications de la Sorbonne, 1996).

[3] These similes are taken from Isaiah 5:27-28. Matthew of Edessa will also borrow the same imagery. See note 42 below.

[4] "Lions," "lion cubs": from Isaiah 5:29; "carrion for the beasts and birds of the air": from Psalm 78:2.

[5] Job 38:11.

learn that not through their own power did they accomplish what they did, but that the hand which powerfully arrested them had also made a way for them to pass.[6]

What interests me here is how Aristakes came to grips with such disasters and what explanations he found for them. Although concentrating on Aristakes, I shall try to put his views into the wider framework of Armenian historical writing and bring out parallels with other Armenian writers.

Very little is known about Aristakes himself.[7] The book for which he is famous is titled, in translation, *History of the Vardapet Aristakes Lastiverttsi Concerning the Sufferings Brought About by the Foreign Races That Surround Us.*[8] This *History* begins with the death of Davit of Tayk in the year 1000 A.D. and ends in 1072 with the death of Sultan Alp Arslan, a year after his victory over the Byzantines at Manzikert.[9] No details about the author's life appear in the narrative, which is not uncommon in Armenian histories. Aristakes does mention, however, that he personally witnessed the revolt of Nicephorus Phocas against the Byzantine emperor in 1022: "I saw with my own eyes" (*achauk imovk tesi*).[10] He later states that he is living "subject to the rule

---

[6] Aristakes, *History*, pp. 64-65.

[7] In addition to the *History*, two short homilies are also ascribed to Aristakes. Full details are in Hakob A. Anasyan, *Haykakan matenagitutyun* [Armenian Bibliography], vol. 2 (Erevan: Armenian Academy of Sciences, 1976), cols. 750-65. For a briefer review, see Robert W. Thomson, *A Bibliography of Classical Armenian Literature to 1500 AD* (Brepols: Turnhout, 1995), pp. 102-03.

[8] *Foreign Races*: Aristakes uses the word *aylaser*, literally "of a different species." In that sense it is contrasted with *homaser* or "homogenous" in Davit Anhaght's *Sahmank imastasirutian*, ed. Sen S. Arevshatyan (Erevan: Armenian Academy of Sciences, 1960), p. 24; reproduced in facsimile with facing English trans. by Bridget Kendall and Robert W. Thomson as *David the Invincible Philosopher, Definitions and Divisions of Philosophy* (Chico, CA: Scholars Press, 1983). *Aylaser* was often used in the same sense as *aylazgi*, a much more common word found in the Armenian Old Testament for Philistines, to mean "Muslim." See Robert W. Thomson, *The Lawcode (Datastanagirk') of Mxit'ar Goš* (Amsterdam and Atlanta: Rodopi, 2000), pp. 47-48. In the title to his *History*, however, Aristakes seems to have both Turks and Byzantines in mind.

[9] This disaster ended the Byzantine occupation of Armenian territories and resulted in Seljuk control of Armenia.

[10] Yuzbashyan, *Patmutiun*, p. 33. All references to Aristakes are to the Armenian text in Yuzbashyan's edition. These page numbers are also marked in the French

of heathens" (*i nerkoy tagavorutean hetanosats*), which means
not that he is living abroad but in Armenia under Muslim domination.[11] Aristakes, unlike some earlier Armenian historians, was
not attempting to glorify the prestige of any person or noble
family. There is no reference to any patron for his work, whereas
many of his predecessors name the individual to whom their
History is dedicated. His *History* was a personal undertaking.
Thus, the narrative frequently turns into a message from a
vardapet to his people, often taking the form of a homily or
exhortation.[12]

At the very end Aristakes indicates his prime purpose in
writing this *History*. First, it is to be a record, *hishatak*, on the
pattern of the old historical chroniclers.[13] The only author he ever
mentions, however, is Asoghik, that is, Stepanos of Taron, whose
own *History* ends with the year 1000, where Aristakes begins.[14]
But their works are very different in character. The idea that
historians leave a "record" is an old one in Armenian historio-

---

translation of Canard and Berbérian and in Yuzbashyan's own Russian translation
(Moscow: Nauka, 1968).

[11] Ibid., p. 144.

[12] It is not insignificant that Aristakes was a vardapet. The training of these
learned clergy was based on biblical study; hence biblical imagery and parallels came
easily to Aristakes. The duties and training of vardapets are discussed at some length
in the *Lawcode* which Mkhitar Gosh composed toward the end of the twelfth
century. See Thomson, *Mxit'ar Goš*, pp. 43-46, for a summary.

[13] It is interesting that Aristakes uses the term *zhamanakagir* (chronicler) rather
than *patmagir* (historian) for his predecessors. Agatangeghos in the Epilogue, §892,
likens his work to those of "chroniclers," but that term is usually applied to
composers of brief notices. It appears in association with the chapter headings of the
Buzandaran, but these are later additions. More significantly, Movses Khorenatsi,
Patmutiun Hayots, uses the term for the biblical genealogies and similar works, for
example, Book I, chaps. 5 and 9. He was much influenced by the fourth-century
Greek *Chronicle* of Eusebius of Caesarea, the Armenian title of which is *Zhama-
nakakank*. For a writer of narrative history, the general Armenian term is *patmagir*,
as used by Agatangeghos in his Preface, §7 and 12, or Movses Khorenatsi, Bk. II,
§92. Eghishe and Ghazar also refer to previous "historians" at the beginning of their
own Histories.

[14] From the earliest times it was common for Armenian historians to think of
themselves as continuing the work of a predecessor. The tradition begins with the
author of the fifth-century *Buzandaran*, was continued by Ghazar, and by the time
of Aristakes in the eleventh century was commonplace. It is therefore all the more
surprising that Aristakes mentions no other historian by name.

graphy. Movses Khorenatsi, for example, stresses the importance of an "immortal record" (*anmah hishatak*), but he is referring to secular rather than spiritual virtues.[15] In stressing fame and glory in this world more than moral values, Movses is unusual among Armenian historians. More typical was the work of Eghishe. In his *History of Vardan and the Armenian War,* Eghishe emphasizes that he wrote down these "records" of the death of the villain Vasak as a reproof of his sinful conduct "so that everyone who hears and knows them may cast curses on him and not lust after his deeds."[16]

Aristakes notes that, beyond the leaving of a record, a second purpose in writing this *History* is that we may understand the cause of those sins that have brought calamities upon us. By recognizing his past sinful conduct, the reader may come to fear God, be penitent, and thus save his soul.[17] In other words, Aristakes' objective is a religious one—not entirely surprising for a vardapet—which brings him into a long, though not universal, tradition of Armenian historical writing.[18]

The *History* of Aristakes covers a period of seventy years, an epoch of dramatic change when the kingdoms of Vaspurakan, Ani, and Kars were incorporated into the Byzantine Empire, at the same time as the Seljuks attacked from the east. The histo-

---

[15] Khorenatsi, *Patmutiun Hayots,* Bk. I, chap. 1.

[16] Eghishe, *Vasn Vardanay ev Hayots Paterazmin* [History of Vardan and the Armenian War], ed. Ervand Ter-Minasyan (Erevan: Armenian Academy of Sciences, 1957), p. 140. Here the word used is *hishatakaran*, which has a collective sense of "records." English trans. Robert W. Thomson, *Ełishe: History of Vardan and the Armenian War* (Cambridge, MA: Harvard University Press, 1982).

[17] Penitence leading to personal salvation is also a major theme in the *Lawcode* of Mkhitar Gosh.

[18] There is a significant bibliography on Armenian historiography. For the early period, see Jean-Pierre Mahé, "Entre Moïse et Mahomet: Réflexions sur l'historiographie arménienne," *Revue des études arméniennes,* n.s., 23 (1992): 121-53; Robert W. Thomson, "The Writing of History: The Development of the Armenian and Georgian Traditions," in *Il Caucaso: Cerniera fra Culture dal Mediterraneo alla Persia (Secoli IV-XI),* vol. 1 (Spoleto: Centro Italiano di Studi sull'Alto Medioevo, 1996), pp. 493-520; Christian Hannick, "La chronographie grecque de l'Antiquité tardive et sa réception dans l'historiographie arménienne," in *La Diffusione dell'Eredità classica nell'Età tardo-antico e medievale,* ed. Rosa Bianca Finazzi and Alfredo Valvo (Alessandria: Edizioni dell'Orso, 1998), pp.143-55. For further works, see Thomson, *Bibliography,* p. 264: "Historiography."

rian ends his narrative with the collapse of Byzantine control in Armenia, only a generation after its establishment. Ani, which had been integrated into the Byzantine Empire in 1045, was captured by the Seljuk Sultan Alp Arslan twenty years later, and in 1071 the emperor Romanus was defeated and captured at Manzikert. What were the reactions to these events of Aristakes, an inhabitant of the region of Karin?

He lived in a time of trouble and anxiety, which is reflected in his woeful narrative. Aristakes often contrasts the idyllic past with the disasters of the present. Regret for the "good old days" is not an Armenian monopoly. Many writers from ancient times on have tended to view the passage of historical time as a decline from a supposed golden age, rather than as a march of progress toward a more perfect happiness. Yet if Aristakes' idyllic picture of the past is exaggerated, it is in order to strengthen the underlying message.

The message is based on a major theme in the Old Testament, that of punishment for backsliding. When Israel forgets God, He brings disasters upon them by means of foreign races; when Israel repents and turns back to God, He saves them from their afflictions.[19] So, it is not surprising that the most obvious characteristic of Aristakes' narrative is the use of biblical imagery. For example, when he describes the situation in 1041 following the death of Hovhannes Smbat, king of Armenia, he looks back on his country as it had been in the days of independence and compares it with the present situation: now the land is abandoned, the towns are uninhabited, the cultivated fields have become grasslands, and the empty houses are occupied by a variety of birds and mythical beasts. The language is a combina-

---

[19] Armenians were not the only Christian writers to see such lessons in the Old Testament. But Armenians drew a very particular parallel between Israel and their own country, most especially in the image of the Maccabees. Just as those heroes fought the Seleucids for freedom to practice their religion and cultural traditions (*aurenk* in Armenian having this double sense), so did the Armenians resist Sasanian efforts to suppress their liberties. This is the theme of Eghishe's *History of Vardan and the Armenian War*, which had a profound impact on later Armenian historians. Aristakes, however, does not draw on this powerful image, contenting himself with exposition of more general Old Testament ideas.

tion of phrases taken from the prophet Isaiah.[20]

In the middle of the *History*, a very long passage describes the Turkish attack of 1047 into Vaspurakan and their advance the following year to the plain of Karin. Again the language is based on biblical expressions, though they are different quotations from those in Isaiah just mentioned.[21] However, more interestingly, this time Aristakes offers an explanation of the disasters and makes his message explicit. Just as in the past the sins of Israel angered God, who in turn brought down punishment through foreign races, so now the anger of God has again been aroused by the backsliding of the Armenians. And once again foreign races are the means of punishment.[22]

In a later passage describing the Turkish attack on Artsn, his home province just north of Karin—an attack that he witnessed in person—Aristakes expands and clarifies his argument. First, he draws an idyllic picture of the past: the city flourished like a beautiful young woman; her princes were benevolent; the judges did not take bribes; the merchants were charitable and honest; there was no fraud in the marketplace; and the priests were fervently pious. Why, then, the sudden ruin and destruction? Each group in society had become corrupted, says Aristakes. In the churches rationalistic thought had supplanted true religion, while among the laity love of money and luxury had blinded the judges and perverted the merchants.[23]

Aristakes describes the actual destruction of Artsn as follows:

Who could describe the multifarious and terrible evils inflicted on our city? As is written concerning the Sodomites: "The sun rose over the earth and the Lord rained down on Sodom fire and sulfur, and he burned it,"[24] likewise here, too, at the rising of the sun over the earth hordes of the impious attacked it like famished

---

[20] Aristakes, *History*, p. 55. See especially Isaiah, chap. 34, for the vivid picture of desolation.

[21] Aristakes, *History*, pp. 65-68. Cf. esp. Isaiah 56:9 and Joel 1:4.

[22] Here for "foreign" Aristakes does not use the term *aylaser*, as in his Preface, but the common *autar* [*otar*].

[23] Aristakes, *History*, pp. 74-79. Cf. Isaiah 3:24 and 5:8-9 for the theme of desolation, and Isaiah 3:16 for pride.

[24] Genesis 19:2.

dogs. They surrounded the city and entered it like harvesters [to reap] the field. They slaughtered the populace, mowing them down until the city was devoid of the living. Those who fled to their homes or churches they mercilessly burned with fire, thinking their deeds benevolence, as previously the Savior said: "The time will come when everyone who kills you will reckon he is offering service to God."[25] And He himself indicated the reasons: "They shall do this to you for my name's sake, because they did not recognize me."[26] The weather assisted that day of destruction, for a powerful wind blew, fanning the fire into a furnace so that the smoke like a pillar reached the sky,[27] and the glare of the fire's light eclipsed the rays of the sun. There, one could witness a pitiable and most terrifying sight. The whole city was filled with the corpses of the fallen—the streets of merchants, the alleys and the broad courtyards. Who could reckon up the number of those burned? All those who fled from the glittering sword and hid somewhere in their houses were consumed by fire. The priests whom they seized in the churches they destroyed with fire. Of those outside, some they slew and in the breasts [of others] they stuffed large pieces of pork in order to insult us and for the derisive mockery of those watching. . . . Here ends the sad history of Artsn. We were not able to describe all the disasters; as for what we have omitted, the inquirer may learn from the ruins. These were the stories of two regions, the mountain and the city. What crimes we saw with our own eyes and experienced, those only have we written down. Whose mind could encompass the afflictions of other provinces and cities? They need a lengthy tale and protracted time. We have shortened our account in conformity with our ability.[28]

The lengthy descriptions of eleventh-century life in Artsn have been strung together from a combination of Old Testament quotations, which in fact give no precise information about Armenia at all. They do reveal, however, a perception of the inherent danger of city life based on the profits of trade— namely, moral corruption through avarice—leading to the oppression of one's fellow men. Aristakes was conscious of writing in

---

[25] John 16:2.
[26] John 15:21.
[27] This is based on Song of Solomon 3:6.
[28] Aristakes, *History,* pp. 78-79.

a long line of Armenian historians, and he takes his general outlook on life from traditional imagery and presuppositions. In previous centuries Armenian writers had always been ambiguous about city life, for cities had not played a predominant role in the social, religious, intellectual, or political life of early Armenia, where the social structure was quite different from that of the Eastern Roman Empire or the world of Islam.[29]

By the eleventh century, of course, traditional Armenian life had greatly changed. But the old ways had not been transformed gradually; the growth of cities like Ani, Kars, or Artsn was a recent and rapid phenomenon.[30] A historian of conservative bent might well regard the social transformations of the comparatively recent past as the prime cause for the collapse of civilized society. Artsn was not the only warning. Other cities such as Melitene (Malatia) were sacked because of the pride of their citizens, who were devoted to luxury.[31] And when Ani fell to Alp Arslan in 1064, although Aristakes did not witness the destruction himself, he dwells at length on the faults of its inhabitants: usury, luxury, and profiting from the sweat of the poor.[32]

Aristakes indicates that not only the Armenians are afflicted when they commit sin. Disasters befall all men. In 1022, for example, the emperor Basil II marched round Armenia to the province of Her to attack the Turks near Lake Urmia. But the severe winter weather decimated his army. In the words of Aristakes:

> While [Basil] was of this intention and all the land of the Persians was enveloped in terror and fear, seeking means of salvation, suddenly the sky grew thick with clouds and torrents of rain

---

[29] On this point, see the important article of Nina G. Garsoïan, "The Early-Mediaeval Armenian City: An Alien Element?" in *Ancient Studies in Memory of Elias Bickerman,* a special issue of *Journal of the Ancient Near Eastern Society* 16-17 (1984-85): 67-83, with evidence from the earliest writers to the tenth century.

[30] For the growth of cities and prosperity in the tenth and eleventh centuries, see Hakob A. Manandian, *The Trade and Cities of Armenia in Relation to Ancient World Trade,* trans. Nina G. Garsoïan (Lisbon: Calouste Gulbenkian Foundation, 1965), chap. 5. Manandian gathers information from Greek and Arabic sources to supplement Armenian evidence.

[31] Aristakes, *History,* p. 115.

[32] Ibid., pp. 134-36.

fell to earth. After this a bitter wind blew from the north, turning
the rain to hail, snow and ice, which covered the ground in dense
layers. The season was indeed apt for that, because it had
reached well into winter. As the fall of snow continued and the
icy cold intensified, the herds of horses and mules became frozen
and were unable to move. From the bitter cold the extremities
of the infantry's feet and hands burned as if by fire and dropped
off. The cords and pegs of the tents stuck to the ground because
of the severity of the cruel tempest and could not be removed.
This, as it seems to me, was their retribution for the merciless
sword which they inflicted on the Christians.[33]

Armenian winters were a constant threat to invaders, as recognized by Plutarch and Tacitus, who describe such difficulties
befalling Roman armies a thousand years earlier.[34] Aristakes sees
in the sufferings of Basil's army a sign of punishment for the
Byzantine treatment of the Armenians. Fifty years later the emperor Romanus was defeated and captured at Manzikert; his pride
was the cause, says Aristakes.[35]

Although his *History* makes depressing reading, Aristakes does
offer the reader some hope. He ends his work with the consola-
tion that God's punishment is not permanent. When our sins
become excessive, God punishes us. But this is a testing in order
to bring us back to our senses, so that we may return to good
works. On reading this present account, says Aristakes, you will
learn that sin was the cause of all that befell Armenia. When you
realize this, you will confess your sins, be penitent, and avoid
punishment. God's love for humanity is infinite, and pardon
comes as soon as we correct our ways.[36]

Such a philosophy of history is quite explicit and has parallels

---

[33] Aristakes, *History*, p. 38. He then quotes Isaiah 47:6: "I shall hand my people
into your hands, and you did not give them any mercy."

[34] Plutarch, *Life of Lucullus* (Loeb Classical Library), §32, notes that winter
weather began as early as the autumn equinox, with snow, frost, and ice, which made
the going very difficult for the horses. Tacitus, *Annals* (Loeb Classical Library),
XIII.35, states that the winter was so severe that the ice-covered ground had to be
dug up before tents could be pitched, and many of the soldiers suffered from frostbite
to the extent of losing limbs.

[35] Aristakes, *History,* p. 138. Here Psalm 33:16 is the key text.

[36] Ibid., p. 144.

in many Armenian writers. It is, however, noteworthy that Aristakes has no very specific framework into which to fit the Armenian present. He picks and chooses his Old Testament parallels in no apparently consistent manner. And he totally refrains from predictions of future well-being. He urges a return to Christian morality, seeing nothing inevitable in what happened in the past or may occur in the future.

In this regard, there is one very significant statement in chapter 9, where Aristakes describes the accession of the Byzantine emperor Michael IV in 1034: "The empires prefigured by the statue in Daniel's vision, which had a head of gold, flanks and hands of silver, a belly of brass, legs and feet of iron mixed with clay—these have all passed away."[37] He is referring to Daniel, 2:32-33, where the prophet retells to Nebuchadnezzar the king's dream which he could not recall. There are several other visions in the book of Daniel which were all interpreted in a similar fashion as referring to successive empires, and some Armenian historians adapted the visions to their own purposes.

Sebeos, for example, uses the four beasts of Daniel, chapter 7, to explain the arrival of the Arabs. Their invasion of the Byzantine and Sasanian empires had been foretold. The Arabs were the fourth and last in a series of kingdoms. But, as Daniel himself prophesied, that beast, too, would be destroyed.[38] Aristakes rejects such hope of salvation from disaster and expectation of future bliss. In his view Daniel's imagery is irrelevant: we have to accept suffering as a trial sent to warn us. Our personal salvation may be gained through penance; the salvation of the nation can only be obtained by a collective action, not by force of arms but by a return to the morality and piety of past days.

Other Armenian historians viewed things differently. Here, I turn to the *History* of another priest, Matthew of Edessa, writing some fifty years after Aristakes, whose explanations—though also

---

[37] Ibid., p. 46.

[38] *Patmutiun Sebeosi* [History of Sebeos], ed. Gevorg V. Abgaryan (Erevan: Armenian Academy of Sciences, 1979), pp. 141-42. Cf. pp. 162, 177, for further quotations from Daniel applied to the Muslims. English trans. Robert W. Thomson and James Howard-Johnston, *The Armenian History Attributed to Sebeos* (Liverpool: Liverpool University Press, 1999), 2 pts.

based on biblical imagery—lead in a different direction.[39]

In his description of the first encounter of the Armenians with the Turks, which he dates to 1018, Matthew explains that the wrath of God was aroused against all Christian peoples and worshipers of the Cross and that a death-breathing dragon (*vishap*) struck those who believed in the Holy Trinity.[40] An Armenian force commanded by the son of King Senekerim of Vaspurakan, Davit, was compelled to turn back because it was unaccustomed to dealing with mounted archers. Matthew describes King Senekerim's reaction as follows:

> Sitting down, he examined the chronicles and utterances of the divinely inspired prophets, the holy teachers, and found written in these books the time specified for the coming of the Turkish troops. He also learned of the impending destruction and end of the whole world. He found written: "At that time they will flee from the east to the west, from the north to the south, and they will not find rest upon the earth, for the plains and the mountains will be covered with blood."[41]

This is not from the Bible, but Matthew ends with a specific reference to Isaiah 5:28: "Their horses' hooves shall be firm," to which he adds: "They are always continually assiduous at drunkenness because of their love and desire for their evil and impure passion."[42]

Some years later a comet appeared and the sun darkened. This frightful omen was interpreted by the learned vardapet John Kozern (Hovhannes Kozern) as the one thousandth year when

---

[39] Matthew of Edessa: *Patmutiun Mateosi Urhayetsvoy* [History of Matthew of Edessa] (Jerusalem: St. James Press, 1869), and *Zhamanakagrutiun* [Chronicle], ed. Mambre Melik-Adamian and Nerses Ter-Mikayelian (Vagharshapat: Holy See of Echmiadzin, 1898). These texts are not identical, but no critical edition has yet been made. For an English translation with commentary, see Ara E. Dosturian, *Armenia and the Crusades, Tenth to Twelfth Centuries: The Chronicle of Matthew of Edessa* (Lanham, MD: University Press of America, 1993).

[40] Matthew of Edessa, *Patmutiun,* Bk. I, §47-48.

[41] See below at note 46 for the source of this passage.

[42] This is the same passage as that used by Aristakes. These similes are all taken from Isaiah 5:27-28. Matthew of Edessa also borrows the same imagery; see note 3 above.

Satan was released from imprisonment. This refers to the book
of Revelation, where it is written:

> I saw an angel come down from heaven, having the key of the
> bottomless pit and a great chain in his hand. And he laid hold
> on the dragon (*vishap*) that old serpent which is the Devil and
> Satan, and bound him a thousand years; and cast him into the
> bottomless pit and shut him up, and set a seal upon him that he
> should deceive the nations no more, till the thousand years
> should be fulfilled. And after that he must be loosed a little
> season.[43]

Today, said John Kozern, Satan has been released, which means
that iniquities will prevail and misfortunes fall upon us. Matthew
explains that John was indeed correct, as shown by the invasion
of the ferocious nation of the Turks, for, as earlier, he equates
the dragon-vishap with those fearsome invaders.

In other words, Matthew did not see any message for personal
reformation that might emerge from a study of the prophecies in
the Bible. The prophets predicted various happenings, which duly
occurred. The Turkish invasions were thus inevitable. But they
do not hold any further significance; they are not regarded as a
trial or punishment which will induce the Armenians to repent
and mend their ways. Matthew interprets other events, too, as the
fulfillment of prophecy. And other prophecies, not just those in
the Bible, can be pressed into service. I shall limit myself here
to two examples, one which Matthew attributes to John Kozern,
and one of his own.

In the year 1036-37, another eclipse occurred portending
frightful events.[44] Once more, John Kozern was asked for an
interpretation. In a long passage he describes coming troubles and
confusion: "Henceforth there will occur invasions by the infidels,
the abominable forces of the Turks . . . and the whole land will
be consumed by the sword. All the nations of the Christian
faithful will suffer through famine and enslavement," and more
in the same vein. However, John continues: "But then the valiant

---

[43] Matthew of Edessa, *Patmutiun*, Bk. I, §52, quoting Revelations 20:1-3.
[44] Ibid., Bk. I, §64.

nation called the Franks will rise up; with a great number of troops they will capture the holy city of Jerusalem." This did indeed happen, in 1099, after John's death. Matthew himself was writing after 1136 and has put his knowledge of these events back to the time of John.

Following this, according to John's prophecy as reported by Matthew, there will be further sufferings and the Persians [that is, the Turks] will grow strong. Eventually, however, the Roman emperor will be awakened and come against them. They will flee, and then the land will see prosperity once more under the dominion of the Roman emperor.

The latest translator of Matthew supposes that the Armenian historian is here putting into the mouth of John Kozern comments about the revival of the Byzantine Empire in the twelfth century.[45] I am not so sure. The idea that the Turks inflict sufferings on the Christians but are then expelled by the Roman emperor who comes in person to the east and inaugurates a time of peace and prosperity is probably derived from the *Apocalypse* of Pseudo-Methodius. This document, composed at the end of the seventh century in Syriac to explain the conquests of the Arabs, was known in Armenia and influenced several writers.[46] The

---

[45] Dostourian, *Armenia and the Crusades*, p. 300, being note 6 to Matthew of Edessa, *Patmutiun,* Bk. I, §64: "If one accepts the rather sure premise that Matthew is talking about the ephemeral revival of the empire under the Comneni (1081-1185), then it is quite obvious that the Armenian chronicler is grossly exaggerating this revival."

[46] Syriac text and German translation are in Gerrit J. Reinink, *Die Syrische Apokalypse des Pseudo-Methodius* (Peeters: Leuven, 1993). Part of the text was known in Armenian to the late-thirteenth century historian Stepanos Orbelian. See chap. 32 of his *History of the Province of Sisakan* in the French translation by Marie-Félicité Brosset, *Histoire de la Siounie* (St. Petersburg: Académie Impériale des Sciences, 1864), pp. 89-94. The Armenian text, *Stepannosi Siuniats Episkoposi Patmutiun Nahangin Sisakan,* ed. Mkrtich Emin (Moscow: Lazarian Jemaran, 1861), was unavailable to me. Stepanos Orbelian claims that the *Apocalypse* was translated by his eighth-century predecessor as bishop of Siunik, the same Stepanos who was known for his translations from Greek made in Constantinople. But no complete text of the *Apocalypse* seems to have survived in Armenian, and the origin of the section quoted by Orbelian remains uncertain. That section includes the ideas of fleeing from east to west and from north to the desert, and the earth being covered with blood, which Matthew mentions in the prophecy attributed to John Kozern. See also chap. XIII of the *Apocalypse* for the theme of the Roman emperor coming to the east and

Apocalypse predicted not only that prosperity would be restored
but that before the Second Coming of Christ at the end of the
world there would occur a final period of woe and affliction
brought about by the Anti-Christ. Both here and in the earlier
prediction of John Kozern concerning the Turks, there are
reminiscences of this influential *Apocalypse*, though it is not
quoted verbatim. As time went by, the original seventh century
Apocalypse, which refers to the Arab invasions, was adapted to
new events: the coming of the Turks and the arrival of the
Crusaders.

In addition to foreign texts, predictions of Armenian origin
were also used by Matthew. In 1097 the Armenians first met the
Crusaders, who were on their way to recover the Holy Places.
Their arrival, says Matthew, was in fulfillment of the prophecy
of Catholicos Saint Nerses I (fourth century), which he spoke at
the time of his death; and it was also foretold by the prophet
Daniel.[47] From Daniel, Matthew adapts to the Turks the imagery
of the fourth beast, which Sebeos had used earlier about the
Arabs.[48] As for the prediction of Saint Nerses, this is found in
the *Buzandaran*. It is there not put to the time of Nerses' death
but to an earlier occasion when the Catholicos is castigating King
Arshak for his evil ways and predicts the division of the kingdom, a fourth-century event.[49] This vision had a long and complicated history and was later applied by numerous authors to the
Crusaders or the Mongols. But let us return to the area of Karin.

My concern here has been to take a local historian, namely
Aristakes from Lastivert, and to see in what framework he places
the unhappy events of his lifetime. As one might expect from a
vardapet, Aristakes not only describes these disasters in biblical

defeating the enemies of Christ.
[47] Matthew of Edessa, *Patmutiun,* Bk. II, §109ff.
[48] *Patmutiun Sebeosi*, p. 177, quoting Daniel 7:7.
[49] *Buzandaran*, Bk. IV, chap. 13. Cf. the later *Patmutiun Srboyn Nersisi Partevi*
[History of Saint Nerses of Partev] (Venice: Mekhitarist Press, 1853), in which this
prediction is elaborated. There are several recessions of this *Life of Nerses*, but a
critical study of the variants has not yet been made. For comments on the later
history of the prophecy of Nerses and similar documents, see Robert W. Thomson,
"The Crusades through Armenian Eyes," in *The Crusades from the Perspective of
Byzantium and the Muslim World,* ed. Angeliki E. Laiou and Roy P. Mottahedeh
(Washington, DC: Dumbarton Oaks, 2001), pp. 71-82.

language, but he uses a basic theme from the Old Testament to interpret them. God is punishing his people for their sins; they must repent, and then they will be saved. By way of contrast, I turned to another Armenian cleric, Matthew of Edessa, who also is strongly influenced by biblical language.[50] He uses prophecy, both biblical and non-biblical, to explain dramatic and unexpected changes of fortune. Both of these approaches to the writing of history have roots in earlier Armenian tradition.

I have called Aristakes a "local historian" in a geographical sense. But one might ask whether the different regions of Armenia had different traditions of historical writing and whether certain styles or approaches to the subject could be associated with particular areas of the country. There were, of course, many a *History* dealing with specific noble families: the Mamikonians had their historians in the author of the *Buzandaran* and Ghazar Parpetsi; the Bagratunis in Movses Khorenatsi; the Artsrunis in Tovma Artsruni. And different regions of Armenia produced local historians: Movses Daskhurantsi wrote the *History* of Aghvank; Stepanos Orbelian, that of Siunik; Hovhannes Mamikonian, that of Taron. But this is not to say that those diverse regions produced different approaches to the writing of history as a literary genre. There are similarities of purpose and approach in all these writers regardless of place of origin.

As for Aristakes, no earlier historian is linked to Karin. Although he mentions by name only one earlier Armenian historian, Stepanos of Taron, known as Asoghik, Aristakes Lastiverttsi was heir to a much longer and broader tradition. History writing was one aspect of Armenian culture which cut across the barriers of local interest and noble rivalry.

---

[50] It is interesting that the use of biblical quotations in Aristakes often does not correspond to that of other Armenian historians. Using the book of Psalms as a reference point, I have noted only three quotations used by several authors, and these are commonplace: Psalms 22:4: "I fear no evil for you, Lord, are with me"; Psalms 63:4: "[Satan] sharpened his tongue like a sword"; Psalms 117:9: "It is better to trust in the Lord than to put confidence in princes." Cf. Robert W. Thomson, "Uses of the Psalms in Some Early Armenian Authors," in *From Byzantium to Iran: Armenian Studies in Honour of Nina G. Garsoïan*, ed. Jean-Pierre Mahé and Robert W. Thomson (Atlanta: Scholars Press: 1997), pp. 281-300. It would be useful to pursue this inquiry further to see whether specific interpretations of biblical verses were often shared among Armenian authors.

❋ 5 ❋

THE ARCHITECTURE
OF THE KARIN/ERZERUM REGION

Christina Maranci

The city of Karin/Erzerum and the region to its north, historical Tayk or Tao, are studded with medieval monuments, including churches, monasteries, and fortifications. These buildings, and the decoration that adorns them, are of key importance in understanding the complex religious and cultural world of Armenia. In the Middle Ages, the population of the region was decidedly heterogeneous, comprising Armenians, Georgians, Seljuk Turks, and Greeks, and the buildings attest to such diversity. Often bearing multilingual inscriptions, they elude easy classification into discrete styles such as "Armenian" or "Georgian." It is perhaps for this reason that they are often excluded from general surveys of Armenian art. Yet these works deserve attention precisely because they challenge the notion of a monolithic and homogenous Armenian architecture. The research of Robert Hewsen,[1] Nina Garsoïan,[2] Michael Stone,[3] and others has demonstrated the ethnic and religious diversity of medieval Armenia, and the monuments of the Erzerum area provide eloquent testimony to

---

[1] See Robert H. Hewsen, *Armenia: A Historical Atlas* (Chicago: University of Chicago Press, 2001), and a series of articles by the same author titled "Introduction to Armenian Historical Geography," in *Revue des études arméniennes*, n.s., 13, 17, 19, 20, 21 (1978-79, 1983, 1985, 1988-89, 1990-91): 77-97, 123-43, 54-84, 271-319, 174-83.

[2] See Nina G. Garsoïan, *L'église arménienne et le grand schisme d'Orient* (Louvain: Peeters. 1999), and "Armenia in the Fourth Century: An Attempt to Re-Define the Concepts of 'Armenia' and 'Loyalty'," *Revue des études arméniennes*, n.s., 8 (1971): 341-52.

[3] Excavations now underway in Armenia under the direction of Michael Stone have uncovered the remains of a Jewish cemetery. Publications are forthcoming.

this position. Hence, seeking out the "Armenian architecture" of the region is probably too rigid an approach. Instead, this discussion will consider a selection of monuments that are tied to the Armenian tradition in a variety of ways. An examination of this group, which includes four churches, a fortress, and Seljuk tomb towers, will demonstrate that medieval Armenians did not remain aloof from their neighbors but rather participated actively in the cultural exchanges that characterized the region.

Church Architecture in Tayk/Tao

Banak

One of the best-known monuments of the group is the church of Banak (Bana; Penek), lying half-ruined on an arid plain some distance to the northeast of Erzerum (Fig. 1).[4] The date of its foundation is a matter of debate: some scholars have maintained that it was constructed in the late-ninth to early-tenth century during the reign of King Adarnase II of Georgia (890s-923).[5] Others, however, including Josef Strzygowski, Tiran Marutyan, and W. Eugene Kleinbauer, have suggested an initial date of the second half of the seventh century, followed by a subsequent period of restoration.[6]

The church holds particular importance for the development of Armenian architecture, as it belongs to a family of buildings

---

[4] For a historical overview and bibliography for the region, see *Armenian Architecture: A Documented Photo-Archival Collection on Microfiche for the Study of Armenian Architecture*, a multi-volume microfiche collection of Armenian monuments (Zug, Switzerland: Inter Documentation, 1980-1990), cited hereafter as *Armenian Architecture*. The set, which is available in a number of American research libraries, was created under the direction of Vasken Parsegian and edited and written by Krikor Maksoudian and several associates. For the area of Erzerum and medieval Tayk/Tao, see vol. 6, fiches 1-61. For an up-to-date list of readings about artistic and sculptural programs in the region, see Antony Eastmond, *Royal Imagery in Medieval Georgia* (University Park: Pennsylvania State University Press, 1998).

[5] The secondary literature on Banak is quite abundant. For commentary and further reading, see *Armenian Architecture*, 6, A-2125, D2, and W. Eugene Kleinbauer, "Zvart'nots and the Origins of Early Christian Architecture in Armenia," *Art Bulletin* 54 (1972): 251ff.

[6] *Armenian Architecture*, vol. 6, A-2125, D2-D3.

commonly referred to as the "double-aisled tetraconch," in which the domed core is screened from an outer ambulatory by means of columnar exedrae (Fig. 2).[7] The most famous representative of the group is the seventh-century church of Zvartnots,[8] but other buildings of the same type include the church of Gregory the Illuminator at Ani, Lekit in historical Caucasian Albania, and a series of fifth-century and sixth-century monuments in Syria and Mesopotamia.[9]

In its dimensions and plan, the church of Banak finds a close parallel in Zvartnots.[10] Yet a number of innovations may also be perceived. For example, the dome is thought to have been erected on an open arcade of columns rather than on a solid drum. Moreover, while the east apse of Zvartnots is defined by solid wall, at Banak it is formed by a fourth columnar exedra (Fig. 3). Finally, between Banak's exedrae are small apsed chambers accessible at the west. Within the thickness of their walls are flights of stairs leading to additional upper chambers, and these walls also serve to support the dome. At the Zvartnots church, this space is occupied instead by solid W-shaped piers. All of these changes serve to lighten the structure, and suggest that the designers of Banak felt confidence in the structural integrity of the building. In a sense, this sentiment was warranted, for unlike other buildings of the same type, at least part of the first two levels at Banak remains standing.

The building is embellished with rich sculptural decoration, carved, like the structure itself, in local tufa. The columns of the exedrae were surmounted with capitals of an Ionic basket variety, in which the base of the capital is encircled with thick bands of sculpture in a woven design (Fig. 4). Above are Ionic volutes, which flank two rows (one upper and one lower) of bead-like motifs. The style of the sculpture has led some scholars to posit an initial seventh-century phase for the church, and some scholars

---

[7] Kleinbauer, "Zvart'nots," p. 251.

[8] For a recent study of Zvartnots, see Christina Maranci, "Byzantium through Armenian Eyes: Cultural Appropriation and the Church of Zuart'noc'," *Gesta* 40:2 (2001): 105-24.

[9] For further discussion of this architectural group, see Kleinbauer, "Zvart'nots," and his "The Aisled Tetraconch," Ph.D. Dissertation (Princeton University, 1967).

[10] In diameter, Banak measures approximately 37 meters (120 feet).

have drawn parallels with the Ionic capitals at Zvartnots. Eugene
Kleinbauer[11] and Dora Piguet-Panayotova,[12] for example, suggest
that the capitals date from the seventh century and were re-used
in the present building.

Ishkhan

The church of Ishkhan (Prince) is located in the district Tortum
to the north of Erzerum (Fig. 5).[13] According to Maksoudian, its
name refers to the fact that the area belonged to the House of
the Mamikonians in the fifth century. Unlike many of the medieval monuments in the area, Ishkhan is mentioned in a number
of primary sources that form a complicated and rather confusing
chronicle of the building history. The seventh-century account of
Sebeos associates the site with Catholicos Nerses III, referring
to Ishkhan as his birthplace. Sebeos also relates that Nerses
returned to the area during a period of exile in 653-58. The
tenth-century Georgian historian Georgi Mertsuli also casts
Nerses as the builder of the church, and in the history of Hovhannes Draskhanakerttsi, Nerses is presented as the former bishop
of Tayk.[14]

Nerses' putative connections with the church have led scholars
to a number of hypotheses regarding its date and present state.
Some believe that the current structure is a later rebuilding and

[11] Kleinbauer (p. 251) believes that "the style of the carved frieze of the ground-
floor walls [and] the schematic treatment of the leaf forms calls to mind mid-seventh
century sculpture in Armenia. The large spiral forms of the capitals also recall the
carved elements of Zvart'nots, but the quite unclassical capitals supporting horseshoe arches in the east conch may be replacements of the beginning of the tenth
century, when the church was rebuilt."

[12] Dora Piguet-Panayotova, "Récherches sur les tetraconques à déambulatoire et
leur decor en Transcaucasie au VII siècle," *Oriens Christianus* 73 (1989): 166-212.

[13] Like Banak, much has been written on this church, and bibliography can be
found in *Armenian Architecture*, 6, A-2081, A1. In particular, see Mine Kadiroğlu,
The Architecture of the Georgian Church of Išhan (Frankfurt and New York: P.
Lang, 1991); Wachtang Djobadze, *Early Medieval Monasteries in Tao, Klarjeti, and
Saveti* (Stuttgart: F. Steiner, 1992), pp. 191-217; Dora Piguet-Panayotova, "L'église
d'Iškhan: Patrimoine culturel et création architecturale," *Oriens Christianus* 75
(1991): 198-253.

[14] Ibid.

that the original seventh-century church resembled Nerses' foundation of Zvartnots, a double-aisled tetraconch.[15] These scholars, moreover, argue that the initial structure was destroyed during the Arab invasions and then rebuilt in the ninth century by the Georgian bishop Saban.[16] Krikor Maksoudian and Tiran Marutyan, however, argue that the bishop only engaged in renovations of the first church. Nikolai Tokarski believes that Ishkhan was rebuilt in the tenth century by Prince David *curopalate*, in imitation of another royal foundation. The tenth-century church of Oshk, a large domed cruciform structure also located in the Tortum area (Fig. 6).[17] A group of wall paintings, seen by Ekvtime Takaishvili in 1917 but now lost, argues for a tenth-century phase of activity at the church and connects it with three royal Georgian figures. The images depicted three men inscribed with the names Adarnase, curopalate, son of Bagrat; Bagrat *magistros*, king of the Kartlians; and Bagrat, *eristav* of *eristavs* (prince of princes), son of Adarnase. From this information, Antony Eastmond and others have concluded that the paintings must have been executed after 958, at which time Adarnase III received the title of curopalate.[18] Because the paintings no longer exist, however, it is difficult to draw firm conclusions regarding the date and founder of the structure.

It is also not clear whether the church was founded and used by Georgians or by Armenians of the Chalcedonian faith, of which there was a sizable population in Tayk. Numerous scholars, including Takaishvili and Eastmond, assume it is a Georgian

---

[15] Nikolai Tokarski and N.P. Severov are among those holding this view. For a further discussion of the secondary literature, see *Armenian Architecture*, 6, A-2081, A-2.

[16] Another renovation is attested by a Georgian inscription on the interior of the church, which relates the refurbishment by Archbishop Antonius in 1032 (*Armenian Architecture*, 6, A-2081, A-3).

[17] Ibid.

[18] Eastmond, *Royal Imagery in Medieval Georgia*, p. 227, writes that "the paintings must have shown Bagrat' I *magistros* and titular king of Kartli (937-945), the third son of Adarnase II, standing between his son Adarnase III (958-961) and his grandson Bagrat', *eristav of eristavs* (961-966)," and concludes that "since Adarnase III only received the title of *kuropalates* in 958, after the death of his uncle Sumbat', the paintings must have been executed after that date, at least eighteen years after the death of Bagrat' I."

monument. Maksoudian, however, asserts that the presence of
Georgian epigraphy attests rather to a congregation of Armenians
who professed Chalcedonianism, noting that they referred to
themselves as "Georgians" and often knew Georgian. Moreover,
he points out the continuity of an Armenian presence in the
region, as witnessed by the seventeenth-century Armenian cleric-
geographer Hakob of Karin, who described the inhabitants of the
region as speakers of Armenian and ethnically half-Armenian and
half-Georgian.[19]

For the present purpose, it is more important to explore the
role of Ishkhan within the history of building traditions in Armenia and, in particular, its peculiar physical characteristics. The
church now stands in the middle of a farming village in a state
of semi-dilapidation. However, enough remains of the building
to discern its elevation. Built on a stepped platform, Ishkhan
bears a domed cruciform plan, with a long western arm crossed
by a shorter lateral arm under the dome (Fig. 7). The method of
dome support is particularly intriguing: the shell-shaped niches
above the piers give the impression of squinches; however, they
are actually spherical triangles (pendentives), to which a sculptural design typical to squinches has been applied (Fig. 8).[20] The
northwest end of the church is occupied by a long, barrel-vaulted
chamber, which, like the nave, is accessible by a portal on the
west facade. According to Takaishvili, at the south side of the
west arm stood an open portico, but no remnants of it now
remain.[21] In the main aisle, large, profiled pilasters run up the
sides of the walls to form transverse arches for the barrel vaults
above. In the central bay, the dome is supported by four thick
shafts; the western pair are cruciform piers of complex profile,
while the eastern are polygonal. The abundance of profiling,
which articulates the walls, vaults, and supports of the structure,
lends the interior an elegant linear effect, typical of churches in
the region.

---

[19] *Armenian Architecture*, 6, A-2081, A-2, A-3. In addition, Maksoudian (6, A-
2081, A7) notes Amiranshvili's discovery of Armenian and Georgian epigraphy in
the main church as well as images of both Armenian and Georgian royal figures.

[20] Contrary to Maksoudian's view, *Armenian Architecture*, 6, A-2081, A6.

[21] *Armenian Architecture*, 6, A-2081, A4.

The interior of Ishkhan was once highly decorated. There is evidence that the walls were completely plastered to create a smooth surface for painting. Remains of the program still survive on the eastern apse, the western end, and in the dome, and are dated by most scholars between the ninth and tenth centuries. Elaborate architectural sculpture adorns the exterior. As at other churches in Tayk, the walls are covered by a system of blind arcading, and windows are surrounded with intricately sculpted frames (Fig. 9). The window frames of the west elevation, for example, feature interlaced bands of geometric motifs, and arched lintels are ornamented throughout with abstract decorative designs. The tympanum of the south portal, which bears a Georgian inscription, is decorated with an unusual pattern resembling waves, and on the surrounding archivolt is a geometricized rinceau (scroll) inhabited by elephants, rabbits, lions, and winged beasts (Fig. 10).

The most intriguing element of the church is the eastern apse, which is flanked by a side chapel to the south, and presumably once also by a chapel at the north. Instead of a solid curve of masonry, the apse is made up of an exedra of columns which screen a straight wall (Fig. 11). Thick and sturdy, the columns support an arcade of horseshoe arches and are adorned with a variety of capital types. Scholars who argue that the present structure of Ishkhan partially preserves Nerses' original foundation point directly to this arrangement and liken it to the columnar exedrae of Zvartnots. It is their contention that this element was original to the seventh-century structure and subsequently incorporated into the new church.

Yet there are a series of problems with this thesis. First, one may point out that many of the capital types used in the eastern exedrae at Ishkhan are far more stylized than those of Zvartnots, featuring large, generalized plant forms, and schematic Ionic capitals, in which the volutes are reduced to two large rosettes (Fig. 12).[22] It is also noteworthy that, unlike at Ishkhan, Zvartnots did not possess an exedra in its east end; rather, the apse was a solid wall. Such an architectural change is by no means trivial,

---

[22] One or two columns do survive with more volumetric proportions, however, which may form part of a rebuilding.

as the apse was the locus of the liturgy and would certainly correspond primarily to functional requirements. Until the absolute and relative chronologies of Zvartnots, Ishkhan, and Banak are made clear, these questions must remain.

Khakhu

The Monastery of Khakhu is situated on the flank of a mountain, surrounded by lush fruit-bearing and flower-bearing trees (Figs. 13-14).[23] Functioning today as a mosque, the complex was originally dedicated to the *Theotokos* (Bearer of God). A precise date and an identification of the religious and ethnic identity of the patron and initial congregation have not yet been established. Some scholars argue that Khakhu was an Armenian monophysite foundation built in the early 860s. Certainly an Armenian presence is attested by an inscription of mixed Armenian and Georgian characters that was detected on the interior of the east apse in the nineteenth century.[24] Nikolai Tokarski notes the bareness of the interior walls, suggesting that it was built by monophysite Armenians, who were disinclined, he asserts, to adorn churches with images.[25] Marutyan adds that the simplicity of the plan of Khakhu is in keeping with traditional Armenian architecture.[26] Maksoudian also argues that the foundation was monophysite Armenian but bases his opinion on Georgian literary sources, specifically two texts that mention the foundation of Khakhu: *The Georgian Royal Annals* (*Kartlis Tskhovreba*) and the *Geography of Vakhutsi*.[27] In the former, the church's foundation is credited to the curopalate David and placed in the second half of the tenth century. The latter source does not mention a date, stating that the church was built by "the *curopalate* David, the stepfather of King David."[28] Maksoudian argues that the latter source does not refer to the tenth-century David but rather to an epony-

---

[23] For further commentary and bibliography, see *Armenian Architecture*, 6, A-2050, B2ff.

[24] Ibid., B3.

[25] Ibid.

[26] Ibid.

[27] Ibid., B2.

[28] Ibid.

mous curopalate who ruled in the late ninth century. He uses epigraphic evidence to support this claim: in the nineteenth century, Nerses Sargisian discovered an inscription on the east wall of the church and deciphered from it a tentative date (in Armenian) of 862. Hence, Maksoudian places the foundation of the church in the 860s. In these years, he suggests, the construction of a monophysite foundation would have been quite conceivable, for the Council of Shirakavan, summoned by Ashot Bagratuni in 862, "established a *modus vivendi* between the Chalcedonian and monophysite Christians of Transcaucasia."[29]

This seems to be the strongest argument in favor of identifying the church as a monophysite foundation. By contrast, Tokarski's argument based on the absence of images at Khakhu is difficult to support, for not only are traces of wall painting actually preserved at the church, but one may also note that numerous medieval Armenian churches bore painting programs.[30] Marutyan's belief that the "simplicity" of the plan indicates Armenian monophysitism is equally problematic, as the layout of Khakhu is in fact quite complex. The greatest challenge to the argument of an Armenian monophysite foundation is the strong link to the tenth-century curopalate David, as attested to by the *Georgian Royal Annals*. Indeed, most scholars credit the foundation of Khakhu to David and date it to 975. Yet, given the presence of Armenian epigraphy at the church, one may also propose a connection to Armenians, perhaps adhering to the Chalcedonian faith.

The architectural features of the church deserve careful attention.[31] Surrounded by a circuit wall, the complex includes three chapels in addition to the main church. Most interesting is the architecture of the latter. In its attenuated dimensions, empha-

---

[29] Ibid., B3.

[30] This is true even in seventh-century foundations such as Talin, Ptghni, and Lmbat. Churches continue to bear painted decoration in the tenth century and onwards. For example, the programs of the monasteries of Datev, Dadivank, and, perhaps the most striking example of all, the elaborately painted interior of the Church of Gregory the Illuminator at Ani.

[31] In addition to its architecture, the monastery is also known for the famous Khakhuli triptych, now located in the Museum of Fine Arts in Tbilisi, which frames an ancient icon of the Virgin composed of Byzantine and Georgian enamels.

sized by a tall, steeply pointed roof, it is typical of tenth-century and eleventh-century building in Transcaucasia. Moreover, in its domed cruciform plan (Fig. 15), the structure resembles the nearby church of Ishkhan. The east end is relatively simple: the apse, decorated with blind arcades, is flanked by two deep side chambers accessible by barrel-vaulted lateral arms. The central dome, supported by squinches, is preceded at the west by three aisles, separated by piers. A series of annexes, believed to be of later date, surround the main body of the church. The north aisle communicates with a long, barrel-vaulted side chamber, and a second room, of similar proportions, stands at the south. This area is accessed through a door in the south aisle and features an open arcade on its south wall, giving entry to a courtyard. A chamber precedes the nave at the west of the church. Relatively narrow in proportion and covered by barrel vaults supported by a pair of columns, it resembles a typical Byzantine narthex. Yet unlike its Byzantine parallels, it does not communicate with the exterior of the church. An additional chamber stands at the corner between the southern portico and the western room, and a small apsed chapel is located just to the east of the portico.

In all these features—the presence of a barrel-vaulted chamber, the use of applied shafts and stepped profiles, the asymmetry of the supports, and the portico on the south side—the church forms part of a larger family of buildings in Tayk/Tao, including the churches of Ishkhan and Oshk. In particular, it is the complexity of the plans that is distinctive. Indeed, tenth-century architecture in Greater Armenia is also distinguished by the introduction of new spaces, particularly side chapels, *gavits* (antechambers to monastic churches), and upper stories. However, in these churches, the chambers are generally laid out within a geometric perimeter wall. In the churches of Tayk, the exterior profiles are often asymmetrical; hence, the church plans suggest aggregations of discrete chambers rather than unified conceptions. Why this type emerged in the northwest region of historical Armenia is uncertain; however, if the churches are Chalcedonian foundations, the layout might attest to the particular exigencies of the dyophysite rite, as it had evolved by the tenth century and beyond.[32]

The decoration of Khakhu is equally striking. On the interior, remnants of the paintings of a *Deesis* scene (Christ flanked by the Virgin and John the Baptist) and portraits of the apostles appear in the apse. On the exterior, huge cornices are suspended in the thickness of the wall, from which project sculpted animal heads. Blind arcades coat the outer walls as well as the tall, twelve-sided drum, which features long, narrow windows with arched lintels on alternating sides (Fig. 16). The frames of the lower elevation windows are particularly ornate, bearing polychrome voussoirs. On the south elevation, the main window is also decorated with twisted colonnettes and a stylized vegetal pattern on its lintel (Fig. 17). An eagle appears above the window carrying a hare in its talons, a subject that also occurs on the south facades at Oshk and the thirteenth-century chapel at Eghvard.[33]

As one of the focal points of the church, the southern portico is heavily decorated with relief sculpture, as seen in the large bunches of grapes adorning the capitals of the arcade. Most interesting, however, are the tenth-century scenes within the portico. On the south wall of the church, an image of the Theotokos appears holding the Christ Child and flanked by angels.[34] The south portal is entirely framed by scenes (Fig. 18). On the right, starting from the bottom, is a cat-like creature, an eagle or peacock-like bird, and a scene of Jonah and the Whale, the latter depicted as a fierce and toothy feline. Just above this image stands a saint with a large key in his left hand, with the Armenian uncial *G* carved at his right. There is debate on the identity of the figure; Marutyan believes it is Gregory (hence the G), while Maksoudian concludes that as the third letter of the

---

[32] It would be particularly important to compare these layouts with contemporary Georgian buildings, as well as Byzantine structures in the vicinity of Trebizond.

[33] Eastmond, *Royal Imagery of Medieval Georgia*, p. 230, suggests that this form might be a heraldic sign of the Georgian kings, but it is important to point out that it occurs with great frequency in Armenian foundations as well.

[34] Maksoudian, *Armenian Architecture*, 6, A-2050, B5, writes that the Virgin's image was still venerated at the beginning of the twentieth century by Muslim women wishing to conceive children, and he points out that such a practice has a long history in Armenia (and, we might add, elsewhere in the medieval world).

Armenian alphabet it refers to the Trinity.[35] Given the prominence of the key, however, it is most probably that the figure
should be identified as Peter. On the left side of the portal,
starting from the top, is a damaged scene of a haloed figure
battling a serpent, a *simurgh* (a mythical winged beast, part-bird,
part-lion in form), and two animals in combat. In the tympanum
are four angels carrying the cross. Certain elements of the program are familiar, such as the scenes of animal combat, the
biblical episode, and the simurgh, which is a frequent theme of
medieval textiles. In its arched composition, however, the portal
sculpture more closely resembles the canon tables of illuminated
manuscripts.

Varzahan

The church of Varzahan, which no longer survives, was located
near the city of Baberd, now Bayburt, and dated to the twelfth
century.[36] Although unknown to medieval sources, the church
does figure in the accounts of nineteenth-century travelers. Small
and domed, Varzahan was octagonal on the exterior, while the
interior space was defined by eight conches, of which the east-
ernmost formed a horseshoe-shaped apse (Fig. 19). The other
conches curved inward only in the upper elevation, and each was
flanked by slender octagonal shafts, which formed the support
for an arch-rib. The structure was illuminated by a pair of narrow
windows in each of the conches, with three openings in the
eastern apse. Three doors, located on the west, north, and south,
provided access to the interior.

In the 1840s, the church still stood, as is attested by the
account of English Assyriologist Austen Henry Layard.[37] En route
to Nineveh, he visited the site and wrote an account of his
impressions of the architecture and paintings. Layard also made
a drawing of the exterior, which was highly decorated, featuring

---

[35] Ibid.

[36] See *Armenian Architecture*, 6, A-3077, A8, for further discussion and bibliography.

[37] Austen Henry Layard, *Discoveries in the Ruins of Nineveh and Babylon, with
Travels in Armenia, Kurdistan and the Desert* (London: John Murray, 1853).

triangular niches with blind arcading, pointed arches, twisted colonettes, and polychrome voussoirs (Fig. 20). Most of the church survived into the early twentieth century as shown in the illustrations of Walter Bachmann, who journeyed through the region in 1911 (Figs. 21-22).[38] What is most important perhaps is Layard's commentary, which is significant for the historiography of Armenian architecture. One of the first to note the Western-looking features of Armenian architecture, Layard remarked that the decoration "calls to mind the European Gothic of the Middle Ages" and suggested that from Varzahan was "probably derived much that passed into the Gothic."[39] The author's observations on the structure convinced him of the important role of Armenian architecture in the development of Gothic architecture:

> The architect, or traveler, interested in the history of that graceful and highly original branch of art . . . should extend his journey to the remains of ancient Armenian cities, far from high roads and mostly unexplored. . . . He would discover almost daily, details, ornaments, and forms, recalling to his mind the various orders of architecture, which, at an early period, succeeded to each other in Western Europe and England.[40]

The often striking parallels between Armenian and Gothic architecture have been a matter of debate for more than a century and a half. The topic, which is extremely complex, has been treated recently by the present author.[41] For the purposes of this overview, it is simply important to note that Varzahan was the first monument to raise European awareness of Armenian architecture and to call attention to its often intriguingly Western features.

---

[38] Walter Bachmann, *Kirchen und Moscheen in Armenien und Kurdistan* (Leipzig: J.C. Hinrich: 1913), Table 8.

[39] Ibid., p. 7.

[40] Ibid., p. 27.

[41] Christina Maranci, *Medieval Armenian Architecture: Constructions of Race and Nation* (Louvain: Peeters, 2001).

Forts and Tomb Towers:
Other Architectural Traditions of the Erzerum Area

The area of Erzerum is also one of the most densely fortified areas of historical Armenia. Numerous fortresses line the mountain passes of the regions of Olti (Oltu) and Artvin, which have been studied extensively by Robert Edwards.[42] He has argued that the presence of certain physical features often reveals the identity of the fortresses' builders. He also observes that Armenian fortifications display several unique features that offered particularly effective defense against intruders. This may be seen in the fortress of Olan, in the Olti-Penek area (Figs. 23-24).[43] The Olan cloister is not geometric in its perimeter wall, but rather conforms to the outline of the mountain on which it stands (Fig. 25). This feature, Edwards notes, makes optimum use of the natural defenses of the mountainous topography, which was often marked by spurs and jagged cliffs. Olan also possesses a bent entrance, which, according to Edwards, is another characteristic of Armenian fortification architecture. Forcing a momentary hesitation before the turn, the bent entrance renders attackers vulnerable to soldiers positioned on upper wall-walks. A third important element protects Olan: rounded wall towers, or bastions, which are common to Armenian military architecture and extremely useful during sieges. Lacking corners, these structures discourage sapping, a term referring to the technique of excavating the corner of a structure to cause it to topple. In its layout and defensive features, the Olan cloister is representative of many other fortifications in the vicinity of Erzerum. In fact, as Edwards himself attests, a number of Georgian fortifications, such as those of Shavshat, Ardahan, and Artvin, also feature rounded towers and non-geometric plans, which suggests, as do the area churches, active relations between the two communities.

Cross-cultural interaction can also be observed within the city

---

[42] Robert W. Edwards, "Medieval Architecture in the Oltu-Penek Valley: A Preliminary Report on the Marchlands of Northeast Turkey," *Dumbarton Oaks Papers* 39 (1985): 15-37.

[43] See *Armenian Architecture*, 6, A-2122, A2.

of Erzerum in three Seljuk tomb towers (Fig. 26).[44] Dating to the tenth and eleventh centuries, the tombs are small, single-unit structures, each consisting of a square chamber capped by a dome and tall, conical roof. Hence, in their configuration, they almost exclusively recall the centrally-planned churches of the Caucasus. The presence of such architectural ideas in a Muslim context might seem rather surprising to the modern spectator, but such cultural exchange can be detected frequently in the medieval monuments of the Near East. One may note that Armenian architecture also appropriated ideas from Islamic architecture: multi-faceted *muqarnas* vaults, for example, are incorporated into the Armenian decorative vocabulary by the twelfth and thirteenth centuries. The Erzerum tomb towers hence offer important evidence that for the Armenian and Muslim inhabitants of the area, architectural ideas could transcend political and religious boundaries.

The monuments discussed above raise more questions than they provide answers. Building histories, foundation dates, and the identities of founders or builders remain, in many cases, unclear. What is certain, however, is that the medieval monuments of the area were not produced in a vacuum but rather participated in a lively exchange among communities of different ethnic, religious, and political backgrounds, including Armenian monophysites, Armenian Chalcedonians, Georgians, Byzantines, and Seljuks. Evading easy classification into modern categories of race and nation, the architecture of the Erzerum area invites us to rethink our notion of the field. Rather than an insular and narrowly circumscribed tradition, the monuments offer a more complicated picture of Armenian architecture, in which architectural production was informed not only by internal forces but also by the process of cultural exchange.

---

[44] For further discussion and bibliography on Seljuk tomb towers, see David Stronach and Thomas C. Young, "Three Octagonal Seljuk Tomb Towers from Iran," 4 *Iran* (1966): 1-20.

Fig. 1. Banak: Reconstruction by A. Kalgin

Fig. 2. Banak: Interior, Looking into Ambulatory

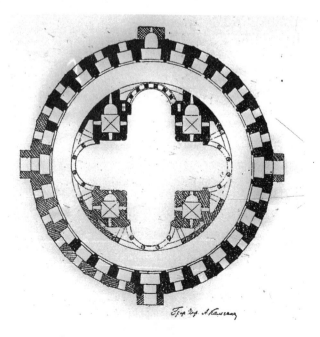

Fig. 3. Banak: Plan, after A. Kalgin

Fig. 4. Banak: Capital of Exedra

Fig. 5. Ishkhan

108

Fig. 6. Oshk

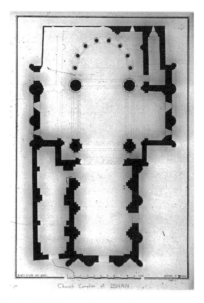

Fig. 7. Ishkhan: Plan, after R. Mertens

Fig. 8. Ishkhan: Interior, Dome

Fig. 9. Ishkhan: West Elevation, Window Frame

Fig. 10. Ishkhan: North Portal, Tympanum

Fig. 11. Ishkhan: Apse

Fig. 12. Ishkhan: Apse, Arcade Capital

Fig. 13. Khakhu: Rendition by Theophile Deyrolle

Fig. 14. Khakhu

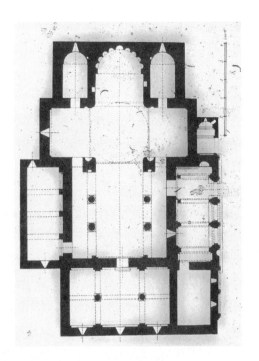

Fig. 15. Khakhu: Plan, after A. Kalgin

Fig. 16. Khakhu: Drum and Dome

Fig. 17. Khakhu: South Elevation, Window

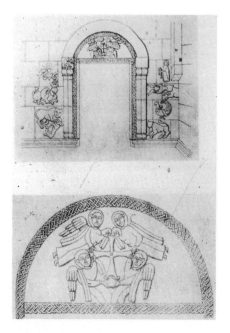

Fig. 18. Khakhu: South Portico,
Portal Decoration, after David Winfield

Fig. 19. Varzahan: Drawing, 1840s, after A.H. Layard

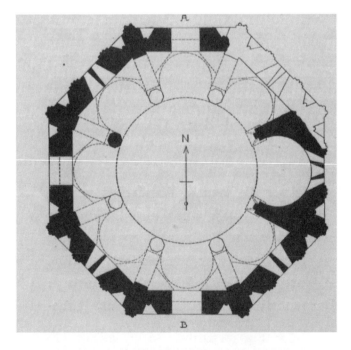

Fig. 20. Varzahan: Plan, after Walter Bachmann

Fig. 21. Varzahan, 1911

Fig. 22. Varzahan Cemetery Monuments

Fig. 23. Olan Cloister

119

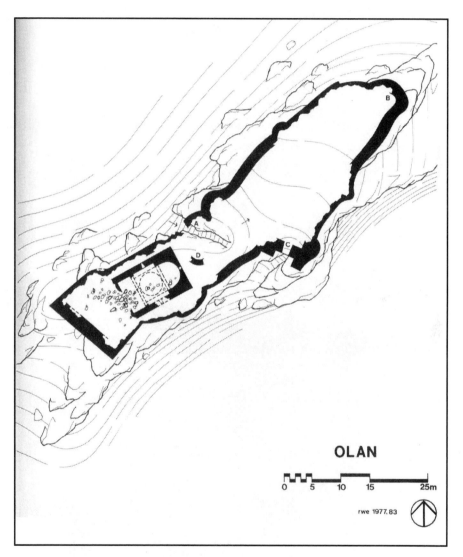

OLAN

0   5   10   15   25m

rwe 1977, 83

Fig. 24. Olan Cloister: Plan, after Robert Edwards

Fig. 25. Olan Church

Fig. 26. Erzerum: Tomb Tower

❋ 6 ❋

THE DECLINE AND REVIVAL OF ERZERUM: SIXTEENTH-EIGHTEENTH CENTURIES

Dickran Kouymjian

Writing the history of an Armenian city such as Karin/Erzerum under Ottoman rule becomes increasingly difficult as the constant flow of revisionist Turkish historiography distorts the evidence of its own official archives and as the selective vision of popular Armenian imagination gets blinded at times by dogmatic positions. The history of Erzerum from the sixteenth to the eighteenth century is that of a city which deteriorated to near extinction, then rose to impressive heights, only to fall once again.

Using three distinct sets of sources—scribal colophons of Armenian manuscripts, Western travel accounts, and Ottoman defters, especially tax registers—I have tried to piece together a narrative of the rise and fall of this ancient fortified city on the Armenian Plateau. In the early 1980s, I statistically charted the output of manuscripts from several localities, including Erzerum, to see if the ups and downs of frequency graphs correspond with moments of prosperity and decline known from purely historical sources.[1] In the case of Erzerum, they do just that. These colophonic data are reinforced by travel reports and, for the sixteenth century, three Turkish defters from Erzerum.[2]

In 1502, Shah Ismail of Iran took Erzerum from the Ak Koyunlu Turkmen dynasty, which had ruled there since the 1460s. Twelve year later, in 1514, Ottoman Sultan Selim (the Grim) assembled a large army, seized Erzinjan (Erznka), Kemakh, and Erzerum, and

---

[1] Dickran Kouymjian, "Dated Armenian Manuscripts as a Statistical Tool for Armenian History," *Medieval Armenian Culture*, Thomas Samuelian and Michael Stone, eds. (Chico, CA: Scholars Press, 1983), pp. 425-39.

[2] Ibid., p. 435, Fig. 3.

engaged Shah Ismail on the plain of Chaldiran. With superior artillery, the Ottomans soundly defeated the Safavids and advanced to Tabriz. In the century-long war that followed, Erzerum, along with Van, served as a primary staging point. Sultan Suleiman (the Magnificent) alone led three important campaigns against Iran, in 1534, 1548, and 1554, all starting out from his major military base at Erzerum.[3]

Erzerum, historic Karin, had been an active Armenian center from early medieval times. Manuscript colophons bear this out. An examination of the catalogues of about half of the surviving Armenian manuscripts, including the largest collection of 12,000 to 15,000 codices that are preserved in the Matenadaran in Erevan, uncovered some 170 from Karin/Erzerum. Ninety percent of these were copied in the city itself or its suburbs, the others in nearby monasteries and villages. There are ten Erzerum manuscripts from the early centuries, one from the mid-eleventh and three each from the twelfth, thirteenth, and fourteenth centuries. But afterward, from 1335 to 1570, there is just one manuscript, dated 1488, underlining the desperate conditions in and around Erzerum during the successive incursions of Turkmens, Safavids, and Ottomans. The low point of scribal activity was in the three decades from 1500 to 1530, a time of violent and merciless combat between Persians and Turks over Armenian lands.[4]

The impression of Erzerum as a prosperous city up to the first half of the fourteenth century is borne out by travelers. Marco Polo writes in 1272: "The noblest of their [the Armenians] cities is Arzinga [Erznka] . . . and then Arziron [Erzerum] and Arzizi [Arjesh]."[5] In 1318, Odoric of Pordenone observes: "I came into

---

[3] For details of the history of this period in historic Armenia, see Dickran Kouymjian, "Sous le joug des Turcomans et des Turcs ottomans (XVᵉ-XVIᵉ siècles)," *Histoire des Arméniens,* Gérard Dédéyan, ed. (Toulouse: Privat, 1982), pp. 341-76, and "Armenia from the Fall of the Cilician Kingdom (1375) to the Forced Emigration under Shah Abbas (1604)," in Richard G. Hovannisian, ed., *The Armenian People from Ancient to Modern Times,* vol. 2 (New York: St. Martin's Press, 1997), pp. 1-50.

[4] Kouymjian, "Armenia from the Fall of the Cilician Kingdom," pp. 14-16, 43, and "Dated Armenian Manuscripts," p. 429.

[5] Henry Yule, *The Book of Ser Marco Polo, the Venetian, Concerning the Kingdoms and Marvels of the East,* 3d ed., vol. 1 (New York: Charles Scribners & Sons, 1903), p. 45, as quoted in Vatche Ghazarian, *Armenians in the Ottoman Empire: An*

Armenia the Greater, to a certain city which is called Arziron, which in time long past was a fine and most wealthy city, and it would have been so unto this day but for the Tartars and the Saracens, who have done it much damage. It abounded greatly in bread and flesh, and many other kinds of victual, but not in wine or fruits. For the city is mighty cold, and folk say that it is the highest city that is at this day inhabited on the whole face of the earth."[6] By the time of Ibn Battuta's visit in 1330, the city was in clear decline: "Arz ar-Rum . . . [is] a place of vast extent, but mostly in ruins in consequence of a factional feud which broke out between two groups of Turkmens there."[7] This impression is confirmed by John Mandeville in 1332: "Artiron [Erzerum], the which was wont to be a good city and a rich and a fair [one], but the Turks have destroyed it."[8] In 1403, Ruy Gonzales de Clavijo, the Spanish ambassador to the court of Tamerlane, gives a very short narrative on the city:

> At midday we had reached the city of Erzerum, which is of the lordship of Timur. It stands in the plain and is encircled by a very broad strong stone wall with many towers; and there is a castle here, but the city is not very populous. We saw also a fine church, for this city formerly belonged to the Armenian kingdom which is Christian, and many Armenians still live here: indeed in the past Erzerum was the richest and greatest city of all those parts. The governor of the town at the present moment is a Turkoman, whose name is Yusuf 'Ali.[9]

Anthology of Transformation, 13th-19th Centuries (Waltham, MA: Mayreni Publishing Co., 1998), p. 7.

[6] Henry Yule, *Cathay and the Way Thither, Being a Collection of Medieval Notices on China*, vol. 2 (London,: Hakluyt Society, 1913), pp. 100-01, as cited by Ghazarian, *Armenians*, p. 8.

[7] *The Travels of Ibn Battuta A.D. 1325-1354*, H.A.R. Gibb, trans., made after the French translation of Défremery and Sanguinette, vol. 2 (Cambridge: Hakluyt Society, 1962), p. 437; cf. Ghazarian, *Armenians*, p. 11. Of course, reference is to the Kara Koyunlu and Ak Koyunlu Turkmen tribes/dynasties, for which see Kouymjian, "Armenia from the Fall of the Cilician Kingdom," pp. 4-8.

[8] Malcolm Letts, *Mandeville's Travels*, vol. 1 (London: Hakluyt Society, 1953), p. 106; cf. Ghazarian, *Armenians*, p. 12.

[9] Clavijo, *Embassy to Tamerlane 1403-1406*, trans. Guy Le Strange (New York and London: Harper and Brothers, 1928), pp. 138-39; cf. Ghazarian, *Armenians*, p. 29.

And then there is silence. There is virtually nothing in travel books about Erzerum for more than two centuries from Clavijo in 1403 to Evliya Chelebi in 1645, unless we count John Newberry's note in 1581 that the city has three gates and one can get plenty to eat there.[10] Of the four dated Armenian manuscripts from our sampling copied in Erzerum in the sixteenth century, three are from after the 1590 Ottoman-Persian Safavid Treaty of Amasia, which left most of Armenia to the Turks. What then was happening to Erzerum and its inhabitants during that long period of war? Thanks to Ottoman fiscal registers of 1523, 1540, and 1591, there is some precise information for the sixteenth century.[11]

The defter of 1523 is perhaps the most striking. Though it shows that the city has twelve quarters (*mahalles*), they are all empty. Erzerum has been deserted because of the havoc of the successive wars of the fifteenth and early sixteenth centuries, explaining the absence of both travel accounts and manuscript production.[12]

The register of 1540 reports the city has three gates and twenty-seven quarters but only twenty-one male householders, and most of these are *sipahi* (cavalry), representing with their families barely 100 souls. None of the quarters, including that of the Erzinjan gate, has a single resident. Erzerum is an enormous, double-walled, fortified city, with mosques, churches, schools, caravanserais, khans, shops, and homes, but they are completely empty except for the garrison. The official responsible for the 1540 tax survey remarks: "Because Erzurum is on the frontier (serhad) . . . the populace (ahali) have been scattered and dispersed (perakende) by the Kizilbaş and the Gürci. The city stands empty and in ruins (hali ve harab)."[13]

---

[10] As quoted by Ghazarian, *Armenians*, p. 50, from Samuel Purchas, *Hakluytus posthumus, or Purchas His Pilgrimes* (Glasgow: J. MacLehose and Sons, 1905-07).

[11] Ronald C. Jennings, "Urban Population in Anatolia in the Sixteenth Century: A Study of Kayseri, Karaman, Amasya, Trabzon, and Erzurum," *International Journal of Middle East Studies* 7:1 (1976): 21-57, largely summarized in Kouymjian, "Sous le joug," pp. 362-63, and "Armenia from the Fall of the Cilician Kingdom," pp. 27-29.

[12] "The icmal defter of 1523 says simply of the city of Erzurum that it is empty and destroyed (hali ve harab)," Jennings, "Urban Population," p. 47.

[13] Jennings, "Urban Population," p. 48. Jennings continues: "Erzurum had been conquered, fortified, and restored by the Ottomans, but even in 1540 no one dared live there. Apparently, despite resounding Ottoman victories, no one felt sure that

There are twenty quarters listed in the third register of 1591, but they are no longer empty. There are now 548 males, representing a total population of about 2,000, still a small number even though twenty times more than a half a century earlier. Of these, 66 percent are Christian, nearly all Armenians, and 34 percent Muslim. Every quarter of the city has inhabitants. Eight of the quarters are Muslim, eight Armenian, and four mixed. The latter are the largest and make up about 55 percent of the total population, indicating that the new inhabitants are generally at ease in a religiously integrated environment. Three *mahalles* that are named after trades are entirely peopled by Armenians: the Debbagan or Tanner's Quarter, the Boya Khane or Dye-Houses, and the Anbar or Granary. The defters also list males by name, making it easy to identify the *zimmis* (protected non-believers) as Armenians: Ovanis, Babajan, Toros, Agob, Asuador, Kirkor, Murad, Hatchik, Karabid, Serkis, Bedros, etc.[14]

The Ottoman account books show that the resettlement of Erzerum by a civil population began in the late-sixteenth century and was dominated by Armenians. Though there are no travel accounts to confirm this until the middle of the next century, the number of contemporary Armenian manuscripts reinforces this notion: three from the last years of the sixteenth century, then seven in the first half and twenty-five in the second half of the seventeenth century. The numbers increase sharply after the 1639 Ottoman-Persian Treaty of Zuhab, which put a definitive end to nearly a century and a half of warfare.

The new prosperity of Karin/Erzerum is confirmed, though sometimes with reservations, by seventeenth-century travel accounts, starting with Evliya Chelebi in 1645. However, his narrative is at times enigmatic: "Erzerum contains seventy quarters of Moslims, and seven of Infidels. There are no Armenians, Copts, or Jews; if any make their appearance they run the risk of being killed."[15] Yet a bit further on he notes: "The inhabitants [of Erzerum] are all Turkomans and Armenian Kurds" [sic]. "Outside

---

the Safavid threat had been removed."

[14] Ibid., p. 47.

[15] *Evliya Çelebi, Narrative of Travels in Europe, Asia, and Africa in the Seventeenth Century*, trans. Joseph Von Hammar, vol. 2 (London: Oriental Translation Fund, 1850), pp. 111-14. This and most of the following citations are taken from the compendium prepared by Vatche Ghazarian, *Armenians in the Ottoman Empire*.

of the gates of the fortress on the east, west and north sides, is the
suburb, inhabited by more than thirty thousand Rayas," presumably
Armenians. The suburb is divided into seven quarters:

> The suburb of the Georgians on the north side is the quarter of the
> rich merchants; here is the custom house where I was employed as
> a clerk: around it are the houses of Persian, Indian, and Chinese
> merchants. Next to the custom-houses of Constantinople and
> Smryna, that of Erzerum is the most busy. The suburb of Erzenjan
> . . . [is] mostly inhabited by Armenians, there are thirteen churches
> here. The Infidels wear variegated turbans, and blue coats, and the
> lower classes wear felt, with coarse shoes called Chark; their
> women wrap white sheets around their heads.[16]

Unfortunately, Evliya Chelebi does not give the exact number
of Muslims. We are at a loss, therefore, to compare the 30,000
Armenian rayas to the total population. If we accept the testimony
at face value, the mixed quarters of fifty years earlier seem to have
disappeared, leaving Erzerum with segregated neighborhoods.
Several other travelers of the seventeenth century help only partially to clarify the situation. In 1648, Alexander of Rhodes describes Erzerum as "the most beautiful and well-known [city] in all
lower Armenia."[17] Jean Baptiste Tavernier is less enthusiastic in
1655: "Erzerom is a frontier town of Turkey toward Persia. . . . If
you take in the castle and the suburbs it may pass for a city, but the
houses are built of wood, without any neatness of proportion. There
are some remains of churches and of the ancient buildings of the
Armenians, by which you may conjecture that it never was very
beautiful. . . . There are in Erzerom several great inns; this city, like
Tocat, being one of the greatest thoroughfares in Turkey."[18] Paul
Rycaut writes in 1666 that the revenue of the pasha of Erzerum is
1,200,660 aspers, the highest for any of the eastern provinces, equal

---

[16] Ibid., pp. 113-14.

[17] Solange Hertz, *The Travels and Missions of Father Alexander de Rhodes in
China and Other Kingdoms of the Orient* (Westminster, MD: Newman Press, 1966),
p. 252.

[18] Jean Baptiste Tavernier, *The Six Voyages of John Baptista Tavernier, a Noble
Man of France Now Living, through Turkey into Persia and the East-Indies,
Finished in the Year 1670 Giving an Account of the State of Those Countries*, trans.
J.P. (London: Dr. Daniel Cox, 1677), p. 8.

to all of Mesopotamia including Diarbekir, and more than Van with 1,032,209 aspers and Sivas with 900,000 aspers.[19]

On the other hand, the Catholic missionary Philippe Avril, who traveled from Aleppo in 1692 disguised as an Armenian, for reasons of security he explains, is very laudatory about Erzerum and its Armenian inhabitants:

> Erzerum, or Arzeron, is . . . seated in a pleasant plain, about seven or eight leagues in circuit. . . . [A] more advantageous situation cannot be picked out by mortal eyes, than that of this city which we have made choice of for the settlement of our new mission. It is near about as big as Marseilles, encompassed with a double enclosure of walls, after the ancient manner. . . . The suburbs are very large and well peopled. The air is wholesome; the water excellent, and in great plenty. In a word, everything concurs to make it one of the best cities of the Ottoman empire.
>
> But that which is most of all to be considered, and which above all things put us upon resolving to settle here, is the vast concourse of all nations that trade in Asia, more especially of the Armenians, who have a particular kindness for this city, which was formerly the seat of their kings; . . . to this day there are to be seen the ruins of the palace where they kept their court, with some beautiful remains of the patriarchal church which they had built in honor of St. John.
>
> The Armenians more especially were so sensible of our zeal, to prefer them before all other nations of the earth. . . .
>
> I had the pleasure during a stay of six months that I made at Erzerum, to see that growing church increasing with so much success that I thought we had no reason to envy the primitive ages of Christianity.[20]

Yet, in the following year, 1693, a somewhat different picture of the city and relations with the Catholics is drawn by Giovanni Francesco Gemelli Careri: "[Near the castle] is the Armenian cathedral, much decayed, excepting two towers built of brick. . . .

---

[19] Paul Rycaut, *The Present State of the Ottoman Empire*, 3d ed. (London: J. Starkey and H. Browne, 1670), p. 53. An asper was a small silver coin, 80 of which were equivalent in value to a large silver piaster.

[20] Philippe Avril, *Travels into Divers Parts of Europe and Asia* (London: Tim Goodwin, 1693), pp. 45-49.

The houses, as also those in the suburbs, for the most part inhabited by Armenians, are low, and made of wood and mud; the streets narrow, and unpaved; the bazars mean; but it is so populous, that there are in the suburbs only, twenty-two caravanserais for the caravans of Persia." He adds that the Jesuits and Dominicans are being driven out by the pasha who has been bribed by the "schismatic" Armenians to prevent the Catholic fathers from settling in Erzerum.[21]

The eighteenth century was even more active culturally than the previous one for the Armenians of Erzerum, with forty-five manuscripts in our survey, a 50 percent increase, fifteen being copied in the city before 1750 and thirty after. At the very beginning, there is the testimony of Joseph Pitton de Tournefort, who passed through Erzerum in 1701 and left a rather substantial description, full of praise for the Armenians. After remarking on the natural beauty of the country and, as a true Frenchman, how awful the brandy and the wine were, he gives an array of population figures:

> It is thought there are eighteen thousand Turks in [Erzerum], six thousand Armenians and four hundred Greeks. They reckon sixty thousand Armenians in the province, and ten thousand Greeks. The Turks who are almost all of them Janizaries, they reckon about twelve thousand there, and above fifty thousand in the rest of the province. . . .
> The Armenians have a bishop and two churches [in the city]. They have some monasteries in the country, [such] as the Great Convent and the Red Convent. They all acknowledge the Patriarch of Erivan. . . .
> This town is the thoroughfare and resting-place for all the merchandise of the Indies.

According to Tournefort, the government of Erzerum yields 300 purses yearly to the pasha, the source of the revenue being a 3 percent duty on merchandise, the sale of offices, and an exit tax of 5 crowns per person for all except Turks, by which he must have meant Muslims. The province yielded 600 purses to the sultan,

---

[21] Giovanni Francesco Gemelli Careri, *A Voyage Round the World by Dr. John Francis Gemelli Careri*, vol. 4 (London: Messrs Churchill for Henry Lintor and John Osborn, 1745), pp. 101-02.

besides 300 purses of *kharaj* (land tax) exacted from the Armenians and Greeks.[22] The pasha also gets 6 percent custom duty on merchandise. Regarding the Armenians, the author states:

> The Armenians are the best people in the world, civil, polite, and full of good sense and probity. I should account them happy in not understanding the use of arms, if it were not by the corruption of mankind become necessary to use them sometimes, purely to defend ourselves against the violence of others. But the Armenians trouble themselves with nothing but trade, which they follow with the utmost attention and application. They are not only masters of the trade of the Levant, but have a large share in that of the most considerable places in Europe.[23]

Near the end of the century, in 1784, Elias Habesci reports that the revenue of Erzerum province is 1,200,000 aspers, the same as Rycaut's figures a century earlier, but higher than that from "Armenia" with 900,000 aspers, and from Kars and Trebizond with 82,000 aspers each.[24]

In the first three decades of the nineteenth century, Erzerum and its Armenians continued to prosper. For just those thirty years, at a time when Armenian printing was replacing almost totally hand-copied books, at least 65 Armenian manuscripts were executed in Karin. The city continued to grow even though Armenians were no longer in the majority. In 1807 a certain Monsieur Tancoigne observes:

> Erzerum, the capital of Turkish Armenia, is, next to Baghdad, the largest city of Turkey in Asia. . . .
>
> It is supposed to contain more than one hundred thousand inhabitants, and is one of the most opulent cities in Asia, from its commerce in copper, furs, madders, drugs, etc., which attract a great concourse of foreigners, especially Persians. Its bazars are the largest and best furnished of any we have seen since our departure from Constantinople, but . . . the streets are dirty and badly paved.

---

[22] In the seventeenth century, a purse was equivalent to about 40,000 aspers.

[23] Joseph Pitton de Tournefort, *A Voyage into the Levant*, vol. 2 (London: D. Browne, A. Bell, 1718), pp. 195-96, 291; cf. Ghazarian, *Armenians*, pp. 108-09.

[24] Elias Habesci, *The Present State of the Ottoman Empire* (London: R. Baldwin, 1784), p. 189.

. . . The suburbs without the ramparts are chiefly inhabited by Armenian artisans.[25]

Nineteenth-century travelers seem more interested in statistics than their predecessors. James Morier, using an Armenian informant, states that in 1808-09, "In Arz-roum there are four or five thousand families of the Armenian [or some 20,000-25,000 individuals], and about one hundred of the Greek persuasion: the former have two churches, the latter one. . . . The Turkish inhabitants of Arz-roum are fifty thousand families [sic; perhaps persons]. This amount of population I give from the authority of a well-informed Armenian."[26] However, five years later, John Kinneir writes:

> Erzeroom . . . is the largest city in Armenia. . . . The houses are small and mean, in some places built of stone, and in others of mud and bricks dried in the sun; the windows being pasted with paper instead of glass. The citadel . . . is three or four miles in circumference; the walls are in good repair, built in the old manner with battlements and angular towers and formed of a gray stone, of a very durable quality, dug in the adjoining mountains. The pasha and the greatest proportion of the Turkish population reside within the walls; there are four gates, but none of them merit a particular description. The inhabitants are said to amount to fifteen thousand families of Mahomedans, three thousand seven hundred [families of] Armenians, three hundred [families of] Armenian Catholicos and three hundred and fifty [families of] Greeks. The Armenians have two churches and a metropolitan.[27]

Morier's "50,000 families" should probably be understood as "50,000 individuals," because 15,000 Muslim families would make just a bit more than that figure. So, too, Robert Ker Porter claims that the population in 1817-20, again according to an Armenian, is

---

[25] M. Tancoigne, *A Narrative of Journey into Persia, and Residence at Teheran*, trans. from French (London: William Wright, 1820), pp. 46-47.

[26] James Justinian Morier, *A Journey through Persia, Armenia, and Asia Minor, to Constantinople, in the Years 1808 and 1809* (London: Longman, Hurst, Rees, Orme, and Brown, 1812), p. 322.

[27] John Macdonald Kinneir, *Journey through Asia Minor, Armenia, and Koordistan, in the Years 1813 and 1814* (London: John Murray, 1818), pp. 365-66.

6,000 Christians and 50,000 Mahomedans.[28] For 1828-29, Thomas Alcock reports: "Arzroom is one of the ancient capitals of Armenia, possessing about sixty thousand inhabitants; it was formerly fortified, but cannot be considered so at present, as the citadel, in the center of the town, is totally dilapidated."[29]

Perhaps the state of the forts contributed to the Russian capture of the city in the autumn of 1828. When the Russian army retreated the next year, an estimated 10,000 Armenian families, a quarter of which were from the city proper, trailed behind, partly in fear of Turkish reprisals and partly because of Russian promises. The city was nearly emptied of its Armenians and, therefore, of its most productive element. The colophons are eloquent witnesses of this: in the 1820s, thirty-three manuscripts from Erzerum are recorded, in the next ten years the number drops to four, and for the rest of the century, only six.

The American Reverend Eli Smith, along with Reverend Harrison O. Dwight, passed through Erzerum in 1830, shortly after these events:

The population of Erzroom, before the severe ravages of the plague a few years ago, was estimated at 100,000. At the time of the Russian invasion it contained, we were told upon authority of the collector of taxes at our second visit, 11,733 Turkish, and 4,645 Christian houses; making a population of about 80,000 souls. Of the Christian inhabitants, 50 houses were Greeks, and 645 papal Armenians, leaving 3,950 houses, or about 19,000 souls, belonging to the proper Armenian church.

Nearly all the Christian population had left before we arrived, and the city was so unsettled that I can do little more than give you a brief account of it as it was. . . . Though the Armenians were so numerous, and their city the largest in Armenia, it is a curious fact that they had but two churches. One of them was very small, and the other so irregular, dark and mean, as to resemble a stable almost as much as an edifice for divine worship. . . . The priests, however, were sufficiently numerous; they amounted to 32. Not far from the

[28] Robert Ker Porter, *Travels in Georgia, Persia, Armenia, Ancient Babylonia etc., etc. during the Years 1817, 1818, 1819, and 1820*, vol. 2 (London: Longman, Hurst, Rees, Orme, and Brown, 1822), pp. 668-69.
[29] Thomas Alcock, *Travels in Russia, Persia, Turkey, and Greece, in 1828-9* (London: E. Clarke and Son, 1831), p. 124.

city are four Armenian convents, each of which was inhabited by three or four vartabeds, and had funds enough for its support; but all of them are now deserted. . . .

Owing to the patronage of the bishop, perhaps, the Armenian grammar school of Erzroom was unusually large and flourishing. Its principal was a layman, who had 5 or 6 assistants; and it contained 500 or 600 scholars, divided into different departments, and studying all the common branches up to grammar and logic.[30]

Smith was told that there was an exceptionally high rate of literacy among Armenian males, as much as 50 percent.

This of course is not the end of the Erzerum story. Armenians gradually returned from Russian exile and migrated from elsewhere, and, as numerous later travelers testify, they began reconstructing community life, opening new schools and other institutions. That, however, is another chapter in the history of Armenians in Karin/Erzerum.[31]

---

[30] Eli Smith, *Researches of the Rev. E. Smith and Rev. H.G.O. Dwight in Armenia, Including a Journey through Asia Minor, and into Georgia and Persia, with a Visit to the Nestorian and Chaldean Christians of Oormiah and Salmas,* vol. 1 (Boston: Crocker and Brewster, 1833), pp. 126-29.

❋ 7 ❋

THE DEMOGRAPHY
OF THE PROVINCE OF ERZERUM:
SIXTEENTH-TWENTIETH CENTURIES

Ashot A. Melkonyan

Between the sixteenth and twentieth centuries, major demographic and ethnographic changes occurred in the region of Karin/Erzerum and throughout all of Western Armenia. The influx of Turkic peoples and Kurdish tribes, the periodic violence and calamities, the forced conversion of countless Christians to Islam, and the flight of masses of people to safer localities all contributed to this development. An overview of these factors based on several contemporary sources and published studies is given in this essay.

During the fifteenth century, the emerging Ottoman Empire, after having already conquered western Asia Minor and much of the Balkans, also turned eastward. Defeating Uzun Hasan and his Ak Koyunlu Turkmen confederation at the battle of Derjan in 1473, Sultan Mehmed II annexed much of the Armenian Plateau, and Sultan Selim (the Grim) extended the empire further in 1514 by overpowering Shah Ismail of Persia (Iran) in the decisive battle of Chaldiran, northeast of Lake Van near Mount Ararat. The administrative divisions of the conquered territories were marked by frequent, destabilizing changes resulting from the political and economic interests of the Muslim ruling elite.

By the 1530s, Western Armenia had been divided into the *eyalets* or provinces of Erzerum (Karin), Sivas (Sebastia), Van, Diarbekir (Tigranakert), Kars, and Akhaltskha.[1] The *sanjak* or *liva* (county) of Bayazed (Bayazid; Bayazit), sometimes mentioned

---

[1] About the administrative divisions of the Ottoman Empire, see Andreas Birken, *Die Provinzen des Osmanischen Reiches* (Wiesbaden: Reichert, 1976).

in the sources as a separate eyalet, actually constituted part of the province of Erzerum but with broad autonomy. This expansive province covered an area of 70,000 to 80,000 square kilometers (27,300 to 31,200 square miles), including the following administrative districts: Erzerum, Upper Basen (Passin), Lower or Interior Basen, Khnus, Kghi, Derjan (Terjan), Erznka (Erzinjan), Baberd (Baiburt), Sper (Ispir), and Tortum, together with the sanjak-liva of Bayazed—the residence of the local pasha—with its four subdistricts: Bayazed, Alashkert (Alashgerd), Diadin, and Khamur.

What was the demographic situation in the central provinces of Western Armenia from the end of the fifteenth century to the middle of the seventeenth century, that is, during the period of the Turkish conquests? Examination of various sources clearly reveals that, in spite of the unfavorable ethnic processes during the preceding period, the territory of the province of Erzerum remained populated primarily by native Armenians. In the course of time, however, ethnically alien groups increased in numbers. Valuable information is preserved in the seventeenth-century chronicle "Shinvats Karno kaghakin" (Structure of the City of Karin) by Hakob Karnetsi, who had profound knowledge of the geography of Bardzr Hayk or Upper Armenia. His chronicle includes demographic information on the twenty-three *gavars* or districts of the Erzerum eyalet in the first half of the century. According to this primary source, most districts remained inhabited almost exclusively by the Armenians. Examples of Karnetsi's descriptions are as follows:

Ghzljan (Kuzijan)—"a most beautiful gavar, the baron's residence, grassy, with ample water, full of animals and sheep and Armenian villages."

Derjan—"has many villages with Armenian dwellings, and land in the form of a plain, full of grain, animals, lard, and honey, and the town of Bagarich on the shore of the Eprat [Euphrates]."

Erznka—"has a broad plain with many villages and towns and twenty-four monasteries. . . . It has the great Armenian city of Erznka, which is full of all manner of wealth, cotton, vineyards, and orchards. And there are now five churches in the city."

Kamakh—"the land of Daranaghi which has villages and towns and a fast, impregnable fortress above the Eprat. . . . And it is a very attractive, fruit-bearing small town inhabited by the Armenian nation and has illustrious churches and monasteries."[2] Similar testimonies are given about Bayazed, Khamur, Diadin, Basen, Erzerum, and other gavars.

According to Karnetsi, in some administrative units there were also peoples of Turkic origin (in Armenian sources identified by the common name of *Tachik* or *Tajik*) as well as Kurds. The Tachiks were found mainly in the northern districts of the province. Hakob Karnetsi wrote the following about the gavar of Gayl or Kelkit: "It has many villages in gorges. It also has the town of Karmri. The inhabitants of the country are Armenians and Tachiks." The neighboring gavar of Sherian or Sharian had "a population consisting of many Armenians and also of the Romans [Greeks] and Tachiks." About the district of Upper Basen, situated in the northeastern part of the province, Karnetsi noted: "The inhabitants are Armenians and a few Turks." It is clearly attested, therefore, that Armenians constituted the majority of the population, with "also Tachiks" or "a few Turks" in some places.

Notwithstanding the fact that some northern districts came to have a mixed Armenian-Turkish population because of the Ottoman government's measures to transfer and resettle Muslim elements there, the area remained largely Armenian populated. Tachiks constituted a relatively small element. This finding is also borne out in the materials published by Turkish researcher İzmet Miroğlu.[3] In the sixteenth century, according to this data, Christians incontestably formed the majority of the population in Baberd, located northwest of the administrative center at Erzerum. Aside from Turks, Kurds made up the other alien element in the Erzerum eyalet, living mainly in the southern districts. There were "many villages and settlements of Armenians and Kurds" in the gavar of Kghi and, to the east, in the gavar of Khnus at the foot

---

[2] Hakob Karnetsi, "Shinvats Karno kaghakin," in *Manr zhamanakagrutyunner (XIII-XVIII dd.)* [Minor Chronicles (13th-18th Centuries)], comp. Vazgen A. Hakobyan, vol. 2 (Erevan: Armenian Academy of Sciences, 1956), pp. 550-51.

[3] İzmet Miroğlu, *XVI. yüzyılda Bayburt sancağı* [The Sixteenth-Century Baiburt Sanjak] (Istanbul: Uçler Matbaası, 1975), p. 119, Table 10.

of the Biurakan or Bingol Mountains. Overall, during the first half of the seventeenth century, the province of Erzerum remained relatively monoethnic. But this situation did not last for long.

In order to establish absolute rule over subjugated peoples, the sultan's government followed a policy of repopulating the conquered territories with Turkish-speaking and Iranian-speaking (mainly Kurdish) tribes. As a result of such measures, the ethnic complexion of Armenia gradually changed. Muslim islands appeared in once-monoethnic Western Armenia. Month after month and year after year, the Armenians were forced to leave their homeland. In 1478, for example, Lala Pasha, the most ferocious general in the Ottoman army, was sent to Baberd, Sper, Tortum, and other gavars stretching along the Pontus Mountains to put the Ottoman administrative machinery in motion, including the imposition of heavy taxation. In a short time, he laid waste to hundreds of villages in Upper Armenia and Tayk and annihilated thousands of people. More than 50,000 Armenians, seeking to escape physical extermination, converted to Islam.[4] Mass slaughter and forced conversions increased during and after the Turko-Persian war of 1512-14. A contemporary author and witness to the events wrote: "While engaging in raids they destroyed and devastated as far as the valleys of Mush, Khnus, and Alashkert, the regions of Diadin and Khamur, Batnots, and Bayazed. They destroyed everything; women and boys were carried off into captivity. They ravaged these fertile lands in such a way that from Erzerum to Erevan only the fortresses remained intact."[5] From this passage, it is seen that the gavars of Karin/Erzerum, Upper Basen, Lower Basen, Alashkert, Bayazed, and Diadin, all the way to the khanate of Erevan were turned into ruins.

Shortly after the Ottoman-Persian treaty in 1639, which brought to an end more than a century of warfare and resulted in a new partition of historic Armenia, the sultan sent Jafar Pasha, a "very

---

[4] Karl Heinrich Emil Koch, *Wanderungen im Oriente während der Jahre 1843 und 1844* (Weimar, Druck und Verlag des Landes-Industrie-Comptoirs, 1846), pp. 75-82, 140-225; Hakovbos Tashian, *Hay bnaktchutiune Sev tsoven minchev Karin: Patmakan-azgagrakan harevantsi aknark me* [The Armenian Population from the Black Sea to Karin: A Historical-Ethnographic Cursory View] (Vienna: Mekhitarist Press, 1921), pp. 3-20.

[5] Hakobyan, *Manr Zhamanakagrutyunner,* pp. 565-66.

unjust, vicious, and severe man" to Erzerum in 1643 to conduct a thorough census for taxation purposes. The burdens of discriminatory taxation and accompanying violence were so onerous that large numbers of Christians in the northern gavars "converted to the law of Muhammad because of great fear."[6]

The brilliant historian-geographer Ghukas Inchichian (1758-1833) described another mass conversion to Islam in the northern part of the province. "Being exhausted by violence and hardships they adopted the religion of the Tachiks." He added that "the inhabitants of Berdagrak were mainly Armenian, [but] then many of them converted to the Tachiks and only a few of them remained Christian."[7]

These forcible conversions were accompanied by the destruction of churches or transforming them into mosques. Hakob Karnetsi has recorded that in 1662, on the initiative of a great mullah by the name of Vani and the grand vizier of the empire, "ten Roman [Greek] and Armenian churches were torn down and destroyed, and every Christian up to Sebastia and Tokat wore black. . . . And taking the church within the citadel of Arzrum, they turned it into their mosque and the Armenian nation sank into great mourning."[8]

Sper, another northern gavar of Erzerum, in 1723 became victim to one of the subsequent Turkish expeditions, during which more than a hundred Armenian villages were reduced to ashes.[9] Each such incursion was accompanied by enslavement of the Armenian population: "Tachik troops captured the Armenians and sold them or forced them to renounce Christ. Some apostatized and those who refused were killed or sold. . . . So many people were carried away from Erzerum that we are incapable of describing it."[10]

Aside from measures to convert and Turkify the Armenian

---

[6] Ibid., p. 554.

[7] Ghukas Inchichian, *Ashkharhagrutiun chorits masants ashkharhi* [The Geography of the Four Parts of the World], vol. 1 (Venice: Mekhitarist Press, 1908), pp. 93, 132.

[8] Hakobyan, *Manr zhamanakagrutyunner*, p. 567.

[9] Atrpet, *Chorokhi avazane* [The Chorokh Basin] (Vienna: Mekhitarist Press, 1929), p. 110.

[10] Matenadaran, Manuscript No. 6332, p. 552.

Christian population, the Ottoman rulers implemented another means to undermine the ethnic structure of Western Armenia. From the beginning of the sixteenth century, the sultans encouraged the influx of Kurdish tribes into the Armenian highlands in order to create a military-political buffer zone. In 1515, Sultan Selim, assisted by the Kurdish chieftain Idrissi, brought into subjugation the nomadic Kurds of Diarbekir and the region to the south. As a reward Idrissi was granted the right to administer those regions. In cooperation with the central government, he pressured many of his people to migrate northward into the province of Erzerum.[11]

In 1635 another migration of Kurdish tribes was organized by Sultan Murad, who directed them to the gavars of Erznka and Derjan. At the same time a mass migration took place to Basen and Alashkert, where many Kurds belonging to the Pasean tribe settled. Writing about the Kurds in Derjan, later Armenian authors noted that they had come from Sekmanapat.[12]

The processes of de-Armenianization continued and intensified in the eighteenth century. If in the initial stages the Kurds moved northward just in the summer months to graze their sheep in Alpine meadows, later they settled permanently in the Armenian villages. During the entire winter the Armenian population had to provide not only for the Kurds but also for their flocks. This unbearable practice, known as *gshlagh*, was sanctioned by the sultan and could not but encourage a greater influx of Kurds, especially in and around the Biurakan Mountains.

Thus, between the fifteenth and eighteenth centuries the Muslim elements increased throughout Western Armenia, including the province of Erzerum, as the result of forced conversion, flight of the native Armenian population, and organized migrations of Turks and Kurds. Many Armenians who were coerced into professing Islam did so only outwardly. The sources show that for a long time they acted as Muslims in daytime and secretly took part in Christian rituals at night. This population became

---

[11] Colonel Trotter, "Malo-Aziiskie kurdy" [The Kurds of Asia Minor], *Izvestiia Kavkazskago otdela* [Bulletin of the Caucasian Department], vol. 7 (Tiflis, 1873): 1-3.

[12] Inchichian, *Ashkharhagrutiun*, p. 97.

known by name of "kes-kes" (half-half), that is, half Armenian Christian and half Muslim Turk.

It is not difficult to surmise that by the eighteenth century the Erzerum eyalet was no longer monoethnic with a predominantly Armenian populaton. Still, at the beginning of the nineteenth century, the Armenians were more numerous than any other ethno-religious group in all gavars except in some parts of Kamakh and the mountainous communities of Khali Yazi and Mrkezar in Alashkert. The province as a whole had 978 Armenian villages and 14 towns with some 400,000 Armenians, of whom 308,000 were peasants and 93,000 were urban dwellers.[13]

The Russo-Turkish War of 1828-29 awakened among the Western Armenians hopes of emancipation from oppressive rule. During the war, the Russian armies occupied parts of the eastern Ottoman provinces, including Erzerum. But immediately after the war, news of an impending Russian withdrawal from most of the occupied territories, under pressure of the European powers, plunged the Armenians into despair. In the months following the conclusion of the Russo-Turkish Treaty of Adrianople in September 1829, approximately 75,000 Armenians abandoned their native villages and moved to the Caucasus, especially into Akhaltska and Akhalakalak or Javakhk, the former Ottoman districts that had just been annexed by the Russian Empire. The emigration of these 9,600 Armenian families further altered the ethnic composition of the province of Erzerum.

From 1830 onward, a new process began that affected the demographic complexion of Western Armenia. The Armenian population of various districts, mainly in the west and north, started to move to areas located near the new border with Russia, particularly to Basen, Alashkert, Nahin, and Bayazed. It was felt that there might be less oppression in districts adjacent to the Russian Empire and that at least this proximity afforded an escape hatch in case conditions became unbearable.[14] Thus, the eastward

---

[13] Ashot A. Melkonyan, *Erzrum: Erzrumi nahangi hay azgabnakchutyune XIX dari arajin eresnamyakin* [Erzerum: The Armenian Population of Erzerum Province in the First Three Decades of the 19th Century (Erevan: Hayastan, 1994), pp. 115-17.

[14] Matenadaran, *Zanazan heghinakneri arkhiv* [Archives of Various Authors], file 54, doc. 13[ii], p. 23b.

movement of population also acquired a political implication. Even during the height of the mass emigration of 1829-30, Armenians from other districts had moved to the east and the southeast and settled in the villages that had been abandoned by those who had departed for the Russian Empire.[15]

It seemed that after the exodus of 1829-30 the depopulated or thinned out villages of Erzerum would never be restored. But already in the 1830s the beginnings of a revival were noted by contemporary authors. In 1830, Eli Smith, a Protestant mission-ary in Western Armenia, expressed anxiety that the region was becoming so deserted that his preaching would be for naught. But in April of 1831, when Armenian immigrants from other regions as well as some natives who decided to return from the Caucasus had begun to bring new life to the half-empty villages, Smith wrote with inspiration: "We doubt not that an Armenian population will again assemble here, and then it may be made an important center for missionary operations."[16]

During the second half of the nineteenth and the first part of the twentieth century, the deepening Armenophobia of the Ottoman rulers and Muslim inhabitants made life increasingly difficult in the provinces of Western Armenia. After the Crimean War of 1853-56, news that the tsar would have to restore to the sultan the territories occupied by the Russian armies led to a new wave of emigration from Erzerum, Kars, Alashkert, and Bayazed.[17] Of the many thousands who crossed the frontier into the Russian Empire, one part settled in the villages of the Talin district, between Alexandropol (Gumri) and Erevan, while others created new homes in the coastal regions of the Black Sea, in the North Caucasus, and elsewhere. Some 4,000 families settled in the region

---

[15] Sukias Eprikian, *Patkerazard bnashkharhik bararan* [Illustrated Topo-graphical Dictionary], vol. 1 (Venice: Mekhitarist Press, 1902), p. 492.

[16] Eli Smith, *Researches of the Rev. E. Smith and Rev. H.G.O. Dwight in Armenia, Including a Journey through Asia Minor, and into Georgia and Persia, with a Visit to the Nestorian and Chaldean Christians of Oormiah and Salmas*, 2 vols. (Boston: Crocker and Brewster, 1833), vol. 2, p. 306.

[17] Russia, Kavkazskaia Arkheograficheskaia Komissiia, *Akty Kavkazskoi Arkheo-graficheskoi Komissii* [Acts of the Caucasian Archeological Commission], vol. 12 (Tiflis, 1904), p. 313.

of Stavropol alone.[18] At the same time, a great number of Caucasian mountaineers, especially after the capture of their leader Shamil, moved to the Ottoman Empire and occupied abandoned Armenian villages. Most of the mountaineers, known by the general name of Lezgin or Cherkez, were purposely settled by the Turkish government in the eastern districts of Erzerum province, particularly in Basen, near the frontier with Russia.[19]

The table at the end of this essay reflects the number of Armenian-populated localities and of individual Armenians in the thirteen gavars of the province of Erzerum. A comparison of the figures for 1809 and 1909 provides a concise picture of the demographic changes that took place during the span of one century.[20] The disastrous state in which the Armenians of the province existed during one century is easily seen from the table. The number of the Armenian-populated localities fell by 58 percent, and the Armenian population decreased by 60 percent. The districts that sustained the greatest losses, Bayazed, Alashkert, Sper, and Erzerum, were located near the Russian border where the retributions following the Russo-Turkish War of 1877-78 and the extreme violence during the Hamidian massacres of 1895-96 were particularly demoralizing. A large proportion of the survivors emigrated to Eastern (Russian) Armenia or other parts of the Caucasus.[21] Meanwhile, in the northern districts of Sper, Tortum, and Baberd, the renewed anti-Armenian persecutions contributed to the further Turkification of the Muslim Armenian "kes-kes."

For several centuries, therefore, up to the time of the Armenian Genocide of 1915, the processes of ethnic elimination—sometimes slowly and at other times very rapidly—were uninterruptedly in motion in Western Armenia. It becomes obvious that the failure of the Armenian national liberation struggle against Turkish dominion and oppression was directly connected with these changes. The de-Armenianization of the Armenian Plateau from

---

[18] Ibid., p. 1389.

[19] Matenadaran. *Zanazan heghinakneri arkhiv*, file 54, doc. 13[i, ii, iii, iv].

[20] Melkonyan, *Erzrum*, pp. 113-17, 158; A-Do [H. Martirosian], *Vani, Bitlisi ev Erzrumi vilayetnere* [The Vilayets of Van, Bitlis, and Erzrum] (Erevan: Kultura, 1912), p. 226.

[21] Matenadaran, *Mkrtich Khrimyani arkhiv* [Archive of Mkrtich Khrimian], file 101, docs. 1, 137, 248; file 102, doc. 639; file 103, doc. 429.

the sixteenth through the nineteenth century, to which insufficient scholarly attention has been given, is in itself strong evidence of the destructive policies of the Ottoman rulers. Bardzr Hayk, like the rest of Western Armenia, was ethnically cleansed over a long period through the intentional policies of forced conversion, assimilation, massacre, and expulsion. The final blow was struck in 1915.

TABLE: ARMENIANS IN THE PROVINCE OF ERZERUM,
1809 and 1909

	Gavar or Kaza	Armenian-Populated Sites		Number of Armenians	
		1809	1909	1809	1909
1	Erzerum	129	52	67,960	34,376
2	Derjan	57	31	32,920	9,128
3	Baberd	79	30	30,960	14,314
4	Erznka (with Kamakh, Kuruchai, and Kerchanis)	124	52	44,760	25,095
5	Kghi	75	50	25,440	18,705
6	Sper	81	18	28,300	3,122
7	Tortum	53	13	16,960	2,829
8	Basen (Upper and Lower)	87	57	35,130	12,404
9	Khnus	59	33	20,960	15,295
10	Alashkert (with Karakilisa)	88	22	28,160	10,248
11	Khamur and Dutagh	23	22	7,360	1,421
12	Diadin	36	7	11,520	1,092
13	Bayazed	40	4	30,800	3,920
	TOTAL	931	391	381,230	151,949

❃ 8 ❃

"HOW THE TURKS RULE ARMENIA"

James Reid

One of the most interesting yet least known aspects of the Crimean War (1853-56) was the work of a British military commission sent to Ottoman Armenia to reform the Turkish army at Kars in an effort to shore up the Anatolian flank of the Allied armies. Led by Colonel William Fenwick Williams, the commission included Humphry Sandwith, a military surgeon who not only left an account of that Russo-Turkish conflict but also later, in 1878, wrote an essay about Armenia under Ottoman control. In that article, "How the Turks Rule Armenia," he concluded that the Ottoman state governed with extreme severity.[1] His comments were based on his experiences in 1854-56 and his many subsequent years of concern about the conditions besetting the non-Muslim minorities under Ottoman rule.

Sandwith began his essay with an appeal to the moral conscience of the British reading public. He asked rhetorically what the reaction of Parliament and the public would be if the prime minister thought he could maintain control over India by annually ordering the sacrifice "of twenty innocent natives of both sexes, with every circumstance of cruelty and indignity which could add bitterness to death."[2] Certainly, the people of Great Britain would

---

[1] Humphry Sandwith, "How the Turks Rule Armenia," *The Nineteenth Century* 3 (Jan.-June 1878): 314-29. For a survey of Western literature about Turkish (Western) Armenia and notably the Erzerum *vilayet*, giving interesting additional information and a bibliographic source for the study of the province, see Jean B. Russo, "Nineteenth Century Armenia and Armenians as Seen Through Western Eyes," *Armenian Review* 36:4 (1983): 27-39. The Russo-Turkish phase of the Crimean War began in 1853, whereas the European powers entered the war against Russia in 1854.

[2] Sandwith, "How the Turks Rule Armenia," p. 314.

reject such a course. By posing the bizarre question to make his point, the surgeon then noted that far worse conditions existed in Ottoman Armenia. In fact, he said, because Great Britain supported the Ottoman regime, which engaged in "the periodical torture and slaughter of 10,000 or 20,000 innocent human beings, to say nothing of other evils which are not periodical, but chronic," Britain itself actually turned into an accomplice.[3] Sandwith made this startling charge to arouse public protest against any measures that supported the repressive Ottoman state.

While Sandwith was on duty at Kars in 1854-55, he had come to know the James Zohrab family, which had served the British Foreign Office as consuls and diplomatic officials in the Ottoman Empire. Although originating in Malta, the family was Armenian.[4] Writing in 1878, Sandwith noted that when his novel *Hekim Bashy* appeared in 1862, "Mr. Consul Zohrab" had penned a reply defending the Ottoman Empire, and "accusing me of exaggerating the vices of the governing class."[5] The Russo-Turkish War of 1877-78, however, changed Zohrab's opinions on the matter. One of his reports, dated November 16, 1877, and published in an official British *Blue Book*, revealed that his disposition had changed radically:

> The demands of the [Ottoman] Government press with crushing weight on all classes. Arrears of taxes (the validity of which no court of justice would admit), current taxes, taxes in advance, aid in money for the war, contributions in kind for the army, means of transport for munitions of war and provisions, are exacted from the Christians and from the Mussulman peasants with pitiless severity, and already thousands of families have been so reduced that they live only by public charity. Unscrupulous employees take advantage of the pressing needs of the Government to augment their own exactions, and as there is no possibility of checking such corruption, seeing that the officers who are supposed to watch over and protect the people (!) are the culprits,

---

[3] Ibid. "In point of morality there really is no difference at all between upholding a system which now and then massacres 20,000 persons, and committing the massacre ourselves."

[4] Edward Vizetelly, *The Reminiscences of a Bashi-Bazouk* (Bristol: J.W. Arrowsmith [ca. 1878-79]), p. 123, states that Zohrab was "of a Maltese-Armenian stock."

[5] Sandwith, "How the Turks Rule Armenia," p. 316.

it is impossible to state what can be done, while Turkish officials have power, to put an end to this systematic spoliation of the people.[6]

Sandwith felt gratified that Zohrab finally concurred with him about the oppression by Ottoman officials. Both men indicated that these conditions existed equally in peacetime and wartime. When a fire destroyed between 800 and 1,000 buildings at Van on December 24, 1876, the Ottoman officials and soldiers, instead of preventing looters from carrying everything away, joined in the plunder. Zohrab wrote the British ambassador: "The Christians complain bitterly of the conduct of the Government officials and soldiers, whom they accuse of having directed their efforts, while the fire lasted, to breaking open, carrying off, and concealing property, instead of endeavouring to arrest the flames."[7] Of course, Ottoman regular soldiers plundered whenever they could because even when they received their wages once every year or eighteen months their officers found ways to reduce and pocket a part of the wages.

Zohrab noted similar outrages occurring all over Ottoman Armenia. For example, on January 30, 1876, he wrote: "Panic in Bitlis district, several murders, many villages devastated, others deserted by inhabitants from dread of Koords, who threaten the town. Inhabitants, Mussulman, Christian watch armed in their barricaded houses."[8] A few weeks later, on March 14, he sent a telegram to the British embassy at Constantinople describing one such event in Erzerum province:[9]

175 Redifs [militia] on the way to Erzeroom, stopped at Gelin-patch, Kahlabar and Hosberik, in district of Bunis; have desecrated church, maltreated priest, beat Christians, outraged women— three violated by about sixty men, left dying. Authorities refuse protection. Villages were deserted, Christians fearing massacre having fled. Military authorities here supine. Christians begin to suffer severely—dread opening their shops. Acts of oppression

---

[6] Ibid.
[7] Ibid.
[8] Ibid., p. 317.
[9] Ibid.

and cruelty occur daily.

A mixed population lived in one of the villages mentioned. The headman was a Turk who quartered 125 militiamen on the Armenians, and only 45 men on the Muslims. Zohrab expanded on the atrocities in a letter that followed the telegram. The soldiers extorted food and money, abused the priest, and beat the Christian males. They then entered "the women's portion of the houses, commenced outraging the women and violating the girls. Three young women were so brutally treated by about sixty soldiers that they were reported dying when the letters, which I have seen, relating these atrocities were sent to the authorities here [in Erzerum]."[10] Sandwith made a significant observation: "These, be it remembered, were not Circassians nor Bashi-Bazouks, they were regular soldiers."[11]

The system of corruption that left the Ottoman soldier a beggar paved the way for such excesses. Authorities had not made disbursements that would provision the soldiers with adequate supplies of food or enable them to march from their home district to Erzerum without resorting to plunder and extortion en route. Corrupt officials and officers kept money and supplies for themselves. The Ottoman general, Zarif Mustafa Pasha, had hoarded most of his soldiers' supplies and sold them back to the army contractors for a fat profit in 1854. Meanwhile, his men ate bad food, from which they grew sick and many died, and had to wear only light summer uniforms without overcoats in the middle of the frigid winter at Kars. More than half of his army died or languished on the verge of death. Indeed, Sandwith himself had treated many of Zarif Mustafa's soldier-victims. As chief of the British commission, Colonel Williams became the nemesis of Zarif Mustafa and the other corrupt generals. In a letter of November 9, 1854, he wrote: "Fancy the Turks who remain outside and who march my way [to Kars], being in white trousers [summer uniforms]. How lucky the Pashas and Colonels are that I do not command, for tomorrow at daylight I would shew them

---

[10] Ibid. Sandwith summarized Zohrab's comments by saying that the same "enormities" were perpetrated in the two other named villages.

[11] Ibid., pp. 317-18.

a gallows tree with at least 10 ropes attached thereto!"[12] Williams did not carry out his threat when he later became the de facto commander of the Ottoman garrison at Kars, though he did stand accusingly at Zarif Mustafa Pasha's court martial. Under Zarif Mustafa, the next generation of Ottoman soldiers in the class of 1876 were to suffer the same deprivations as did their predecessors. In fact, common soldiers, especially the *redîf* or militia, were a generally abused lot. This mistreatment not only caused their morale to sink but also removed the normal restraints regarding plunder and atrocities by regular armed forces.

Without realizing it, Dr. Sandwith had described the condition that most affected the Armenian population. Corruption of Ottoman officers deprived the soldiers of supplies, wages, and other necessities and abused the men with exceedingly severe punishments. These conditions break the soldiers' morale and morality, which played hand in hand with one another. In a seminal study about the Franco-Prussian War of 1870-71, Thomas Rohkrämer considered the question of what would lift the restraint that normally prevented regular army soldiers from committing atrocities.[13] He cited instances when Prussian soldiers lost self-control because civilian partisans called *franc tireurs* attacked and killed stragglers and made hit-and-run attacks on isolated patrols. Extraordinary events caused German soldiers to punish civilians harshly in the war. Otherwise, Prussian soldiers kept discipline and generally did not harm civilians (except in instances where artillerymen received orders to bombard cities and towns). With Ottoman soldiers of the regular army, however, the factors that broke their restraint on a continuing basis were the abuses inflicted on them by their officers, and most of all the deprivation of food, supplies, and clothing that made them search for these things among the civilian population. Prussian and French soldiers did not face these problems normally, but Otto-

---

[12] W.F. Williams, "Letter to My Dear Hanson, Camp near Kars, November 9th, 1854," Manuscript from the collection of James J. Reid, pp. 2-3.

[13] Thomas Rohkrämer, "Daily Life at the Front and the Concept of Total War," in Stig Förster and Jörg Nagler, eds., *On the Road to Total War: The American Civil War and the German Wars of Unification, 1861-1871* (Washington, DC: German Historical Institute, and New York and Cambridge: Cambridge University Press, 1997), pp. 496-518.

man soldiers experienced privation virtually all the time. This situation only became worse in more remote provinces such as the Erzerum *vilayet.*

Sandwith's commentary gave significant evidence of atrocities—pillage, murder, rape—based on his personal experiences in historic Armenia in 1854-55 and on the reports of a personal friend in the 1870s, the Maltese-Armenian, James Zohrab. Long before World War I, Armenians in the region of Erzerum lived in intolerable circumstances according to Sandwith: "The most industrious and largest portion of the inhabitants are Armenians, who, treated like dogs by their Moslem fellow-citizens, are often accused of being 'disloyal'."[14] At the time of the Crimean War, Sandwith had not felt much sympathy for the Armenians. His memoir of the campaign portrayed the Armenians and other local Christians as "the spiritless, cringing Christian of the East."[15] This comment was associated with an incident in which a "western Christian," here a French captain, wished to fight against some Muslim bandits. He was a "spirited Christian," in contrast with the Armenians and other Eastern Christians who had little will to fight against their oppressors. Even though Sandwith's view originated in a bias against Eastern Christians as being less developed spiritually than occidental Christians, it is apparent that some truth existed in the notion that Armenians and even many Muslims lived in perpetual fear and insecurity and did not have the military capacity to resist either Ottoman regular troops or the mounted *zaptiye* irregulars.

Whether biased or not, Dr. Sandwith had ample opportunity to observe Ottoman rule in Armenia as an eyewitness in an official capacity. His comments on the corruption of Ottoman officers and the oppression of Armenians at Erzerum and Kars during the Crimean War came from direct observation of the terrible conditions and the efforts of his own senior officer, Colonel William Fenwick Williams, to combat this corruption and malfeasance. Sandwith assisted Williams in drawing up the

[14] Sandwith, "How the Turks Rule Armenia," p. 324.
[15] Humphry Sandwith, *A Narrative of the Siege of Kars, and of the Six Months' Resistance by the Turkish Garrison under General Williams to the Russian Army* (London: John Murray, 1856), pp. 46-47.

very documents that gave details and statistics regarding the various dishonest activities of Zarif Mustafa Pasha, Ahmed Pasha, and other officers of the Erzerum-Kars region.[16] His perception of corrupt Ottoman officers led him to the understanding that if the Armenians appeared downtrodden they were in fact genuinely unable to resist their oppressors, who had fallen into chaotic conditions in the nineteenth century, making the situation all the more unbearable.

To emphasize the point made by Sandwith and ultimately accepted by Zohrab, one can cite the condition of the Mush district (then in the Erzerum vilayet) in the 1860s as an example.[17] While insecurity prevailed throughout Erzerum province, it was at its worst at Mush in the south. Kurdish tribes dominated their respective spheres by force. Armenian villages were often raided to extract plunder but equally to impose total obedience. Rival Kurdish chieftains executed raids against each other's Armenian villages to weaken their enemies or to lay claim to disputed territory. Actions of this type had occurred for centuries in the historic Armenian lands but increased or waned in cycles. The 1860s, a period of great uncertainty throughout the Ottoman Empire, placed Christians in many places in heightened jeopardy. The Mush district became one of the most seriously affected areas. Insecure Kurdish chieftains and their people—facing encroachment by Ottoman officials—countered by asserting their claims through attacks on Armenians. Defenseless trav-

[16] William Fenwick Williams, "Letters, 1854-1855," in [Henry] Atwell Lake, *Kars and Our Captivity, with Letters from Sir W.F. Williams, Major Teesdale and Captain Thompson* (London: R. Bentley, 1856), p. 148, describes briefly Sandwith's assistance to Williams in collecting documents and writing letters.

[17] Louise Nalbandian, *The Armenian Revolutionary Movement: The Development of Armenian Political Parties through the Nineteenth Century* (Berkeley and Los Angeles: University of California Press, 1963), p. 79, gives a concise summary of the harassing raids against Armenian villages in the Mush district between 1863 and 1865. Ottoman references to the insecurity of Armenians under Turkish rule are few indeed. Mahmud Jelaleddin Pasha, *Mirat-i hakikat, tarihi hakikatların aynası* [The Mirror of Reality: Mirrors of Historical Realities], İsmet Miroğlu, ed. (1908; repr. Istanbul: Berekat Yayinevi, 1983), pp. 578-79, translated one of the articles of the Treaty of San Stefano in 1878 which referred to the need to address the insecurity of the Armenians under attacks by Kurds and Circassians. Zarif Mustafa Pasha did not seem to acknowledge that Armenians or Greeks even existed.

elers, primarily Armenians, were set upon and killed.[18] The Armenian population of the district paid a heavy price in these years when exactions were commonplace, and raids merely represented the most obvious and violent form of oppression. Armenian petitions were sent to the provincial government in Erzerum but with no result. Delegations went to Constantinople in order to present the villagers' grievances to the imperial government, but the last such delegation ended its journey in prison. When complaints came from the Armenian villagers of Bulanik to the grand vizier in 1867, the principal representative of the so-called Tanzimat reform era replied bluntly: "If the Armenians do not like things as they are in these provinces, they may leave the country; then we can populate these places with Circassians."[19] Such an answer pointed toward a mentality of ethnic cleansing.

Frederick Millingen, who commanded an Ottoman garrison in the Kotur district near Van, felt sympathy for the Armenians and helped them to organize some of their delegations. The problem proved extremely complicated. The governor of Erzerum in the mid-1860s was the Albanian Ismail Pasha, an outsider who could count upon the factional support of his Albanian irregular cavalry (zaptiyes). Like most Ottoman governors, he was adept at creating social gridlock by promoting internal conflicts among the Kurdish tribes under his jurisdiction, who in turn victimized the Armenians, Assyrians, Yezidi Kurds, and Jews of the region. Ismail Pasha did not rule by outright and direct oppression but by having others fight for the spoils. Ottoman governors and generals had ruled Kurdistan in this manner for several centuries. His primary mode of operation, the creation of Kurdish feuds, led to the persecution of the Kurdish losers and the subject populations beset by the feuding sides.

In his memoir of Ottoman army life in the early 1860s, Millingen described the Machiavellian manipulation of groups

---

[18] Frederick Millingen, *La Turquie sous la regne d'Abdul-Aziz (1862-1867)* (Paris: A. Lacroix, Verboeckhoven, 1868), p. 168; idem, *Wild Life among the Koords* (London: Hurst and Blackett, 1870), pp. 264-65.

[19] Nalbandian, *Armenian Revolutionary Movement*, p. 79. The grand vizier was Ali Pasha. See Roderic H. Davison, *Reform in the Ottoman Empire, 1856-1876* (New York: Gordian Press, 1973), p. 110n86.

and persons by Ottoman officials and commanders. In this regard, both Kurds and Armenians fell victim to this practice throughout the nineteenth century. In the political game played by the Ottoman pashas, the Armenians were at a distinct disadvantage. Millingen observed: "As for the peasants they are always the losers in any bargain. Their only safety from the depredations of the Koords lies in clearing out of the country by emigrating to Constantinople or to the Russian frontier."[20] Accustomed to seeing the trend in hostilities from his war experiences, Millingen could determine that Ottoman Armenia was already down the road toward ethnic cleansing, and it would be the Armenians who would be the victims. Ottoman rule promoted both Kurdish feuds and Kurdish raids on Armenians and other villagers. The whole process of rule, in his view, was characterized by a cynicism more ominous than pure and simple evil. He saw Ismail Pasha as an *eminence grise*, pulling strings and waiting to take advantage of the weakest and most vulnerable.[21]

The Kurdish raids of 1863 on Mush were a case in point. Because the Armenian villagers did not have money or diplomatic support, their representations to the governor and the grand vizier received no favor. The principle of divide and rule did not rest on the threat of military force or on the concept of following the dictates of public opinion; rather, it required the official or the commander to gauge the political atmosphere that favored an alliance with one or another person or group. According to Millingen's measure of political operations in Ottoman Armenia, if it became necessary to allow a Kurdish band to massacre and destroy an entire Armenian village or district and if the political repercussions were nil, then the pasha conspired with the Kurdish chief to meet his end. If, on the other hand, a Kurdish chief stood to lose revenues from an Armenian village because an enemy chief sought to extort sheep or grain and kill peasants, then the pasha would favor whichever of the chiefs had the greatest influence.

In the end, the governor managed his province or the general his army as though it were an *iltizam* or "tax farm." He bribed

---

[20] Millingen, *Wild Life among the Koords*, p. 263.
[21] Ibid., pp. 263-64.

officials in Constantinople to obtain his office, and he sought to make a profit by grabbing whatever funds came his way. In some cases, this meant the governor would take bribes or share the loot seized in Kurdish raids or else deprive his own soldiers of rations, winter coats and uniforms, and good billets in order to obtain his profit. This insidious procedure made everyone a potential victim of the avaricious pasha and his officers, whose chief motive was profit, not justice or good administration.

Ottoman Pashas and European Generals

Anyone riding between Baiburt and Erzerum could not but notice one incontrovertible fact, a picture of desolation as seen by Humphry Sandwith in 1855:

> As the traveller wends his way across interminable plains, he sees nothing on which the eye can rest with pleasure. True the scenery is often, nay, always grand; but it is a desolate grandeur, palling upon the senses; it is like a world without life,—like a Mussulman landscape painting, in which no visible thing is depicted. You wander on from hour to hour, from day to day, and still the same huge mountains bound the horizon; and the same broad plain, without a tree, a city, or a village, lies before you. You may imagine yourself the Last Man wandering over the blank of an unpeopled world.[22]

Why should the region seem unpeopled? The answer appears to be deceptively simple. Villages that once lay astride primary routes found themselves the way stations for "travelers" of all sorts who demanded "hospitality." Soldiers marching to and from Erzerum, officials of every description, and foreigners riding in one direction or another expected billets and food at the very least. Often soldiers extorted more from the peasants. Why continue life as a target? The villagers moved their abodes to remote places that could not be seen from the road. In this way, they hoped to avoid oppressive levies of the extraordinary type that left them on the brink of starvation by winter's end. But

---

[22] Sandwith, *Siege of Kars*, p. 47.

even remote villages came to be affected. One of the causes of the depopulation was the method used by the Ottoman army to quarter its troops in winter. The poorest villages, those that could not afford to bribe army officers, were assigned more troops to billet than other villages. Such an arrangement only led to the impoverishment of both peasants and soldiers and the abandonment of many a village—"one more roofless hamlet, attesting the misery of avaricious misrule."[23]

Had the problem just been the practice of billeting soldiers on the poorest villages, Ottoman Armenia would have suffered less, but the very remoteness of Erzerum and Kars made conditions ideal for extremely corrupt government. The Tanzimat reforms may have extended the promise of greater equality to non-Muslim subjects and honesty in government, but the Ottoman bureaucracy was not efficient enough to supervise the governors and army commanders in distant and inaccessible regions. The best window into the management of affairs in the province of Erzerum appeared in the period of the Crimean War. Both Ottoman and European documentation is plentiful for this era. Insight into the government of the province must begin with the memoirs of the governor (*vali*), Zarif Mustafa Pasha, who became commander of the Fourth Army (*ordu*).

The governor held the rank of *vizier*, and his *pashalik* included the *sanjaks* (counties) of Erzerum, Kars-Childer, Bayazid (Bayazed; Bayazit), Van, and Mush. In 1854 the population of these districts was estimated at 800,000, with about 1,500 villages spread throughout the large province.[24] An indication of the lugubrious functioning of the Ottoman system in Armenia comes from Zarif Mustafa Pasha himself. The first task assigned to him as governor in 1853 was the mustering of troops at the provincial capital for the distribution of six months' arrears in pay (*alti aylik*). Most nineteenth-century armies had difficulties in paying their soldiers on time, but the Ottoman paymaster proved far more dilatory in this respect. During the Crimean War, soldiers

---

[23] Ibid., p. 207.

[24] Ibid., pp. 59-60. For the sanjaks of Erzerum in 1875, Nalbandian, *Armenian Revolutionary Movement*, p. 199n64, lists Bitlis instead of Mush and adds Hakkiari and Dersim.

in the Anatolian army went without pay for eighteen months and in some cases for as long as three years. Zarif Mustafa recounted the steps he took to implement the grand vizier's decree (*irade*) ordering the distribution of wages. The battalions and companies of the army were stationed in many places throughout the province. These far-flung units to the number of 25,000 to 30,000 men had to march through difficult mountain passes in severe climate simply to collect their wages. One could well question why soldiers guarding the crucial points of the border from Russian encroachments or disturbances by brigands should have to abandon their posts, leave the border and other regions in grave insecurity, and march to Erzerum simply to collect pay. Would it not have been easier for the paymaster (*defterdar*) to send protected agents to the outposts to pay the troops? This method was finally put into use at Kars two years later in 1855, as it was impossible for soldiers to leave these forward positions exposed during wartime.[25]

In most other armies, the state would have considered such a vast movement of soldiers as an unnecessarily heavy financial burden. But since the men had obviously lived by their own devices for six months and their generals had quartered them on the 1,500 villages of Ottoman Armenia where they requisitioned food and supplies, the government apparently was not overly concerned. But there was more than simple inefficiency and incompetence in this mismanagement and chaos, as deep and ineradicable corruption (*fesad*) held the governor and his generals in its grip. The governor and the local field marshal (*mushir*) could better organize their pilfering of the treasury with the army gathered together and fully enrolled. Why should they allow junior officers or highway robbers the opportunity to grow richer on a small scale when they could enrich themselves on a grander scale as the sultan's representatives in the province at large? As came to light later, payroll fraud proved one of the most lucrative forms of money-making for the pashas, who cared little for their soldiers and even less for the subjects under their jurisdiction.

---

[25] "Zarif Paşa'nın hatıratı, 1816-1862" [The Memoirs of Zarif Mustafa Pasha, 1816-1862], Enver Ziya Karal, ed., *Belleten* 4 (1940): 443.

The fact that no one knew the exact number of soldiers in the Fourth Army in 1853 before the outbreak of the Crimean War facilitated the creation of a false, padded muster roll. Paymasters could issue wages for some exaggerated number of soldiers, with the many men beyond those actually present being paid in name only; that is, the governor, generals, and colonels would pocket the wages of the phantom troops. Scarcely one year later, Zarif Mustafa Pasha was caught in just such a fraud along with his predecessor as army commander, Ahmed Pasha. Colonel Williams had received orders to reform the already notoriously corrupt Fourth Army, which was "defending" Ottoman Armenia against the Russian forces headquartered at Gumri (Alexandropol). Williams, at first accompanied only by Humphry Sandwith, made a thorough inspection of the army and later received assistance from other British officers who formed the British military commission. He made an accurate count of the troops in the Fourth Army and discovered a huge discrepancy. Zarif Mustafa's muster rolls listed 22,574 men, while in point of fact only 14,600 soldiers were actually still alive and on duty. Williams and his commission, including the Armenian translator James Zohrab, proved that Zarif Mustafa Pasha had tampered with the muster roll.[26] They took the enriched general to an Ottoman court martial, which removed him from his command. Thereafter, Williams became the de facto commander at Kars and made reforms through an honest titular commander, General Vasif Pasha.

Colonel Williams' British military commission discovered an even more serious problem. Zarif Mustafa Pasha, Ahmed Pasha, and other officers had conspired to deny the common soldiers the

[26] "Report of the Military Board to the Seraskier on the Corps d'Armée of Kars in September and October, 1854," in Great Britain, Foreign Office, *Papers Relative to Military Affairs in Asiatic Turkey* (London: Harrison and Sons, 1856), no. 119, encl. 3, art. 1, pp. 110, 112. On the muster-roll fraud, see also Charles Duncan, *A Campaign with the Turks in Asia*, 2 vols. (London: Smith, Elder, 1855), vol. 1, pp. 110-16; Williams, "Letters, 1854-1855," in Lake, *Kars and Our Captivity*, vol.1, p. 147, and vol. 2, pp. 148-49; Sandwith, *Siege of Kars*, p. 92. For parallel examples, see Lt. Col. Nathaniel Stevens, *The Crimean Campaign with "The Connaught Rangers," 1854-55-56* (London: Griffith and Farran, 1878), p. 137. On a similar muster-roll fraud right after the Crimean War, see Millingen, *Wild Life among the Koords,* p. 336.

very supplies they needed for survival. After the Ottoman military commissariat had issued cheaper summer uniforms, it finally received more costly winter uniforms and military overcoats, but the generals intercepted and sold back the shipment to the army contractors for a huge profit. Many other necessities either did not reach the soldiers or came in such bad shape that they proved useless. Ahmed Pasha, for example, had conspired with a Greek baker named Kosmas (Cosmo) in Kars in a scam from which the soldiers suffered immensely. The baker accepted payment for his highest quality, most expensive bread but actually distributed adulterated bread from which the soldiers became gravely ill. He and Ahmed Pasha shared a large profit in their kickback scheme.[27] Thus, Ottoman soldiers died from illnesses caused by exposure to extreme cold in flimsy summer uniforms, unsanitary conditions and crowding in squalid living quarters, and inferior food. All the commentators except the Ottoman pashas wrote at length about the sufferings of both the regular and irregular soldiers.

Why should this discussion of the misery of the Ottoman soldiers matter in a discussion about the Armenians in the province of Erzerum? Quite simply and bluntly, the greater the misery of the soldier, the more the suffering of subjects of all types, especially Armenians and Greeks. Correspondent Charles Duncan, who was at Kars with the Ottoman army before Williams "Pasha" arrived, had enough to say on this matter. In late March 1854, Duncan observed firsthand that the people of Kars, a majority of whom were Muslim "colonizers," as he noted, "not only dreaded being pillaged by the Russians, but also by their own countrymen, should the latter have sustained a defeat."[28] He

---

[27] In addition to the letter written by W.F. Williams, other sources also note the lack of warm uniforms for soldiers in the severe winter conditions at Kars. See Duncan, *Campaign with the Turks*, vol. 1, pp. 150-52, and *Papers Relative to Military Affairs in Asiatic Turkey*. On Ahmed Pasha's bread scheme and other forms of corruption, see Duncan, *Campaign with the Turks*, pp. 110-16. Sandwith, *Siege of Kars*, p. 126, saw no improvement in the coarse, adulterated black bread. The bakers filled the flour with artificial substances to cut costs and increase profits. By early October 1854, at the very beginning of winter when food stores should have been plentiful, Zarif Mustafa Pasha had not stockpiled any food supplies.

[28] Duncan, *Campaign with the Turks*, vol. 2, p. 8.

witnessed the effect that the Ottoman army had on the civilian population of the region. Army agents voraciously seized grain supplies, while terrified peasants secreted their flocks of sheep to escape further confiscation. The same villagers no longer ploughed the land or sowed the fields. "In a word, the greatest misery speedily followed in the track of the Ottoman army, destitute as it was of a regular commissariat or of an able chief."[29] Lacking any organized system of provisions, the army's regular and irregular formations became a heavy and overpowering burden on the inhabitants. It was apparent to even the casual observer that the poorest villages bore the brunt of the exploitation and paid dearly for the "defense" of their homeland.

The most neglected of soldiers were the irregular cavalry called *bashi-bozouks*. During the Russo-Turkish wars, large contingents of irregulars flocked to the front, and in "peacetime" the Ottoman government appointed permanent bands of irregular zaptiyes to act as "rural police." Ottoman Armenia was no exception, especially as it became a primary war zone in any conflict between the Ottoman and Russian empires. Ottoman military commanders, except those of European origin, maintained that the irregulars should supply themselves. This attitude survived from the medieval past when the prototype for irregular cavalry, *timarli sipahi*, received tax districts from the central government, then taxed the subjects and used the money to supply, maintain, and feed a garrison of cavalry. When the sipahis disappeared, irregular military formations did not. Failing to receive supplies from the authorities, they were left to their own devices and usually resorted to pillage as the primary means of providing for themselves.

Coming upon a Muslim village, the bashi-bozouks would use a ruse to create panic among the villagers, forcing them to flee and leaving their goods unprotected and open to looting. In Christian villages, the irregulars engaged in murder, rape, abduction, and burning the place. These extreme measures were most common in wartime but also occurred less frequently in peacetime. In the Russo-Turkish wars, the Armenian villages between Kars and the Russian frontier suffered most terribly. What the

---

[29] Ibid., vol. 1, pp. 139-40.

irregulars did not destroy or steal, the Cossacks carried away. General Giorgi (Jerzy) Kmety (alias Ismail Pasha) commanded the bashi-bozouk advance guard two hours' ride from Kars. When Charles Duncan visited him at a former Armenian village, Kmety told Duncan that he often spent the night in some ruined village or another deserted by its inhabitants. All the villages where General Kmety stayed had been Armenian. Irregular bands —bashi-bozouk and Cossack—had destroyed them in their repeated skirmishes for control of the area.[30] The practice of allowing the irregulars to forage for their own supplies without regard to administrative procedures or regularized forms of taxation originated, of course, with the local governor or the army commander—usually both.

The Ottoman provincial official treated his domains, even in the nineteenth-century Tanzimat reform period, as if he were a tax-farming *multezim* of the seventeenth and eighteenth centuries. Even though tax-farmers generally ceased to exist as a result of a series of reforms beginning in the late eighteenth century, the mentality of their operation persisted. A tax-farmer purchased his iltizam tax district at a high price from the government. He was then free to tax his district at will without interference. If the multezim no longer existed on the Ottoman scene in this form during the Tanzimat, many officials and officers continued to obtain their posts by bribery and purchased promotion all the way to the highest levels regardless of their qualifications to govern people or command armies. This method of "administration" worked in the case of Zarif Mustafa Pasha, both as governor of Erzerum vilayet, and as the commander of the Fourth Army. Thus, the corrupt, moneymaking schemes described by various eyewitnesses originated in the personal profit mentality that had its roots in the defunct multezims. Before the era of genocide, there was the era of the corrupt governor and army commander. The casualty rate among subjects was not as high in this period as later, though the harassment of the subjects was a constant bane, and many casualties occurred.

A study of the part of Zarif Mustafa Pasha's memoir concerned with his position as governor of Erzerum demonstrates

[30] Ibid., p. 170.

that he did not even acknowledge the existence of Armenians. He wrote of military matters, chiefly the deployment of troops on the border to meet any Russian invasion at the beginning of the Crimean War. He described raids and counter-raids by the bashi-bozouks, the movements of troops, and the actions of army officers.[31] Only on two occasions did he discuss civilians in this section. In the first instance, the Russian army had expelled the Muslim villagers of the Childir district. The Russians, he complained, had committed aggressive acts (*tejavuz*), that is, atrocities in these villages (*karyeler*). The men fled with their wives and children (*choluk chochukları*) seeking protection, and Ottoman troops went to confront the enemy.[32] In the second instance, Zarif Mustafa wrote that troops of the imperial army had protected villages and districts (*köy ve kazalar*) of the Kars region from bashi-bozouks and fleeing soldiers. It is interesting to note that he did not mention the idea of protecting civilians until a European officer arrived at the Kars front and began to make persistent efforts to reform Ottoman military practices. The officer, identified as Hurshit Pasha in Zarif Mustafa's memoirs, was actually an Irish soldier of fortune named Richard Gahan, who had married into the Hungarian aristocracy and commanded rebel armies in the Hungarian revolution of 1848-49.[33] Even then, Zarif Mustafa did not concern himself with the identities of his subjects, referring to them only as *raya* who had been attacked, stripped of their belongings, and forced to flee. The callous indifference he showed toward his own soldiers indicated that he cared little even for Muslim peasants. With such disregard for "favored" subjects, it follows that the pasha had even less regard for non-Muslims.

The primary purpose of Zarif Mustafa Pasha's memoir was to discredit his critics, the *Avrupa jenerallari* (European Generals: Gahan or Guyon and Williams) and to show that he acted in the best interest of all. The food supplies that he requisitioned had made it possible for the soldiers to have their *chorba* and *pirinc* (soup and rice). His officers assertedly had made reim-

---

[31] "Zarif Paşa'nın hatıratı," pp. 473-84.
[32] Ibid., p. 478.
[33] Ibid., p. 482.

bursements for these requisitions (*mevjut pusulasi*) in cash money.[34] He made every effort to discredit Guyon, who had died from cholera in 1855, and simply ignored Williams in this part of his memoir.[35]

Colonel Williams, who had been promoted to the rank of general in Ottoman service, did not ignore Zarif Mustafa Pasha. In his report to British Ambassador Stratford de Redcliffe in October 1854, Williams devoted an entire section to the pasha. "The said Zarif Mustafa, Kerim, and Veli Pashas are altogether reprehensible characters, because the extensive frauds which they have committed are deserving of severe punishment."[36] He criticized Zarif Mustafa for provoking a battle with the Russians when the Ottoman army was not prepared to fight. The entire report listed the depredations of Zarif Mustafa and the other officers of his army. Of the points made by Zarif Mustafa in his memoir, Williams had an entirely different view. In the matter of pay, he reported: "A portion of the army has not received its pay for twenty-two months, another for eighteen, and another for fifteen."[37] The pay for muster in the previous year had benefited the corrupt pashas, not the soldiers. Wounded or sick soldiers who were unable to assemble languished in total neglect and received no money at all: "Privates, maimed and wounded in action, are obliged to beg their bread in the street."[38] As for food, Williams wrote: "There is barely food enough for one day, and not three days' provisions in store."[39]

On October 10, 1854, Williams wrote the Earl of Clarendon, Principal Secretary of State for Foreign Affairs, directly detailing his dealings with Zarif Mustafa Pasha.[40] In point six, he observed: "Sandwith brought me, two days ago, a loaf of black dough, full of all sorts of impurities, and quite unfit for a human

---

[34] Ibid., p. 485.

[35] Ibid., pp. 484-94.

[36] Williams, "Report of the Military Board," no. 119, encl. 3, art. 30, p. 116.

[37] Ibid., art. 32, p. 117.

[38] Ibid.

[39] Ibid., art. 4, p. 111.

[40] George Villiers, 4th Earl of Clarendon, acted as the ultimate authority for the British ambassador in Constantinople, Sir Stratford de Redcliffe, and apparently also for Colonel W.F. Williams.

being. This was taken from a sick man. I enclosed it to the Mushir [Zarif Mustafa], who said it had been sent to the hospital as food for the attendants, and not for the sick."[41] The point of these reports is that the poorly-fed, poorly-clad, and poorly-paid soldiers survived by making "requisitions" of their own from civilians. If there were no non-Muslims nearby, then they fleeced Muslims. The Muslim inhabitants of Kars, even sick ones, were forced to vacate their homes in October 1854 to provide winter billets for Ottoman soldiers.

Colonel Williams began to threaten and intimidate Zarif Mustafa, who refused to make any move to implement his suggestions. Soldiers continued to receive bad food, sutlers did not issue winter coats and uniforms, and numerous other deficiencies persisted. When Williams wrote the Earl of Clarendon to complain of Zarif Mustafa's inaction, he had every sentence and paragraph read and translated to the Ottoman general by James Zohrab, the Maltese-Armenian who would later come to play an important role as British consul in Ottoman Armenia.[42] In very fact, one might say that this ugly dispute between Williams and Zarif Mustafa Pasha enlightened Zohrab about the attitude of the Ottoman ruling elite. They conducted affairs solely for their own personal gain. If 12,000 Ottoman soldiers died from illnesses caused by lack of supplies, these losses seemed to matter little to them. Even more important, it became apparent to Zohrab that abused soldiers proved a heavy burden to a civilian population.[43] The condemnation of Zarif Mustafa Pasha's neglect of his army prompted Foreign Secretary Clarendon to instruct the British ambassador to "demand of the Porte the punishment of Zarif

---

[41] "Colonel Williams to the Earl of Clarendon, Camp near Kars, October 10, 1854," in *Papers Relative to Military Affairs in Asiatic Turkey*, no. 41, p. 38.

[42] For the case of Armenag Haigouni, who was another Armenian in British service as an Ottoman army interpreter during the Crimean War and who later translated a work by Edward Young into Armeno-Turkish, see Vahé Oshagan, *The English Influence on West Armenian Literature in the Nineteenth Century* (Cleveland: Cleveland State University Press, 1982), p. 15.

[43] "Colonel Williams to the Earl of Clarendon, Camp near Kars, October 11, 1854," *Papers Relative to Military Affairs in Asiatic Turkey*, no. 42, p. 39, states that Zohrab had translated this dispatch to Zarif Mustafa and notes that the pasha felt unsettled and disturbed by these comments.

Pasha," among others.[44] A court martial convicted Zarif Mustafa in due course, though the only punishment he received was a short period of exile.

The situation remained much the same in the Russo-Turkish War of 1877-78. The Ottoman commanding general of the Fourth Army was Ahmed Mukhtar Pasha. He concerned himself with military affairs far more than did Zarif Mustafa Pasha, but, aside from being more honest, he followed many of the practices of his not-so-venerable predecessor. He spread his troops all over the Armenian countryside, with towns and villages, especially around Kars, forced to support the regiments.[45] One of the chief reasons for Ottoman defeats, including those in 1877-78, was the fact that Ottoman generals rarely concentrated their forces in the face of the invading Russian armies. Even the best Ottoman generals, Omer Pasha and Ahmed Mukhtar Pasha, tended to distribute their troops over a broad area. Ahmed Mukhtar deployed contingents at Bayazid, Ardahan, Batum, and elsewhere during the war. This practice proved particularly disastrous for the Armenian and other Christian populations, as the scattered ill-provisioned detachments engaged in unchecked pilfering. Even when Mukhtar Pasha was made aware of these excesses, his measures to halt them were ineffectual.

Ahmed Mukhtar, like Zarif Mustafa Pasha, showed little regard for Ottoman subjects of any type, Muslim or Christian. The Russian attack on Bayazid was a rare occasion when he mentioned the "Turks" (Anatolian Turkish provincials) of the region. These people fell into a chaotic condition during the offensive because they had no leader, no organization, and lacked

---

[44] "The Earl of Clarendon to Lord Stratford de Redcliffe, Foreign Office, November 9, 1854," *Papers Relative to Military Affairs in Asiatic Turkey*, no. 43, pp. 39-40. See also "Lord Stratford de Redcliffe to Ali Pasha, November 28, 1854," no. 59, encl., p. 56.

[45] Ahmet Muhtar Paşa, *Anadolu'da rus muharebesi, 1876-1877* [The Russian Campaigns in Anatolia, 1876-1877], Enver Yaşarbaş, ed., vol. 1 (Istanbul: Petek Yayınları, 1985), pp. 82-83. A communication from Ismail Hakki Pasha to Ahmed Mukhtar (pp. 224-26) actually referred to this "scattered" (*peruşan* = *perushan*) condition and made suggestions for a rationalized concentration that did not fully come into being. *Perushan* can also mean disheveled, disordered, bewildered, or wretched, but when used to describe an undefeated military force, the term usually means scattered.

accord among themselves. The Russian army's occupation (*mevchut*) was devastating, as the town was reduced to ruins and the inhabitants were driven away and scattered. General A.A. Ter-Ghukasov's Russian troops took the residents of the place and carried them away.[46] This last reference did not mention Armenians by name, but in fact the uprooted population who followed the Russian army were the Armenian inhabitants of Bayazid. The context of the passage suggests that Ahmed Mukhtar considered the Armenians of this distant town to belong to the classification "*Turkler*," by which he would have meant rustic and backward peasants in a derogatory sense. Whether he intended this slur or not, it is certain that Ahmed Mukhtar had no intention of discussing subject elements of any type, even though his strategic and tactical operations directly impacted the already miserable existence of the population.

Pashas and generals engaged in policies that disrupted the lives of both Muslims and non-Muslims in Erzerum province, with Christians suffering the most. This oppressive rule, terrible in peacetime and unbearable in the extreme in wartime, prevented Erzerum and the rest of historic Armenia from progressing beyond a primitive existence. Ottoman Armenia remained provincial, with much of the population seeking security by relocating to isolated and inaccessible places or by moving to distant cities and lands.

Armenians Caught in War

Any war between the Russian and Ottoman empires caused serious problems for the Armenian populations from Bayazid through Kars and Erzerum. Armenians and Greeks in the region either came under Russian "protection" or the suspicion of the Ottoman generals. On December 12, 1854, Colonel W.F. Williams reported to the Earl of Clarendon: "I am happy to announce the withdrawal of the Russians from Bayazid to Erivan, after having burnt the greater part of the town and the fine old palace of the ancient hereditary Pashas, together with many

---

[46] Muhtar Pasha, *Anadolu'da rus muharebesi*, vol. 1, p. 228: "isteyen ahaliyi dahi alarak götürmüştür" (He carried off the inhabitants who wished to leave).

villages, and carried off the Armenian population."[47] To be claimed as an ally of the Russians was a mixed blessing. In winter and spring 1854, the Ottoman army's advanced posts were a short distance to the east of Kars. The forward troops were all irregular cavalry, the infamous bashi-bozouks, under the command of the Hungarian expatriate Kmety, now Ismail Pasha.[48] These Arab, Kurdish, Turkmen, Albanian, and other irregulars had never treated the local population upon whom they were billeted with any degree of civility. Armenians living in the villages between Kars and Gumri suffered in particular, being driven to abandon their homes, which were plundered either by the bashi-bozouks or Cossacks or by both.[49]

The Russians sometimes did incite the Armenian villagers, not excluding coercive measures, while from the other side, the Ottoman irregulars always behaved as if the Armenians were conspiring with the Russians to throw off Muslim rule.[50] Caught between these two forces, the Armenian villagers either had to flee or to rebel in self-defense. The area between the Ottoman outposts in Kars and the Russian garrison at Gumri constituted a virtual no-man's land where neither state nor army dominated and in which the Armenian and Greek villages tottered on the perilous precipice of death and destruction.

In April 1854, General Kmety received intelligence that the Armenian villages in the no-man's land two hours from his base at Perghet had revolted. As these villages lay near the Ottoman-Russian border, Kmety anticipated much difficulty in suppressing this revolt. The Armenian villagers had constructed their houses of heavy thick stone, with small entry doors that forced horsemen

---

[47] "Colonel Williams to the Earl of Clarendon, Erzeroom, December 12, 1854," *Papers Relative to Military Affairs in Asiatic Turkey*, no. 72, p. 67.

[48] The operations at Kars under Zarif Mustafa Pasha, assisted by General Guyon (Gahan), are described in Michal Czajkowski (Mehmed Sadyk Pasza), *Moje wspomnienia o wojnie 1854 roku* [My Reminiscences of the War of 1854], Jozef Fijalek, ed. (Warsaw: Wydawnictwo Ministerstwa Obrony Narodowej, 1962), pp. 75-76. General Kmety (1810-1865) commanded the bashi-bozouk troops on the frontier and engaged in constant skirmishes with the Nizhni-Novgorod Dragoons and Cossacks. Czajkowski received this information from Polish eyewitnesses who observed affairs in the Kars garrison during the spring of 1854.

[49] Duncan, *Campaign with the Turks*, vol. 1, p. 170.

[50] Ibid., p. 291.

to dismount and bend in order to enter. One or two large, unlit stables would greet the soldier upon his entry, and these rooms served as places of ambush. The defenders could barricade the central rooms in such a manner as to allow those besieged within to have the maximum advantage in firepower, while attackers were unable to find easy targets. Kmety told Duncan that the only means of entering the house safely was to attack its weakest point, that is, to make a hole in the roof, which was constructed of wood topped by earth. The assaulting troops could then toss in "hand-grenades." Duncan heard from his Hungarian friend that he intended "to summon the insurgents to disarm in return for an amnesty, but in case of refusal one village would be razed as an example to the others."[51] This strategy stopped short of ethnic cleansing but did reflect the policies of European armies waging so-called "small wars." Irregular soldiers and partisans, it was thought, could not stand in a pitched battle with a regular army. The primary goal of the regular army commander, then, was to attack and destroy rebels and irregulars at every possible point until they begged to submit.

On April 24, 1854, some 250 Cossacks crossed the Arpachai (Akhurian) River and entered Ottoman Armenia. Duncan made the following assessment regarding the Cossacks and Armenians:

> Their presence was probably to carry off the stores collected in those villages, and which, it was feared, might fall into the hands of our irregulars. Part of their project was, perhaps, to persuade the inhabitants to enter Georgia and become Russian subjects —that having been a favourite and successful policy of Prince Vorontsov [Viceroy for the Caucasus]. Its success was doubtful this time; for, in my opinion, these villages had accepted arms from the Russians more with the intention of repelling the outrages of the Turkish bashi-bazooks, irregulars, than from a wish to change masters.[52]

From the other direction, an Ottoman officer rode with an escort of bashi-bozouk cavalry to confront the intruders and the Armenian villagers. Duncan continued his narrative of these

---

[51] Ibid., p. 268.
[52] Ibid., pp. 290-91.

events with the following commentary:

> A few Cossacks, who had brought ammunition to the villagers,
> fled at the sight of the Turkish party, whilst the inhabitants
> opposed its advance by an irregular fire. The bashi-bazooks,
> however, dashed into the village at a headlong gallop, routed the
> villagers, and took six prisoners. These were brought to Kars,
> but, as a measure of policy and reconciliation, were sent back
> to their homes after they expressed their repentance at having
> taken up arms against their legitimate sovereign. After having
> restored order in this village after their homely fashion, the
> bashi-bazooks evacuated it, and returned to their former
> quarters.[53]

As interesting as it is, this narrative leaves much unanswered.
What did Duncan mean exactly when he said that the irregular
cavalry had restored order in the village "after their homely
fashion"? He and others spoke of the "outrages" perpetrated by
the irregulars in all their dealings with villagers, townspeople,
and even European soldiers. The attackers must have looted the
village with much destruction and perhaps even killed persons
unable to hide. One can never know in this instance, because
Duncan either was not fully apprized of what had occurred or
he chose not to record all that he knew. The Ottoman Empire,
after all, was an ally of Great Britain.

One learns that the Russians used the villages in this zone as
a protective shield against an Ottoman offensive. At the time of
the Turkish action against the village, for example, a Russian
column advanced across the Arpachai from Gumri and encamped
at the village of Uzun Kilise. This force attacked the Ottoman
outpost at Ergine (Argina) village, drove away the irregular
cavalry there, and then drew back across the Arpachai, "taking
with them all the inhabitants of the revolted villages."[54] Duncan's
observation was that "the revolted villages offered a favourable
screen, and facilitated the concentration of troops."[55] In short,
some Armenians had taken arms as a response to the unbearable

---

[53] Ibid., vol. 2, pp. 3-4.
[54] Ibid., p. 6.
[55] Ibid.

circumstance of being trapped between two warring antagonists in a no-man's land.[56]

The Zohrab Family:
Armenian Officials for Great Britain

The Zohrab family rested at the pinnacle of Armenian society in Erzerum vilayet from 1854 until after the Russo-Turkish War of 1877-78. Their status came as a consequence of their inviolable position in the service of Great Britain. The family had a long association with both London and Erzerum in the nineteenth century. When Reverend Horatio Southgate visited Erzerum in 1837, he engaged in dealings with the British consul there, Mr. Brant, and his interpreter, Mr. Zohrab. They gave Southgate much assistance in making his travel preparations through eastern Anatolia.[57] This Mr. Zohrab must have been a close relative of James Zohrab, who became an interpreter first class for the British officers at Kars in 1854, when he was still quite young.

As consul for Great Britain in Erzerum in the 1870s, James Zohrab assumed a distinguished position in the province. He brought British influence to Erzerum and gave a measure of protection to Christians wherever he could. Charles B. Norman, who knew Zohrab personally, held a very high opinion of him:

> It is extremely gratifying to find our country represented by a man like Mr. Zohrab, a gentleman in every sense of the word— well read, thoroughly versed in all Oriental languages, with an accurate knowledge of the country-people, their manners, customs, and history. There is no man, I believe, in Asia Minor more respected by Turks and Christians alike. It is pleasing to know that in their distress the people of Erzeroum turn to Her Majesty's representative for counsel and assistance. It is well to find that such a representative is able and willing to advise them effectually and determinedly; that he can soothe their discontent,

---

[56] The "small war" and skirmishing in this no-man's land continued, as indicated in the letters of Captain Henry Langhorn Thompson. See Lake, *Kars and Our Captivity*, pp. 73-75.

[57] Horatio Southgate, *Narrative of a Tour through Armenia, Kurdistan, Persia and Mesopotamia,* 2 vols. (New York: D. Appleton, 1840), vol. 1, p. 183.

appeal to their better feelings, and by his cheerful bearing, and by the noble disregard of danger displayed by him in keeping his family at a post of much difficulty, hardship, and trial, show them that things may not be so black as they are painted. No living man knows this part of the country as well as he does. For twenty-two years he has been intimately associated with its history.[58]

Charles Duncan met James Zohrab at Erzerum in February, 1854, when he held the rank of official translator (*terjuman*) first class or the equivalent of a captain in the British army. He often translated for the British consul or other dignitaries in their dealings with the Ottoman governors or generals in the Erzerum region. From this time on, Zohrab made his career as a British civil servant in Ottoman Armenia. He could function under the protection of the British government, though he had little influence on the imperial scheme of things in the British Empire. While his background and linguistic abilities made him a well-suited candidate for holding the post of British consul, he initially received little notice in London.

With the resumption of war in 1877, however, Zohrab gained more respect, as shown in the narrative of C.B. Norman. He served as the local representative of British benevolent organizations and gained permission and arranged for British doctors to perform operations in the Turkish military hospital. In addition, the consul acted as postal agent, meaning that he controlled the mails received and dispatched under British protection, and he was the forwarding agent for any English residents in his jurisdiction. Norman recounted: "I have travelled with him through the district, and can bear testimony to the way in which the lower classes, the agriculturalists, turn to him as a guide and friend, and welcome him in their villages. Thoroughly acquainted with their language, with their manners and customs, he is at home among them, ever ready and willing to hear their smallest trouble, and never forgetting a promise."[59] Norman clearly saw that James Zohrab had become a political figure of stature among

---

[58] Charles B. Norman, *Armenia and the Campaign of 1877* (London: Cassell, Petter and Galpin [1878]), pp. 60-61.

[59] Ibid., pp. 314-15. See also pp. 342-43.

the villagers of Ottoman Armenia. Both Muslims and Christians regarded him as a significant personage, who as British consul had some power to help them.

During the crisis that gripped Ottoman Armenia amid the Russo-Turkish War of 1877-78, Zohrab dealt with many problems and attempted to maintain a high humanitarian standard. He belonged to a world dominated by an Ottoman multicultural consciousness, and for this reason Muslims as well as Christians showed him respect. When Ottoman authorities proved unyielding, inept, or corrupt, he received petitions from both communities.[60] Despite this position, Zohrab himself sympathized most clearly with Armenians and other Christians. This inclination became especially evident when the war erupted in 1877, as can be deduced from the account of Sandwith and the strange comments of Edward Vizetelly. The latter had joined a group of Circassian cavalry and identified so closely with the irregular soldiers of "my" band that he wore a Circassian outfit and purchased a sixteen-shot Winchester repeating rifle. When he called at the Erzerum consulate with another British subject, he was given a bad reception. "To us he [Zohrab] showed himself as boorish and discourteous as Sir Edward, his nephew, is genial and obliging, and his reception formed a striking contrast to the affable, though officially reserved, attitude of Sir Alfred Biliotti at Trebizond."[61] Vizetelly observed further that Zohrab "curtly inquired what we wanted," and finding that they had come to announce their arrival, Zohrab said he did not wish to see their passports "and abruptly brought our visit to an end."[62]

Vizetelly heard at a later date that Zohrab had made the remark that, considering that England was not at war with Russia, "he regarded me as little more than a cut-throat, and that if I was caught and hanged it would serve me right; adding that in such an eventuality he would not raise a finger to save me."[63] It is not difficult to discern the reason for Zohrab's hostility. Cir-

---

[60] Ibid., p. 59. Both Muslim and Christian deputations in a state of alarm came with petitions to Zohrab on May 31, 1877. These notables from the city of Erzerum complained about the Ottoman government's ineptness.

[61] Vizetelly, *Reminiscences of a Bashi-Bazouk*, p. 123.

[62] Ibid.

[63] Ibid., p. 124.

cassians victimized both Muslim and Christian villages on a grand scale during the war, and naturally Zohrab could only despise Vizetelly's admiration of the murderous irregulars.[64] If Shamil's resistance in the Caucasus Mountains to the imperial Russians had captured the imagination of the British, French, and Germans in the 1840s and 1850s, Circassian depredations in Bulgaria and throughout Anatolia revealed the ugly, unromantic side of the irregular cavalry to most former admirers. Clearly, Vizetelly's Burtonesque adventure of "going Circassian" seemed not only anachronistic to persons like Zohrab but also gave sanction to a dangerous mentality that prevailed among irregulars who engaged in murderous operations against the village population, the very people they theoretically were there to defend.

Kurdish raiders made a sweep through a district of Armenian villages in June 1877, as recounted by C.B. Norman. Numerous reports of murder, rape, and pillage found their way to Zohrab's office.[65] Vizetelly had arrived after these events, in the company of Circassian bashi-bozouks. Was it any wonder that he received a blunt and unpleasant acknowledgment from Zohrab? In November 1877, Zohrab nearly lost his life while helping to care for the wounded on the battlefield. Erzerum itself had come under Russian attack after the retreat of the Ottoman army. When Zohrab prevented a Turkish soldier from bayoneting a wounded Russian, the soldier turned his bayonet on Zohrab, who was saved only by the fortuitous arrival and intervention of an Ottoman officer.[66]

---

[64] Lieutenant-Colonel [John] Fife-Cookson, *With the Armies of the Balkans and at Gallipoli in 1877-1878* (London: Cassell, Petter and Galpin, 1880), p. 160, gives the eyewitness testimony of a Muslim peasant woman who was the only person to remain in her village after the killing, rape, and looting by the Circassians. These practices were said to be universal among the thousands of Circassian irregulars retreating with the Ottoman army in 1877. See also Bilal Şimşir, ed., *Rumeli'den türk göçleri: Belgeler* [Turkish Emigrations from the Balkans: Documents], vol. 2 (Ankara: Türk Kültürünü Araştırma Enstitüsü, 1970), pp. 320-29. Circassians who were resettled at Adabazar in 1878 spread mayhem throughout this district near Constantinople. They attacked Muslims as well as Christians.

[65] Norman, *Armenia and the Campaign of 1877*, p. 89.

[66] Ibid., p. 407. Turkish writings say nothing about the Zohrab family but rather treat Erzerum as a breeding ground of sedition and revolution in 1877-78. Such writings generally ignore the strong attachment to multiculturalism even among the

Zohrab had two sons, Reginald and Percy, who evidently assisted their father in his consular duties at Erzerum and helped as hospital attendants.[67] James Zohrab's nephew, Sir Edward Zohrab, was associated with the British diplomatic service at Cairo. The Zohrab family had achieved a prominence in Erzerum not previously attained even by the wealthiest merchants. Yet, one must consider it the bitterest of ironies that an Armenian could enjoy the freedom of his person and property in his own historic homeland only through the protection afforded by a foreign government, in this case Great Britain.

Professionals, Merchants, and Artisans

Before the administrative reforms of the Tanzimat had abolished the iltizam tax farms, some Armenian bankers and merchants had gained wealth from the purchase and sale of tax-farm properties and associated revenue-producing transactions. Bankers and merchants called *amiras* were most prominent in Constantinople, but their affairs and activities extended throughout the Ottoman Empire, even to distant Erzerum.[68] A new Armenian middle class emerged in the nineteenth century, located primarily in Constantinople and Izmir (Smyrna), though some of the merchant houses in Erzerum and other interior cities had links with these communities. This group furthered the Armenian cultural renaissance, whose effects, however, were not felt strongly in the provinces

---

highest of the Armenians in the province. For an example of the dogmatic view of Armenians as plotters of revolution or as partisans (*komitajilar*) in Erzerum province between 1877 and 1890, see İhsan Sakarya, *Belgelerle Ermeni sorunu* [The Armenian Question in Documents] (Ankara: Genel Kurmay Basımevi, 1984), pp. 94-95. Sakarya's treatment fails to give specifics. If there were some persons in illegal societies, they certainly did not have the prominence of the Zohrab family or of the mercantile houses of Erzerum.

[67] Norman, *Armenia and the Campaign of 1877*, p. 406.

[68] For a fuller discussion of the amira class, see Vartan Artinian, "The Role of the Amiras in the Ottoman Empire," *Armenian Review* 34:2 (1981): 188-94; Lillian Etmekjian, "Armenian Cultural and Political Contributions to Reform in Turkey," *Armenian Review* 29:2 (1976): 167-91; Benjamin Hendricks, "Une famille arménienne au service des Ottomanes: Les Missakian, amira et effendi," *Mésogeios, Méditerrannée* 1 (1998): 97-103, which includes a genealogical document of the nineteenth century.

until the period after 1877-78. The middle class lacked the stature of the amiras and had less influence in the administration of the Armenian confessional community or *millet* through the Patriarchate of Constantinople or in the Ottoman state as a whole, but it reflected the winds of change associated with the Tanzimat period.

Armenian merchants and craftsmen held prominence in the cities of Ottoman Armenia. The towns of Bayazid, Kars, and Erzerum benefitted from the caravan route that stretched from Tabriz to Erzerum, whence Armenian and other Ottoman merchants shipped goods to other points in the empire. This trade included cloth, wool, dyes, carpets, and other specialized items. The Persian trade brought currency and coins of all types into Armenia, thus making moneychangers indispensable even in the middle of the nineteenth century. By that time, the armorers of Karin/Erzerum had long ceased to operate as such, though metalworking remained important.

Ottoman officials had difficulty getting loans from merchants in peacetime, primarily because they developed a reputation for either failing to make timely repayment or in the end not repaying at all. If most officials made some repayment in peacetime, none ever repaid wartime loans. For this reason, Armenian and other merchants at Erzerum felt as though they had become targets for loan-seeking officials and generals, and they tried to evade such obligations in wartime. This refusal extended into the ranks of lesser entrepreneurs as well, petty merchants who refused to sell goods to soldiers for script issued when funds were short, and muleteers who did not hire out their animals to haul military goods. Corrupt pashas in particular sought means to appropriate all available funds for themselves, and under such circumstances everyone had to protect his own resources.

The Armenian cloth merchant Hovhanes Marinoghlu epitomized the survival mentality that prevailed among the merchants of Erzerum. His offices and caravanserai (*khan*) were located near the Erzerum bazaar in 1854. In February, Marinoghlu received a visit from Charles Duncan, who bore a letter from Alexander Pirjantz, an Armenian merchant of Trebizond, extending credit to Duncan for the purchase of a variety of goods and necessities, including a horse. When a customer had firm credit, he received consideration, and Marinoghlu accommodated Duncan.[69] Marinoghlu also agreed to act as the agent for both Duncan and Colonel Thorne, who came to the Anatolian war zone as correspondents of the London *Times*. Runners took Duncan's dispatches and personal letters to Marinoghlu in Erzerum, who in turn sent them to Pirjantz in Trebizond, where the mail went to England. Conversely, all mail from England to Duncan or Thorne passed through Pirjantz and Marinoghlu.[70] Persons with money and the official backing of European states or firms obtained excellent credit and service. The mercantile network centered on Erzerum extended from northwestern Persia to Trebizond, the point for shipping trade goods to the west. Pirjantz, who had lived in London and Vienna for some time, thus acted as a banker and middleman for many of the merchants at Erzerum and other places in the interior.[71] This network, with its international connections, could serve in its own best interests and could protect itself to some degree from the economic short-comings and problems created by the Ottoman state and army. Its sources of income were partly international and therefore somewhat immune from economic decline in Ottoman Armenia.

Not all merchants belonged to an international network with links to Trebizond, Constantinople, Western Europe, or Russia. Many Armenian merchants participated in the Persia-Erzerum or the Erevan/Tiflis-Erzerum trade route with mainly local implica-tions. This class of merchants maintained a far more precarious existence, as had been their fate for centuries. For example, Kurdish raiders killed Hampardzum and Sarkis, two Armenian merchants from Bitlis, at the village of Qaya in June 1877 as they traveled on business. Kurdish marauders raided the village and were engaged in looting when the unfortunate merchants happened along. After killing the two men, the raiders plundered their belongings as well.[72] Such casualties need not have be-longed to a broader campaign to eliminate Armenians but were typical of the brigandage that plagued the caravan routes on a

---

[69] Duncan, *Campaign with the Turks*, vol. 1, p. 79.
[70] Ibid., p. 263.
[71] Ibid., p. 18.
[72] Norman, *Armenia and the Campaign of 1877*, p. 295.

perennial basis. Victims of all backgrounds, including Europeans and army officers, lost their lives. If a merchant became wealthy enough and developed the proper connections, he might attempt to shift from the caravan trade to international mercantile ventures and thus make his life safer.

Traders and Caravan Workers

Much of the urban Armenian population belonged to two basic vocations. Some Armenians functioned as independent, petty traders who joined caravans for safety and traveled to Persia, Trebizond, Jerusalem, and all points inside Russia. Unlike the independent muleteers who hauled freight belonging to others, the petty merchant owned the merchandise. The second group working in the caravan trade or as independent keepers of donkeys or mules engaged in transporting goods. Associated with this group were the Armenian porters (*hamals*), who carried the loads after donkeys, mules, or camels had taken the goods as far as possible.[73] Narrow streets required such persons to bear heavy loads from caravanserai to inner city. Camel-drivers and muleteers often lived away from the city center on the outskirts of town, since they represented the most transient part of the population. They did not belong either to the urban or the rural sector. Hamals usually inhabited the same quarter as the muleteers, though they were not necessarily transient.

The scout-translator acted as an essential functionary in the long-distance trade and travel routes in Ottoman Armenia. Charles Duncan hired a Pontic Greek named Giorgos "who spoke fluently some ten languages." He was, moreover, "an excellent cook and general servant."[74] He also acted as a scout and dragoman (translator) along the route, having traveled the road from Trebizond to Erzerum many times. His knowledge of the road proved invaluable as he took Duncan through the deep snow that blanketed the region during the entire winter. The party left

---

[73] Duncan, *Campaign with the Turks*, vol. 1, p. 98, wrote that Armenians controlled the profession of hamal in Constantinople. For a description of the hamals, see Stevens, *The Crimean Campaign*, pp. 14, 31.

[74] Duncan, *Campaign with the Turks*, vol. 1, p. 28.

Trebizond in January 1854, led by Giorgos, who assisted Duncan in all the journey's hardships and acted as translator in each of the villages—Armenian, Greek, and Turkish—to which they came and in interviews with Ottoman soldiers.[75]

Duncan gave very little information about Giorgos' background. He had a wife and family. The prospect of a Russian attack in late April 1854 frightened Giorgos, who stated that "he could not, in justice to his wife and family, remain at Kars any longer."[76] The dragoman relented, however, and stayed with Duncan as his translator and servant. Giorgos had some experience beyond that offered by an eastern Anatolian villager. In addition to his "ten languages," he had also traveled outside his Pontic homeland. At each village where the party stopped for the night, Giorgos told stories. Duncan thought his talent for oral narration was quite remarkable, especially his description of a train: "My dragoman (who, I already said, was a very ingenious fellow) created a constant sensation by his dramatic description of a railroad. He would commence with a whistle, then imitate the noise of the engine, and conclude with the nervous cries of elderly ladies in passing through a tunnel. He would accompany the dramatic acting with a suitable libretto in Turkish."[77] His oral account of a train, meant to amuse, also demonstrated the highly provincial nature of this northeastern region, where the newer technology and other progressive developments were slow to be introduced.

One of the most colorful of characterizations among the Crimean War narratives of the Armenian campaign came from the pen of Charles Duncan. He had hired an Armenian muleteer or "groom" to help transport his baggage from Erzerum to Kars and act as his personal servant. The groom lived with his family in Erzerum. On cold, wintry nights when Duncan returned from *soirées* with his European friends in Kars, the Armenian servant carried the lantern that lit the way back to his house.[78] The *katerj* (muleteer) specialized in travel through rural and mountainous

---

[75] Ibid., pp. 51-67, 90-99.
[76] Ibid., p. 10.
[77] Ibid., p. 136.
[78] Ibid., pp. 47-48, 52.

regions. The muleteers of Armenia could find tracks in the snow, and Duncan recorded that his "cattergis" saved his life once by finding a path to Baiburt through a new snow. While he thought that even the lowliest "cattergis" possessed "an air of dignity," he held such grooms (*sais*) in rather low esteem because they were "often morose and always indolent."[79] A hierarchy existed in the profession. The chief groom (*seyis-bashi*) walked alongside the horse of the rich pasha or merchant, conveyed his orders to the other grooms and supervised their activities. Duncan hired six grooms in May 1854, beginning with the one-eyed Armenian groom from Erzerum. He also engaged a Russian Armenian groom from Gumri, whom the authorities deported when they discovered his place of origin. The other four grooms employed at Kars included two Arabs, who abused or neglected the horse, a Kurd, "who attempted to decamp to the hills with two of the horses," and a Polish noncommissioned officer who had "an invincible aversion to work."[80] The one-eyed Armenian groom proved the best of the lot despite his comical failures in preparing cuisine.

The Armenian became friendly with the new servants whom Duncan hired. These men were orderlies, pipe-bearers (*chibukji*), and lantern-carriers. Duncan resided in the top floor of the house, while these men with the Armenian groom and Giorgos slept on the bottom floor in the room next to the stable where the sheep were kept. This arrangement in a wealthy Muslim or Christian household was common, and their servants included Armenians, Greeks, Turks, Kurds, Assyrians, and others:

> The groom, who was a wit in his way, favoured the company below stairs with descriptions of his travels and adventures. He had been as far as Jerusalem in his time, and was gifted with great descriptive powers. This I presumed from the mirth indulged in by the assembled orderlies and pipe-bearers, whose laughter must have been peculiarly distressing to the sheep who were confined in the next room.[81]

---

[79] Ibid., pp. 250-52.
[80] Ibid., vol. 2, p. 10.
[81] Ibid., vol. 1, pp. 242-43.

This anecdote illustrates a number of factors important in this level of Armenian society. First, not every Armenian living in the eastern provinces—Ottoman Armenia—had limited horizons or remained trapped in a perpetual village existence. Certain sectors of rural society engaged in trades that took them to many places outside their homelands. Chief among the lesser occupations was that of the caravaneer and muleteer, who would sometimes travel far distances in his line of work. Second, there was a lively oral culture that possessed as much or even more power than written literature. This culture included not only songs and orally-recited poems and epics but also descriptions of personal experiences, jokes, riddles, and other forms of oral communication. Turkish, Armenian, and Armeno-Turkish were often used interchangeably.[82]

Duncan's fortuitous willingness to describe more than just the war preserved an insight into the level of Armenian society that must have been very important but that has received little attention. A relatively large population of Armenian caravan-workers and muleteers maintained links with communities outside Armenia and helped to take at least a part of Armenia beyond provincial rural horizons. Far from desiring capture by the Russians, Duncan's Armenian groom feared a renewed Russian attack on Kars and wanted to return to his family in Erzerum.[83] The two characterizations of a Pontic Greek and an Armenian illustrate well the prevailing problems of living in Erzerum. Travel over high mountains proved difficult even in summer, but in winter a person could lose his way and die in trackless snow. Both Greeks and Armenians played a critical role in the travel and transport economy of the region, and European travelers in their adventurous accounts gave some of their best descriptions of this class of person.

---

[82] Sandwith, *Siege of Kars*, p. 186. Armeno-Turkish was a mixture of Armenian and Ottoman Turkish: "A patois generally spoken or understood throughout the Turkish Empire."

[83] Duncan, *Campaign with the Turks*, vol. 2, p. 9.

Artisans and Small Merchants of the Marketplace

The Armenian artisans of the main cities in Erzerum organized themselves into guilds (*esnaf*)—coppersmiths, tailors, shoemakers, bakers, masons, blacksmiths, and so forth. In the empire's eastern-most reaches, Erzerum had 331 Armenian shopkeepers in 1829, and these petty merchants and artisans were formed into a number of esnafs.[84]

Armenian tradesmen have received inadequate attention, but numbers of them existed. European authors have little to say about them, because the Armenians with whom they normally engaged in business were the merchants (for credit and other needs), grooms and caravaneers (for transport), and peasants in whose houses they lived while traveling. This category was obviously much larger than the available sources have represented. The majority of the urban Armenian population in this province belonged to this socioeconomic community, but information is generally lacking. Until the latter half of the nineteenth century, the Armenian writers of Constantinople and elsewhere had little interest in recording the provincial life that they considered backward, even though it was their own homeland. Ottoman sources are entirely misleading, since corrupt pashas and other officers (including some Armenians and Greeks) created false statistics and used archaic categories to suit their own purposes. It is possible to study certain aspects of Armenian society in Erzerum province with more depth for the sixteenth century than it is for the nineteenth century.

Villages, Peasants, and Farm Workers: Security in an Insecure World

The great mass of the Armenian population in Erzerum lived in villages. The estimate that placed the peasant population at 70 percent of all Armenians in the Ottoman Empire may be a bit high, however, since a number of trades and vocations existed

---

[84] Reported in the Armenian newspaper of Tiflis, *Mshak*, no.127 (1890), as cited in Vartan Artinian, *The Armenian Constitutional System in the Ottoman Empire, 1839-1863* (Istanbul: n.p. [1988]), p. 25.

on the margins of rural society.[85] The descriptions of Armenian peasantry from the period of the nineteenth century are quite limited. The primary method of survival in villages constantly vulnerable to attack from all sides was through the building of intruder-resistant structures. Villagers constructed the basic peasant dwellings of Armenia, Georgia, Azerbaijan, Iran, and much of Anatolia with defense in mind. In the event of an attack by raiders, shepherds or guards outside the village would give warning. Women, children, and elderly would hasten to secret hiding places. The entrances to these hideaways often proved so narrow and short that the larger men could not readily enter and needed to find other places to conceal themselves. If, however, attackers caught the villagers by surprise, the houses were like small fortresses with difficult access. Residential rooms, located in the rear or center of the compound, had no direct entry from the exterior. Horsemen mounted upright on their steeds could not get in. The front room or lower storey was a stable for animals, for which a bigger door was necessary, but entrance to the house had to be gained through the smaller, inner door, which was fortified for defense. Inside the house itself, the inhabitants could as a last resort seek refuge in a well-hidden cellar, also built with difficult access.

Such defense saved lives but could not always succeed in

---

[85] An important primary source is *Endhanur tsutsak Tajkastani hayabnak gava-rats, kaghakats, ev ereveli giughoreits* [General Table of Armenian-Inhabited Provinces, Cities, Towns, and Prominent Villages in Turkey] (Constantinople: n.p. 1864). Hagop Barsoumian, "The Eastern Question and the Tanzimat Era," in Richard G. Hovannisian, ed., *The Armenian People from Ancient to Modern Times*, vol. 2 (New York: St. Martin's Press, 1997), pp. 192-95, describes economic conditions of the peasantry, villagers, sharecroppers, and other farm workers in Ottoman Armenia. Susie Hoogasian Villa and Mary Kilbourne Matossian, *Armenian Village Life before 1914* (Detroit: Wayne State University Press, 1982), present a historical sociology and anthropology of Armenian village life using surviving informants, one of whom was born as early as the 1870s but most of whom were born in the 1890s. These oral sources were supplemented with various travel accounts from the 1850s to the early twentieth century. An important study of Pontic Greek villages in the vilayet of Trebizond may be used as a model of future study of Armenian villages in the nineteenth century. See the series of articles by Anthony Bryer et al., "Nineteenth-Century Monuments in the City and Vilayet of Trebizond," *Archeion Pontou, Syngramma Periodikon* 28 (1966-67): 228-308; 29 (1968-69): 89-132; 30 (1970-71): 228-385; 32 (1972-73): 126-310.

preventing the ultimate tragedy. Raiders intent on immediate plunder would not linger long to harass the hidden occupants, but irregulars or others seeking to harm the inhabitants could finally have their way. A short siege might force the villagers out of their cramped quarters, or if the attackers were impatient the usual method was to find the secret hiding places and incinerate the huddled masses.[86] The best method of escape, of course, was to flee the village and get to the high mountains where raiders or parties of soldiers felt less inclined to follow.

An Assessment

Provincial culture in the nineteenth century did not have much in the way of professional differentiation, division of labor, progressive social, economic, and technological change, or understanding of the industrial revolution in Europe. The further into the interior of the Erzerum vilayet one traveled, the more this provincialism became evident. Armenian society in the nineteenth century seems deceptively similar to its predecessor in the sixteenth century. The archaism of Armenian social institutions

---

[86] Shaykh Husayn ibn Shaykh Abdal-i Zahidi, *Silsilat al-Nasabl-i Safaviyah* [Geneology of the Safavid Dynasty] (Berlin: Chapkhanah-'i Iranshahr, 1343 [1924]), pp. 12-14, recorded a seventeenth-century Georgian raid on a Persian village in fourteenth-century Azerbaijan. Peasant houses were all built with secret crawl spaces, and hidden sanctuaries with difficult access existed outside the village for women, children, and the elderly in case of a raid. These hiding places contained ceramic jars with grain in the event of emergencies. See also the discussion of Persian Armenia in the 1820s by George Bournoutian, *The Khanate of Erevan under Qajar Rule, 1798-1828* (Costa Mesa and New York: Mazda Publishers and Bibliotheca Persica, 1992), pp. 183-84, which gives James Morier's description of Armenian village houses, and Sedad Hakki Eldem, *Türk evi: Osmanli dönemi* [Turkish Houses, Ottoman Period], vol. 2 ([Istanbul]: Türkiye Anit, Çevre, Turizm Degerlerini Koruma Vakfi, 1984), pp. 88-95. A photograph of the Pontic Greek village at Maurana, mostly remains from the nineteenth century, shows a house with no visible entry and high, small windows. See Anthony Bryer, Jane Isaac, and David Winfield, "Nineteenth-Century Monuments in the City and Vilayet of Trebizond: Architectural and Historical Notes," *Archeion Pontou* 32 (1972-73): 210. On the burning alive of a large group hidden in the basement of a village school, see Januarius MacGahan and Eugene Schuyler, *The Turkish Atrocities in Bulgaria* (London: Bradbury and Agnew, 1876), p. 28, who saw the "bones and ashes of 200 women and children burned in the schoolhouse at Batak by Circassian zaptiyes."

belonged primarily to the Ottoman policies that encouraged a tradition-bound social philosophy. For all the celebrated discussion of Tanzimat reform, the reality was that Ottoman provincial society was subject to an extremely regimented structure. Yet real changes did occur from generation to generation. These did not, however, receive adequate recognition in Ottoman administrative sources. Ottoman Armenia, in being ignored even by the cosmopolitan Armenians of Constantinople, was neither well understood nor properly portrayed.

During this period Ottoman Armenia dwelt in a state of nihilistic desolation. The essence of this overwhelming disorder carried a deep contradiction within itself. On the one hand, all the worst possibilities evoked by a dehumanizing state and military establishment came to be realized. Armenians, Greeks, and other non-Muslims as well as certain Muslim elements living on the margins of society languished in an environment filled with negative symbols. In a society oppressed and forced to conform to crude and shriveled community ideals, the possibilities for major philosophical expressions or creative innovation seemed to lack valid meaning. Some Armenians attempted to breach the pattern by adopting religions of personal expression as espoused by the Protestant missionaries, who believed that most Armenians merely followed ritualistic practices imposed on them by centuries of custom and priestly hierarchy.[87] The literary renaissance that captured the imagination of Armenians in Constantinople and the coastal cities and gradually spread to the provinces also reflected a yearning for both greater personal and community fulfillment in a society that was beginning to reject continued conformity to a rigid pattern.[88]

---

[87] Mrs. E.C.A. Schneider and Reverend B. Schneider, *Letters from Broosa, Asia Minor, with an Essay on the Prospects of the Heathen and Our Duty to Them by Rev. B. Schneider* (Chambersburg, PA: Rev. Samuel Gutelius, 1846), p. 91, wrote of the lack of a "religion of the heart" in Greek and Armenian congregations. While stationed at Bursa, they also referred to a mission of their church at Erzerum where, in their view, similar conditions prevailed (p. xii). Despite their bias, their message of a personal religion that would offer a sense of salvation or fulfillment attracted a number of followers.

[88] See Oshagan, *English Influence on West Armenian Literature*; Frank Andrews Stone, "The Educational 'Awakening' among the Armenian Evangelicals of Aintab,

Among the Armenians living in Erzerum province, change occurred in other ways. The stolidly provincial mentality that might have characterized any rural area at this time slowly lost its limiting isolation. Individual foreigners and groups of officers or missionaries from Europe or America became catalysts for change. Moreover, many persons who had left their villages for a period and then returned brought a new view of the outside world. The episode of the Greek Giorgos and his amusing imitation of the railroad was one example of a preliminary assault on the provincialism of Ottoman Armenia. New or mixed fashions, for example, became the mode and entered into daily life, replacing the older styles prescribed by custom and the limitations of the provincial social structure. Many men at first insisted on clinging to their old-style weapons and rejected the less adorned pistols and rifles, but, once the supremacy of the new weapons was demonstrated, the flintlocks were relegated to decorations on the walls of village houses. These changes in the external aspect of life signified a slow and grudging change in the internal perceptions and reflected a desire to humanize society.

Humanity had long been denied to the Armenians by the Ottoman ruling hierarchy. The main flaw of nineteenth-century authoritarian society was its emphasis on the privileged power of the elite and its marginalization of the remainder of the population. If Ottoman generals starved, beat, and flogged Muslim soldiers and denied them the basic necessities of life and occasionally drove them into battle at the tip of their sabers, how could one expect non-Muslim peasants to receive better treatment? If Ottoman culture had frozen into an obsession with past forms and did not recognize the emergence of new social and psychological realities, how could even gifted individuals create contemporary categories? The archaizing view of the Ottoman past and traditional Ottoman society gave little room for new developments to grow into an intellectual and literary framework.

Any effort to study Turkish, Armenian, Greek, or Kurdish society in Erzerum province in the nineteenth century is doomed to failure if one emphasizes only Ottoman, Armenian, or Greek sources. Whether or not Armenians at the time would have

---

Turkey, 1845-1915," *Armenian Review* 35:1 (1982): 30-52.

desired to study their own rural society, Ottoman censorship prohibited the publication of almost everything ethnic or personal. These strict regulations and absence of respect for the people have deprived following generations of a more precise and thorough understanding of provincial Armenia in its human and social aspects. The failure to develop a human history of the Ottoman Empire in general heralded the terrible events of the period from 1876 to 1923, during which dehumanization was carried to its fullest and most extreme extent in many levels of the dying Ottoman society.

�֍ 9 �֍

"A CALL SOUNDED FROM THE ARMENIAN MOUNTAINS OF ERZERUM"

Rubina Peroomian

Western Armenians experienced a social, cultural, and political renaissance in the second half of the nineteenth century. The manifestation of this reawakening was felt especially in Constantinople, the intellectual and communal administrative center of the Western Armenians. Indeed, the revitalized cultural life, the prospects of the Armenian religious minority's newly adopted Azgayin Sahmanadrutiun (National Constitution or Statutes, 1863) to regulate the affairs of the community (*millet*), and the pledges of the European powers to intercede with the sultan for the amelioration of the unbearable conditions in the interior Ottoman provinces (*vilayets*) had created an atmosphere of hope and optimism among the intelligentsia.

The picture was dramatically different, however, in the eastern provinces, where cultural life was stifled, political activity suppressed, and national expression censored. In a land where the perniciousness of the local Turkish or Kurdish authorities was the prevailing way of life, the Armenian National Constitution had little bearing. As stated by Bishop Mkrtich (Mgrdich) Khrimian (known affectionately as "Hayrik"), who was elected Patriarch in 1869, the Constantinople intelligentsia, which had invested so much time in drafting the statutes, knew Europe better than the geography and the physical makeup of Armenia. The people whom the Sahmanadrutiun should have served lived not on the shores of the Bosporus but in the remote Armenian provinces.[1] Aside from its intrinsic shortcomings, the Constitution

---

[1] Khrimian's views on the *Sahmanadrutiun* are cited in T.E.G. (Bishop Torgom

lacked the power and means to put an end to the harrowing conduct of Kurdish chieftains against their Armenian subject *raya*s, the seizure of their crops and cattle, the abduction of their daughters, and the usurpation of their lands. The government officials or the army units stationed in every province turned a blind eye and in some instances even helped the Kurds in their plunder of the Armenian villages.[2]

Despite the reform measures promulgated by the sultans, such as the *Hatt-i Sherif* or Noble Rescript of 1839 and the *Hatt-i Humayun* or Imperial Rescript of 1856, which guaranteed the equality of all subjects before the law,[3] the government with its agrarian policies and tax-collection practices actually facilitated the transfer to Muslims of Armenian-owned lands in places such as Van, Mush, Bitlis, and Bardzr Hayk or Upper Armenia, with the city of Karin/Erzerum as its center.[4] The practice was common and gradually intensified to the extent that even the properties of the Armenian Church were not exempt. Eremia Tevkants, who undertook a fact-finding mission in Bardzr Hayk and Vaspurakan (Van), reported to Patriarch Mkrtich Khrimian in 1873 that the Turks and Kurds were usurping the lands of Armenian villagers and that repeated complaints to the local officials were unavailing.[5] In fact, there was evidence that the

---

Gushakian), *Khrimian Hayrik* (Paris: Imprimerie Artistique, 1925), p. 51.

[2] During the Russo-Turkish War of 1877-78, Charles B. Norman, the special correspondent of the London *Times*, regularly sent detailed reports from the battlefront, including much information on the local demography and the overall situation, past and present. His reports, which also contain descriptions of the deplorable condition of Armenians and other Christians in the eastern provinces, are compiled in C.B. Norman, *Armenia and the Campaign of 1877* (London: Cassell, Petter and Galpin [1878]), esp. pp. 70-71, 317-31.

[3] For a discussion of the two reform edicts, see Hagop Barsoumian "The Eastern Question and the Tanzimat Era," in Richard G. Hovannisian, ed., *The Armenian People from Ancient to Modern Times*, vol. 2 (New York: St. Martin's Press, 1997), pp. 180-82.

[4] Haykaz M. Poghosyan, *Vaspurakani patmutyunits (1850-1900)* [From the History of Vaspurakan (1850-1900)] (Erevan: Armenian Academy of Sciences, 1988), p. 64. Citing an article in *Aragats* (Constantinople, 1920, no. 51, p. 708), Poghosyan adds that in 1870 the government granted permission to the Kurdish aghas and beys to "purchase" Armenian lands, paying next to nothing, through a special arrangement ("legal *tapu*") to legitimize the transfer of land to the new owner.

[5] Ibid., p. 52.

government facilitated the Kurdish actions.

During the June 14, 1877 session of the Ottoman Parliament, Hamazasp Pallarian (Ballarian), the Armenian representative of the province of Erzerum, addressed this issue and expressed discontent with the government's failure to halt the Kurdish exactions and constant harassment of Armenians.[6] His investigation about this situation had revealed the state's high political reason (*hikmet-i hükumat*), which was to keep the Kurds content in order to use them against possible Armenian insurgency or to fight against the Russians in case of war.[7]

Living in the comparative peace and comfort of the capital city, Armenians in Constantinople knew very little about the existing plight in the eastern provinces. Thanks to the efforts of Patriarch Khrimian, information from the provinces, especially the "Report about Exploitations" that included an extensive list of violations of rights, discrimination, and persecution, exposed the true face of the prevailing conditions. The socio-cultural renaissance that was so enthusiastically extolled in the press and in artistic literature in the capital had made little headway among the Armenian masses in the eastern provinces.

The situation was unbearable in Erzerum. Only a half century earlier, Erzerum was the heart of the largest of the three *pashaliks* on the Armenian Plateau (the others being Diarbekir and Kharput or Kharpert) and encompassed most of the historic lands

---

[6] The Ottoman Parliament was convened with 86 deputies, of whom 38 were Christian. Daniel Kharajian represented the city of Erzerum, and Hamazasp Pallarian, the province. For a list of other Armenian representatives, see Eghishe Geghamiants, *Hayeri azatagrakan sharzhumnere XIX darum, kam Haykakan Hartsi hingerord shrjane* [The Liberation Movements of Armenians in the Nineteenth Century, or the Fifth Phase of the Armenian Question] (Baku: Erevantsian Elektr. Press, 1915), p. 321.

[7] Ibid., pp. 318-21. Geghamiants notes that Pallarian's exposé so moved the representatives that the Parliament called on the Sublime Porte to take immediate measures to stop the Kurdish excesses. The petition was left unanswered. Pallarian's address, published in the journal *Masis* on June 19, 1877, is also cited by Mikayel Varandian, *H.H. Dashnaktsutian patmutiun* [History of the A(rmenian) R(evolutionary) F(ederation)], vol. 1(Paris: Imp. de Navarre, 1932; repr. Tehran: Varandian Press, 1981), p. 38, and by Ghazar Chareg, *Karinapatum: Hushamatian Bardzr Hayki* [Karin: Memorial Volume of Upper Armenia] (Beirut: Garin Compatriotic Unions of the United States and Lebanon, 1957), pp. 184-86.

of Armenian Bardzr Hayk.[8] In some Turkish annals and maps, this region was called *Ermenistan* (Armenia). In an analytic survey of the Armenian Question, Krikor Zohrab (Grigor Zohrap), writing under the pseudonym Marcel Léart, shows the *eyalet* of Erzerum as having the heaviest concentration of Armenian population. After the Russo-Turkish War of 1877-78, the Ottoman government partitioned the region to form the vilayets of Van, Erzerum, Bitlis, and Mamuret ul-Aziz (Kharpert). To these vilayets were attached heavily Muslim-populated districts.[9] Moreover, large numbers of Muslims were encouraged to settle in Bardzr Hayk, and the Armenian population, living in wretched conditions, gradually became a minority. From time to time, such as during the Russo-Turkish War, the persecutions would intensify and the traumatic effect would linger for a longer period. The reports of London *Times* correspondent C.B. Norman best captured the scene. More than that, Norman's dispatches were desperate calls to his own government to intervene to put an end to "the desolation that reigns throughout Kurdistan [including Erzerum][10]—villages deserted, towns abandoned . . . and this is not the work of a power whose policy of selfish aggression no man can defend, but the ghastly acts of Turkey's irregular soldiery on Turkey's most peaceable inhabitants."[11]

---

[8] Poghosyan, *Vaspurakani patmutyunits*, pp. 7-8, citing Edward Dulaurier.

[9] Marcel Léart, *La Question Arménienne à la lumière des documents* (Paris: Librairie Maritime et Coloniale, 1913), p. 9. Zohrab adds that in 1880, when the Armenian Question was under discussion, the Ottoman government published statistics showing Armenians to be an insignificant minority in the nine eastern vilayets of Aleppo, Adana, Trebizond, Erzerum, Van, Bitlis, Diarbekir, Mamuret ul-Aziz, and Sivas, with 762,760 Armenians and 283,000 other Christians as opposed to 3,619,625 Muslims (pp. 9-10). Zohrab, who became an Armenian deputy in the Ottoman Parliament after the Young Turk revolution of 1908, was murdered in 1915 during the first stages of the Armenian Genocide.

[10] The name Kurdistan for this area was relatively new. F.D. Greene provides an interesting explanation: "The term Kurdistan, which in this region the Turkish government is trying to substitute with the historical one Armenia, has no political or geographical propriety except as indicating the much larger area over which the Kurds are scattered. In this vague sense it applies to a stretch of mountainous country . . . between Erzingan and Malatiah, and sweeping east and south over into Persia as far as Kermanshah." See Frederick Davis Greene, *The Armenian Crisis and the Rule of the Turk* (London: Hodder and Stoughton, 1895), p. 46.

[11] Norman, *Armenia and the Campaign of 1877*, p. 294.

Only a small number of youth in Erzerum, who gathered around educational institutions and clubs, considered ways to cast off the oppressive yoke. They sensed the impending encounter of the Turkish and Russian armies and foresaw the danger Armenians would face. There is evidence that even before the outbreak of war in 1877, many Armenians in Erzerum expected the tsarist armies to cross the border and liberate the Christians of the Ottoman Empire. Some Armenians began to prepare themselves, including a few merchants who secretly bought arms and had them transported to Erzerum to distribute among the populace.[12] But arming Armenians was not an easy task. Few Armenians were mentally or physically prepared to move.

A large faction of the Armenian leadership, especially in Constantinople, opposed any form of resistance. For this group, the path to emancipation and freedom lay only through enlightenment by establishing schools and spreading education among the ignorant masses. This approach, however, was seen as inadequate by some, including a small but influential segment of the clergy, which in general was very conservative. Khrimian Hayrik and Eghishe Vardapet Ayvazian, for example, were among those who favored resistance and tended to believe that education alone could not save the nation.

In Erzerum, many notables and young intellectuals undertook initiatives to raise the collective self-awareness of the masses through education and cultural programs. The Krtakan Enkerutiun (Educational Society) pioneered the movement in 1876 with lectures and Sunday classes in its *varzharan* or school.[13] Even this modest endeavor aroused the suspicion of the authorities, ironically precipitated by the fears and complaints of the conservative Armenian primate of Erzerum, Bishop Harutiun, and the society was soon dispersed.

---

[12] See Hakob M. Nshkian, *Arajin kaytser: Ej me Karno zartonken* [The First Sparks: A Page from Karin's Revival] (Boston: Baikar Press, 1930), pp. 26-27.

[13] The Azatutiun Hayrenasirakan Miutiun (Liberty Patriotic Society), organized in 1874 by Khachatur Kerektsian, is not considered here. The short-lived group is discussed briefly in Rafik P. Hovhannisyan, *Arevelahay azgayin azatagrakan sharzhumnere ev Karini "Pashtpan Hayreniats" kazmakerputyune* [The Western Armenian National Liberation Movements and the "Protectors of the Fatherland" Organization of Karin] (Erevan: Armenian Academy of Sciences, 1965), p. 88.

In the Web of Ideas and Approaches

In the 1860s Armenian political thought was taking its first steps toward the subsequent manifestation of political parties. However, while the shared vision of political thinkers was the deliverance of the Armenian people, the means to reach that goal differed greatly. Some believed that Armenians should trust the government and solicit European intercession with the Sublime Porte, never aggravating the government or giving it a pretext to use force. Such thinking prevailed especially among proponents of the Armenian National Constitution who had put so much effort into its formulation and adoption and who attached great hope to its application. According to Krikor Odian (Grigor Otian), one of the principal authors of the Sahmanadrutiun, revolution required blood, and Armenians did not have the blood to spare. A second group, mostly youthful hardliners, pushed for revolution, arousing the masses, organizing demonstrations, defending people's rights, even if this meant "beating up a Turk every day," they jested. As Hakob Nshkian attests, in Erzerum that was a favorite pastime of a certain Avetis Pashmagchian, whom everyone knew and called *barekargich* (discipliner) or, as the Muslims labeled him, *Islamlare terbie idior* (He disciplines the Muslims).[14] A third group advocated working with the Armenian populace to awaken in them the aspiration for freedom and justice. It was not necessary to preach revolution, this group believed, as people themselves had to come to the realization that resistance was unavoidable.

The reverberations of all these thoughts and currents reached Karin/Erzerum and found followers. In keeping with the third school of thought, Nshkian and a few of his friends sought to purchase a large piece of land in the Basen district. The location in the eastern reaches of the province was carefully chosen because it was surrounded by Armenian villages. The group, which called itself the Erkragortsakan Enkerutian Varchutiun (Agricultural Society Administration), planned to build a model farm with modern agricultural machinery and through that farm to work among the peasantry, but the undertaking was stymied

---

[14] Nshkian, *Arajin kaytser*, p. 112.

by interference and threatened prosecution by the authorities. While there were different approaches and ideas, one thing was clear for active youth in Erzerum, as in all parts of the Ottoman Empire: the situation was intolerable and something had to be done. The outbreak of the Russo-Turkish War in 1877 was a turning point in the history of the development of political thought and the future struggle for freedom among the Armenians of Erzerum.

The Impact of the Russo-Turkish War

In November 1877, while the war was raging, Sultan Abdul-Hamid II ordered a general conscription of all eligible men from seventeen to forty-five years of age. Through Patriarch Nerses Varzhapetian, he also called for Armenian volunteers. The Armenian National Assembly (Azgayin Zhoghov), representing the Armenian millet, took a daring step by declining the request, rationalizing that Armenians had already paid their required military exemption fees and had made financial contributions to the army beyond their means. Besides, it was argued, Armenians were not mentally and physically prepared to participate because they had never been allowed to serve in the regular armed forces.[15] The sultan viewed this decision as a sign of disloyalty, as he had a year earlier when the Armenian National Assembly had forwarded the report about exploitations in the provinces. In truth, the high hopes of the Constantinople Armenian intelligentsia and the National Assembly regarding the government's good will had ebbed by this time. Conditions clearly showed that the Armenian National Constitution had little impact in the provinces. The Armenian population gained no new rights and was not protected against Turkish and Kurdish excesses, and the government showed no interest in alleviating the situation. Moreover, with the war as a pretext the sultan made no attempt to prevent new waves of Kurdish violence against the Armenians. Mistrust had grown on all sides.

---

[15] For more details on the Armenian National Assembly's deliberations and reasoning regarding the degree of voluntary Armenian participation in the war, see Geghamiants, *Hayeri azatagrakan sharzhumnere*, pp. 325-35.

Under such conditions, many Armenians welcomed the entrance of the victorious Russian army into Erzerum. C.B. Norman explained:

> Scarcely an Armenian village in the country has escaped their [the Kurds] heavy hands. They do not content themselves with stealing, plundering and murdering their weaker and unarmed fellow subjects, but they outrage and violate every girl on whom they can lay their hands. The stories that reach us—stories from too authentic a source to admit of doubt—are perfectly unfit for publication. The Ottoman Government are showing great want of policy in encouraging, arming and feeding these men, who, useless in action, are causing all the Christians of Armenia to turn with thankfulness to the Russians as their deliverers, instead of aiding the Government with all the means in their power to repel the Muscovite aggressor.[16]

This assessment runs counter to the Turkish contention that Armenians were traitors who sided with the enemy and also challenges Soviet Armenian historiography, which ascribed the enthusiastic Armenian reception of the Russians and later the mass migration to the Caucasus to an unequivocal love for and trust in the Russians.

The rejection of the call for troops by the National Assembly did not prevent the government from fleecing Armenians under the pretext of offsetting the expenses of the war. Many Armenians were forcibly conscripted to carry heavy arms and machinery. There was no conspiracy against the government, no cooperation with the Russian army, no volunteers from Turkish Armenia fighting on the Russian side. Nevertheless, Armenians could not avoid the repercussions of the war. Norman reported:

> Hordes of fanatics led by Moolahs have joined the Turkish army; their fury, daily fed by the exhortations and addresses of the priests, who have denounced the war as a menace to the Ottoman religion, leads them to commit every conceivable excess against the defenceless Christians, whom they accuse of furnishing information to the enemy. Facts prove the reverse, for as yet not

---

[16] Norman, *Armenia and the Campaign of 1877*, p. 137.

a single Armenian spy has been discovered by the authorities, while several Kurds and Circassians, preferring money to faith, have paid for their treachery with their lives; in short, every spy hanged during this war has been a Mohammaden.[17]

These circumstances caused many Armenians to rejoice with thoughts of deliverance and freedom during the Russian occupation of the eastern provinces. Some intellectuals even began to contemplate the future structure of an autonomous Turkish Armenia with Erzerum at its center. Grigor Artsruni, a prominent Eastern Armenian political thinker, suggested that with the realization of an autonomous Armenia, the National Assembly should be moved from Constantinople to either Van or Erzerum.[18] The scheme for an autonomous Turkish Armenia was reportedly also accepted by the sultan. Although the sultan's acquiescence seems unbelievable, the speculation was, as Zohrab put it in hindsight, that the Ottoman government, in fear of losing the eastern provinces to Russia, encouraged the Armenians to seek autonomy under Ottoman sovereignty for the Armenian-populated provinces. Zohrab added that the decision was prompted by despair and that once the crisis had passed the idea was quickly dropped.[19]

Anticipation ran high. Karapet Ezian (Ezov) and many other Armenian conservative intellectuals in Russia looked to the tsar to liberate Western Armenia just as earlier tsars had emancipated the Armenians and Georgians of the Caucasus from Persian and Turkish rule.[20] In the same vein, Ezian viewed the Treaty of San Stefano that concluded the Russo-Turkish War in March 1878 as a major breakthrough. Even earlier, in a letter to Ezian in December 1877, another Russian Armenian conservative thinker expressed the hope that the Great Powers would extend their protection over the Armenians, that Armenians would prosper,

---

[17] Ibid., p. 234.

[18] Norayr Sarukhanyan, *Haykakan Hartse minchkhorhrdayin hay hasarakakan kaghakakan mtki ev patmagrutyan mej* [The Armenian Question in Pre-Soviet Armenian Civic Political Thought and Historiography] (Erevan: Genocide Museum and Institute, 1997), p. 54.

[19] Léart, *La Question Arménienne*, pp. 5-6.

[20] Sarukhanyan, *Haykakan Hartse*, p. 163.

not dispersed throughout the Ottoman Empire but in Armenia proper, and that Armenia would become not just a historical and geographical term but an administrative entity.[21] The issue of Armenian autonomy was dropped in the Treaty of San Stefano. Rather, Erzerum was to be returned to the Ottoman Empire, although there was at least a strong clause requiring reforms in the Armenian provinces.

Political speculations and hopes for the future—as well as fear and disappointment—surged, with a direct effect on the Armenians in Erzerum. The Russian occupation of the region had made a difference in the lives of the Armenians. They came into contact with Russian Armenian military commanders, such as the generals M.T. Loris-Melikov, I.I. Lazarev, and A.A. Ter-Ghukasov, as well as many lower ranking officers who encouraged them to take action, arm themselves, and defend their honor and their possessions. They were awed witnesses to the confidence of these professionals. The presence of an Armenian, Kostandin Kamsarakan, as the assistant military governor of Erzerum (later Russian vice consul there and then at Van) was also impressive. Coincidentally, Tserents (Hovsep Shishmanian), the noted Armenian novelist and political activist, was also in Erzerum, spreading his aura with analytical articles and authoritative opinions on the present situation and the future of Armenia. His novels, although historical in context, were examples of patriotism and heroic self-defense for contemporary Armenians to emulate. The Armenians of Karin stirred with excitement.

Optimism regarding the good will of the European powers was still strong. The newspaper *Meghu Hayastani* editorialized: "It is not possible even to think that the Great Powers would deceive a poor, powerless nation in need of protection. And why should they deceive? What is there to fear?"[22] Was this political naiveté or credulity based on despair? Whatever the case, the turn of events led to the revision of the Treaty of San Stefano and its favorable terms through the Treaty of Berlin in July 1878. The article relevant to the Armenians was now stated in general

---

[21] Ibid., p. 49.
[22] *Meghu Hayastani* [Bee of Armenia] (Tiflis), 1878, no. 26, cited in Sarukhanyan, *Haykakan Hartse*, p. 49.

terms, that is, that the sultan would implement reforms in the Armenian-inhabited provinces, which were not specified, and that responsibility for overseeing the reforms, instead of devolving upon Russia while the imperial armies still stood in Erzerum, would fall on the European powers collectively after those armies had withdrawn.[23]

During the brief Russian occupation of Erzerum, cultural life had blossomed. A theatrical group, for example, the Taterakan Enkerutiun (in some sources, Taterasirats Enkerutiun), was organized. A novelty in the eastern Ottoman provinces, the dramatic troupe intended to entertain and enlighten Armenians, but it had the capacity to reach out to Turks as well. The performances were also attended by Russian army officers and European officials in Erzerum. The choice of repertoire was significant, mostly pieces by playwrights such as Petros Durian (Bedros Turian) and Mktrich Peshiktashlian (Mgrdich Beshigtashlian), whose works embodied the heroic past of the Armenian people and aimed at instilling national pride. Other groups formed to spread enlightenment in the region of historic Karin included the Ghevondiants, the Mamikoniants, and the Bardzr Hayots societies.[24]

Reaction to Despair

The withdrawal of the Russian army from Erzerum in August 1878 left the Armenians in despair. Renewed atrocities ensued, as Muslim mobs, free of the constraining Russian presence, vented their rage against the Armenian population.[25] Previously, General Lazarev ordered the hanging in Geul-Bash of two mullahs who had incited bloodshed, but the effect was only temporary. Norman reported: "As long as Kurd Ismail Pasha is at the head of a Turkish force, so long will the Kurds be allowed to

---

[23] For a discussion of the treaties of San Stefano and Berlin, see Richard G. Hovannisian, "The Armenian Question in the Ottoman Empire, 1876-1914," in Hovannisian, *The Armenian People*, vol. 2, pp. 208-12.

[24] Abraham Giulkhandanian discusses the activities of these groups in "Heghapokhakan sharzhume Karini mej" [The Revolutionary Movement in Karin], *Hairenik Amsagir* 17 (July 1939): 125.

[25] For details of this new wave of violence, see Norman, *Armenia and the Campaign of 1877*, pp. 285-99.

carry on their war of creeds with impunity."[26] He sanctioned the outrages of Sheikh Jalaleddin. Horrified by the prospect of continued persecution, Armenians began a mass exodus toward the Russian frontier. Significantly, however, both Turkish Armenian and Russian Armenian leaders opposed this relocation as being tantamount to political suicide.[27] Indeed, the mass migration to the Russian Caucasus would alter the demographic ratios of Erzerum province and make implementation of reforms all the more difficult. General Lazarev's appeal to the populace not to follow his army but to remain on the ancestral lands was of no avail. It is ironic that Lazarev asked Ismail Pasha, formerly *vali* (governor) of Erzerum and now the commandant of the right wing of the Turkish army, for help in dissuading the Armenians from leaving.[28]

The initial hope for reforms under the supervision of the Great Powers quickly dissipated. There were no signs that the government would undertake such a program or that the European powers would intervene. Meanwhile, oppression increased. To secure his rule, Sultan Abdul-Hamid systematically restricted the rights of Christians and encouraged assaults on them. On the occasion of a brawl between Turks and Armenians in Erzerum, Mkrtich Pallarian, a member of the Armenian National Council (Azgayin Varchutiun), expressed his conviction that Muslim religious fanaticism would be a major obstacle to the implementation of reforms.[29] The government's policy was to decrease the Armenian concentration in the eastern provinces by sporadic harassment and massacre to encourage expatriation. These tactics, together with falsifying statistical and demographic data, were

---

[26] Ibid., p. 299. After a personal interview with Ismail Pasha in Erzerum, Norman wrote (p. 69): "I left him, impressed with the idea that the Porte could not have found a more bigoted, fanatical or worthless man for the post of *Vali* of Erzerum. "

[27] Giulkhandanian, "Heghapokhakan sharzhume," p. 123.

[28] Lazarev's letter to Ismail Pasha is cited in Giulkhandanian, "Heghapokhakan sharzhume," p. 123, using Leo (Arakel Babakhanian), *Tiurkahay heghapokhutian gaghaparabanutiune* [The Ideology of the Turkish Armenian Revolution], vol. 1 (Paris: Pahri Eghbarts, 1934).

[29] Excerpt from a letter to Nshkian, July 14, 1879, in Nshkian, *Arajin kaytser*, pp. 74-75.

used to evade reforms and European intervention.[30]

As predicted, conditions grew worse after the Russian departure and especially after Fazli Pasha arrived as the new military
commander of Erzerum. Gatherings were banned; petitions were
scorned; protests were punished. All the previously active Armenian organizations in Erzerum, such as Krtakan Enkerutiun,
Taterakan Enkerutiun, and Mamikoniants, were dissolved. In
these difficult times rumors began to circulate that Russian
Armenian volunteers were gathering beyond the border to come
to the rescue of their Turkish Armenian brethern. Nshkian cites
one of Khrimian Hayrik's letters in which there is a hint of such
a movement. Volunteers may indeed have existed, but they soon
dispersed, perhaps because there was no commensurate action by
the Turkish Armenians or because of obstacles created by the
Russian government.[31] Individual initiatives nonetheless continued.

Erzerum was closer to Constantinople than was Van, the other
center of Armenian political action, and with merchants constantly traveling to and from the capital news reached Erzerum
quickly. Erzerum was also near the Caucasus and became the
first major stop for Russian Armenian activists who crossed the
border to come to the homeland, the *erkir*, to devote themselves
to the cause of the Western Armenians. One of these young men
was Ter Grigor Abrahamian. A priest and a revolutionary activist,
he was sent by a group in Erevan which, according to Abraham
Giulkhandanian, maintained contact with Khrimian Hayrik.
Abrahamian entered the Erzerum vilayet in 1880 and circulated

---

[30] According to Giulkhandanian, in 1881 the Armenian Patriarchate of Constant-
inople provided the ambassador of Austria with the following data on the population
in the province of Erzerum: Armenians, 136,147; Turks, 105,565; Kurds, 65,644;
Kizilbashes, 23,858; Circassians, 1,202; Greeks, 1,315, for a total of 333,731.
Zohrab (Léart, *La Question Arménienne*, p. 59) cites another statistical table of the
Armenian Patriarchate in 1882, showing the Armenian population of the Erzerum
vilayet to be 280,000 and of the six Armenian vilayets together to be 1,630,000.
Lynch, on the other hand, gives the following figures for the Erzerum vilayet based
on data of the Ottoman government: Armenians, 106,768; Muslims 428,495; Greeks,
3,270; other races, 5,969, for a total of 544,502. For the statistical data above, see
Giulkhandanian, "Heghapokhakan sharzhume," p. 124, taken from the official Russian *Orange Book* (St. Petersburg: Ministry of Foreign Affairs, 1915).

[31] Nshkian, *Arajin kaytser*, pp. 114-15.

in the villages of the Alashkert district to encourage people to take up arms in self-defense.[32] Individual field agents and those who set a personal example of armed defense were instrumental in sensitizing some of the Erzerum youth, who saw that no reforms would be forthcoming and that conditions would only become worse unless they were willing to take matters into their own hands.

In May of 1881, six men came together to form the core of what was to grow into the first quasi-revolutionary organization in the Erzerum region. Khachatur Kerektsian, Karapet Nshkian, Hakob Ishgalatsian, Aleksan Etelikian, Hovhannes Asturian, and Eghishe Tursunian, with Hakob Nshkian as adviser, formed the Pashtpan Hayreniats (Protectors of the Fatherland),[33] identified in some sources as Gaghtni Enkerutiun Bardzr Hayots (Secret Society of Upper Armenia).[34] The society's goal was the defense of the Armenian villages against Kurdish raids by arming in complete secrecy multiple units of ten able and trustworthy men.[35] The arms were procured through contributions or loans of wealthy Armenians in Karin. According to Hakob Nshkian, the "membership" reached into the hundreds within two to three months, and there was a demand for arms from all over the province. Bishop Maghakia Ormanian, who at the behest of the Erzerum Armenians had finally succeeded the ill-famed prelate, was aware of this organization and cautiously supported it. Tacit encouragement also came from Patriarch Nerses Varzhapetian, who upon learning about the organization's goals and activities, is reported as saying to Nshkian: "I wish you people of the

---

[32] Giulkhandanian, "Heghapokhakan sharzhume" (Aug. 1939): 60.

[33] The most detailed information about this organization is provided by Nshkian, *Arajin kaytser*, pp. 115-46.

[34] See Giulkhandanian, "Heghapokhakan sharzhume," pp. 54-62, who names Kara-Melik (Barsegh Melik-Grigorian) as a person with reliable knowledge about the organization. Giulkhandanian refers to Kara-Melik's *Zinagorts kahana* [Gunsmith Priest], published in Vienna in 1896.

[35] For precautionary reasons, the organization adopted a system in which each member of the core group would delegate his very trusted friends to form their own groups of ten and these ten would know only their own group leader. They would take an oath to serve the organization in secrecy. The most capable and trustworthy men within these groups would in turn be delegated to form new groups of ten, allowing the organization to multiply in secrecy.

provinces had thought of working independently much sooner and did not wait for plans and ideas to come from Constantinople."[36] Even before that, Khrimian Hayrik had encouraged the first faltering steps of the Erzerum youth. In a letter to Nshkian he noted the example of Van where the youth "were now armed with guns and with hope." He alluded to the revolutionary activities in Van and to the optimism that the change of government in England had inspired. William Gladstone, regarded as a friend of the Armenians, had replaced Benjamin Disraeli, and Armenians hoped that his cabinet would be more favorable to the Armenian cause.[37] Hence, while the moral support was there, finding the means to procure arms to meet the increasing need remained a problem.[38]

The popularity of this secret organization tempted the leaders to neglect the extreme caution and secrecy that were originally observed. They composed a pledge of allegiance, which ended with the phrase, *Azatutiun kam Mah* (Liberty or Death). The pledge, by which the members were inducted, was printed on attractive leaflets with a coat of arms at the top showing two swords crossed and two hands held together as a symbol of unity. The pledge was distributed among the members to sign and return. Ormanian did not approve of this and viewed it as bravado. Years later, in a biography of Father Garegin Vemian (the gunsmith priest known as Avetis), Barsegh Melik-Grigorian (Kara-Melik) wrote about a meeting of the organization that he attended. Avetis criticized the organization's tactics, arguing that the Armenian peasants were ignorant; they would sign the pledge and then do nothing, think nothing, and, like soldiers, wait

---

[36] See Nshkian, *Arajin kaytser*, p. 119.

[37] Ibid., p. 94.

[38] Giulkhandanian, "Heghapokhakan sharzhume" (July 1939): 127, refutes Leo's statement that Bagrat Navasardian, a prominent physician in Tiflis (now Tbilisi), came to Erzerum to help establish the new organization and became a major financial supporter of the Protectors of the Fatherland (Leo, *Tiurkahay heghapokhutian gaghaparabanutiune*, p. 139). Giulkhandanian contends that there was only a one-time contribution of 1,300 to 1,500 rubles and no steady relationship between the group and the Tiflis intellectuals. On the other hand, Giulkhandanian (Aug. 1939: 58) also cites Kara-Melik, according to whom Grigor Artsruni and Bagrat Navasardian belonged to a group in Tiflis which sent Kara-Melik to Erzerum to learn about the new organization and collaborate with its leaders.

for orders to come from above, while the organization would have nothing to tell them. Weapons were what they needed, he insisted, and there were not enough to arm the people. Avetis pointed out that of the more than 2,000 guns he had made, sadly, less than 100 had been bought by Armenians. The Turks and the Kurds knew that in order to live in this country they needed to be armed. Avetis believed that the organization should act quickly to train and arm the people for self-defense.[39]

The leaders finally realized that the written material was a liability because it would expose the group. They collected and burned the papers, but, as Nshkian attests, one leaflet remained in the hands of an adventurer, and with the help of Armenian informers the government laid hands on it.[40] The arrest of 70 to 80 members followed in late November 1882. Homes in the city and the villages were searched, and some guns and documents were discovered. Fifty-two members were charged and imprisoned. Writing about the trials, Sarukhan, an eyewitness, cites the charges read by the prosecutor, stating that the group intended through revolution to detach the Erzerum region from the Ottoman Empire.[41] The interrogations and the lengthy trial of the prisoners reverberated throughout the country and abroad. It became a phenomenal event, actually the first political trial of Armenian activists in the empire. The proceedings were reported

---

[39] Giulkhandanian, "Heghapokhakan sharzhume" (Aug. 1939): 56-57, provides a brief account of Avetis' adventurous life. After the suppression of the Protectors of the Fatherland, in order to help the Armenians of Erzerum, the gunsmith became a priest. But even in his religious garb he brought together young men, trained them to use arms, and circulated with them from village to village to defend Armenians against Kurdish assaults. He was loved by the people, but the conservatives of Karin considered him a threat to their own safety, fearing that his conduct would give the government the pretext to exercise force. Driven out of Erzerum, he became a bandit under the name of Khurshud Chavush and joined Ibo, the Kurdish brigand. Together, they attacked and robbed Turkish officials, especially tax collectors. In 1892, when the Armenian Revolutionary Federation (ARF; Dashnaktsutiun) became active in Karin, he became Father Garegin, joined the party, and acted as a field agent.

[40] Giulkhandanian cites Kara-Melik and Sarukhan (another historian of the organization), both of whom point to Father Mikayel, a wicked priest, as the traitor who out of spite turned in the names. Nshkian, however, believes that Boghos Sarafian, a government agent, was the culprit.

[41] Sarukhan's account was published in the journal *Gorts* [Work] in Baku in March 1917. See Giulkhandanian, "Heghapokhakan sharzhume" (July 1939): 130-31.

with exaggerated pathos in Armenian papers everywhere. The size and activities of the organization were also exaggerated. The group was lauded and idealized to become a source of inspiration for Armenian student movements, especially in Russian universities. For example, the Hay Usanoghneri Enkerutiun (Society of Armenian Students), organized in Moscow in 1883, was directly inspired by the Protectors of the Fatherland.

In the wake of the exposure of the Pashtpan Hayreniats, the situation grew worse. The prelate Ormanian, suspected of collaboration with the conspirators, was ousted. The government reacted promptly and harshly, looking upon the revolutionary activities as evidence of an empire-wide insurgency movement, even though it soon became apparent that the organization worked alone with no connections beyond Erzerum. The prisoners were given heavy sentences, but, through the intervention of influential Constantinople Armenians, most were released by September 1886. Thus, the armed struggle of the Erzerum Armenians was stifled almost from the outset. Political activities were paralyzed for several years. The government's repression caused another relapse in the slowly evolving Armenian revolutionary movement, but it also brought to the fore the need for a better and stronger organization to stand against oppressive rule and the exploitation of the Kurdish and Turkish beys and aghas.

A Period of Preparation

The period between 1883 and 1890 was one of self-realization and self-education in Karin/Erzerum. The main sources of inspiration were the admonitions and encouragement of Khrimian Hayrik through his words and messages. His writings about the deplorable reality in Erzerum, such as *Haygoyzh* (Armenian Lament) on the massacres of Armenians in Alashkert and Bayazit (Bayazed) in the aftermath of the 1877-78 Russo-Turkish War, were especially effective. These were complemented by the novels of Raffi (Hakob Melik-Hakobian), such as *Jalaleddin* (the name of a Kurdish chieftain) and *Khente* (The Fool), in which the theme of armed struggle and self-defense is dominant.

During this period, the Armenakan society, the first formal Armenian political party (organized in 1885) emerged at Van.

The Hnchakian Revolutionary party, founded in Geneva in 1887, did not become active in the eastern Ottoman provinces until the 1890s.[42] The first political group to be formed in Erzerum was the Droshak (Banner) committee, organized in early 1890 by Tigran Okonian, a member of the Tiflis (Tbilisi) branch established in 1889. The Droshak circle expanded into a union called the Hay Eritasardats Enkerutiun (Society of Young Armenians), which later became an important component of the Hay Heghapokhakanneri Dashnaktsutiun (Federation of Armenian Revolutionaries). Immediately after the founding of the Dashnaktsutiun in Tiflis in 1890, Aram Aramian (Ashot-Tatul) and Keri (Arshak Gavafian) were also sent to their native Erzerum to organize revolutionary cells.

The government thought it had eradicated all political activity in Erzerum when it squelched the Protectors of the Fatherland. But the continuing oppression and lingering bitterness was to instigate new action. A new organization formed by school principal Gevorg Chilingirian and a number of students in whom he had instilled patriotism was joined by former members of the Protectors of Fatherland. The group met regularly in the prelacy's reading room until it was discovered by informers and had to change locations. It dispatched Tigran Kerektsian (brother of Khachatur Kerektsian, a founding member of the Protectors of the Fatherland) to Constantinople to inform and consult with Khrimian Hayrik. On his return, Kerektsian met with Ruben Khan-Azat (Khanazatian), one of the founders of the Hnchakian party and the principal of an Armenian school in Trebizond. Khan-Azat suggested that the group join the Hnchakian party, and he sent a letter to Gevorg Chilingirian in that regard. The proposal was accepted and the activities of the Hnchakian party in Erzerum got off the ground.[43]

---

[42] The Hnchakians organized impressive demonstrations and manifestations of self-defense before the party suffered a major debilitating split in 1896. Rostom, an ARF founder, asserts that after 1896 there were no Hnchakian bodies in Erznka (Erzinjan), Karin, or Van. The Hnchakian party's centralized system and its leadership located in faraway Geneva, London, and Athens, impeded full-scale participation in the political and revolutionary activities in the heart of the homeland. See *Rostom* (Beirut: Hamazkayin Press, 1979), p. 124.

[43] See Giulkhandanian, "Heghapokhakan sharzhume" (Aug. 1939): 55.

Despite such small-scale secret activities during this period, the government's watchful eyes rendered any manifestation of political or revolutionary activity in Erzerum, as elsewhere, extremely difficult. Levon Sargisian, a member of a student group at Moscow University, came to Erzerum in 1888 to test the waters and to return with suggestions for a plan of action in Armenia. The atmosphere was so tense and government surveillance so tight, however, that the local Armenians shunned him. He was begged to leave in order not to endanger his own life and the lives of others. Sargisian returned to Russia after only eighteen days in Erzerum. Under such oppressive conditions, the unrest in the city on June 20, 1890, was a significant event, an outburst against persecution and the defiling of the Armenian church.

The Sublime Porte, in receipt of news that the Erzerum Armenians had stored a large quantity of arms in their cathedral and in the Sanasarian school, ordered the vali to take immediate action. According to Giulkhandanian and Mikayel Varandian, both of whom recorded similar accounts of the event, on Sunday, June 20, the police and the army raided the church premises and began their search in a most crude and insulting manner. Aggravated by their sacrilegious conduct, Armenians attending the mass confronted the intruders. The police, with bayonets bared, tried to force the demonstrators to disperse. Then gunfire sounded and soon, as if by prearrangement, the Turkish mob joined in. After three hours of fighting that left casualties on both sides, the clash came to an end. Armenians suffered heavy losses, with an estimated 100 dead and 200-300 wounded. Arrests were made and the city remained under martial law for weeks, during which the police and the army circulated freely, disregarding law and order, conducting house-to-house searches and making arbitrary arrests. Many individuals who feared arrest, Chilingirian among them, fled the city.[44] The details of this event may vary slightly in different sources, but what is important is that all sources close to the Dashnaktsutiun describe the event as a spontaneous reaction to Turkish provocation. According to Varandian, the

---

[44] See Varandian, *Dashnaktsutian patmutiun*, pp. 53-54. See also Giulkhandanian, "Heghapokhakan sharzhume" (Aug. 1939): 55-57.

Dashnakist Vartkes Serengulian (Vardges Serenkulian), a future member of the Ottoman Parliament and a victim of the Genocide of 1915, took charge of the situation and led the resistance. Hnchakian sources, on the other hand, maintain that the uprising was organized by the Hnchakian body in Trebizond and carried out by local comrades Hakob Ishgalatsian and Khachatur Kerektsian. These sources indicate that Ruben Khan-Azat believed the event would prompt action by the European governments and was disappointed that this did not occur.[45]

Echoes of the unrest spread beyond the Ottoman Empire. This was the first time that the Armenians of Erzerum were shedding blood in acts of resistance to the Turkish authorities. Although the bloody Sunday in Erzerum was a modest manifestation of protest, the news appeared in the European press and attracted reporters to the area. Excitement also gripped Armenian activists, for example, inspiring Sargis Kukunian, a university student in St. Petersburg, to abandon his studies, travel to the Caucasus to recruit a large group of young men, and embark on what became an ill-fated expedition across the Russo-Turkish frontier to fight for the cause of Western Armenians. The Erzerum event also inspired the *fedayi* (partisan) song, *Dzain me hnchets Erzrumi hayots lerneren* (A Call Sounded from the Armenian Mountains of Erzerum).[46] The inherent excitement and romanticism of the song are further evidence of the exaggeration that led to overestimating Armenian power and underestimating the government's resolve to crush the movement, a continuing miscalculation that was to end in frustration and disappointment. A month after this incident, the Hnchakians organized the Kum Kapu demonstration in Constantinople to protest the government's mishandling of the unrest in Erzerum. The response once again, however, was violent supression.

---

[45] Hrand Gangruni (Hrant Kankrouny), *Hay heghapokhutiune osmanian brna-petutian dem, 1890-1910* [The Armenian Revolution against Ottoman Oppression, 1890-1910] (Beirut: [H. Kankrouny], 1973), pp. 104-07. Gangruni also names Hakob Nshkian as a member of the group of local comrades who supposedly carried out the uprising. Nshkian, however, had been in the United States since 1888 (*Arajin kaytser*, p. 10).

[46] In some historical sources, this song is ascribed to the Protectors of the Father-land organization.

Romanticism and Frustration

The 1890 disturbance in Erzerum was an isolated event, a manifestation of genuine protest and the development of political thought and aspirations among the Erzerum Armenians. It was followed by the increased boldness of individuals who formed their own fedayi groups and launched a daring campaign to defend Armenian villages against raids. Two such groups around Erznka (Erzinjan) were led by Galust Arkhanian and Ruben Shishmanian, known as Keri of Dersim (Dersimi Kerin). After two years of acting separately, the groups met in the nearby Monastery of Surb Grigor Lusavorich (Saint Gregory the Illuminator) some time in 1892. With the help of Aram Achekbashian, a Hnchakian field agent present at the meeting, a plan of joint action was drawn up. The groups were reinforced and reorganized to undertake the defense of the region of Erznka. Arkhanian's unit had a short life. The troop of 52 men was arrested and imprisoned in 1893. The fedayis were charged with the crime of sedition in their trial in April 1894, resulting in death sentences for the leaders, later commuted to life imprisonment, and long prison terms for the others. Arkhanian became ill and died in prison in 1905. The rest were freed after the Young Turk revolution in 1908.

Keri and his men joined the Dashnaktsutiun in 1895.[47] For three years, from 1896 to 1899, Keri tried to gain the collaboration of the Kurds in the Dersim district. This was part of a bold Armenian strategy to reach an understanding with the Kurdish people, who were repeatedly used by the Ottoman rulers to suppress the Armenians.[48] But the government was determined to abort any such rapprochement by punishing the implicated

---

[47] See Gabriel Lazian, *Demker hay azatagrakan sharzhumen* [Figures from the Armenian Liberation Movement] (Cairo: Houssaper, 1949), pp. 20-26.

[48] The first such attempts were Kara-Melik's activities in Karin, Erznka, and Dersim. After joining the Dashnaktsutiun, he engaged in transporting arms to the *erkir* and continued to preach Armeno-Kurdish cooperation. In 1895, the supreme executive body of the Dashnaktsutiun, the Bureau, sent Kara-Melik to Erzerum to further that mission, but he arrived only to become a witness to the massacres. For more details on his activities, see *Rostom*, pp.102-03, and Giulkhandanian, "Heghapokhakan sharzhume" (Aug. 1939): 58-59.

Kurds and Armenians. Keri, too, was arrested by the authorities and after four years in chains in solitary confinement was hanged in Erzinjan in 1903. His efforts may have helped to bear some fruit years later during and after the Armenian Genocide.[49]

The period from 1890 to 1895 was characterized by romantic plans, goals, and ideas, unrealistic expectations, ideological disputes and conflict within the leadership, dangerous factionalism, unwillingness and unpreparedness of the masses to become engaged, and reluctance of the wealthy to finance the resistance movement. The government's repression of the least attempt at self-defense added to the frustration. Not only were the implicated punished, but whole communities of men, women, and children were subject to the government's severe punitive actions.

In the atmosphere of idealism and total devotion to the *Surb Gorts* (Sacred Work), political clairvoyance and calculations had little place, leading to overestimation of Armenian power, revolutionary momentum, and the readiness of the masses to rise up against tyrannical rule. At the same time, the Ottoman government's means and determination to crush the Armenian movement were underestimated. The idealistic assessment of the possibility of a general insurrection and the unfounded optimism of some political elements prompted them to make pompous declarations on placards and leaflets posted on walls in towns and villages, arousing fear and anger among ordinary Turks. The government and religious leaders exploited those sentiments to rouse the Muslim population against the Armenians even in the remotest villages. Reverend Edwin M. Bliss, who was born in Erzerum in

---

[49] Lazian, *Demker*, pp. 16-18. Lazian notes that Keri, a native of Erznka, was very much loved and respected among the Kurds of Dersim. The seeds of friendship and harmony he had sown may have germinated during the 1915 deportations and massacres of the Armenians of Erzinjan. Kurds in Dersim gave refuge to and saved the lives of many deportees. Still later, when the Russian army occupied Erzinjan and approached Dersim in 1916, the local Kurds collaborated with Kaytsak Arakel, Keri's comrade in arms, who was sent to that region by partisan commander Sebastatsi Murad to rescue Armenian survivors sequestered in Muslim households or forcibly converted to Islam. After Keri's arrest and incarceration, the Dashnaktsutiun continued to negotiate with the Kurds, especially in Taron/Mush and Van, trying to work with their notables to curb the Kurdish penchant for killing and plunder. On earlier negotiations and occasional collaboration, see Varandian, *Dashnaktsutian patmutiun*, pp. 211-14.

a family of American missionaries and came to know Turkey intimately over the years, wrote that there was "general fear of an uprising of Christians, probably to be supported by the European governments." He added: "It was absurd, for not one Christian in a hundred, scarcely one in a thousand, had a weapon, while comparatively few Turks were unarmed."[50]

Another characteristic of this period was the lack of control and discipline, which can be attributed to the individual initiatives aimed at eliminating all obstacles in the path of revolution. This sometimes led to unfounded accusations and hasty punitive measures. One such example was the assassination in 1891 of Khachatur Kerektsian, a founding member of the Protectors of the Fatherland, who was accused of treacherous acts against the Dashnaktsutiun. The assassination, decided upon by the party's Erzerum central committee without the sanction of the Bureau in Tiflis, was carried out by Aram Aramian.[51] Later, in 1892, during the Dashnaktsutiun's General Congress in Tiflis, Aramian, representing the Erzerum committee, was summoned to answer for his action. He rationalized the murder and went even further to propose that terror, especially against Turkish government officials, be adopted as a tactic of the organization. His experience in Erzerum had convinced him that it would be impossible to bring about a general insurrection in the Ottoman Empire in the way the Dashnaktsutiun had envisioned during the party's founding meeting in 1890. His proposed tactic, which was rejected at the congress in 1892, involved the inevitable arrest and execution of the terrorist, for Aramian proposed that the person carrying out the act should not try to escape but rather should surrender in order not to endanger the lives of innocent persons.

The distance between romanticism and frustration is short, and

---

[50] Edwin Munsell Bliss, *Turkey and the Armenian Atrocities* (n.p.: Edgewood Publishing Co., 1896), p. 556.

[51] Dashnaktsutiun's Bureau in Tiflis warned the Erzerum central committee against that action and after the assassination acknowledged wrongdoing and expressed regret. Martiros Shatirian ascribes this assassination to Okonian and mentions his murder by Kerektsian's brother in Tiflis as an act of revenge. See Shatirian's memoirs, "Hayots hasarakakan sharzhumnerits" [From the Armenian Social Movements], transcribed by N. Hangoyts [Nikol Aghbalian], *Hairenik Amsagir* 1 (March 1923): 35.

in that agitated period, when there were so many heavy losses and failures, frustration was unavoidable. Indeed, ultimate devotion to the Armenian cause had crashed against the fear and aloofness of the masses on whose account lives were being sacrificed. Wealthy Armenians did not honor their word to finance the purchase of arms and other revolutionary activities. The government's reaction was more brutal than anyone could have anticipated. The British consul general in Erzerum, Clifford Lloyd, summarized in a dispatch of October 1890 the condition of the country under the following headings:

I.   The insecurity of lives and properties of Christians.
II. The insecurity of their persons, and the absence of all liberty of thought and action.
III. The unequal status of Christian and Mahometan in the eye of the Government.[52]

In this period of disillusionment, confusion and uncertainty clouded the goals. What were these? Reforms, autonomy, independence? What would these entail? Freedom? Freedom of what or from what? These terms had different meanings for different people. For the ordinary Erzerum Armenian, freedom meant relief from the heavy taxes exacted by authorities, the Kurdish chieftains, and Turkish absentee landlord beys and aghas or the right to move beyond the Russian border with their possessions. Frustration translated into animosity among the various classes of people. The pattern was true everywhere: antagonism among revolutionary activists, the wealthy, the conservative intellectuals, the cautious merchants, the city dwellers, and the peasantry.

Reverend Bliss made the following assessment:

Next to Van, Erzrum has been looked upon by the Armenians as belonging peculiarly to them, and as was natural the revolutionary party sought to exert their influence in it. That they so signally failed is but another proof of the inherent weakness of

---

[52] Cited in J. Castell Hopkins, *The Sword of Islam, or Suffering Armenia, Annals of Turkish Power and the Eastern Question* (Brantford and Toronto: Bradley-Garretson, 1896), p. 313.

the movement and the general conservatism of the nation in regard to aggressive action against the Turkish Government.[53]

The Massacres of 1895

The city and province of Erzerum did not escape the widespread massacres of 1894-96. Ironically, the massacres were perpetrated without restraint in a city with so many international offices, including the French, British, Russian, and German consulates and the American mission house.

In September 1895, Rostom, a cofounder of the Dashnak-tsutiun, entered Erzerum disguised as a merchant. He came with the mission to oversee the distribution of arms and the training of the people for self-defense. The party was deeply involved in trafficking arms and ammunition from Persia to the Ottoman Empire, and Rostom's presence in Erzerum was crucial. The arms were transported mainly through Alashkert, with Erzerum becoming an important center for distribution. As it happened, while in Erzerum, Rostom witnessed the massacre on October 30, 1895. The wave of bloodshed that had spread from Trebizond to Gumushkhane and Baiburt (Baberd) now reached Karin.[54]

As an eyewitness, Rostom described the commotion in the city.[55] About 20,000 Lazes, Circassians, Kurds, and other Muslims from the outside had joined the mob in the streets, looting, murdering, stripping and mutilating the dead, and burning the wounded.[56] A comparison of the size of the mob, even if somewhat exaggerated, with the total population of the city reflects the horrific impact of the rabble. Edwin Bliss estimated the population of the city before the massacres of 1895 at 40,000, with the majority being Turks. He described the Armenian com-

---

[53] Bliss, *Turkey and the Armenian Atrocities*, p. 415.

[54] Ibid., pp. 416-26, for details of the massacre. Bliss recorded the eyewitness account of William N. Chambers, the resident American missionary in Erzerum. See also Johannes Lepsius, *Armenia and Europe* (London: Hodder and Stoughton, 1898), pp. 5-7, 51-53; Hopkins, *The Sword of Islam*, pp. 366-67.

[55] See *Rostom*, pp. 50-54.

[56] Bliss, *Turkey and the Armenian Atrocities*, p. 416, states that these outsiders were "heroes" of the massacres of Trebizond, Baiburt, Erzinjan, Kemakh, and other places, who had come to Erzerum for "another similar game."

munity as "strong, both in numbers, wealth and character."[57] In spite of the enormity of the murderous horde, the slightest resistance, returning rifle fire from inside a house, was often enough to scare many looters away. But then the army interfered, cutting down those who dared to resist. It was in such a situation that Father Garegin (Avetis, the gunsmith), cut off from his comrades, fought alone in a house under siege. The soldiers, believing that a large troop was shooting from inside the house, did not dare to enter for a long time. When they finally charged, they found that they had killed one lone defender.

In Baiburt, where Armenians constituted a minority of the population, the slaughter did not start until an army unit arrived from military headquarters in Erzinjan to break the resistance and open the way for the mob to engage in the carnage. Many villages around Baiburt were wiped out without difficulty, but at Lus Hank, a young man fought back single-handedly, armed with the only gun in the village. Frightened by the unexpected fire, the mob scattered.

Rostom asserted that the massacres were not as thorough in the city of Erzerum and the surrounding villages because in some places the Armenians defended themselves. The British consul general also reported to his ambassador in Constantinople that the Turks avoided places where they knew the Armenians were armed.[58] In view of the fact that most of the Armenian villages in Erzerum were surrounded by Turkish and Kurdish settlements, the comparatively lower number of losses in the district is a significant phenomenon. Another important contributing factor was the benevolent conduct of some Turks in the city and some Kurdish beys and aghas in the villages. Rostom affirmed that even in the city, where the government troops were most active and where anti-Armenian agitations had been stoked for years, some quarters were spared, and many notable Armenians took refuge in Muslim homes.[59]

According to reports and eyewitness accounts, the role of the

---

[57] Ibid., p. 415.

[58] The letter, dated April 12, 1897, is cited in Varandian, *Dashnaktsutian patmutiun*, p. 226.

[59] Bliss, *Turkey and the Armenian Atrocities*, pp. 421-22, gives a similar account.

mob in the massacres was secondary to that of the army, which in many places initiated the assault and committed most of the killing. The mob, on the other hand, with religious fanaticism and an appetite for Armenian belongings, looted and completed the murderous process. Bliss explained: "Political fear, religious fanaticism, lust for booty, have all entered in varying proportions in different places."[60] Ironically, at the time that Rostom was writing his report in February 1896, Van was still peaceful. There were no signs of an impending assault. Rostom warned that Van would not be an exception and that the government was only in a period of watchful waiting, because the Armenians of Van were more organized. Rostom had intended to stay in Erzerum for at least a year, but the massacres interrupted his mission. With the Armenian schools in which he was to teach closed, he left the city in November 1896, not to return until 1910.

The massacres added to the disillusionment and apprehensions of the Armenian activists:

First, the perpetrators were not punished; instead, the authorities forced the Armenian civil and religious leaders to sign fabricated affidavits that the Armenians had instigated the violence. Johannes Lepsius reported that in the case of Erzinjan, the Armenian bishop and council refused to buckle under the pressure to dispatch a telegraph to the sultan placing the blame on the Armenians. The arrest and imprisonment of many leaders followed.[61]

Second, the revolutionary movement had not been able to stir the Armenian masses to a general rising. Instead, with few exceptions, the Armenian population allowed itself to be victimized without showing strong resistance.

Third, the revolutionary activists were largely blamed for the calamities not only by European observers but also by the Armenians themselves. Indeed, there were those who believed the massacres to be the direct consequence of the Armenian underground movement. Many deemed it wise to stop all political

---

[60] Ibid., p. 557. The descriptions and assessments of Bliss, Lepsius, and Rostom are very much alike.

[61] Lepsius, *Armenia and Europe*, p. 63.

activity and give no further occasion for the government's vengeance. Condemning the Armenian massacres while also severely
criticizing the revolutionaries, Frederick Davis Greene differenti-
ated between the peaceful Armenian masses and the revolutionist
minority: "The real spirit and aim of the Armenian race, as a
whole, is unfortunately obscured, in the mind of the public, by
utterances and acts of a few irresponsible Armenian hot-heads,
who have imbibed nihilistic views in Europe, and are trying, in
a very bungling way, to apply them."[62] Reverend Bliss deplored
the role of Hnchakian revolutionaries and termed as absurd
Hnchakian plans to create an independent Armenia. He nonetheless asserted that "in not one single instance can it be fairly said
that the great massacres, as at Erzrum, Harput, Diarbekir, etc.,
had any excuse in the presence of Armenian revolution. Granted,
however, that the Huntchagist movement did harm, and it certainly did, it must be remembered that it was an almost inevitable
development."[63] The singling out of the Hnchakians, aside from
their open and irritating threats, was probably influenced by the
fact that Bliss was stationed in Cilicia where the Hnchakian party
was very active. Reverend Greene, for his part, explained the
revolutionary movement as "the natural outcome of the horrible
situation in Armenia since the treaty of Berlin" and warned that
"the disease is bound to grow more virulent and contagious until
the European doctors apply vigorous and radical treatment to the
'Sick Man' [Ottoman Empire]."[64]

Fourth, the massacres demonstrated the inability or unwillingness of the European powers to prevent, to intervene, or to halt
the outrages. Russia, Great Britain, France, Germany, Austria,
and Italy each had political and economic interests, and pushing
the sultan too hard for the sake of the Armenians would only
hinder their objectives.

Thus, once again the Armenians felt abandoned, their hopes
and dreams shattered. Their incipient armed struggle to gain
freedom and security had been thwarted.

---

[62] Greene, *Armenian Crisis*, p. 69.

[63] Bliss, *Turkey and the Armenian Atrocities*, pp. 557-58.

[64] Greene, *Armenian Crisis*, p. 83.

The Apex of Political Activism

The revolutionary movement in Erzerum and the cultural, socio-economic, and political life in general in that region resumed after the restoration of the Ottoman constitution in 1908, particularly during the years from 1910 to 1914. New educational establishments such as the Hripsimian girls' school were opened. The highly-regarded Sanasarian school flourished, and Karin became an important cultural center for the Armenian provinces. It had also become an exclusive field of influence and activity of the Armenian Revolutionary Federation. During this period, Rostom returned to Erzerum, now as a representative of the supreme party Bureau, political field agent, and superintendent of the Armenian schools in the province. Other prominent Dashnakists in Karin were Simon Vratzian, Armen Garo (Garegin Pasdermajian), Dr. Hovsep Ter-Davtian Dr. Hakob Zavrian, Astvatsatur Khachaturian, and Eghishe Topchian.[65] The upsurge of party activities stirred the antagonism of Armenian conservatives. As a result, the trustees of the Sanasarian school decided in 1912 to close the institution, expel students labeled as troublemakers, and transfer the school to Sebastia (Sivas), even though the benefactor's will stipulated the maintenance of a modern educational institution in Erzerum.[66] Rostom and some of the faculty strove

---

[65] Vratzian stayed in Erzerum for a year before departing for Boston to assume the duties of editor of the *Hairenik* (Fatherland) newspaper. He returned in 1914 to participate in the Dashnaktsutiun's Eighth General Congress and to take Rostom's place. Shortly after the outbreak of war he was arrested and imprisoned but as a Russian citizen was then expelled to Russia. For his ordeals in the Turkish prison and the trying experiences on the way to the Russian border, see Simon Vratzian [Vratsian], *Kianki ughinerov* [Along Life's Ways], vol. 1 (Cairo: Houssaper, 1955), pp. 162-88. Rostom had also invited Zapel Esayan, the well-known Western Armenian writer, to join the Sanasarian faculty, stressing the importance of the presence of an educated woman. By the time Esayan arranged to move to Erzerum, however, the world war erupted. See Esayan's article in *Rostom*, pp. 24-29.

[66] Lazian, *Demker*, p. 138. For more details, see the articles by Hovakim Arshakuni [Hovakimian] and Vratzian on Rostom in the volume *Rostom*, pp. 276-81, and pp. 193-209. Vratzian notes that during the Russian occupation of Erzerum in 1916, Rostom visited his erstwhile field of educational and revolutionary activity and was able to retrieve a number of papers and documents from the Sanasarian school building. He was deeply affected by the sight of the devastated city and its once-thriving Armenian life.

to keep the doors of Sanasarian open. The New Sanasarian began operations in September of that year. Through the efforts of Simon Vratzian, who was then in Boston as editor of *Hairenik,* the Educational Union of Karin (Karno Usumnasirats Miutiun) was organized in 1912 and began to provide financial support for the schools in Erzerum.

In this brief period of optimism, there were great enthusiasm and flights of imagination regarding the future. The Armenians of Karin had their own periodical press, *Harach* (Forward) from May 31, 1909 to early 1914, sponsored by the Dashnaktsutiun's Eritasardakan Miutiun (Youth Union) and edited consecutively by Eghishe Topchian, Simon Vratzian, Shavarsh Misakian, and Pilos.[67] *Alik* (Wave) daily replaced *Harach* in the spring of 1914 but was published only until mid-July. *Erkir* (Homeland), published briefly in 1914, was also a continuation of *Harach.* Other periodicals were *Sirt* (Heart, 1911), a monthly in Karin and the organ of the Dashnaktsutiun's Union of Workers, and *Aror* (Plough, 1909-14) in Erznka/Erzinjan. And these were only the party-sponsored papers in the province of Erzerum.

The active periodical press was a sign of socio-cultural progress and the advancement of political thought in Erzerum. The arming of the people and their training for self-defense continued along with the cultural activities.[68] Pilos, in the city of Erzerum, and Dro (Drastamat Kanayan), in Bayazit, among others, were engaged in that activity. In a letter to Simon Vratzian in Boston, Rostom gave assurances that the Dashnaktsutiun was not only involved in educating the Erzerum Armenians but was also engaged in an arms-training program. Constantinople Armenian leaders, Rostom stated, were so taken with a new reform plan

---

[67] Just before the Ottoman Empire entered the war in 1914, Pilos and other young Armenian leaders in Erzerum enlisted in the Turkish army, thinking that their gesture would demonstrate the good will of the Armenians toward the government. Shortly thereafter, Pilos was arrested and being an officer was sent to the military prison, where it is likely he was murdered. See Vratzian, *Kianki ughinerov,* pp. 156-80.

[68] There were plans, as Rostom revealed in a letter, to gather every year at the Monastery of Surb Karapet (Saint John the Precursor—the Baptist) in Mush to revive the Navasardian athletic competitions, which in pre-Christian Armenia had been held annually to mark the New Year in the month of Navasard. See *Rostom,* p. 182.

that they could not see the reality. He was certain that reforms would never be implemented and that the Armenians had to rely on their own strength.[69]

Karin, in the heart of the *erkir*, had become a vital center of Armenian political life in the Ottoman Empire. A combination of factors had made the Dashnaktsutiun the predominant political force in the region.[70] The party's Eighth General Congress was held in Erzerum during the summer of 1914 to plan future activities and to devise strategies to function within the alarming atmosphere of an impending war. For some, the expectations based on the promulgation of a reform measure in February 1914 and the appointment of European inspectors-general to be headquartered in Erzerum and Van were high. However, the specter of a world conflagration was felt stronger with each passing day. Vratzian, writing from Erzerum, described the "hellish situation" as follows: "All men are drafted into the army. There are no shops open, no trade, no schools. Cultural life is at a standstill. The government has confiscated sugar, coffee, kerosene, rice, flour and has handed out receipts in return."[71] There was also a deterioration in the attitude of the Turks since early summer, an escalating mistrust and animosity toward the Armenians. Turkey was preparing to enter the war against the Entente Powers and viewed the Armenians as an important factor, or rather, a worrisome impediment.

This was the state of affairs when the ominous events began to unfold. The Young Turk government's policy of eliminating all obstacles to the realization of its objectives, which entailed above all the annihilation of the Armenian population of the empire, was implemented with horrific force. The eradication of Armenian life in Erzerum brought to an end the development of Armenian political thought and movements in the region except

---

[69] Ibid., pp. 188-89.

[70] In a letter to the ARF Central Committee of America, dated August 25, 1914, Vratzian noted that the Sahmanadrakan Ramkavar (Constitutional Democrat) party opened a center in Karin, but it closed within a few months. See Simon Vratzian [Vratsian], *Hin tghter nor patmutian hamar* [Old Papers for Modern History] (Beirut: [Mshak], 1962), p. 78.

[71] The letter, dated September 1, 1914, was addressed to the ARF Central Committee of America. See Vratzian, *Hin tghter*, p. 81.

for a brief flicker in 1916-18, when Erzerum was under Russian occupation. By the end of World War I, Erzerum was entirely Turkish. Armenian Karin ceased to exist.

Dersimi Kerin
(Ruben Shishmanian)

Keri
(Arshak Gavafian)

Armen Garo
(Garegin Pasdermajian)

Vardges
(Vartkes Serengulian)

222

Rostom with Hripsimian School Faculty

Dashnaktsutiun Building and Editorial Offices of *Harach*

❊ 10 ❊

THE W.L. SACHTLEBEN PAPERS
ON ERZERUM IN THE 1890S

Gia Aivazian

In the 1960s, a man was driving along one of the residential streets of Houston, Texas, when he noticed a rather strange sight in front of a house.[1] A bonfire was raging in the yard, and a workman was tossing boxes filled with unwanted things from an attic window into the fire. As the driver slowed down to watch, he saw one box fall away from the fire and its contents spill all around. These seemed to be sheaves of paper and photographs. Being a photography buff, he stopped the car and got out to see what was in the box. To his surprise, there were not only note-books and batches of manuscripts written in a small hand from one edge of paper to the other and not only numerous photographs of distant lands, but also hundreds of negatives neatly packaged and placed in envelopes with descriptions of the contents and dated in the same hand as the manuscripts. The dates covered the years from 1891 to 1896. Excited, he asked the workman if he could have them and upon receiving an affirmative response, he rewarded the workman and took off with the rescued box.

A decade later, in the 1970s, this collection came into the possession of Mrs. Jean Zakarian of Carpinteria, California. Having married into an Armenian family, Jean was particularly interested in the items relating to Turkey. Reading the texts and

---

[1] Since I began research on this paper for the conference on Armenian Karin/ Erzerum in 1998, some new and interesting discoveries have been made regarding W.L. Sachtleben's biography, the court trials revolving around the murder of Frank G. Lenz (the reason for Sachtleben's presence in Turkey in 1895-96), and the photographs and photographers of the Erzerum massacre.

examining the photographs, she learned that the original owner of the material was one William Lewis Sachtleben, who had been an eyewitness to the Erzerum massacre of Armenians on October 30, 1895. Not only had he written pieces on the subject, but he also had negatives of scenes of the event.

Wisely, Mrs. Zakarian had new negatives made from the original nitrate film and seventeen prints from these new negatives. As time went by, she realized that the material needed to be in an appropriate archive for use by interested scholars and decided that UCLA was the place to preserve them. The UCLA Research Library gratefully accepted the gift and placed the archive in its Special Collections. From the very first day, I became intrigued by the contents of the collection and the man who was responsible for its existence. It has been both an exciting and challenging experience to learn more about W.L. Sachtleben and what business he had in Erzerum which placed him in the midst of the 1895 massacre. Although there were hundreds of negatives and photographs, the texts were few and incomplete. All the texts, except for a couple of notebooks dating from the spring of 1891 during a stay in Greece, are either from mid-1895 to the spring of 1896 or not dated but relate to Erzerum in 1895-96.

The reason for Sachtleben's presence on the Armenian Plateau became apparent through one of the incomplete texts titled "Trip to Alashgerd," covering the period September 24 to early October 1895, showing that he had come to the area in search of an American cyclist named Frank G. Lenz who had crossed the Persian-Turkish frontier in May 1894 and whose trail had disappeared in an Armenian village in the Alashgerd (Alashkert) plain.

What was there to explain some 137 photographs of two cyclists in many different towns and villages with people in various types of Eastern apparel when there was no identification on the back of the photographs? Fortunately, there were two pieces of text dating after 1896 that offered a key to the mystery. One was a letter addressed to Sachtleben in 1934, which placed him in Houston, Texas. The other was a four-page printed brochure with his photograph on the first page announcing the "1899/1900 Season" and that Sachtleben would present a series of illustrated lectures of his adventures in the Orient. There were quotations from various newspapers about his exploits, and he was described as being the author of four works:

- "Across Asia on a Bicycle"
- "In Search of Frank G. Lenz"
- "Ascent of Mt. Ararat"
- "The Armenian Massacres"

I began by assuming that these were all books and soon came across the first title—*Across Asia on a Bicycle: The Journey of Two American Students from Constantinople to Peking* by Thomas Gaskell Allen and William Lewis Sachtleben, first published in 1894. The UCLA library happened to have a copy of the 1897 second edition. It was exciting to look through it and find there a number of the photographs that were in our collection. Briefly, two young men, on the day after graduation from Washington University in Saint Louis, Missouri, left for New York and thence set sail for Liverpool on June 23, 1890, on their way via England, France, Italy, and Greece to Constantinople. It was at this point that they took to their wheels, in April of 1891, cut across the Ottoman Empire into Persia, past the Gobi desert into China, all the way to Peking. From Shanghai they sailed to Japan and then to California, arriving in San Francisco on Christmas night of 1892. They then "wheeled" by way of Arizona, New Mexico, and Texas to New York—having covered 15,044 miles on bicycle, thereby laying claim to "the longest continuous land journey ever made around the world."[2] In the preface of the book, they assert that they never "employed the services of guides or interpreters," although they did have to procure official permits and letters of introduction.

One portion of this trip is of relevance here—their use of the town of Erzerum as a link for their route into Persia. This was via one of the five important roads that connected Karin/Erzerum to other parts of the Ottoman Empire and neighboring countries,

---

[2] Thomas Gaskell Allen and William Lewis Sachtleben, *Across Asia on a Bicycle: The Journey of Two American Students from Constantinople to Peking* (2d. ed., 1897; New York: The Century Co., 1894), pp. xi-xii.

as described in Eprikian's dictionary.[3] They first journeyed from
Constantinople to Izmid, Angora (Ankara), Kaiseria (Caesarea),
and Sivas (Sebastia) and then joined the Trebizond-Erzerum road
at Baiburt. In Erzerum they met several Europeans and the *vali*
or governor of the Erzerum *vilayet* (province), to whom they
presented their letter of introduction from the Ottoman grand
vizier himself and requested permission to proceed to Bayazit
(Bayazed) whence they planned to climb Mount Ararat. Their
goal was realized in July of 1891 with the help of Kurdish
guides and an Armenian muleteer.

As no book with the title *Ascent of Mt. Ararat* could be
found, this apparently was a chapter by the same name in
Sachtleben's *Across Asia on a Bicycle*. The entire adventure of
the climb is vividly brought to life in those forty pages. Did
Sachtleben publish this chapter as a separate article in a periodical as the list of publications in the brochure seems to suggest?
No evidence for this has been discovered, but he certainly did
present many illustrated lectures on the subject.

The following titles from the UCLA Sachtleben Collection
give an idea of things that interested him and about which he
wrote:

1. "Sultan Abdul Hamid" (23 pages). Written over a period
of two months in November-December 1895, Sachtleben evalu-
ates the political situation, the sultan, his actions, and his person-
ality, and often cites materials from the British and American
press.

2. "The Conditions in Armenia as a Result of European Non-
Interference" (8 pages). This article focuses on the repercussions
of Article 16 of the Treaty of San Stefano (February 1878),
showing how both the sultan and the European powers did not
honor the provisions for essential reforms in the eastern provinces. The views expressed are similar to those of many other

---

[3] The roads led to Constantinople via Erzinjan, Sivas, Tokat, and Samsun; to
Trebizond and the Black Sea via Baiburt; to Bayazit and Persia via Hasankale and
Toprakkale; to Kars via Hasankale and Soghanlu; and to Akhaltskha and Georgia
via Olti and Ardahan. See Sukias Eprikian, *Patkerazard bnashkharhik bararan*
[Illustrated Topographical Dictionary], vol. 2 (Venice: Mekhitarist Press, 1907), p.
304.

American and European authors and closely parallel those in missionary accounts before and after the Armenian massacres of 1895-96: Turkish abuses and cavalier treatment of Christian subjects—particularly the Armenians, on the one hand, and verbal threats, procrastination, and non-action on the part of the European powers, on the other hand. The calamitous effect of the revision of Article 16 of the Treaty of San Stefano by Article 61 of the Berlin Treaty (July 1878) was foreseen by many from the very beginning.

3. "The Kurds: Alashgerd Stories" (3 pages). This is a short piece on the origins, language, religion, and customs of the Kurds and some specifics about two or three tribes.

4. "Long Article on Erzerum" (only pages 20-24 exist, with those before and after missing). This small fragment is not very helpful, as much of it is repeated elsewhere in Sachtleben's writings.

5. "On Armenia" (34 pages). The article has subdivisions on such topics as reforms, persecutions, injustice, character, and taxation and includes fascinating views on various subjects and positive and negative characterizations of Armenians, Turks, and Kurds.

6. "Armenian Marriage Customs" (6 pages). Based on personal observation, Sachtleben compares Armenian customs of courting with those of Americans and Europeans without being judgmental. He does show sympathy for girls married off at thirteen or fourteen years of age, with no say in the choice of husband, although village girls have more freedom in this regard. Sachtleben is invited to an Armenian wedding in Erzerum during which the girl is completely silent from beginning to end. He also has much to say about the mother-in-law. He relates the following small episode (page 1) involving his interest in an Armenian girl (he was twenty-nine years old and single at the time):[4]

---

[4] W.L. Sachtleben was born in Alton, Illinois, in 1866, attended Washington University in St. Louis (graduated in 1890), married Mae Merriman in 1903, and moved with his wife to Houston, Texas, in 1911. He was a theatrical manager and insurance executive until his retirement. Sachtleben died in December 1953 in Fort Lauderdale, Florida, where he had been living for three years. He was buried in Houston, his home for forty years. These findings are the result of research in the

Another rather pretty and charming girl, whom I knew intimately, when I was leaving Erzeroum after a year's stay, I asked her if she would not kiss me good-bye. "Why, that would not be nice. But, the American girls wouldn't do that for you," she added. "Oh, yes they would if they liked you," I replied; which seemed so strange to her that she did not believe me, but I leave it to my fair American readers if this is not so.

This last sentence indicates that he intended the piece to be published.

The Sachtleben Collection currently consists of the following materials:

- 450 negatives;
- 316 prints organized into three groups:
- 54 4-1/2" x 5-1/2"mounted and unmounted silver prints with notes on the back;
- 115 9" x 7" unmounted, mainly platinum, prints, with most of them having notes on the back;
- 137 4" x 4" sepia tone silver and cyantype prints of the first voyage to the Orient in the early 1890s but with no notations on the back;
- 2 small notebooks with a total of 317 pages;
- 107 manuscript pages in various groupings.

"In Search of Lenz"

Among these papers, the most interesting are the photographs, the piece titled "In Search of Lenz," which has not yet been found in any periodical, and various "Letter to the Editor" pieces concerning the Erzerum massacre. Only three of these letters, very similar to the ones in the collection, seem to have appeared in print, namely in the London *Times*.

The article "Trip to Alashgerd" is the section (pages 17-31) of a larger work, "In Search of Lenz," meaning that more than half the account of an event that was the reason for Sachtleben's presence in Erzerum in 1895 is missing. I have been able to

Houston Public Library and the Office of the County Clerk of Harris County, Texas, during a fact-finding trip in the summer of 2000.

piece together some of the facts from tidbits within the text and from notes on the back of a couple of the photographs and some external sources. Whatever the case, William Sachtleben's unhappy mission was instrumental in his witnessing the massacre in Erzerum on October 30, 1895, his having photographs taken of the bodies in the Armenian cemetery, and his submission of shocking descriptions and photographs to the English-language media. Both his articles and photographs were subsequently used in other periodicals and books as well.

W.L. Sachtleben arrived in Erzerum in May of 1895—one year after the disappearance of Frank G. Lenz.[5] He had been sent on behalf of Lenz's family and *Outing*, a sporting magazine published in New York, to ascertain the whereabouts of Lenz (1867-1894), "the wheelman who was murdered in Asia Minor," in the words of the *Illinois State Register*, January 17, 1899.[6] Lenz, who was employed by *Outing* magazine, had been traveling in an east to west direction, had crossed the Persian-Turkish frontier, and then disappeared after arriving at the Armenian village of Chilkani (Tchelkani) in the Alashkert district.[7] This was in May 1894, just before the massacre of Armenians in Sasun,

---

[5] "Trip to Alashgerd," p. 17. His arrival in the spring of 1895 is also attested by William Nesbitt Chambers, *Yoljuluk* (London: Simkin Marshall, 1928; repr. Paramus, NJ: Armenian Missionary Association of America, 1988), p. 33.

[6] Quoted on page 4 of the "Special Announcement" of Sachtleben's lecture tour in the 1899/1900 season.

[7] Frank Lenz's articles and photographs sent from the various stages of his trip are in *Outing: An Illustrated Monthly Magazine of Sport, Travel and Recreation*, beginning with volume 20, August 1892, and ending with volume 28, July 1896, under the title "Around the World with Wheel and Camera: Illustrated from Photos by the Author." Although the July 1895 issue printed Lenz's obituary, his articles continued to be published for another year. Lenz's route and job were picked up by *Outing*'s "Special Correspondent" (six articles August 1896-January 1897), who traveled from Tabriz to Erzerum. While this person seems to have completed the trip to Constantinople, his submissions to *Outing* stop with his arrival in Erzerum as described in his last article. It is uncertain if this "Special Correspondent" can be identified with Sachtleben, because he started from Tabriz in July (presumably 1895), while Sachtleben arrived in Erzerum in May 1895 and was constrained to remain in the city until September. It is possible to assume that there were two correspondents sent out by *Outing* magazine. In fact, in Lenz's obituary in the July 1895 issue, the editor wrote that "the correspondents of *Outing* continue at work to determine what has been done with the body and effects of poor Lenz."

where, as American missionary William Nesbitt Chambers notes, the Kurdish tribes were in ferment.[8] Now, sixteen months later and following a four-month wait in Erzerum, Sachtleben is finally allowed to visit Alashkert by no less a personage than Shakir Pasha, who has been appointed by Sultan Abdul-Hamid as the high commissioner for reforms in the eastern vilayets. In fact, Sachtleben is invited to join the pasha's entourage on his fact-finding mission in the areas beyond the provincial capital of Erzerum. Sachtleben, in his turn, asks Chambers, who heads the American mission house in Erzerum and is Sachtleben's host, to accompany him as a supportive mentor and interpreter.

Extensive literature exists on the subject of reforms in the Ottoman Empire and about the negative consequences of the Treaty of Berlin in 1878.[9] Article 61 of that treaty placed the responsibility for guaranteeing the security of the Armenians

---

[8] Chambers, *Yoljuluk,* p. 33.

[9] For relevant sources on the reform plans and massacres, especially European and American official documents such as ambassadorial and consular dispatches and correspondence, see the bibliographic references to chapter 3, "Turkish Armenia," in Richard G. Hovannisian, *Armenia on the Road to Independence, 1918* (Berkeley and Los Angeles: University of California Press, 1967), pp. 265-67. For some of the more specific Erzerum-related histories, see Hakob Kosian, *Bardzr Hayk: Teghagrutiun, patmutiun ev sovorutiunner* [Upper Armenia: Toponymy, History, and Customs], 2 vols. (Vienna: Mekhitarist Press, 1925-1926); *Karno Hishatakin: Kotoratsits araj, Karno kotoratse, Hovhannes Korkotian ev Zinagorts Kahana* [In Memory of Karin: Before the Massacre, the Massacre of Karin, Hovhannes Korkotian and the Gunsmith Priest] (Vienna: Armenian Revolutionary Federation, 1896); Ghazar Chareg, *Karinapatum:Hushamatian Bardzr Hayki* [Karin: Memorial Volume of Upper Armenia] (Beirut: Compatriotic Unions of Garin of the United States and Lebanon, 1957) and the shorter English version by Hratch A. Tarbassian, *Erzurum (Garin):Its Armenian History and Traditions,* trans. Nigol Schahgaldian ([New York]: Garin Compatriotic Union of the United States, 1975); Hovhannes Zatikian, *Karin* (Erevan: Hayastan, 1991). Other relevant sources, aside from contemporary newspapers and periodicals and the account by Chambers, include Edwin Munsell Bliss, *Turkey and the Armenian Atrocities* (n.p.: Edgewood Publishing Co., 1896); Felix Charmetant, *Martyrologe arménien: Tableau officiel des massacres d'Arménie dressé après enquêtes par les six ambassades de Constantinople et statistique dressée par des témoins oculaires....* (Paris: Bureau des Oeuvres d'Orient [1896]); *Les massacres d'Arménie: Témoignages des victimes* (Edition de Mercure de France, 1896); Jeremy Salt, *Imperialism, Evangelism and the Ottoman Armenians, 1878-1896* (London and Portland, OR: Frank Cass, 1993); W.J. Wintle, *Armenia and Its Sorrows* (London: Andrew Melrose [1896]).

collectively on the European powers, but they soon turned away from the "Armenian Question" and abandoned the Armenians to intensified persecution. The revolutionary movement among the Armenians in the last decade of the century does not seem to have been very effective among the merchants and the masses in the hinterland who sought the safeguarding of person and property through political, social, and economic reforms. A detailed reading of the contemporary European press and other publications and the correspondence of consular officials of various governments shows that the Ottoman government claimed revolutionary activity as the root cause of the general unrest and constantly retaliated, while foreign observers, including Sacht-leben, considered these mere excuses because there was no Armenian action to justify the merciless punitive measures taken by the government and its regular and irregular armed forces.

The Sasun massacre in the summer of 1894 shocked the world and moved the European powers, notably Great Britain, France, and Russia, to devise a new reform plan in the spring of 1895. After procrastinating as long as possible, Abdul-Hamid sud-denly announced that he had prepared his own reform program for the eastern vilayets and had appointed Shakir Pasha as the high commissioner. In September 1895, Shakir Pasha arrived in Erzerum, where Great Britain, France, Russia, Italy, and Persia had consulates or consular representatives.[10] There was no United States consulate but there was an American missionary station directed by William N. Chambers, who had been in the provin-cial capital since 1881, the year of the founding of the noted Sanasarian school. U.S. interests were officially represented by the British consulate, as often noted by Consul Leo Bergholz during the 1897 trials for the murder of Lenz. Observing Shakir Pasha's activities in Erzerum, Sachtleben writes that the Ottoman high commissioner "had evidently not finished his Herculean task of reforming abuses in Erzerum governmental affairs . . . and with his work half-finished he was preparing to leave for new

---

[10] United States, National Archives, *Despatches from United States Consuls in Erzerum, 1895-1904*, 2 vols. (Microfilm, 1961), Bergholz to Department of State, Oct. 17, 1896. Bergholz arrived in Erzerum on July 10, 1896, but was never officially confirmed as consul by the Sublime Porte.

fields where reform was equally necessary and, if anything, far more abundant."[11]

Alashkert lies east of Karin/Erzerum and is described as having been a rich and fertile plain. Many Armenians had left the district in the aftermath of the Russo-Turkish wars of the nineteenth century, and the remainder lived in extreme poverty and oppression. In the 1890s a traveler would encounter bad roads, bridges in disrepair, abject poverty, frightened and wary Christians, and aggressive and suspicious Muslims.

What had happened to Lenz? As Sachtleben's text is read, it becomes clear that he already knows that Lenz has been murdered and by whom. He is now bent on proving it and finding Lenz's grave. With him are Chambers, his carriage driver (Misag), and his Arab interpreter (Khedouri). The entourage leaves Erzerum on the morning of September 24, 1895, as it begins to snow. About 4 miles out of the city, they are met by a young man, about twenty-five years of age, whom Sachtleben describes as "a red-hot Hunchagist (Revolutionist)," adding: "I had induced him to go along and be prepared to do any and all kinds of spy-work. His brother was as strong a nation[al]ist as himself and during the past winter he had volunteered to go to Sassoun to glean information for the English Consul [Robert W. Graves]." Sachtleben's secret plan is to have Aram surreptitiously talk to an Armenian, one Apro, in the village of Gedikan. They are really looking for one Musteh Neseh (Mustehneseh), a notorious Kurdish brigand and Lenz's lead murderer, according to Sachtleben and Chambers and later Bergholz as well as witnesses that would expose him.

What follows is a remarkable adventure through the countryside of historic Armenia. Traveling from the plain of Erzerum eastward toward Alashkert, they pass through many villages, several towns such as Hasankale, forts, dangerous mountain passes, and swift-flowing tributaries of the Euphrates and Araxes rivers. En route, they interrelate with Turks, Kurds, and Armenians, allowing Sachtleben to make telling remarks about politics, economics, social and religious matters, and racial hatreds. Some he records in a detached manner, some with humor, but more

---

[11] "Trip to Alashgerd," p. 24.

often with strong emotion—anger, disgust, pity, indignation, fury. Occasionally, he waxes poetic about sudden beauty glimpsed in an otherwise gloomy setting. The party is put up in the homes of Armenians, Kurds, and Turks. Sachtleben observes the poverty and squalor, the exhaustion of the formerly fertile land, the desolation all around. He deplores the plight of the Armenians, denigrates the Kurds, and is contemptuous of the Turks as indolent exploiters and manipulators of others. Both Kurds and Turks, he insists, are inveterate liars, quite ready to lie even under oath. Armenians lie, too, but this is primarily out of their great fear of murderous reprisals.

After four days of arduous journey, the party reaches its destination. "It was to this plain of Alashgerd that my attention had been directed ever since the return of my reliable spy Khazar to Erzerum on June 8.[12] For four weary months I had been within 100 miles of the spot where Lenz was killed but the Turkish authorities had successfully prevented me from ap-proaching any nearer until good fortune and the Armenian Question brought it to pass."[13] At the mixed Armenian-Kurdish village of Hashian on September 27, Sachtleben learns that Shakir Pasha has orga-nized a commission headed by Tewfik Bey, the procurator-gen-eral of Erzerum, to investigate the Lenz matter. The commission is to include two other Turks (one of them the district governor or *kaimakam* of Toprakkale), together with a Kurd, an Armenian, and Chambers and Sachtleben. The next six pages, 25 to 31, of "Trip to Alashgerd," where the text abruptly stops, are devoted to the description of a Turkish criminal in-vestigation where the worst offender, in the eyes of Sachtleben, is the procurator-general. The investigation is a farce, as every effort is made to persuade Chambers and Sachtleben that Lenz had never come that way, or, if he did, he must have returned to Persia. Wit-nesses, Kurd and Armenian alike, swear under oath with a curse attached that they never saw a man come to the village of

---

[12] Khazar was the Armenian who had secretly collected information on Lenz's murder while Turkish officials kept Sachtleben in Erzerum under various pretexts. It follows then that there were two men involved in gathering information—Khazar and Aram, the "red-hot Hunchagist."

[13] "Trip to Alashgerd," p. 24.

Chilkani riding a *"jansız araba"* (soulless carriage).

Only an Armenian peasant whom the village headman had ordered to give Lenz lodging tells the truth. To Sachtleben's great joy, the Armenian confides that Lenz had come from Karakilisa and departed toward Erzerum the next day. Here was the proof that was sought. But now the procurator Tewfik tries to place the blame on Armenian bandits. After an impasse lasting two weeks, Sachtleben and Chambers start going from village to village to investigate but with no results until at Churokh, they are given to understand that only the Kurds have the answer to the desired information. Here the text ends. Fortunately, Chambers also wrote on the issue and has given the following additional information:

> It was impossible to get anything out of them, though we were convinced they knew all about it and that one of the murderers was a neighbor to them. . . . We continued our journey as far as Mt. Ararat. Having established the fact of the murder, I said to the law officer, the president of the judicial commission, that on our return journey we would like to put the men of this village under oath again. He agreed, and called the same men, administered the oath, "the truth, the whole truth, and nothing but the truth." They confirmed our contention, declaring that the whole village turned out to see the wonder of a man riding a wheel, and that after spending the night in an Armenian village he was murdered the next day at the ford of the river. The village notables did not seem to think that there was any inconsistency—not to say moral obliquity—between the solemn oath that they knew absolutely nothing about the matter and ten days later the declaration under oath that they knew all about it.[14]

---

[14] Chambers, *Yoljuluk*, pp. 33-34. This account varies from the report of Consul Bergholz (despatch no. 97, Dec. 10, 1897) stating that Sachtleben had persuaded the Armenian witnesses, who had been silent because they feared reprisals from the Kurds and unjust punishment from the Turks, to come forward with the truth by giving assurances that they would be protected and therefore the impression that he represented the United States government. There is also a third version of the promised protection. The priest, Der Arsen, who was the main witness in the trial in December 1897, claimed that Shakir Pasha had guaranteed him protection (Bergholz despatch no. 104, encl. 2, April 1, 1898). See also Fig. 3.

The fifteen-page section (17-31) of "Trip to Alashgerd" entails a detailed record of the commission regarding the murder of Frank Lenz which had taken place a year and a half earlier. Although the evidence points to the Kurdish chieftain Musteh-neseh and his men, five Armenians and three Kurds are arrested and thrown in prison in October of 1895. One Armenian dies there and two Kurds escape—including Mustehneseh. At some point, the remaining prisoners are released on bail. A second Armenian dies of wounds sustained while in prison, and the other three escape to Russia.[15]

In November 1896, warrants are issued for the three fugitive Armenians and the three Kurds (two of whom are now also fugitives in Russia, while Mustehneseh, the leader, is in hiding), and the trial is set for March 1897. Because no one is appre-hended, the proceeding is termed "trial by default" and a "not guilty" verdict is pronounced for lack of evidence.[16] Owing to certain irregularities by the criminal appeals court of Erzerum in the trial by default, the Ministry of Justice orders a new trial, slated for December 25, 1897. This time, warrants are issued for the five Armenians (two of whom have died) and one Kurd (Mustehneseh), while six Armenians from the village of Chilkani and one Kurd, namely Mustehneseh's son, are summoned as witnesses. Sachtleben is present and insists that the real criminals are six Kurds led by Mustehneseh, all of whom should be ar-rested and tried, not the innocent Armenians. But the verdict is that three Armenians and Mustehneseh are to go to prison in chains for fifteen years.

Since the three Armenians have fled the country, they are declared fugitives from justice and their properties are ordered sequestered. Mustehneseh goes free as he is considered untouch-able because he is serving in the Turkish army in the mounted Kurdish Hamidiye units. The details of the trial are reported in April 1898 by Leo Bergholz, who also considers the outcome unjust and recommends a U.S. appeal for a retrial in Constantino-

---

[15] Chambers, *Yoljuluk*, p. 34. There is much information on the trials in US National Archives, *Despatches from United States Consuls in Erzerum*.

[16] Bergholz despatch no. 64, May 3, 1897, with Turkish and English texts of the trial.

ple.[17] At one point, Bergholz writes to the U.S. Legation in Constantinople, stating that he knows that Washington is claiming damages from the Turkish government for the murder and requesting that the verdict against the innocent Armenians be quashed.[18] The first of the two volumes of Bergholz's dispatches —which comprise several hundred pages—are for the greater part concerned with the Frank Lenz murder and trials.

William Chambers fills in the blanks about what had occurred at Chilkani in 1894. Lenz arrives at the village, which turns out in force to gaze in wonder and amazement at the "*atsız araba*" (horseless carriage) and the foreigner that sits upon it. He is put up in a separate room (*oda*) in the house of an Armenian. While he is reclining on a mat with his beautiful silver mounted revolver (a gift of the "Wheelmen of America") next to his head, Mustehneseh comes in and picks up the revolver to examine it. Chambers writes that Lenz did not understand the situation and did not show the proper respect toward the Kurdish bey of the village. Lenz grabs the revolver "and with a wave of his hand shows him the door." For that insult, he pays with his life. The next morning three Kurds wait in ambush at a stream he has to ford, kill him, take his possessions, and smash his bicycle to pieces.[19]

As to the sequel, Chambers notes that in the end "the Kurds went unpunished and only the wretched and, I believe innocent, Armenians suffered seriously for the murder of Lenz."[20] Finally, when indemnity was demanded and received by the U.S. government, "a small amount was assigned to cover certain indemnities including that to Mrs. Lenz" (the mother of Lenz).[21] Moreover, William Sachtleben has written on the back of a photograph of an Armenian priest, Der Arsen Hagopian, that he had helped in the investigation and had received a reward from Mrs. Lenz but that the Kurds had later robbed him and sought to murder his family (see Fig. 3).

---

[17] Bergholz despatch no. 104, April 1, 1898.
[18] Bergholz despatch no. 97, Dec. 7, 1897.
[19] Chambers, *Yoljuluk*, pp. 32-33.
[20] Ibid., p. 34.
[21] Ibid., pp. 34-35.

Massacre in Erzerum, October 30, 1895

The most shocking materials in the Sachtleben Collection are text and photographs depicting the massacre of October 30, 1895.[22] These include a ten-page letter addressed "To the Editor of ——— ," dated "Sat. Dec. 14 '95," which is entirely on the massacre, and several other short pieces similarly addressed without identifying the newspaper. The four-page brochure on his lecture series identifies Sachtleben, among other credentials, as formerly correspondent to the London *Times*. Lengthy searches in the *Times* yielded unsigned letters by an Occasional Correspondent sent from Erzerum. The dates of the letters are November 2-3 (he added a page on November 3 and posted the letter via Trebizond that day) and November 9 and 16, 1895. These appear in the issues of November 16 and 27 and December 9, 1895. Some of the manuscripts in the UCLA collection have their parallels in the letters to the *Times*. Further, Sachtleben was apparently one of only two Americans in Erzerum at the time, along with William N. Chambers. The most telling evidence is, of course, the collection of photographs in the archive.

Had William Sachtleben not been in Erzerum by force of circumstance, had he not been the *Times* Occasional Correspondent, the visual as well as starkly detailed information on the massacre of October 30, 1895, would not have been shared with the world within days of its perpetration. There were, of course, the official reports and dispatches that the European consulates sent their governments via their embassies in Constantinople.[23] These are generally short, dry, factual official dispatches, parts

---

[22] The date is often cited in Armenian sources as October 18, according to the Julian calendar, which was still used in both the Ottoman and Russian empires.

[23] I consulted the correspondence of the British consul, H.A. Cumberbatch, to Ambassador Sir Philip Currie to compare and verify the information in Sachtleben's writings. I have limited myself to two publications of the British government covering the events of September 1895-February 1896: *Correspondence Respecting the Introduction of Reforms in the Armenian Provinces of Asiatic Turkey*, Sessional Papers, 1896, XCV, c. 7923, Turkey No. 1 (1896), pp. 117ff., and *Correspondence Relative to the Armenian Question and Reports from Her Majesty's Consular Officers in Asiatic Turkey*, Sessional Papers, 1896 XCV (A and P), c. 7927, Turkey No. 2 (1896).

of which were fed to the press whose pages included frequent
reports sent by their correspondents in Constantinople.[24] Few of
these compare, however, to the three lengthy, meticulously detailed, compassionate yet conscientiously objective letters that
Sachtleben sent to the London *Times*. Each sequential piece gives
the chronologic details of what the writer did and saw and what
other eyewitnesses shared with him. His effort to maintain objec-
tivity is reflected in his first letter, written three days after the
massacre:

> All the above account can be relied upon. It is culled from a
> mass of material that came to my ears. These people have the
> Oriental love of exaggeration. The simple truth is bad enough,
> without a bit of exaggeration. I relate merely what I learned, with
> no attempt at rhetorical effect, and striving to lessen and not to
> increase the stories. What I myself saw this Friday afternoon is
> forever engraven on my mind as the most horrible sight a man
> can see. . . .[25]

The stark, graphic descriptions he gives of the burial scenes
of the hundreds of Armenian men, women, and children are
chilling. If Armenians exaggerate and missionary eyewitnesses
or reporters misinterpret a situation and also exaggerate, as
contemporary historian Jeremy Salt maintains in urging caution
in examining massacre-related reports so as to "create a balanced
picture of what was happening," then Sachtleben's reports may
go a long way to allay suspicions and biased claims of overstate-
ment.[26]

Sachtleben's descriptions of the Erzerum massacre are so
vividly detailed that authors writing on the events in the Armenian provinces and elsewhere in the Ottoman Empire in 1895-96
could not but quote directly or paraphrase passages from his

---

[24] In the *Times,* November 14, 1895, page 5, there is a reference to the fact that
a report of the paper's Constantinople correspondent had been censored. On that
page and on page 9, it is reported that the Turkish embassy in Paris had issued a note
contradicting accounts of foreign correspondents and terming the events (1895
massacres) "local scuffles."

[25] *Times*, Nov. 16, 1895, p. 6.

[26] Salt, *Imperialism, Evangelism and the Ottoman Armenians*, p. 97.

letters. I have been able to identify two such books: Edwin Munsell Bliss, *Turkey and the Armenian Atrocities*, narrates (pp. 416-26) in his own style a combination of the three letters of Sachtleben and, without giving names, states that "an eyewitness . . . went with one of the cavasses [guards] of the English Legation, a soldier, his interpreter, and a photographer (Armenian) to the Armenian Gregorian Cemetery" and then describes the scene the same way Sachtleben has in the letters to the *Times*. Further, Bliss has used two of the Sachtleben photographs.[27] The other source is W.J. Wintle's *Armenia and Its Sorrows,* which quotes directly from the first letter of Sachtleben (referred to as "the *Times* Correspondent") and uses a photograph identified in the Sachtleben Collection.[28] The caption in the book reads: "A grim corner of the cemetery at Erzeroum (from a photograph)." Further, two of the three photographs in the memorial volume, *Karno Hishatakin,* are identical to two in the Sachtleben Collection.[29]

Before reading excerpts of Sachtleben's reports on the Erzerum massacre, it would be relevant to see how *Outing*'s second cycler-correspondent portrayed the city. In his concluding article in the series "Lenz's World Tour Awheel" (title slightly changed from the original), he writes:

> From the valley of the Passin Su I wheeled slowly up, late in the afternoon, to the summit of the Deve Boyun Pass, when the City of Erzerum, the Armenian capital, broke suddenly into view. It was here, in this pass, that the Turkish army, in November, 1877, [during the Russo-Turkish War] made their last gallant attempt to stem the tide of disaster that had, by the fortunes of war and the incompetency of their commanders, set in irresistibly against them.
>
> Filled with the thoughts suggested by these historical associations, I descended with the setting sun toward the Persian gate of the fortified city.[30]

---

[27] Bliss, *Turkey*, description on p. 424, and photographs on pp. 526, 643.

[28] W.J. Wintle, *Armenia and Its Sorrows* (London: A. Melrose [1896]), quotations on pp. 84, 87, and photograph on p. 85.

[29] *Karno Hishatakin*, unnumbered pages 21 and 33.

[30] A traveler coming from Tabriz, as the second *Outing* correspondent was doing,

My first impression of Erzeroum was of earthworks of im-
mense size extending for miles, with dismounted guns upon
them, frowning forth like watchdogs stationed to guard the city;
of a deep ditch and a lofty rampart pierced by a fine granite
tunnel; of more earthworks, and of forts covering all the heights
directly above the city. Patches of snow lingered on the
Palantokan Mountains, a few miles to the south; the Deve Boyun
hills looked down on the city from the east; the broad valley of
the West Euphrates stretched away westward and northward,
terminating at the north in another mountain range. Between the
fortifications and the town there is a great deal of open ground,
sprinkled with rifle-pits, powder magazines, and artillery, cavalry
and infantry barracks, very substantially and neatly built. After
passing through cemeteries containing thousands of gravestones,
I abruptly entered the principal street, wide and somewhat
European-looking, in which are some of the consulates and the
Protestant Armenian Church and schools, and was at once directed to the Armenian hostelry or semi-European hotel.[31]

... As compared with Persian towns Erzerum looks solid and
handsome, and its uncovered bazaars seem fairly busy. The
through traffic between Trebizond and Tabreez, chiefly in British
goods, is very heavy. The Custom-House was in sight from my
hostelry windows, and in one day I counted as many as seven
hundred laden camels passing through it, besides horse and mule
caravans. There are about two thousand Persians in the city, and
the carrying trade is mainly in their hands. The present population is estimated at from twenty thousand to twenty-four thousand, including, besides Persians, Turks, Armenians, Russians
and Jews. The Armenians are not very numerous but their enter-
prise as traders gives them an importance out of proportion to

---

would enter the city through its southeastern gate, which was also known as Kars
Kapusi/Tabriz Kapusi. According to *Karno Hishatakin* (p. 24), there were four
principal gates to the city: Kars Kapusi to the southeast, Gurju (Georgian) Kapusi to
the northeast, Stambul (Istanbul/Constantinople) Kapusi to the northwest, and
Erzinjan Kapusi to the west. Eprikian (note 3 above) and other sources refer to five
main routes leading from the city, so that the Kars/Tabriz Kapusi served for the
routes both to Kars and to Tabriz. Some variations in the names of the gates appear
in the sources.

[31] According to Kosian, *Bardzr Hayk*, vol. 1, p. 40, there were very few wide
streets in the city. The rest were narrow, twisted, and unpaved. The street referred to
here may be Gumruk Sokak on which the consulates, the American mission house,
and several schools were located.

their numbers."[32] The Armenian cathedral, the "Pair of Minarets", the "Single Minaret", and the castle, which stands on a height in the middle of the city and contains a small Saracenic chapel, are among the chief "sights."

But the most interesting object of all is the Sanassarian College, founded and handsomely endowed by the liberality of an Armenian merchant. The fine buildings are of the best construction and are admirably suited for educational purposes, and the equipments are of the latest and most complete description.[33]

The bazaars and shops, including the businesses of the Armenian merchants, were located in the central area, while the Armenian quarters, a fifteen- to twenty-minute walk from the center, lay in a semi-circular arrangement from the city's inner walls next to Kars/Tabriz Gate in the east to near the Ilija/Stambul Gate in the north and northwest.[34]

Sachtleben's Reports

Sachtleben was shocked by the massacre in Erzerum and like many other authors became convinced that the mayhem had been fully prearranged, just as it was in a hundred other Armenian-inhabited towns and villages in 1895-96: "Many things which happened before the massacre of Wed. Oct. 30th 1895, as well as the particulars of the horrible event, go to prove that the massacre of Armenians in this city was carefully planned beforehand, and that it was, just as Sassoun, a political massacre organized and carried out by government orders."[35] In his first letter to the *Times*, written on November 2-3, Sachtleben reports:

For some days the Turks had been threatening to kill the Christians. Heroes from the Trebizond massacre, from the pillaging

---

[32] Bliss, *Turkey,* p. 416, places the population of the city at 40,000, of whom 30,000 were Muslim and 10,000 were Armenian. He may have taken this information from one of Sacthleben's letters to the *Times* in November 1895.

[33] *Outing* 29 (Jan. 1897): 386-87.

[34] *Karno Hishatakin*, pp. 24-25.

[35] W.L. Sachtleben, ten-page manuscript letter, "To the Editor of ——— ," Sat. Dec. 14, 1895, Erzeroum, Turkey in Asia, p. 2, in W.L. Sachtleben Collection, UCLA.

at Baiburt, from Erzingan and Kamakh, and from other places
had come to Erzerum as the most likely place for another similar
game. These men had boasted how much they had got, and all
had the gold fever with a vengeance. In spite of all these premo-
nitions, I had always had faith in Shakir's ability to keep the city
free from rioting. The fact that he, together with the aid of Raouf
and his other officers, could not control the military is another
proof of the rottenness of the Turkish Empire.[36]

The blow descends with stunning swiftness. On Wednesday,
October 30, at the noon hour when the Muslim faithful are
pouring out of the mosques, a bugle call signals the beginning
of the killing and looting. "At the Serai (Government office), all
was empty [see Fig. 2]. The officials had gone and left only the
fanatical mob." The soldiers are shown to have taken an active
part in the massacre: "A dragoman [interpreter] of one of the
Consulates, who saw the firing for two hours in the bazaars, said
that all the soldiers were out, fully armed, to the number 3,000.
They were not content with shooting a man once, but they fired
each one three and four times. He boldly declared that the
Government officials had ordered the soldiers to begin to kill."[37]
The Armenians have no means to defend themselves, and when
they run to soldiers for protection they are shot instead. The
killing lasts until sunset while the plunder continues into the
next day. The number of dead is estimated in the hundreds by
November 3 (the day Sachtleben sends his first letter to London),
and there are so many wounded that the hospitals cannot care for
them all.

In his second letter to the *Times*, dated November 9, Sachtleben reports on the material losses:

On Thursday, November 7, ten days after the frightful massacre,
I went up to the Serai, going by one route and returning by
another, so as to see all the ruined bazaars. Although it was ten
days after the affair, we did not see a Christian. The bazaars
were one succession of ruins. . . . A moderate estimate of the
number of Christian shops, great and small, in Erzerum, is 2,000,

[36] *Times*, Nov. 16, 1895, p. 6.
[37] W.L. Sachtleben, "To the Editor of ——— ," Dec. 14, 1895, p. 3.

of which about 200 escaped being plundered. . . . The number of houses of Armenians in Erzerum is about 2,000, the same as the number of shops, for some of the shops are kept by people from other villages. . . . Of these 2,000 houses, about 1,500 to 1,800 are completely emptied of their contents. Many families, formerly well-to-do, are now completely in poverty. . . . With their means of earning a living gone and no money to buy any more, winter coming on, and no work to be had to earn a living, the lot of the Christians this winter needs no comment from me. No harder fate could be meted out to any one by the most barbarous people. The Turks are too blind to see that in destroying the Christian shops they have ruined their own city and made the collection of taxes almost impossible.[38]

The Story of Garabed Fidanian

There is a long litany of tragic stories, some Sachtleben has witnessed, others about which he has been told, and still others about which he learns while walking around the city after the stabbing and shooting have ceased. Only two examples are recounted here. The first is concerned with the amazing survival of the young man, Garabed Fidanian: "Garabed is a strong well-knit lad of 16, but he looks older. He is a bright, pleasant fellow, without the feeling of fear and bore the pain consequent on dressing his wounds in the hospital heroically."[39] The American correspondent narrates Garabed's story after the youth has left the hospital:

At noon on the fatal 30th of Oct., he was about to go to his dinner when the Turks began the massacre. At that moment he was in front of the Serai (the Government Building where are the offices of the Governor General and his assistants) and he quickly ran into an Armenian shoemaker's shop and locked the door. Six besides himself had taken refuge here. They heard firing and noise outside, but were not given a long respite. The Bashi-bozooks [irregulars] broke open the door, when the

[38] *Times*, Nov. 27, 1895, p. 6.
[39] W.L. Sachtleben, two-page manuscript letter, "Story of Garabed Fidanian," Sat., Jan. 11, 1896, Erzeroum, Turkey in Asia, p. 1, in W. L. Sachtleben Collection, UCLA.

"zaptiehs" [militia], men, women and children entered and emptied the shop. Then they turned their attention to the fugitives.

They first called the proprietor, searched him all over, took away a "lira" from him and did not injure him at that time. Then they seized Garabed, saying, "This is the best one, this is a young man," and a zaptieh cut him over the head with his heavy sword making the blood flow freely. Garabed did not wait for a second blow. He ran out and made for the bazaars which led toward the Christian Quarter of the city. But he had fled only a few hundred feet when he met some soldiers whom he tried to dodge, at the same time holding his hand to his head in order to wipe the blood from his eyes, when a bullet from a Martini passed through his hand within an inch of his head. Running through the yard of the so-called Pashas' Mosque, as he was leaving by the outer door a Turk with a heavy cane struck him over his bloody head. Then a soldier outside cut him over the neck and back which wounds bled profusely. Next a "Dervish," whom he encountered, made a lunge at him with a dagger in the side, but struck his left leg just above the knee and started more blood.

Now he had reached the "Uch-Meidan," an open place in the bazaars, which was thronged with Moslems killing and looting the Armenians. The "Dervish" was after him, and he ran to a soldier who protected him, although he had his gun raised to shoot him. But this soldier . . . recognized him as the son of an Armenian who was his friend and who had done good service in the Turkish ranks in the Russo-Turkish war. For this reason he protected the Armenian's son, or at least, didn't shoot him. . . . So, covered with blood he tried to cross the open space but he was struck again, it became dark before his eyes and he fell down in a faint, pretending death. Some of the Turks said, "he's dead", and pulled him by one leg aside. Afterwards some Turks came and searched him, took off a good pair of shoes he had on and coat, and left him for dead. This was about 2:00 p.m.

They did not take his pants which were burning from the discharge of the Martini, and one of the soldiers said "who's going to stand this bad air?"and threw two buckets of water over him. There he lay for two hours in blood and water and became chilled. But he was not dead and looking between his fingers he saw the Moslems murder every man who ran into the square. Three corpses were laid beside him, all cut up and bloody, and afterwards they brought three more horribly mutilated bodies. And 20 more were laid in a row a little above him.

Finally 3 Turkish boys came up to the dead bodies and after looking at them one of them said, pointing to Garabed, "this man's alive, let's cut off his head." But an old Turk, who was passing by said, "he's dead, why do you dirty your hands with Ghiaour [infidel] blood?" and so he was saved again. Then a big village Turk with a heavy cane came up and struck him a hard blow on the bottom of his feet, put his hand to Garabed's nose to see if he was breathing and then hit him again on the flat of his foot as a final test, but left him for dead.

Then came the call to prayer (about 4:00 p.m.) when a Tellal [town crier] passed through the square crying publicly that there was to be no more killing. But this didn't stop the Turks who went on killing until sunset. At the meantime he narrowly escaped death. He saw between his fingers, as he held his hand over his eye, a soldier at a distance take aim at him with his Martini and fire. The bullet struck a rock near his right temple, splintered, a piece entered between the skin and the bone. Afterwards in the hospital this festered and from his position in bed the lead worked itself down to the lower part of his right jaw where the Dr. extracted it.[40]

Garabed sustains some fifteen wounds to his head and body. The Good Samaritan soldier finding that he is still alive carries Garabed to the hospital, where he is told that Shakir Pasha had been in favor of killing all but that the vali, Raouf Pasha, had interceded, saying: "It's enough, stop it." After telling Sachtleben his story, Garabed exclaims: "Is there to come a time when we can kill the Turks? I am not afraid." Sachtleben is taken aback by the socio-religious preconditioning for killing: "In all the accounts I have heard from survivors of the massacres it is a curious and suggestive fact, the part which Turkish boys, even of a tender age, took in the bloody work. They are thoroughly taught by their elders the part they are destined to play in the body politic against the Christian. We can hope for no change in the Turk under such conditions."[41]

Sachtleben apparently sent or attempted to send Garabed's story and photograph to a newspaper. Unfortunately, the photo-

---

[40] Ibid., pp. 1-2.

[41] W.L. Sachtleben, one-page manuscript letter, "To the Editor," Sat. Feb. 1, 1896, Erzeroum, Turkey in Asia, in W.L. Sachtleben Collection, UCLA.

246   *Gia Aivazian*

graph is missing from the Sachtleben Collection, but Garabed is
in another photograph taken in the hospital, together with other
patients and hospital staff (Fig. 9).

At least one episode, as related by Sachtleben, puts a spark
of humanity into this starkly brutal canvas of evil:

> In another house not far from us the soldiers broke and pillaged.
> There were two young Armenian brides, whose beauty aroused
> the lust of the Turks. While they were disputing as to who
> should have these prizes, a Turkish Mollah entered and defended
> them. "None of you shall have these girls except over my dead
> body." What led a Mollah to perform such an act of kindness to
> Ghiaour women is a mystery.[42]

At the Armenian Cemetery

On Friday, November 1, 1895, the bodies of many of the victims
are buried in the Armenian cemetery.[43] The following description
comes from Sachtleben's first letter to the *Times*, published on
November 16:

> What I myself saw this Friday afternoon [November 1] is forever
> engraven on my mind as the most horrible sight a man can see.
> I went with one of the cavasses of the English Legation, a soldier,
> my interpreter, and a photographer (Armenian) to the Armenian
> Gregorian Cemetery. The municipality had sent down a number
> of bodies, friends had brought more, and a horrible sight met my
> eyes. Along the wall on the north, in a row 20 ft. wide and 150
> ft. long, lay 321 dead bodies of the massacred Armenians. Many
> were fearfully mangled and mutilated. I saw one with his face
> completely smashed in with a blow of some heavy weapon after
> he was killed. I saw some with their necks almost severed by a
> sword cut. One I saw whose whole chest had been skinned, his

---

[42] W.L. Sachtleben, "Letter to the Editor —— ," Sat. Dec. 14, 1895, p. 8.

[43] There is frequent mention of bodies buried in other parts of the city, as well as
intimations that the Turks disposed of many bodies in hastily dug trenches. In at least
one instance, a Turkish witness asked for money to show where about 50 of the slain
were buried. The first count of dead in the cemetery was 321, but the final figure was
estimated to be between 800 and 1,000. In the following days, the toll of women was
placed at more than 60.

fore-arms were cut off, while the upper arm was skinned of flesh. I asked if the dogs had done this. "No, the Turks did it with their knives." A dozen bodies were half burned. All the corpses had been rifled of all their clothes except a cotton undergarment or two. These white under-clothes were stained with the blood of the dead, presenting a fearful sight. The faces of many were disfigured beyond recognition, and all had been thrown down, face foremost, in the dust of the streets and mud of the gutters, so that all were black with clotted blood and dust. Some were stark naked, and every body seemed to have at least two wounds, and some a dozen. In this list of dead there were only three women, two babies, a number of young children, and about 30 young boys of 15 to 20. A crowd of a thousand people, mostly Armenians, watched me taking photographs of their dead. Many were weeping beside their dead fathers or husbands. The Armenian photographer saw two children, relatives of his, among the dead. Some Armenian workmen were engaged excavating a deep trench 20 ft. square close by to bury the corpses. Here, too, was a peculiar scene. The space of this trench contained many graves, and on one side were a number of skulls, perhaps 20 in all, and a pile of bones found in the excavating. I left the sad sight sick at heart. . . . The last thing I heard tonight ere sleep closed my eyes was the metallic clanking of the swords of the soldiers in the street, the very sound of which made me wish for some means of protecting these poor Christians. To be killed in battle by brave men is one thing; to be butchered by cowardly armed soldiers in cold blood and utterly defenseless is another thing.[44]

The Sachtleben Photographs of the Massacre

Among the 450 acid-nitrate negatives dating from the 1890s, eighteen are of photographs taken on Friday, November 1, 1895, during the mass burial of the Armenian victims, or possibly during the whole three days from October 31 to November 2. The headline in the December 7 edition of the London-based *The Graphic: An Illustrated Weekly Newspaper,* reads, "The Massacre at Erzeroum, October 30, 1895: From Photographs Taken on the

---

[44] *Times,* Nov. 16, 1895, p. 6.

Three Following Days."[45] This may imply that Sachtleben went
to the cemetery, aside from the day of the funerals on November
1, also on Thursday, October 31, while the bodies were being
collected and deposited and the digging of the trenches for the
mass grave was under-way. His second letter to the *Times* con-
firms that he visited the cemetery on November 2 as well.

The photographs in this study are from the prints made in the
1970s by Jean Zakarian, the donor of the Sachtleben Collection.
In addition to the original negatives in the collection, there are
also print photographs connected with the massacre. Among these
are photographs of the serai or government building (Fig. 2), two
priests who had assisted in the search for Lenz (Fig. 3), the
cemetery (Fig. 8), the wounded in the hospital (Fig. 9), and
several others also at the cemetery. The photograph of the serai
is large (10" by 7") compared with the others and may not be
from Sachtleben's camera.

An Armenian photographer did accompany Sachtleben to the
cemetery on November 1. In addition, Sachtleben mentions the
crowd's watching him as he took photographs of the bodies. It
is probable that both photographers worked together at the site
and Sachtleben sent them all abroad to develop. It is important
to link W.L. Sachtleben with the ten photographs published in
The Graphic. Six of these are connected with the burial, with
five being part of the UCLA Sachtleben Collection. The one
missing image is that of an Armenian woman standing over the
bodies of two women and weeping. The caption in *The Graphic*
reads: "Lying apart from the long rows of the bodies in the
cemetery were those of two women who were killed by the
soldiers and the mob. When the photograph was taken [on
November 1] a woman was standing by the corpses weeping, and
as our correspondent passed her, she, seeing that he was English,
stopped her tears for a moment and cursed him: 'May your
house fall on your head! You English have deceived us'." The
captions in the illustrated weekly either were derived from
Sachtleben's letters to the *Times*, as the story of the weeping
woman (published on November 27), or, in view of the fact that
the *Times* did not use photographs then, were supplied directly

[45] *The Graphic* 52 (Dec. 7, 1895): 725-27.

by Sachtleben with the captions on the backs of the photographs. The editor of *The Graphic* himself makes the following connection with the *Times* and Sachtleben:

> The whole truth about many of these massacres will never be known, as no trustworthy eye-witnesses have survived to tell the tale; but some idea of them may be gained by the ghastly story which has been given to the world through the columns of the *Times* of the massacre at Erzeroum on October 30. Hitherto, moreover, the accounts of these heartrending scenes have been frequently denounced as exaggerated and highly coloured for personal or political reasons. At Erzeroum, however, one correspondent brought the camera to bear upon the results of the massacres, and by this witness, which cannot exaggerate, fully confirmed the truth of his terrible statements. It is the duty of the pictorial as well as the literary journalist to chronicle all world-important incidents whether they be agreeable or otherwise, and these photographs are of such historical importance that we feel bound to reproduce them, unpleasant as they may appear in many of their details.[46]

The study by Tessa Hofmann and Gerayer Koutcherian of photographs of the massacres of 1894-96 and of the Genocide of 1915 proved important in linking the *Times* correspondent with the supplier of the Erzerum massacre photographs in *The Graphic*.[47] One point, however, needed resolution. Referring to two of the photographs reproduced from *The Graphic*, they write: "These photographs [Figs. 109 and 110] are often connected to the Genocide of 1915-16. In fact they were published as early as 1895 in the illustrated British journal *The Graphic*, along with other photographs and drawings on the massacre of October 30, 1895, in Erzerum. A few photographs of the illustrated report carry the name Meisenbach on the lower left corner, from which one may conclude that the photographer or the photographic operation was German."[48] Figs. 109 and 110 (identical

---

[46] Ibid., p. 725.

[47] Tessa Hofmann and Gerayer Koutcherian, "'Images that Horrify and Indict': Pictorial Documents on the Persecution and Extermination of Armenians from 1877 to 1922," *Armenian Review* 45:1-2 (1992): 175-76.

[48] Ibid., p. 175.

to Figs. 4 and 8 in this chapter) reproduce the captions in *The Graphic*. Both photographs have the name "Meisenbach" in the lower left corner. An examination of all ten photographs in *The Graphic* revealed that three showed this name and one used only "M," the first initial. All four of these photographs as well as the negatives are in the Sachtleben Collection, but the German name does not appear on any of these.

The "Meisenbach" mystery needed resolution. Was there a German consulate or a German visitor with a camera in Erzerum at the time? I was able to establish that there was no official German presence, but it was still necessary to remove the least doubt.[49] After a lengthy search, the question was answered by accident. *The Graphic* is a magnificent journal. Leafing through its pages is a pleasure. The illustrated weekly frequently covered events in Turkey, especially with photographs from Constantinople. Looking through hundreds of pages of illustrations, captions, and credits in the half-year volume for July-December 1895, I suddenly noticed that the name "Meisenbach" appeared on the lower left corner of a photograph totally unconnected with Erzerum or the Armenians. After this exciting discovery, a scramble through the pages of the journal revealed "Meisenbach" on the lower left corner and an illustrator's name on the right lower corner of a number of photographs. One page displayed six photographs of rooms in a mansion where two or three of the photographs showed "Meisenbach," bringing me to the conclusion that he was actually a photogravurist employed by *The Graphic* to prepare photographs and other types of images for publication. In short, Meisenbach had never been in Erzerum and was not the author of the photographs taken there.

All of Sachtleben's writings make fascinating reading, even though some pieces are gruesome. His language is picturesque and his style absorbing. The writings and the photographs are one more addition to the treasury of primary historical sources on the

---

[49] Consul Leo Bergholz, in a communiqué of October 17, 1896 to the Department of State regarding "Powers Represented in Erzerum," listed consuls general for Russia and Persia, consuls for Great Britain and the United States (the latter not confirmed), and a vice consul for France. The Italian consulate had been closed on October 1 of that year.

dark history of this area and provide visual and textual information on the social settings, costumes, laic architecture, and the
customs and traditions of bygone days of an important part of
the Middle East.

The illustrations that follow are from the William L. Sachtleben
Collection at UCLA. Those at the Armenian cemetery were
photographed on the three days (October 31-November 2) following the massacre of October 30, 1895. Figures 2-3 and 8-9 are
from prints, and Figures 4-7 are from negatives. The captions of
Figures 4-8 are from *The Graphic* (December 7, 1895, pp. 725-
27).

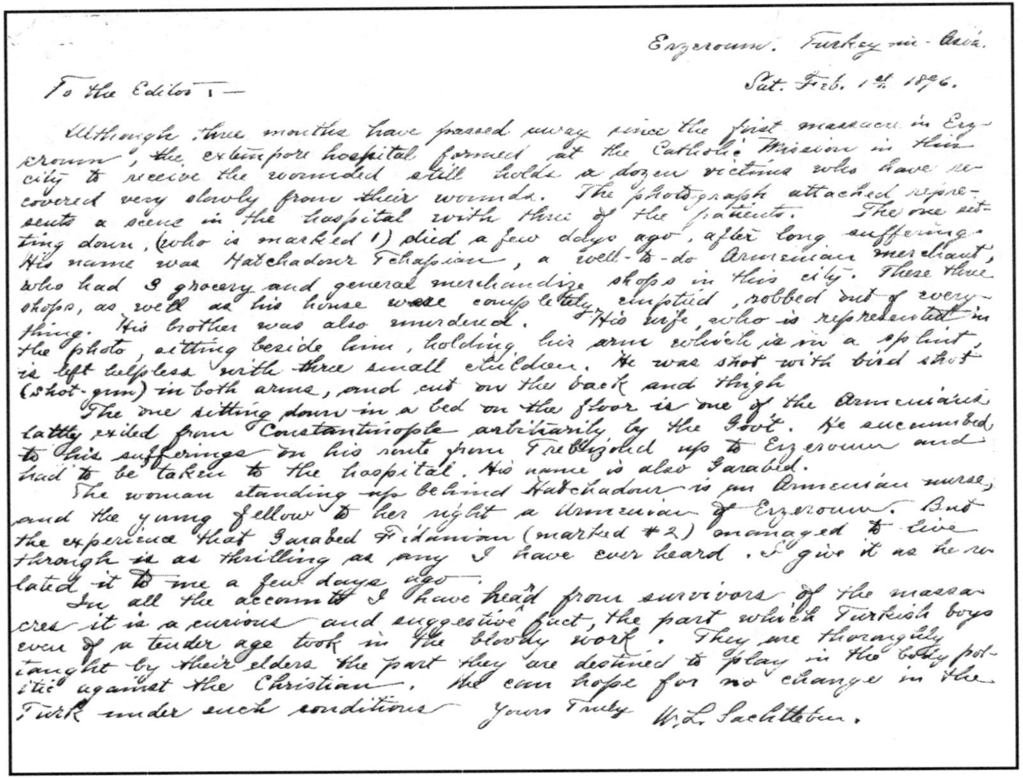

Erzeroum. Turkey-in-Asia.

Sat. Feb. 1st 1896.

To the Editor:—

Although three months have passed away since the first massacre in Erzeroum, the extempore hospital formed at the Catholic Mission in this city to receive the wounded still holds a dozen victims who have recovered very slowly from their wounds. The photograph attached represents a scene in the hospital with three of the patients. The one sitting down, (who is marked 1) died a few days ago, after long suffering. His name was Hatchadour Tchapian, a well-to-do Armenian merchant, who had 3 grocery and general merchandize shops in this city. These three shops, as well as his house were completely emptied, robbed out of everything. His brother was also murdered. His wife, who is represented in the photo, sitting beside him, holding his arm which is in a splint, is left helpless with three small children. He was shot with bird shot (shot-gun) in both arms, and cut on the back and thigh.

The one sitting down in a bed on the floor is one of the Armenians lately exiled from Constantinople arbitrarily by the Govt. He succumbed to his sufferings on his route from Trebizond up to Erzeroum and had to be taken to the hospital. His name is also Garabed.

The woman standing up behind Hatchadour is an Armenian nurse, and the young fellow to her right a Armenian of Erzeroum. But the experience that Garabed Fidanian (marked #2) managed to live through is as thrilling as any I have ever heard. I give it as he related it to me a few days ago.

In all the accounts I have heard from survivors of the massacres it is a curious and suggestive fact, the part which Turkish boys even of a tender age took in the bloody work. They are thoroughly taught by their elders the part they are destined to play in the bloody politic against the Christian. We can hope for no change in the Turk under such conditions. Yours Truly W.L. Sachtleben.

Fig. 1. Sample of W.L. Sachtleben's Handwriting

Fig. 2. "The Serai in Erzeroum, the chief government building, the official residence of the Vali (Governor-General) of the Erzeroum Vilayet, and his chief officers. The massacre of the 30th Oct. '95, of the Armenian Christians, began in this building, where the priest of Tevnik was shot by the Turks." [note on back of photograph]

254

Fig. 3. "Two Armenian Village Priests–Der Arsen, of Tchelkani, assisted me materially in my search for Lenz and was liberally rewarded by Mrs. Lenz. Kurds in revenge robbed him of all he had, plundered his village and sought to kill his family. Der Garabed of Karakillissa (my host) was strangled by a Turkish officer for the purpose of robbing him and pleasure of killing another Armenian. No one was punished (of course) otherwise it wouldn't be Turkey." [note on back of photograph]

Fig. 4. "The Trench Dug for the Bodies of the Victims: A Scene in the Cemetery. This photograph shows the horrible spectacle presented to the visitors to the Armenian cemetery two days after the massacre. Two rows of dead, thirty-five deep, had already been laid down and partially covered with the earth by labourers. When the photograph was taken, four men had just deposited another corpse, and so started a third row. The open spaces between the bodies were filled up with the skulls, thigh-bones, and other human remains from the graves disturbed by digging a huge grave fifty-three feet square for the reception of the slaughtered Armenians."

256

Fig. 5. "Some of the Innocent Victims of the Massacre. Lying together in the Armenian cemetery, awaiting burial, were the bodies of two children who had been killed in the general slaughter of Armenians by the Turks on October 30. The corpse of the mother to be seen close by."

Fig. 6. "An Unceremonious Burial: On the Way to the Grave. The burial of most of the victims took place on November 2. There was no funeral ceremony at all. The photograph shows four Armenians half-dragging and half-carrying a corpse from the rows of bodies about 300 feet away to the large trench dug for the burial of 350. The carrying of so many dead in this manner made a beaten path from the two rows of the bodies to the grave."

Fig. 7. "An Unceremonious Burial: At the Graveside. The four Armenians are here depicted having arrived at the deep trench with their gruesome burden, which they are handing over to four companions. On every side of the large grave were crowds of people watching with anxious face the sad work going on . . . ."

Fig. 8. "A Grim Corner of the Cemetary. Nothing could be more convincing as to the truth of the reports of massacres than the sight of corpses laid out in the cemetary waiting until one large common grave had been dug for their reception. It is impossible to state the exact number of the killed, but one correspondent heard of 400, and it is probable that the total reached about 1,000." The note on the back of this photograph, not derived from a negative, reads: "Another scene in the cemetery of corpses awaiting interment."

260

Fig. 9. "Makeshift Hospital after the Massacre: Hatchadour Tchapian [seated man], Garabed Fidanian [standing, left], Garabed [of] Constaninople [on mat]." [note on back of photograph]

❋ 11 ❋

THE SANASARIAN VARZHARAN:
MAKING A PEOPLE INTO A NATION

Pamela J. Young

The development of education among the Ottoman Armenians made great strides at the end of the nineteenth century with the creation of academic institutions and the spread of literacy among the masses. At the same time there was a rise in national consciousness, and, with the establishment of political parties, ferment spread within the Armenian community. Many places in the eastern provinces were known for their connections with the emerging nationalist sentiment. This study will explore the link between education and national consciousness in Erzerum.[1]

This theme makes it imperative to focus on the internal communal dynamics. Within the Armenian community there was a growing desire to maintain a national identity and to pass traditions on to younger generations through knowledge of language, history, and religion. The educational programs were not solely confined to Armenian subjects. Rather, educational leaders brought forth a vision of greater societal and world understanding through instruction in Western languages, history, literature, and current affairs.

Previous research has argued that the presence of foreign

---

[1] An expanded discussion on Ottoman Armenian education is found in Pamela J. Young, "Knowledge, Nation, and the Curriculum: Ottoman Armenian Education (1853-1915)" (Ph.D. Dissertation, University of Michigan-Ann Arbor, 2001). I wish to thank the staff at the State Literature and Arts (Charents) Archives in Erevan, especially Anahit Astoyan and Sona Mikayelyan, for helping me to navigate through the Sanasarian archives; Raymond H. Kévorkian, Director of the Bibliothèque Nubar in Paris, for his assistance in locating materials; and Razmik Panossian, for his steady support and encouragement. Proper names in this chapter are usually given in Western Armenian forms if the individuals were natives of the Ottoman Empire.

missionaries, together with the increasing Westernization and modernization of the Ottoman Empire, had a strong influence on the growth of Armenian education. The missionaries did, of course, play a significant role in creating schools in the region, but by the 1860s the Ottoman Armenians themselves had begun to create an educational infrastructure and organizational plan for developing schools. Although the curriculum and teaching methods underwent important changes, these were the result of numerous factors, only one of which was a response to missionary activities. The second argument, which centers on the role of Ottoman Westernization and modernization, seems to be more cogent. The Armenians were exposed to both formal and informal societal influences within the Ottoman Empire, including also the censorship of textbooks and regulations on course offerings. The Armenian schools were nonetheless created and administered by community intellectuals who received their pedagogical training, not from the Ottoman authorities but rather from other Armenians, be they clergy or lay teachers. Many others were educated in foreign institutions.

Therefore, the general dynamics between Western ideas, Armenian traditions, education, and the development of national consciousness must be taken into consideration. The hypothesis is that education was a hybrid of Western knowledge which combined with Armenian traditions both from the Eastern Armenian centers in the Caucasus and the native Western Armenian provinces. The evidence for supporting this conclusion is established by examining the educational system in Erzerum and more specifically in one institution, the Sanasarian *Varzharan* (School, Academy, Collège), its curriculum, faculty, and students.

Provincial Education in Erzerum

Education among the Armenian community of Erzerum in the early part of the nineteenth century was the product of religious and lay teachers. Because Armenians living in the inner provinces were peasants, education was often viewed as a luxury with little practical purpose. Attendance was therefore sporadic as students usually attended classes for a few months or would leave after one or two years of study. Only a few students continued on to higher education.

By the end of the nineteenth century, these early forms of education began to evolve into a more formalized system. In Constantinople, the Azgayin Usumnakan Khorhurd (National Educational Council) served as a central academic coordinating body, and benevolent societies such as the Miatsial Enkerutiun Hayots (United Society of Armenians) provided the basis for growth and reform.[2] New schools focused on elementary education and started to make use of instructional materials such as textbooks, blackboards, and desks. In the past, schools were often held in informal settings—private homes, churches, or in the back of shops, with students sitting on mats.

During the nineteenth and continuing into the twentieth century, the Armenian Patriarchate of Constantinople, the local Armenian communities throughout the Ottoman Empire, and the National Educational Council collected statistical records for taxation purposes and for monitoring community activities. The

Table 1

Partial Educational Statistics for Erzerum Sanjak

	1901	1909	1913
Number of Schools	93	134	211
Number of Students	6,938	7,547	13,932

figures in Table 1 reveal a substantial growth in the number of students in the *sanjak* or county of Erzerum between 1901 and 1913.[3]

---

[2] The National Educational Council was formally established in 1863 by the Armenian Constitution (Sahmanadrutiun), and the Miatsial Enkerutiun Hayots was established in 1881.

[3] This study concentrates only on the sanjak of Erzerum, as the statistics are more complete for the period under review than are those for the entire province. The sanjak included the districts or *kazas* of Erzerum, Narman, Khnus, Terjan, Ispir (Sper), Kiskim, Passin (Basen), Tortum, Baiburt (Baberd), and Kghi. The statistics for 1901 do not include the kazas of Narman and Tortum. The statistics for 1909 exclude Kghi, Narman, and Tortum, and the figures for 1913 exclude Baiburt and Tortum. For 1901, see *Vijakatsoyts gavarakan azgayin varzharanats Turkio* [Statistics of the Provincial National Schools in Turkey], vols. 1-2 (Constantinople: H. Matteosian,

As remarkable as this growth may seem, the statistics also reflect larger societal issues. For example, in 1901 a devastating earthquake struck Erzerum, making it likely that the figures for that year are under-reported because of the widespread destruction. Moreover, the impressive growth between 1909 and 1913 probably reflects the optimism associated with the Young Turk revolution and restoration of the Ottoman Constitution in 1908.

Educational Life in the City of Erzerum

With the increase of educational activity in Erzerum, the young people were afforded a widening scope of opportunities, as new schools, including the Sanasarian Varzharan, were established to meet their needs.[4] By the beginning of the twentieth century, there were ten community-sponsored schools in the city of Erzerum alone.[5] These included the Artsnian school for boys established in 1811,[6] the Kedronakan Jemaran (Central Academy),[7] and the coeducational Msrian,[8] Der Azarian,[9] Aghabalian,[10] and Kavafian[11] institutions. Throughout the later part of the nine-

---

1901-1903), vol. 1, pp. 14-16, vol. 2, p. 12; for 1909: A-Do (H. Ter-Martirosian), *Vani, Bitlisi ev Erzrumi vilayetnere* [The Vilayets of Van, Bitlis, and Erzerum] (Erevan: Kultura, 1912), pp. 166-67; for 1913, Archives du Patriarcat de Constantinople, Documents Officiels et Rapports, in Bibliothèque Nubar, DOR 3/1, DOR 3/2, DOR 3/4.

[4] See Ghazar Chareg, *Karinapatum: Hushamatian Bardzr Hayki* [Karin: Memorial Volume of Upper Armenia] (Beirut: Garin Compatriotic Unions of the United States and Lebanon, 1957), pp. 161-269.

[5] In my definition of community-sponsored schools, I do not include those established by the Catholics or American missionaries.

[6] The school was named in memory of Artsn, a nearby city destroyed by the Seljuks in the eleventh century.

[7] The Central Academy was established in 1874. The faculty included three university-educated teachers from Constantinople.

[8] The Msrian school operated from 1888 to 1914 and was named for its benefactor. Coeducational, it had two buildings for kindergarten and elementary education, a playground, and dining hall. After graduation, students could attend either the Sanasarian Varzharan or the Hripsimian school.

[9] The Der Azarian school was a coeducational kindergarten and elementary school that operated from 1860 to 1914.

[10] The Aghabalian school was named after its principal, Mgrdich Aghabalian. The school provided elementary education to boys and girls until 1914.

[11] The Kavafian School was a coeducational elementary school established by

teenth and early twentieth century, these schools expanded to accommodate the growing student population. Figure 1 shows that the number of students enrolled in the city schools increased twofold from the period of 1872 to 1913.[12]

Figure 1[13]

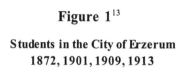

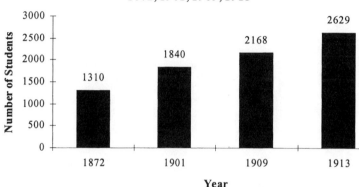

The Armenians in Erzerum and elsewhere in the Ottoman Empire clearly had a progressive attitude toward education. This was apparent through the open-minded attitude regarding the introduction of coeducational classes, a concept that some Western countries did not embrace until the middle of the twentieth century, and the growing focus on the education of women. The rise in female education in Erzerum began with the establishment of the first girls' school, Surb Targmanchats (Holy Translators),

---

Mardiros Kavafian in 1905.

[12] The figures for 1913 include 34 Armenian students in Ottoman state schools and 521 students in Catholic and Protestant schools.

[13] Sources: for 1872, *Hamaratvutiun Azgayin Kedronakan Varchutian 1872-1873 ami ar Azgayin Endhanur Zhoghovi* [Report of the National Central Executive for the Year 1872-1873 to the National General Assembly] (Constantinople: H. Miuhendisian, 1874), pp. 39-74; for 1901, *Vijakatsoyts gavarakan azgayin varzharanats Tiurkio*, vol. 1, pp. 14-16, vol. 2, p. 12; for 1909, A-Do, *Vani, Bitlis ev Erzrumi vilayetnere*; for 1913, Archives du Patriarcate Constantinople, Documents Officiels et Rapports, DOR 3/1, DOR 3/2, DOR 3/4 BNP.

in 1870. The second school, Hripsimian, was founded in 1875 as a middle school but eventually expanded to include a high school and a teacher-preparation program. During the period between 1872 and 1909, the number of girls enrolled in schools in Erzerum doubled as shown in Figure 2.

Figure 2[14]

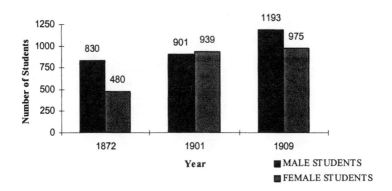

With the educational gap between boys and girls closing, the attainment of formalized knowledge became progressively less of a gendered experience. Western educational institutions, both French and American, were also a part of the academic scene in Erzerum. The Armenian Franciscan fathers operated a French *lycée* with a curriculum that included Armenian, Turkish, French, the sciences, and music (with a noted string orchestra). The school attracted students from various religious backgrounds.[15] A Catholic boys' school was also established in 1867, and a Catholic girls' school was attached to the Anarat Hghutiun (Immaculate Conception) convent operated by Armenian nuns. The curriculum in both schools included Armenian, French, the

---

[14] Sources: for 1872, *Hamaratvutiun Azgayin Kedronakan Varchutian*, pp. 37-74; for 1901, *Vijakatsoyts gavarakan azgayin varzharanats,* vol. 1, pp. 14-16, vol. 2, p. 12; for 1909, A-Do, *Vani, Bitlisi ev Erzrumi vilayetnere*, pp. 166-67.

[15] The school enrolled not only Catholics but also Armenian Apostolics and Turks (including the two sons of the *vali* or governor, Tahsin Pasha).

sciences, and religion. Meanwhile, the American Board of Commissioners for Foreign Missions financed a Protestant boys' school and girls' school.[16] While the religious component of these Western institutions was certainly evident, they also continued to cultivate a national awareness among the students.[17] The history of all of these schools, Armenian- and Western-sponsored, ended abruptly in 1915 with the Armenian Genocide.

The Makings of Sanasarian Varzharan

Sanasarian Varzharan was the most visible and prominent Armenian school in Erzerum because it was an institution of higher learning and catered to students from a wide area. Lord Warkworth, a British traveler, wrote of his visit to the Sanasarian Varzharan:

> The School of San Saurian [sic] . . . is an important and flourishing institution. Besides a large dormitory and classrooms it contains a natural history museum, and a good workshop in which instruction in turning and carpentering is given. It provides accommodation for one hundred and fifty scholars, and the education, conducted on the German plan, comprises in its curriculum among other subjects, the teaching of French, German, Turkish and Armenian, ancient and modern.[18]

The initial support for the school came from Mkrtich Sanasarian for whom the school was named. Born in 1818 in Tiflis of parents from Van, he attended the noted Nersesian Academy.[19] In the 1840s, Sanasarian moved to St. Petersburg where he became an ardent advocate of education. With his financial backing, the Sanasarian's organizational structure was

---

[16] The Protestant boys' school, Mancheru Bartsragoyn Varzharan (Superior School for Boys), was known as the Masiats Varzharan until 1897.

[17] Hratch A. Tarbassian, *Erzurum (Garin): Its Armenian History and Tradition,* trans. Nigol Schahgaldian ([New York]: Garin Compatriotic Union of the United States, 1975), p. 113.

[18] Lord Warkworth (Henry Algernon George Percy), *Notes From a Diary in Asiatic Turkey* (London: Edward Arnold, 1898), p. 81.

[19] The Nersesian Academy was established in Tiflis in 1824 and served as a leading center for training young Armenians in the Caucasus.

shaped through the assistance of Karapet Ezian (Eziants; Ezov), who had studied at the Lazarian Academy (Jemaran) in Moscow and at St. Petersburg University. A specialist in Oriental languages, Ezian was employed in the imperial ministry of education in St. Petersburg. Under the guidance of these two founding fathers, the first seeds of Western educational ideas were planted within the walls of the Sanasarian Varzharan.

The Western approach to education continued to grow when nine young men were sent abroad to study in the 1870s.[20] The plan was that they would return to Karin/Erzerum to teach at Sanasarian and become the institutional leaders. While abroad, the students frequently corresponded with Ezian. They provided detailed information about their studies and the books they purchased for the school.

At the same time, the Eastern Armenian connection also began to develop. Students in both Tiflis and Echmiadzin were being trained as specialists in Armenian language, history, and literature.[21] Thus, these two groups, one trained in the Russian Empire and the other in Europe, converged on Erzerum to begin the work of educating future intellectuals in the heart of historic Armenia. Sanasarian Varzharan opened in 1881 as a boarding school for boys with nineteen students. The school remained in Erzerum until 1912 when it was moved to Sivas (Sebastia). It was organized as a German *Realschule* and licensed by the Ottoman government as an *école secondaire lycée*.[22] According to the institutional regulations, the school's role was to educate Armenian children in keeping with the spirit and regulations of the Armenian Church as well as to provide instruction in crafts and industrial knowledge.[23] With this guide, Sanasarian was

---

[20] This development follows along with the European influence on educational activities in Constantinople in the 1850s when young Armenian men returned to the Ottoman Empire from study abroad with ideas inspired by the French Revolution.

[21] In Echmiadzin, this training was provided at the Gevorgian Academy.

[22] The German *Realschulen* were also known as *Bürgerschulen*, trade and technical schools. These schools focused on practical training. Students learned commercial and manual skills as well as mathematics, sciences, and modern languages. See James C. Albisetti, *Secondary School Reform in Imperial Germany* (Princeton: Princeton University Press, 1983).

[23] See *Himnakan kanonadrutiun Sanasarian Varzharani* [Fundamental Regula-

divided into two sections. The first focused solely on academic education, and the second on vocational training. The school was both a public and private institution within the Armenian community. It drew students from the general public, serving as a boarding school and a day school. But it was also a private institution in that it remained independent of the National Educational Council and therefore had more flexibility with its curriculum and organizational structure.[24] During its first few years, Sanasarian was housed in the Erzerum prelacy (*Arajnordaran*) until it was transferred to the newly-built Hripsimian girls' school. This space was quickly filled, and a new building was constructed to house additional classrooms, the craft-house, directors' offices, and physics and chemistry rooms.

Institutional management was divided among the school administration, a local management committee in Erzerum, a board of trustees in Constantinople, and the institutional benefactors.[25] The religious hierarchy of the Armenian Church also played an active role in the school's management. For example, Maghakia Ormanian was involved with Sanasarian from its inception, first as prelate of Erzerum (1880-87) and then as the Patriarch of Constantinople (1896-1907) when he served on the board of trustees. Each branch of management had clearly defined roles and responsibilities. The trustees in Constantinople administered the school's financial resources, while the institutional leadership oversaw daily affairs. There was, however, constant tension between the institutional directors in Erzerum, the benefactors in St. Petersburg, and the trustees who lived in Constantinople. Those distant from Erzerum were far removed from everyday life and were constantly criticized for not understanding the school's daily problems.

---

tions of the Sanasarian School] (Constantinople: Onnik Barseghian ev Vordi, 1910), pt. 1, art. 3, p. 1.

[24] Because of its status as a private institution, Sanasarian was initially criticized for taking students away from the Armenian community schools. However, the argument was refuted as the national schools were not equipped to provide the same type of higher education and the qualifications that students needed in order to continue their studies in Constantinople or abroad.

[25] An academic council was created in early 1903 under the leadership of Sarkis Soghigian but was disbanded several years later.

Sanasarian Varzharan's entrance requirements in the early years remained relatively lenient. The guidelines mandated that students be able to read, write, and speak in Armenian and to solve mathematical problems. Institutional evolution and a desire to raise the academic standards led in 1909 to a noticeable change in the admissions policy. At that time, entering students were given examinations in religion, Armenian, Turkish, mathematics, and the sciences.[26]

The guidelines for admission provide insight into the institution's curricular leanings. Clearly, the school required the knowledge of the Armenian language. Based on these foundations, Sanasarian's goal was to expand the minds of the students in order to create educated and well-rounded individuals.

Curriculum

When Sanasarian first opened, there were classes in religion, Armenian language, geography, history, natural history, arithmetic, drawing, singing, and physical education. There were twenty-six hours of instruction per week and no alternatives to the core courses. In the following years, the rise in student enrollment and the addition of grades resulted in an increase in the variety of subjects offered and the number of class hours per discipline. Hence, the course outline expanded to offer classical Armenian, Ottoman language and history, French and Turkish translations, geometry, and, as electives, piano and violin. Courses were later added in Church history, physics, chemistry, bookkeeping, algebra, trigonometry, health, and agriculture.

Even with the addition of new courses, Armenian subjects remained the core curriculum. Institutional regulations mandated that all classes, aside from foreign languages, be conducted in Armenian. Therefore, even the sciences and mathematics instilled in students a deeper understanding of the language.[27] While class-

---

[26] *Karamia teghekagir Sanasarian Varzharani, 1906-1910, Karin* [Four Year Account of the Sanasarian School, 1906-1910, Karin] (Constantinople: Shant, 1911), pp. 18-19.

[27] Sanasarian followed the lead of the Armenian national schools whose primary language of instruction was Armenian, whereas the American missionary schools,

room instruction was in Armenian, foreign languages, especially German and French, had an ever-present effect through the use of textbooks in those languages. Many of the books served as reference guides, as the teachers supplemented the curriculum with Armenian textbooks or even created their own. The list of course offerings reveals the continual mixture of Western approaches to education with Armenian-centered realities.[28]

A comparison between the course hours for third year students in 1884-86 and 1907-09 bears out the growing Westernization of the curriculum. During Sanasarian's first years, there was very little instruction offered about the West. But as changes took place in the Ottoman Empire, there was a significant increase in foreign language instruction, grammar, translations, and world history.[29] Sanasarian offered both French or German.[30] These languages were rational choices given that French was used throughout the Ottoman territories in trade and governmental affairs, whereas German was valuable for trade and science and was popular among professors who had studied in Germany. While the institutional leaders noted the importance of language training, providing such instruction was a heavy burden. The need to attract teachers was a constant concern as it often meant recruiting qualified persons from abroad. The location and cli-

---

depending on location, alternated between Turkish, Armenian, and English. See *Himnakan kanonadrutiun Sanasarian Varzharani*, pt. 1, art. 13, p. 2.

[28] In the mid-1800s textbooks on various subjects were printed in Armenian. The most striking example of a textbook prepared by a teacher is one on the Armenian language written by Professor Goriun Mgrdichian. The textbook also served as a guide for teachers, with preparatory lectures, suggested poems, songs, stories for the students to learn, and work assignments.

[29] The Armenian classes included the modern and classical languages and grammar. The Turkish classes included language and grammar and Ottoman history. Included in the Western division were the French and German languages, history, French and Turkish translation, and grammar.

[30] Beginning in 1885 students could choose French as an elective; four years later German was offered as an alternative third language, in addition to the required Turkish and Armenian. Efforts were also made in the 1880s to introduce English, but as no students registered for the course the idea lapsed. At one point the school also found itself without an Armenian language teacher when in 1901 Astvatsatur Khachaturian departed for Germany. Attempts to find a replacement failed because of a cholera epidemic in Erzerum. Therefore, other courses such as religion and history were expanded to include additional Armenian reading.

mate of Erzerum did not make it a very attractive place for foreign teachers. Therefore, the retention rate of these faculty members was quite low, with many staying a year or less. On more than one occasion, the school went without foreign language teachers.

Sanasarian's formalized course offerings were supplemented by informal outings, celebrations, and access to literary works in a wide array of subjects and languages. In the school library, students perused a collection of more than 7,000 German, Armenian, and French language books.[31] Outside of school, students went on outings with faculty members to the villages surrounding Erzerum so that they might enjoy the fresh air of the mountains and become familiar with the surrounding rural economy. Students also observed the religious traditions and practices of the Armenian Apostolic Church, beginning the day with morning prayers and singing and ending in the same manner. Students attended church every Sunday and on feast days and fasted during Holy Week and as prescribed by the religious calendar. The Sanasarian Varzharan also celebrated numerous holidays, such as the annual commemoration of the sultan's enthronement, Christmas, Easter, Barekentan (eve of Lent), and Vardanants day. On these occasions students and faculty participated in the presentation of musical selections and speeches.

The Role of the Faculty

Educated at leading institutions for higher education in Europe and Russia and to a lesser extent in Constantinople, the institutional directors and faculty played a large role in shaping Sanasarian's pedagogical orientation. These faculty members were classified into three groups: directors or head teachers, principal teachers, and assistants.

The foremost proponents of Western approaches were head teachers Sarkis Soghigian, Kevork Abulian (Gevorg Apulian), and

---

[31] The books numbered by language: German, 2,900; Armenian, 1,450; French, 1,102; Turkish, 398; English, 119; Russian, 55. In addition, there were 400 books of the student society and 942 bound and unbound manuscripts, for a total holding of 7,366 items. *Karamia teghekagir Sanasarian Varzharani*, p. 37.

Hovsep Madatian, who also served as institutional directors. Soghigian, a native of Kharpert, completed his studies in Germany before moving to Erzerum where he taught religion, French, German, and piano. In addition, his official duties included representing the administration on the academic council, implementing institutional reforms, writing newspaper articles, serving as the library director, and corresponding with students and parents. Abulian, a native of the Caucasus, was born in Tiflis where he graduated from the Nersesian Academy. At a young age, he went to Switzerland and graduated from the École Normale of Zurich, then studied in Germany from 1875 until 1881 and for a year at Cambridge University. Upon returning to Sanasarian, Abulian taught history, geography, German, and physical education. His official school duties also included financial operations and correspondence between the school leadership and local management committee. A large part of his time was spent writing to Karapet Ezian. Following the Armenian Genocide, Abulian relocated to Paris and there helped to create an alumni association, the Sanasarian Miutiun (Sanasarian Union). Madatian, a native of Samsun, taught natural sciences, health, German, drawing, chemistry, and geometry and organized the school's museum and craft school. He also served as the institution's liaison with the government because of his friendly relationship with Turkish officials and his fluency in Turkish.

Aside from the primary institutional leaders, the most active and influential teacher was Astvatsatur Khachaturian, who was educated at the Gevorgian Academy in Echmiadzin and then at the University of Strasbourg. He taught classical and modern Armenian, literature, history, and geography. Not only did Khachaturian play an active role in ensuring the central place of Armenian in the curriculum, but he also became a leader in the nationalist movement. He was a member of the regional central committee of the Armenian Revolutionary Federation (ARF; Dashnaktsutiun) and in 1919 was elected to the Parliament of the newly-created Republic of Armenia at Erevan and served as an advisor of the Republic's delegation to the Paris Peace Conference.

Throughout its existence, the Sanasarian Varzharan sent students and teachers to Western academic institutions. Among them

was Simon Aghabalian, who was born in 1874 and educated at
the Artsnian and Sanasarian schools. After becoming a teacher,
he studied mechanical engineering and physics in Germany until
1900 and was then sent to Vienna by the Constantinople trustees
of Sanasarian to study pedagogy, mineralogy, geology, and chemistry.[32]

Among the teachers sent to France was Aram Hagopian. After
receiving degrees from the École Normale Primaire and St. Cloud
École Normale Superieure in Paris, he returned to Erzerum to
teach French. Sanasarian faculty also came from other institutions. For example, Sarkis Manougian, a native of Kghi and a
graduate of the Gevorgian Academy in Echmiadzin, went on to
St. Petersburg, Berlin, and Leipzig to study Armenian, philosophy, and religion. In 1910 he came to Sanasarian to teach classical Armenian (*grabar*) and moral philosophy.

Student Population

Sanasarian students came from a variety of backgrounds. They
ranged from those born into wealthy established families to poor
pupils supported by scholarships. In order to provide educational
opportunity to all Armenians, the school leaders attempted to
draw students into the academic community from the larger
general Armenian population. Despite school notices appearing
in newspapers and journals in Tiflis, Constantinople, and Smyrna,
however, most of Sanasarian's students were from the interior
regions: Arabkir, Tokat (Evtokia), Trebizond, and Van.[33] Students
from the sanjak of Erzerum constituted the largest number from
any one region and were a majority of those enrolled in the

---

[32] Among the teachers sent to other institutions were Aram Vahanian in carpentry, Hagop Melkonian as a locksmith, Kevork Chiyerchian in chemistry, and
Levon Paspanian in French. There were also those who stayed closer to home. In
1906-07, Khosrov Babayan, a Sanasarian graduate, taught politics in the Erzerum
middle school before moving to Constantinople for training in teaching Ottoman
Turkish. After receiving a university certificate, he returned to Sanasarian in 1909
to teach Turkish.

[33] From 1881 to 1910, there were 59 students from Arabkir; 51 from Trebizond;
31 from Tokat; 25 from Van.

vocational crafts school.[34] Thus, with most students hailing from the provinces, the school fulfilled its mission of providing educational opportunity to youth in the less developed interior regions.

Through the years, Sanasarian's existence was marked by changes in student enrollment, as reflected in Figure 3. In many cases, enrollment fluctuations coincided with societal problems

Figure 3[35]

Number of Sanasarian Students
1881 - 1910

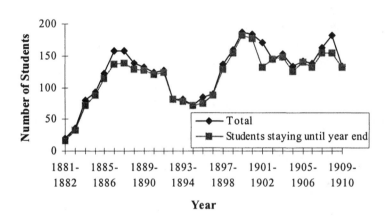

and conflicts beyond the school. For example, the decline in the number of students between 1891 and 1897 is a reflection of the cholera epidemic in Erzerum and the Hamidian massacres of 1894-96. The figures also reveal that, for the most part, students

---

[34] From 1881 to 1910, out of a total of 772 students at Sanasarian, 286 were from the sanjak of Erzerum (218 from the city of Erzerum, 26 from Khnus, 15 from Kghi, 14 from Baiburt, 5 from the Erzerum plain, 4 from Basen, 3 from Terjan, and 1 from Kiskim).

[35] Sources: *Ksanamia teghekagir Sanasarian Varzharani, 1881-1901* [Twenty Year Bulletin of the Sanasarian School 1881-1901] (Constantinople: Ter Nersesian, 1903); *Hngamia teghekagir Sanasarian Varzharani 1901-1906* [Five Year Bulletin of the Sanasarian School 1906-1910] (Constantinople: Ter Nersesian, 1908); *Karamia teghekagir Sanasarian Varzharani, 1906-1910,* p. 29.

remained at the school until the end of the year. A clear exception was in 1901, when a devastating earthquake struck the region. Years later uncertainty about constitutional guarantees caused the suspension of classes because of fear of arrest by the Turkish authorities.

Political activity and the beginnings of a revolutionary spirit began to emerge among the students by the beginning of the twentieth century. One group banded together to form the Sanasarian Ashakertakan Miutiun (Sanasarian Student Union), which published a handwritten journal *Sirt* (Heart) between 1904 and 1906. The journal provided a literary outlet for students and contained short stories, poems, essays, and biographies of national figures such as the inspirational writer Mikayel Nalbandian and Archbishop Maghakia Ormanian. *Sirt* also contained numerous translations of poetry, stories, and historical and pedagogical ideas from both Germany and France. These works provide insight into the developing Armenian national consciousness among the student population as well as the influence of their Westernized education.[36]

Ardashes Hovsepian (Malkhas) and Hovhannes Siuzmejian later formed another secretive group, Enkerakan Sirt (Heart of Comraderie), with the help of the carpentry teacher Aram Vahanian. Under the banner *Droshak* (Banner), they held meetings and wrote provocative letters to other schools in an attempt to establish organizational connections. However, since the students were constantly under the watchful eye of the institutional leaders, the letters were soon discovered and the students punished by being locked in their rooms.

In the early 1900s, Sanasarian students were also engaged in dramatic productions. They presented, among other pieces, *Depi azatutiun* (Toward Freedom), *Charshele Artin Aghan* (The Peddler Artin Agha), Garegin Levonian's *Anonts mahe* (Their Death), and Hagop Baronian's (Hakob Paronian) satirical *Arevelian atamnabuzh* (Oriental Dentist). When after the Young Turk revolution in 1908 the students were again able to form a student union, they opened their own library with 400 volumes.

---

[36] For more detailed analysis of this journal, see Young, "Knowledge, Nation, and the Curriculum," cited in note 1 above.

By 1910, 235 of the 772 students (including one woman) who had enrolled at Sanasarian had completed their studies and graduated.[37] Most of the graduates became educators, community leaders, professionals, merchants, and railroad and tobacco administration officials. One such example was Aram Aramian, a native of Erzerum, who was the secretary of the Armenian prelacy and one of the early members of the Dashnaktsutiun.

Other students remained in the provinces working as teachers and promoting the nationalist cause. In fact, as Table 2 reveals, among the graduates the largest number served as educators. Some of them also became leaders of the Dashnaktsutiun,[38] including Levon Karakashian, Khachadur Gordodian, Stepan Shehrian, Hovhannes Poghsoyian, and Andranik Yesayan.[39]

The collective impact of the teachers, training, and everyday institutional life formed the seeds of national leadership that also grew among the Sanasarian students. Many of them used their training to spread ideas of resistance among the greater Ottoman Armenian population. Influenced by revolutionary ideologies from abroad, several students went on to become prominent members of the Dashnaktsutiun party, including Garegin Pasdermajian (Armen Garo), Dikran Khachigian (Arzuman), Khosrov Babayan, Ardashes Hovsepian, Mgrdich Barsamian, and Paylag Sanasar.

---

[37] The one female student was Nevart Madatian, who graduated in 1904.

[38] The Dashnaktsutiun organized affiliates throughout the Diaspora and among both the Ottoman Armenians and Russian Armenians. The party was organized in 1890 and held its first congress in 1892 in Tiflis.

[39] Karakashian, a native of Erzerum, was educated at Sanasarian and became a lecturer there, teaching Armenian, geography and national and general history. He was deported in 1915 but survived and became the director of the Azgayin Miutiun (National Union) in Aleppo from 1919 to 1925, principal of a national school in Beirut, and teacher at the Melkonian Institute in Cyprus. He wrote several articles in the *Hairenik* monthly and published a book on the local Erzerum dialect. See N.D.S. Tashjian, "Sanasariantsinere Dashnaktsutian mej" [Sanasarianites in the Dashnaktsutiun], *Hairenik Amsagir* 9 (Feb. 1931): 126-33.

Gordodian was an ARF party member who after graduating from Sanasarian returned to Sivas/Sebastia, where he spent fourteen years working as an educator in the national orphanage and national schools

Shehrian was principal of Hirpsimian girls' school in Erzerum and the schools in Kghi under the Miatsial Enkerutiun Hayots.

Poghsoyian was a teacher and an ARF activist.

Yesayan taught at Sanasarian.

Table 2

Occupations of Sanasarian Graduates, 1910[40]

Profession	Number
Educator (Principal, Teacher)	61
Merchant, Commissioner, Peddler, Shopkeeper	57
Leader (Railroad, Tobacco, Government, Health, School, Factory, etc)	29
Student (Pedagogy, Medical, Agriculture, Law, etc.)	27
Artisan (Carpenter, Locksmith, Tentmaker)	25
Deceased	10
Engineer, Mathematician, Economist	7
Doctor	6
Ottoman Representative	1
Painter	1
Priest	2
Housewife	1
Dentist	1
Profession Unknown	7
TOTAL	235

Pasdermajian, Khachigian, Hovsepian, and others were active in student societies while they lived or studied abroad and then returned to Constantinople in 1908 after the Young Turk revolution and restoration of the Ottoman Constitution that had been suspended since 1878.[41]

---

[40] Source: *Karamia teghekagir Sanasarian Varzharani 1906-1910, Karin*, pp. 92-102.

[41] Armen Garo was admitted to Sanasarian in 1891 and spent several years studying there. In 1894 he traveled to France to continue his studies and with other Armenian students joined the revolutionary movement. In 1896 he played an important role in the occupation of the Ottoman Bank in Constantinople. After being given safe conduct abroad, he traveled to the United States for a short period before transferring to Tiflis in 1901. With the restoration of the Ottoman Constitution in 1908, Pasdermajian returned to Erzerum where he was elected as an Armenian deputy to the Ottoman Parliament. During the first Armenian republic, he acted as

As shown in Table 3, most students stayed in the eastern provinces after graduating from Sanasarian, taking positions especially in large cities such as Erzerum, Van, Trebizond, and Samsun. Born and raised in the provinces, they remained attached

Table 3

Locations of Sanasarian Graduates, 1910[42]

Location	Number of Graduates
Erzerum	88
Provinces (Van, Samsun, Arabkir, Trebizond, Smyrna, etc.)	62
Western countries (Switzerland, France, United States, Germany, Italy)	39
Constantinople	25
Russia and Caucasus	13
Egypt	2
Unknown	6

to the land. Of those who did move on, most ended up in Western countries such as the United States, France, and Germany rather than in Constantinople or Russia.

Hence, most Sanasarian graduates left the institution equipped with a strong desire and will to work in the interior provinces where they had been born. They were filled with the knowledge and love of the Armenian language, history, and literature and

the Armenian plenipotentiary to the United States. Ardashes Hovepian, the later noted writer who used the pen-name Malkhas, came to Sanasarian in 1887 but stayed only two years before returning to his birthplace at Trebizond. In 1894 he enrolled again at Sanasarian but shortly thereafter went on to Samsun, where he became a close friend of the ARF leader, Ardashes Tevian. In 1896, Hovsepian traveled to America and then in 1903 to Geneva before finally returning to Constantinople at the time of the restored Ottoman Constitution. He later served in the Parliament of the first Armenian republic.

[42] Source: *Karamia teghekagir Sanasarian Varzharani, 1906-1910, Karin*, pp. 92-102.

of a greater Ottoman society in which they lived. At the same time, however, they were increasingly affected by a combination of intellectual currents from the Russian Empire and Western approaches to education, pedagogy, and thought.

Conclusion

Sanasarian Varzharan was one of the hundreds of Armenian schools in the Ottoman Empire. This and other schools in Erzerum are examples of a hybrid national consciousness combining Western subjects and the ways of the Armenian people of Erzerum. Modeled after the German Realschule, Sanasarian fostered a consciousness based on Armenian national ideals and greater world knowledge.

While the curriculum stressed the study of Armenian subjects —language, literature, religion, and history—students were also exposed to foreign languages and world history. Many Sanasarian graduates continued their studies at foreign institutions, and a large number of them eventually returned to teach at their alma mater and other Armenian schools in the interior provinces. Thus, as educational leaders, they played a significant role in passing on their ideas and beliefs to the masses and building a national consciousness among the Armenian people.[43]

---

[43] For additional materials relating to the Sanasarian Varzharan, see *Hngamia teghekagir Sanasarian Varzharani, 1901-1906*; *Ksanamia teghekagir Sanasarian Varzharani, 1881-1901*; *Sanasarian Varzharan Karno usumnakan teghekagir 1891-92 ev 1892-93 tarineru ev tntesakan teghekagir 1892-93 tario* [Educational Bulletin of the Sanasarian Academy of Karin for 1891-92 and 1892-93 and Economic Bulletin for 1892-93] (Constantinople: Nerses J. Aramian, 1894); *Elevmtakan ev usumnakan teghekagir Sanasarian Varzharani Karno, 1893-1894 tario* [Financial and Educational Account of the Sanasarian Academy of Karin for the Years 1893-1894] (Constantinople: Sahak Nikoghosian, 1895); Hovhannes Shavarsh, "Sanasarian Varzharan," *Arevelian Mamul* [Oriental Press] 20 (Oct. 5, 1897): 682-85; Vahan Kuyumjian, "Anhetatsogh demker: Gevorg Apulian" [Vanishing Personalities: Kevork Abulian], *Harach* (Paris), Oct. 10, 1933, p. 2; Mkrtich Parsamian, "Simon Aghapalian," in the M. Parsamian Fund, no. 264, State Literature and Arts Archives (Charents), Erevan.

The Sanasarian School

Mkrtich Sanasarian

Karapet Ezian

Kevork Abulian

Hovsep Madatian

Sarkis Soghigian

Simon Aghabalian

Graduates with Photograph of Mkrtich Sanasarian

Collège Sanassarian.

Programme.

De la séance de Distribution des Diplômes
du jeudi 9/16 juillet 1903.

1. Marche Impériale, par la fanfare du Collège.
2. Marche: Entrée des Lauréats. id. m.
3. Discours en turc, par Diktran Amsian.
4. "Quatrième Sonate en mi bémol" de Mozart, piano et violon.
   par Onnik der Bogossian e Arm. Madathian.
5. Discours d'adieu en arménien, par Yéprème Soxénian.
6. a) "Lohengrin" de Wagner: Chœur des Noces, piano et violons.
   par plusieurs élèves
   b) "La Dernière Rose", chant populaire irlandais, piano et violon.
   par Mᵉ Nevart Madathian et Arm. Madathian
7. Discours en turc, par Sérope Noradounguian. piano et violons
8. "Le Calife de Bagdad" de Boïeldieu, par plusieurs élèves, sur
9. Discours en français, par Arménak Madathian.
10. "Festival", Chœur en français: par Mᵉ Osketchian et L. Karakachi
11. Discours en arménien, par Garabet Ulubékian.] élèves
12. a) "La Vallée Tranquille" de Gantz, chœur en allemand par plusieurs
    b) "Le Chant du Matin" de Grégor, chœur en allemand ... id.

La séance est suspendue pour 10 minutes.

13. Hymne à Sa Majesté, chœur en turc, par les élèves.
14. Discours en turc, par Mᵉ Madathian, directeur du Collège.
15. Distribution des Diplômes.] directeur du Collège.
16. Allocution aux Lauréats, en arménien, par Mᵉ Solikian.
17. Chant religieux, en arménien, accompagné par l'orgue.
18. Prière.

Graduation Ceremony Program, 1903

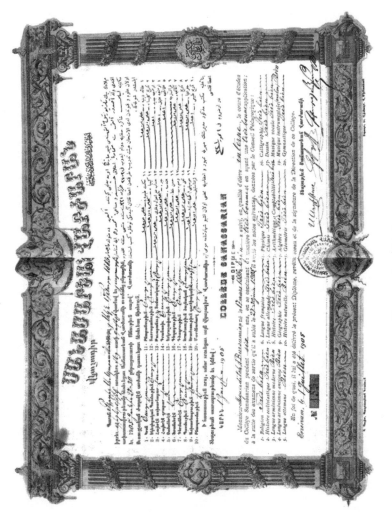

Sanasarian Diploma

287

Sanasarian Graduate Hripsime Madatian

Hripsimian School Principal Eghishe Dursunian and Students

Hripsimian School Faculty and Students, 1911

Anarat Hghutiun (Immaculate Conception) School

American Mission House

Armenian Teachers of American Mission School

❊ 12 ❊

ARMENIAN VILLAGE LIFE
IN THE PLAIN OF KARIN

Vartiter Kotcholosian Hovannisian

Who can foretell our future?
Spare me the attempt
We are like harvest reaped
by bad husbandry men
amidst encircling gloom and clouds

John Catholicos
Tenth-Century Armenian Historian

This opening quotation, appearing on the title page of H.F.B. Lynch's *Armenia*, contemporizes the need to rediscover the past, which is the record of today's ephemeral future. The present essay is not a scholarly research paper. Rather, it has grown out of years of gathering memoirs and accounts of survivors of the 1915 Genocide who had one common denominator. They all were natives of the village of Dzitogh (Tsitogh) in the plain of Karin/Erzerum. Some escaped certain death by happening to be in the Russian Empire at the outbreak of World War I. Others were children who miraculously cheated death on the long, bloody forced marches to the distant deserts of Syria. They lived out their lives in various countries in widely different political and economic environments. Of the relatively few who survived from this large village of some 3,000 souls, most found new homes in Armenia, Georgia, the North Caucasus, Russia, Ukraine, Iran, Iraq, Syria, Lebanon, France, and the United States. Because of the turbulence of the twentieth century, some had to relocate two, three, or even four times.

My early years were spent among rapidly assimilating, mostly Russian-speaking Armenians in the eastern Ukraine. The Armenian church and school of Kharkov were shut down during the Stalin Terror, and the most-promising youth found themselves in the Pioneer and Communist Youth Association (Komsomol). Still, the several families that had originated in Dzitogh maintained a special mutual bond, whether by a blood relationship, by employment, or by nostalgia. It was not until after World War II and our re-Armenianization process that began in a Displaced Persons' camp in Germany that life in Dzitogh became livingroom and table conversation. Since my father, Hovakim Kotcholosian, survived not only the 1915 Genocide but also the frostbite and wounds received in his service in the Armenian Fourth Volunteer Battalion organized in the Caucasus, his accounts of the first two decades of the twentieth century were detailed and vivid.

It was at the urging of his two daughters that Hovakim began to record his experiences, resulting in a long and significant memoir. It was then that I decided to seek out other Dzitoghtsis (natives of Dzitogh) around the world to ask each one to submit an account of his or her own experiences during that critical period. Some failed to respond; others promised to write but never did, but still others did expend the time, effort, and emotion to recount village life before and during the genocide and the difficult, often turbulent years that followed. On the basis of these contributions, I compiled, edited, annotated, and published in 1972 the volume in Armenian titled *Dzitogh Dashti Karno.*[1] Much of the information in the current essay has been gleaned from these accounts, together with a few published studies relating to the province of Karin/Erzerum.[2]

---

[1] Vartiter Kotcholosian Hovannisian, *Dzitogh Dashti Karno* [Dzitogh in the Plain of Karin] (Beirut: Hamazkayin Press, 1972).

[2] See Hakob Kosian, *Bardzr Hayk: Teghagrutiun, patmutiun ev sovorutiunner* [Upper Armenia: Toponymy, History, and Customs], 2 vols. (Vienna: Mekhitarist Press, 1925-1926); Hakovbos Tashian, *Hay bnakchutiune Sev tsoven minchev Karin: Patmakan-azgagrakan harevantsi aknark me* [The Armenian Population from the Black Sea to Karin: A Historical-Ethnographic Cursory Overview] (Vienna: Mekhitarist Press, 1921); Hamazasp Oskian, *Karin u Karnetsin ev Karno vankere* [Karin and the Karnetsi and the Monasteries of Karin] (Vienna: Mekhitarist Press, 1950);

The *vilayet* of Erzerum was one of the six Turkish Armenian or Western Armenian provinces of the Ottoman Empire, while the city of Erzerum (Garin or Karin) was and still remains the largest urban center in the area. The region's importance as a critical military, economic, and cultural crossroads has made it a theater of perpetual geopolitical fluctuations. One constant and fundamental factor, however, has outlasted the sway of all incursions, conquests, and natural disasters. That has been the tenacity with which the Armenian inhabitants have clung to this mother soil since antiquity. Adapting to the ever-changing social, economic, and political environment, the agrarian population of Karin remained deeply rooted in this land.

Because of the turbulence of the Armenian experience, there is no uninterrupted narrative history of Karin. Hence, oral tradition, with its unbroken chain extending from generation to generation, becomes ever more valuable. But this indigenous repository, which was preserved largely by the peasantry, was abruptly and irreversibly severed in 1915. Even the record of that great crime became the victim of a malevolent process.

The Plain of Karin

To the north of the elevated, once-walled fortress city of Karin/ Erzerum unfolds a picturesque plain, running about 35 miles east to west and 25 miles north to south (60 by 40 kilometers). It is bounded by high mountains and watered by the upper branch of the Euphrates River, the Sev Jur (Turkish: Kara Su, meaning Black Water) and its many tributaries. It is known by this name because when the ice breaks in the spring, the gushing water is very murky, but soon the river becomes sparkling clear and pure. The highland plain, at an altitude of around 6,000 feet or nearly 2,000 meters, has been described by early travelers and explorers as a sanctuary of never-before-seen hues and flowers, a bird

---

Ghazar Chareg, *Karinapatum: Hushamatian Bardzr Hayki* [Karin: Memorial Volume of Upper Armenia] (Beirut: Garin Compatriotic Unions of the United States and Lebanon, 1957); Hratch A. Tarbassian, *Erzurum (Garin): Its Armenian History and Traditions* ([New York]: Garin Compatriotic Union of the United States, 1975); Hovhannes Zatikyan, *Karin* (Erevan: Hayastan, 1992).

paradise (some 170 varieties were listed by Robert Curzon in the nineteenth century),[3] a water wonderland with brooks, streams, waterfalls, and hot springs, and an area rich in untapped mineral deposits. The plain of Karin has been called an open-air museum, containing numerous religious edifices, some of which may still be seen in a vandalized state.

In studying the foundations of rural Armenia, an imposing reality becomes evident, that is, the symbiosis of church and people. That deep-rooted relationship survived centuries of devastating foreign incursions and conquests. It was disrupted, however, by the unprecedented violence of the late nineteenth and early twentieth century. Then history suddenly stops in 1915 and its study is forced to conform to the dictates of an unrepentant regime. The extirpation of an entire people is followed by the attempted obliteration of a thick cultural layer and the digging in its place of a deep "memory hole."

Military and political vicissitudes notwithstanding, Armenians remained rooted for centuries in some 100 villages of the plain of Karin. The brief Russian occupation in 1828-29 was followed by an Armenian exodus prompted by growing socioeconomic oppression. The renewed exodus after the Russo-Turkish War of 1877-78 and the Hamidian massacres of 1895-96 resulted in a further decrease of the Armenian element. Toward the end of the nineteenth century, only about 50 villages were left, many with mixed Armenian and Turkish or else Islamized inhabitants.

The following Armenian composite sketch map of the villages of the plain of Karin is based on information provided by the last generation of Armenians to have lived there. The map happened to serve as a guide for a group of California educators who in 1995 set out to discover their roots in the historic Armenian provinces now in Turkey, especially in view of the fact that official publications and tourist brochures intentionally omit any reference to these places and their former inhabitants. For the

---

[3] Robert Curzon, *Armenia: A Year at Erzeroom, and on the Frontiers of Russia, Turkey, and Persia* (London: John Murray, 1854), pp. 150-54. The list is divided into the following categories: Raptores (Birds of Prey); Insepores (Perchers); Scansores (Climbers); Rasores (Gallinaceous Birds); Gralle (Waders); Palmepedes (Web-Footed Birds).

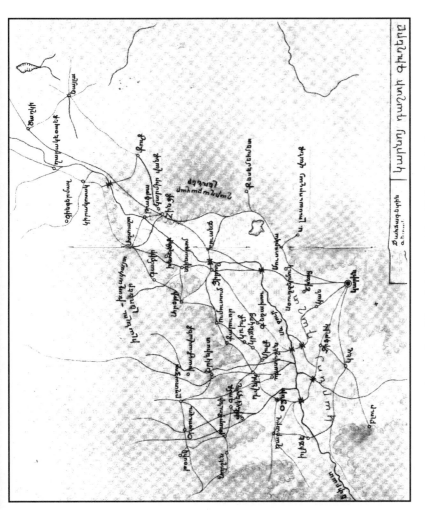

Armenian Sketch Map of the Plain of Karin

teachers, the pilgrimage to their parents' extinguished hearths became a contemporary lesson in political reality and reinforced the trauma caused by the state's concerted efforts to erase the record of the ages-long Armenian presence in the region.

The use of oral tradition and memoir literature provides vital information about village life. Moreover, these genres transcend changing boundaries, as demonstrated by comparative research into local, neighboring, and distant cultures. Unexpected commonalities and cross-cultural similarities between these peoples surface in mythology, philology, art, and other areas. A glimpse into the life of the villages of Karin supports that observation, while revealing the distinct colorama of Karin within the elusive rainbow of the universe. The village of Dzitogh may be used as the basis for examining the way of life in the plain of Karin/ Erzerum.

Dzitogh in the Plain of Karin

Dzitogh was one of the largest Armenian villages of the plain, having some 300 hearths. Located about a three-hours' walk from Erzerum city to the northeast, it was situated in a low-lying position between a large swamp and marshland called the *shamp* and one of the tributaries of the Euphrates. Water was always abundant, although the village did not have fresh water springs and depended on a large communal well known as *tulumba* for drinking water. From the vegetation in the shamp, the villagers made mats, cushions, and other products, used dried reeds to cover their roofs, and gathered feed for their animals. They hunted small animals and eggs amid the reeds and enjoyed an abundance of fish in the summer when the receding water level created numerous large and small ponds. The arable land of Dzitogh was insufficient for such a large village, especially as some fields were kept fallow on a rotating basis. There was a complex pattern of land ownership, with some peasants holding title to their plot of land, others being share-croppers on lands that had come under the control of Turkish notables called *begs*, and quite a few having no land of their own because of usurpation and therefore having to work as hired hands (*maraba*). The shortage of land and deteriorating socioeconomic and political conditions compelled many young men to seek their fortunes in Russia, where more often than not they were employed in or became proprietors of bakeries. Not all Dzitoghtsis were farmers but rather made their living as skilled artisans—blacksmiths, carpenters, masons, tanners, weavers, tailors, and weapon makers —and were also able to meet the needs of surrounding smaller settlements. One street in the northern quarter of Dzitogh had several shops and served as a marketplace.

There are several versions relating to the name of the village, one of the most popular being that it was the place where pilgrims left their horses (Dzi-togh or Dzi-toghk) en route to the nearby Monastery of Madnavank (Matnavank). It is believed that the village belonged to that monastery or to the more famed Karmir Vank near Hindzk (Hintsk), another large Armenian village. Whereas down through the centuries some of the nearby villages had converted to Islam and become Turkified, Dzitogh maintained its Christian faith. It was always alert to potential danger from the neighboring predominantly Muslim settlements of Tvanj, Dinarkom (Dinargom), and Umudum. The spirited nature of the Dzitoghtsis was well known in the area and just as the villagers proceeded cautiously in groups when journeying to and from the city, so, too, did the Turkish travelers go out of their way to avoid the bounds of Dzitogh.

Climate largely dictated the course of life in Dzitogh and all of the plain, which is surrounded by mountain ranges that give rise to the Euphrates and several other rivers. This high plateau is blanketed with snow for nearly half of the year. Before contemporary times, therefore, life virtually came to a standstill during the long winter, interrupted only by the foreboding howl of ravenous wolves. A mandatory lifesaving semi-hibernation set in during which the children were trundled off to school and, after the livestock was fed and the cows milked, there was much time for rest and story-telling. Those who ventured out for long had to wrap their heads in a heavy wool shawl known as a *ghapalagh* and to wear wool or leather gloves, several layers of socks and clothing, and an outer sheepskin coat with the wool turned inward and the hide, dyed red or yellow, turned outward. Not surprisingly, constant care had to be taken to avoid frostbite.

Nature dictating the course of life, there were recognized

omens portending all kinds of events. For example, when in early spring the stork returned to the village with a bloody rag in its beak, war was imminent; if a dead lizard or rodent was held, another massacre was in the making; if it was a husk or leaf, the grain harvest would be bountiful. When enjoying a respite from hard work or hard times, the light-hearted peasant would spontaneously break out into song and fervent dance, both the ceremonial solo and the energetic, intricate steps of group dancing. There was an incisive sense of humor and a tendency to make fun of the traits of the inhabitants of other villages as, for example, in the rhymed verse nicknaming the various villages in the plain of Karin. The accompanying table in Armenian gives sample stanzas sung in unison during a slow circle dance, accompanied by *daul* and *zurna* (drum and reed flute).

The Work Cycle

The spring and summer seasons were filled with arduous labor in a cycle of plowing, sowing, cultivating, reaping, and threshing, interrupted briefly by festivals, in the age-old pattern of eking out a living from Mother Earth. There were no trees in Dzitogh, where the majority of the peasantry was occupied in growing grain—wheat, barley, oats, and rye, while other villages were noted for their livestock and dairy culture or for their vegetable gardens and orchards. As soon as the ice cracked and the roofs were cleared of snow, the animals were taken out of their indoor stables to become acclimated to the brisk air. Following a light-hearted celebration with joyous dancing to the sound of the daul-zurna to mark the approach of spring and to beckon all to come out of their winter hideaways, the villagers began to prepare the hard ground with crude plows. When the time had come to sow the fields, which had to be completed by the end of April to have a full harvest, the eldest male member of the family would perform the ritual of facing to the east, blessing himself, and kissing the soil three times. Beseeching God, he would take handfuls of grain from his apron, scattering the seed right and left while exclaiming, "This one for the birds; this one for the government, this one for the church," and so forth until the last handful he claimed for his own family.

Stanzas of Light-Hearted Village Song

Երգրումը մեծ նահանգ է
Մեծ ու փոքր գիւղեր ունի
Թարձր ու գած տներ ունի
Երկար ու կարճ մարդիկ ունի
Ամէն մի գիւղ անունն ունի։

Արծթի բարձր տեղ է
Ճուրը հիւանդի դեղ է
Ուզող – ուզողին չեն տար
Այս ինչ անօրէն գեղ է։

խաչկավանձը ուխտի տեղ է
Թասմաձորը մահ տեղ է
Սրտաձորը սեյրի տեղ է
Քեսեմեհմետ թուրբի գեղ է
Իլինէ սեյրի տեղ է
Արեւ չունի Գինկերմազը։

Քուղայ բաճնող (երգրումցիք) բաղբեցիք
Ոսկոր կրծող ուստա Կանցիք
Ճիլ կրծող են Մուտուրիկեցիք
Գորտի մաճատ Գիխսախորցիք (կամ)
Կախ-կախ ոռ են Գիխսախորցիք
Ճիթոտ կոնակ Ուծուտուունգցիք
Սարի սինրիլ Րգտսաձորցիք (կամ)
Աղա շալվար Րգտսաձորցիք
Քելի ետմաղ Թարքունեցիք (կամ)
Թարեք չունէն Թարքունեցիք
Կուլյոտ կոնակ Գոմֆցիք
Պատ շարող են Պատուիշէնցիք (կամ)
Պարձենկոտ են Պատուիշէնցիք
Ուստա մարդիկ են Դվենիկցիք (կամ)
Փուտչուլուղ ուտող են Դվենիկցիք

Ղարաչուխայ Օձնեցիք (կամ)
Կախ-կախ շալվար են Օձնեցիք
Սիսլի հագնող Ղարարգցիք
Փուտչուլուղի գող Կեզագցիք
էշ վռնտող Չիֆֆթլիկցիք
Թորակ լիզող Սոուդջերմունգցիք
Մոթնւ չունեն Քեսեմեհմեթցիք
Թուրֆի վասատակ Թունաննցիք
Դիրասեկ ձակող Հնձացիք
Փոխսինդ ունող Տիննարգումցիք
Ճիգեար ունող Թասմաձորցիք
Երկար բոյով են Կրիչֆցիք
Երդիկ չունեն երկնիստացիք
Մարապա են Ալպըննեցիք
Ճերնուկ ունեն Իլինեցիք
Սումին ունող Ղոզլըֆիլիացիք
Կաթողիկ են Շիփեկցիք
Հալ գոցգող են Հեչուելելմեկցիք
Մատակ ունող են խաչկավանֆցիք
Լախսան ունող են Կրնննգցցիք
Սոված փորով են Ծանկեցիք
Գարի հաց ունող Կարպակեոպելցիք
Շաղկամ ունող են Շխնցիք
խորոզ խաղգնդ Ղուտենիցիք
Լոյսի տեղ է Կարմիր Վանճ
Կարմիի բարի տեղ է Գամպիր
Աղա շալվար են Չիթողցիք
Կախ շալվար են Չիթողցիք
Ճանն Չիթողցիք, եար Չիթողցիք
Ոսկի կախող են Չիթողցիք։

From May until August, the oxen and horses needed for farm-
work grazed in the village pasture, but almost all of the cattle
(the village had no sheep) were taken to Dzitogh's distant mountainous summer campsite (*yaila*) to escape the oppressive heat
and mosquito infestation and allow the cattle to graze in the
lush alpine meadows. There were also traditional celebrations at
the yaila, but it was necessary to be ever-alert to lurking danger
and sometimes to ward off wild animals and predatory bands
and nomads. In the village, meanwhile, some members of the
household weeded and tended the fields under the scorching
summer sun, and others, with sickles in hand, cut the grass and
plants that had grown tall in a part of the pasture and at the edge
of the shamp. Women and children raked and spread the grass
to dry and then bundled and carted it to the hay loft for winter
feed. At the end of July, the first grain to ripen was oats, followed by winter wheat, rye, spring wheat, and linseed. The
sheaths of grain were carted to the threshing ground (*gal*), where
the primitive rotating wheel was drawn by two oxen or cows or
a single horse. Then followed the separation of chaff from the
grain with pitchforks and sifters. The harvest had to be in by
September before the sudden arrival of winter. By that time the
herdsmen and helpers who had taken the animals to yaila returned with the cows, new calves, and large quantities of cheese
and butter for the winter season. Women of the household, aside
from daily baking in the clay oven—*tonir*—and other chores,
busily prepared all sorts of preserves—pickles, cabbage, tomato,
turnip, cured beef, boiled beef in lard-filled crocks, dried fruit,
and so forth.

The Household

In the plain of Karin, dwellings were built to keep out both the
cold and hostile elements, including the hungry wolf, the deadly
antagonist in local lore. Stone was used for building near the
foothills where it was abundant, while in the central plain clay
and sun-baked brick predominated as building materials. Stone
and wood pillars (some decorated with the carved initials of the
family) supported the roof beams, the spaces being filled with
branches and reeds, which were plentiful in the centrally located

great swampland, the shamp, which once had been a lake. The soil that was excavated in preparing the foundation of the house was used to cover the roof. The flat roofs of adjoining houses were connected, thus creating a continuous surface for an extensive block of homes, at a second-storey level. Small outlets in the roofs made possible communication among the inhabitants during the snowbound winter and at times of hostile intrusions. The stable, which was divided into separate corrals for each kind of animal, the hayloft or barn, and the storage room (*maran*) were all connected with the living quarters for pragmatic reasons —security, economy of space, and heating. The entrance to each structure was from an inner courtyard. In the storage room were both utensils and food for the household, including strung vegetables, garlic, and grain. The living quarters were divided into a baking room with its tonirs, a central room with an eating area, one or more rooms with high or low lofts for sleeping, a place for carpets, mats, and pillows, and often an upper room with cradles for the babes of the extended family.

Karin peasants dressed simply, reflecting their meager means. Men normally wore coarse dark pants with a blue jacket, a belt and perhaps a red shawl and a red fez. Like villagers everywhere they wore moccasin-like leather footgear known as *drekh,* which they removed at the entrance to the living quarters. Women dressed in long skirts with a red or dark-colored breast-plate, long sleeves, an ankle-length apron, and a decorated headpiece known as a *yazma.* Unlike Muslim women, they ordinarily did not wear a full body covering and veil.

Political and economic factors and deep-rooted traditional values may explain in part the fact that the Armenian rural family was the largest among all other surrounding ethno-religious communities. In the village, it was not at all uncommon for a family of more than thirty members of three or four generations to live under a single roof. While the family was patriarchal in structure, a widow or older woman would assume the role of head of household when there were no sons ready for that responsibility.

The multi-member household had a built-in division of labor. In the field, men toiled with primitive implements; a pair of oxen would spare many a back and raise the family's social status.

Women, too, worked from dawn to dusk, both in home and field. An unwritten code of family relationships with specific domestic chores was in place—cleaning and washing, child care, daily baking, cooking, preparing preserves and staples for winter, and weaving (larger families had their own loom). Even children participated in this hierarchy of labor by delivering simple meals to the workers in the field.

The tradition of village self-reliance was based on communal cooperation. Many families had barely enough milk for their daily needs, especially for culturing *matsun* (yogurt), a staple of the Armenian diet. Not having sufficient milk to make cheese and butter for themselves, the villagers developed an efficient economic practice known as *khab*. For a certain period of time, a cluster of families would deliver most of their daily milk to a designated family, which would be able to produce in bulk from the large volume of milk thus collected. Each participating family would then receive the final product proportional to the amount of milk contributed. The *hokhank* was another occasion for mutual help. When a peasant completed building the walls of a new house and the installation of the roof was next, the town crier would summon the entire village. Those who were able, with shovel in hand, hastened to cover the roof with a layer of soil nearly two feet thick. When the task was completed, a celebration with food, drink, music, and dance would ensue.

The Church

The history of Christianity in the plain of Karin leads back at least to the fourth century. According to local tradition, upon the return of Gregory the Illuminator from Caesarea, where he was ordained bishop and the first patriarch of the Armenian Church, he founded Karmir Vank (Red Monastery) near the village of Hindzk. Other sources show that the monasteries of Khachkavank, Lusavorchavank, and Karmir Vank were among the numerous religious edifices built or renovated in the tenth century during the predominance of the Bagratuni dynasty. Aside from their spiritual, intellectual, and educational mission, these institutions played an important socioeconomic role in village life. In the past, the peasantry not only worked the monastic

lands but also supplied the church with needed artisans, craftsmen, and supportive services.

Pilgrimages to these and other holy sites were a part of the
yearly cycle. After performing the religious rituals and making
their pious offerings and sacrifice (*matagh*), hundreds of peasants
would join in festivities, including games and dance. The city
folk of Karin, with their assumed haughty societal superiority,
their advanced educational-cultural establishments, and their
relative Westernization, nonetheless also perpetuated the traditions of folk culture. During certain *deri* (feast) days, families
in well-supplied carriages would travel to monasteries or retreats.
The Lusavorchavank was the closest to the city, and the lively
Koch Kochan stream in the valley nearby was the favorite
swimming, washing, and amusement site for young maidens and
women. Men preferred the deep natural pools below the rainbow
spray of the breathtaking Koch Kochan waterfall.

The center of Dzitogh was dominated by Church of the Holy
Mother of God—Surb Astvatsatsin. Unlike the city and other
villages, Dzitogh had no Catholic or Protestant families and
remained monolithically attached to the Mother Armenian Apostolic Church. There were normally six priests, one for each of
the parishes in the village. Remodeled with red stone on the
façade in 1860, Surb Astvatsatsin was a large edifice with three
altars adorned with pictures of the Madonna and Christ Child
and other holy personages. The interior was plastered white, with
lanterns hanging from the ceiling and the floor covered with
small carpets and mats, where individual families each had their
place. The church was proud and protective of the five manuscripts in its possession. As was the custom, men and women
separated upon entry into the sanctuary, with the women and
girls taking their place in the upper-storey loft. From the large
belfry, the peel of the church bells could be heard in neighboring
villages. The elderly attended morning and evening services
throughout the year, but the regularity of attendance by the
villagers was also dictated by the agricultural cycle.

Christmas and Easter were the most eagerly-awaited holidays.
On Christmas Eve, January 5, the choir strolled with lighted
candles through the village, stopping at individual homes to sing
Khorhurd Mets ev Skancheli (Great and Sublime Mystery) and

to receive sweets and gifts in return. On Christmas Day, the entire family was in church to celebrate the birth and baptism of Christ and to partake of Holy Communion and of the blessed holy water for health throughout the year. The eve of Lent provided a final opportunity for merrymaking, as the boys went from house to house, singing and dancing, and receiving *gata*, a sweetbread that would not be tasted again for seven weeks. On the first morning of Lent, an *akhloj*, a large onion pierced with seven chicken feathers, six white and one black, was hung from the skylight. Each week a white feather was removed until only the black one remained for Holy Week and until the celebration of the resurrection of Christ. Forty days after Easter, the feast of the Christ's Ascension (Hambardzum) was marked by picnics and circle dances to the shrill daul-zurna music outside the church.

All the milestones of life—birth and baptism, matchmaking and the contractual dinner (*khosk-kap*), the meticulously observed wedding rituals, and funerals drew together much of the village. An age-old custom, which in modified form still continues, is the mourning ritual for the deceased. Neighbors and relatives joined in preparing the deceased and accompanying the family to the church for the religious rites, to the cemetery for burial, and back home to share in the memorial meal—*pededi hats* or *hogejash*.

Education and Self-Defense

Schools were opened in the villages of the Karin plain in the second half of the nineteenth century. Beginning in the earlier part of the century, Roman Catholic and Protestant missionaries made their appearance in Erzerum, establishing their religious outposts for missionary and educational endeavors. Forbidden by Islamic law to proselytize Muslims, they turned their attention to the Christian Armenians. In due course, the city had the Catholic boys' school, the Catholic girls' school and kindergarten, the Protestant boys' school, the Protestant girls' school and kindergarten, and the French lycée, aside from the several national (*azgayin*) schools of the Armenian Church. The Sanasarian *Varzharan* (School or Academy), a bastion of contemporary learning since 1881, boasted a distinguished teaching staff and graduates.

The Sanasarian and other schools in Erzerum and in Constantinople were out of reach to almost all peasant families. An occasional fortunate village boy would be taken into a seminary. Particularly renowned was the Karmir Vank seminary (*zharangavorats*) where ecclesiastical and cultural luminaries such as Grigor Vkayaser, Grigor Magistros, Ohan Odznetsi, Anania Shirakatsi, Khosrov Andzevatsi, Grigor Narekatsi, Aristakes Lastiverttsi, and Mekhitar Sebastatsi (founder of the Mekhitarist order) are said to have studied or taught. The monastery also operated an orphanage, a hospital, and a sanctuary for lepers.

By the end of the nineteenth century, many villages in the plain had schools, though primitive and with a limited curriculum. In Dzitogh, there were both a boys' school with about 160 students and a girls' school with about 150 students. The boys' school situated on one side of the church was an impressive structure with red stones, while the more modest school for girls was located on the opposite side of the church. At first there were no desks or books, and each student had to bring a mat or sheepskin upon which to sit, but the teachers were progressive, graduates of the Nersesian Academy of Tiflis and of the Karmir Vank seminary, providing instruction in the Armenian and Turkish languages, mathematics, and religion. At the turn of he twentieth century and especially after the restoration of the Ottoman constitution in 1908, educational activity took a great leap forward. The United Armenian Alliance in Constantinople sponsored numerous schools in the provinces and for a time assumed responsibility for the boys' school in Dzitogh. The school was renovated and furbished with desks, chairs, and blackboards. The principal was Arshavir Shamlian, an enlightened pedagogue from Karin who had studied in Constantinople, and then Haik Zhamkochian from the Nersesian Academy. Other teachers, including Arsham Sirunian (the future Archbishop Mampre, Prelate of Egypt), were graduates of the Sanasarian Varzharan or Karmir Vank. The four-year curriculum included Turkish and Armenian, reading and composition, history, geography, mathematics, penmanship, art, and music. The girls' school was directed by Nvart Ghenevizian, who was assisted by three graduates of the Hripsimian school in Karin city.

The growing insecurity and oppression in the Ottoman Empire, coupled with the increasing enlightenment of the population, contributed to socio-political movements among the Armenians in the nineteenth century. Numerous societies were formed in Karin/Erzerum—educational, cultural, social—including establishments for counseling youth, married people, and alcoholics, and groups distributing political tracts relating to human rights and personal and collective emancipation. Several of these groups spilled over into the villages. In Dzitogh, one of the earliest political organizers was Aram Aramian, who was affiliated with the short-lived clandestine society known as Pashtpan Hayreniats (Protectors of the Fatherland). After the formation of regular Armenian political parties between 1885 and 1890, the village adhered overwhelmingly to the Dashnaktsutiun—Armenian Revolutionary Federation (ARF)—with two or three families being sympathizers of the Hnchakian party. Several ARF cells operated in the village, becoming most active during the lull in the agrarian cycle in late autumn and winter. They acquired and hid various kinds of guns and ammunition, with the activist Harutiun Der Vartanian becoming legendary for his resourcefulness in transporting weapons across the border from Russia. Party field workers from Karin city and from abroad always found a cordial welcome and haven in Dzitogh.

The villagers were put to the test in 1895, when at the end of October they could see dark smoke rising above the Armenian quarter of Karin. The massacres of 1895-96 had begun in Trebizond at the beginning of the month and spread rapidly to the towns and villages in Erzerum province. The youth of Dzitogh, resolving to defend the village, hastened to the empty irrigation canals that they used as trenches in face of the rabble approaching from Umudum and Dinarkom, where the few Armenian homes had been plundered and burned. After several days, the frustrated attackers withdrew, sparing Dzitogh and several Armenian settlements to its rear. Yet a few months later, gendarmes entered the village, searching for weapons and hauling a number of suspected revolutionaries off to prison for one to five years. In 1904 the village was again attacked and again resisted. It also dispatched a group of armed young men to defend the yaila from encroachments by neighboring Turkish settlements.

1915

The Young Turk revolution in 1908 offered hope to the Armenian villagers, as Garegin Pasdermajian (Armen Garo) was elected to represent the Armenians of Erzerum in the Ottoman Parliament. In this period of optimism, newspapers were published, reading rooms (*entertsaran*) and lecture halls (*lsaran*) were opened, and theatrical groups, composed mostly of students, made exchange appearances. For a brief time, the Armenians, together with many other elements in the Ottoman Empire, thought that the slogan, "Liberty, Equality, Justice," would ring true. But war clouds soon gathered again. Already during the Balkan wars in 1912-13, thousands of young Armenians from Erzerum province were drafted into the Ottoman army while many others evaded military service by slipping over the Russian frontier. The eruption of World War I in the summer of 1914 led to a general mobilization in the Ottoman Empire, taking even more young people away from the native village. Most foreign residents left Erzerum and the routes of communication were closed for Armenians. In August, the plain of Karin witnessed with great apprehension a two-minute solar eclipse. Foreboding became reality when Turkey openly joined the conflagration two months later at the end of October 1914.

Before the Turkish attack on Russia, the Ottoman Third Army concentrated in Erzerum province. In September, the 11th Division made Dzitogh its headquarters and forced the Armenian villagers to billet and feed the troops. Unheeded protests about offensive behavior toward women led many families to send younger women to neighboring villages or to the city. In November, the 11th Division left for the front but the respite was brief because the dreaded irregular mounted *chete* soon appeared to harass and plunder. What was worse, a command was received in mid-December for the population to leave the village in two days' time. Winter had already set in, the youth was gone, and few oxen and wagons remained. The villagers could do nothing more than to scatter to other Armenian villages in the plain or try to find shelter in the city. The military authorities turned Dzitogh into a hospital-sanitarium, as countless wounded and frostbitten soldiers from Enver Pasha's ill-fated Sarikamish campaign were brought there to languish and die. When in March of 1915 the villagers were allowed to return, they found corpses and utter devastation in every home. But with their ageless patience, they cleaned home and church and again prepared for the sowing season.

The hope of resuming a semi-normal existence was quashed at the beginning of May when gendarmes surrounded Dzitogh and ordered the inhabitants to prepare to depart. The confused villagers sent messengers to the Armenian prelacy in the city to give notice that they were prepared to resist, but the Armenian national administration cautioned against aggravating the situation for everyone and advised submitting to temporary relocation. Thus, the Armenians of Dzitogh, Dinarkom, Hindzk, Tvanj, and Artsuti were driven westward under a torrential rain lasting for three days. They were not allowed to halt until they had reached Ilija. The caravan was attacked by Muslim refugee *muhajir*s and chete bands, and as it moved toward Mamakhatun was joined by deportees from many other villages. The oxen and wagons were soon seized, and the elderly, weak, and children who could not continue the journey began to fall victim to the cruelty of the gendarmes. By the time the Dzitoghtsis arrived at a place known as Jebije Boghaz, the number of deportees from the province reached into the thousands. They were attacked repeatedly by chete bands and Kurdish tribesmen. Those who survived the murder and mayhem were driven onward to the plain of Erzinjan where the killing continued, now with machine guns. At the treacherous Kemakh gorge, nearly all of those still surviving were ambushed and cut down or thrown off the cliff into the Euphrates River. The same fate awaited the inhabitants of Karin city in June and July.

The caravans of death were routed to the "convenience stations" of the Syrian desert, Deir el-Zor, the intended definitive resting place for the Armenian nation, prepared by the xenophobic triumvirate of Talaat, Enver, and Jemal and their enthusiastic cohorts. The few Dzitoghtsis who completed the decimating trek and those who were taken into Turkish, Kurdish, and Bedouin households eventually made their way to far-flung places, where all that was left to them from the homeland were their memories of a seemingly unending cycle of life that had ended.

311

Plain of Karin from the City

Approach to Dzitogh

Dzitogh Boys' School

Artsuti Armenian Catholic Church

Dinarkom Armenian Apostolic Church

314

Plain of Karin Peasant Dress

Karin City Formal Dress

Karmir Vank near Hindzk

Lusavorchavank near Mudurga

✻ 13 ✻

KGHI VILLAGE EDUCATIONAL ASSOCIATIONS IN NORTH AMERICA BEFORE 1915

Isabel Kaprielian-Churchill

In the late nineteenth and early twentieth centuries, Armenian migrants to North America established secular organizations that they could easily transplant with them wherever they moved.[1] Political associations, cultural and charitable groups, athletic unions, and compatriotic societies, unlike churches, could readily accompany a highly mobile work force. Among these, the regional or compatriotic societies played a role in bringing together Armenians from the same hometown or village and served as agents for various activities in the new world. But they also had a major impact on the educational and economic life of the old country.

Regional associations were not unique to Armenians. Almost every ethnic group created such organizations often called *landsmannschaften*. The pre-1915 Armenian regional associations, differed, however, from those of most other ethnic groups. The main objective of Jewish, Italian, and Slovak societies was to facilitate the immigrant's adjustment to the new world. By banding together, village men could help one another defray costs during illness or burial and provide assistance to widows and orphans or they could act as credit unions and loan societies. By contrast, the Armenian compatriotic societies were grassroots efforts directed primarily towards the old world. According to the constitution and bylaws of three village societies from the district of Kghi (Keghi), the principal objectives were to help build and

---

[1] Parts of this essay will appear in Isabel Kaprielian-Churchill, *Like Our Mountains: A History of Armenians in Canada*.

maintain a school in the village and enhance the education and culture of village children. Even the names of their organizations reflect the emphasis on education: Darman Village Educational Society, Khoups Village Educational Union, Osnag Village Educational Union, Astghapert Educational Association.[2]

A Brief Background

Kghi was an administrative district (*kaza*) of the county (*sanjak*) and province (*vilayet*) of Erzerum. A mountainous region, it had but one town, Kghi-Kasaba, the district seat, and 363 large and small villages, including 51 Armenian villages.[3] Citing a 1908 study, Simon Vratzian, a prominent figure of the Armenian Revolutionary Federation (Dashnaktsutiun), estimated the population of the district to be around 60,000, with about half being Armenian. Based on Ottoman statistics for 1913-14, another study showed the Armenian population of Kghi to be about 20,000.[4]

Prior to the nineteenth century, monastic schools dominated the educational scene in Kghi.[5] During the nineteenth-century

---

[2] The records of the villages of Osnag, Astghapert, and Darman have been utilized for this article. I would like to thank Hasmig Injejikian and Eugenie Shehirian for their assistance in reading some of the handwritten passages.

[3] Arevigian, "Endhanur aknark me Kghiin vra" [A General Overview of Kghi], *Taregirk* [Yearbook] (Detroit: Compatriotic Society of Kghi, 1937), p. 19. In the same volume, "Kghii giughere" [The Villages of Kghi], p. 4, there are 302 villages with more than ten inhabitants listed in the kaza. The number of Armenian villages is given by Raymond H. Kévorkian and Paul B. Paboudjian, *Les Arméniens dans l'Empire ottoman, 1894-1915: La veille du génocide* (Paris: Éditions d'Art et d'Histoire, Arhis, 1992).

[4] Simon Vratzian, "Depi Kghi" [Towards Kghi], *Taregirk*, pp. 49-72. Arevigian, in the same yearbook, gives the population of the kaza as 100,000, with half being Armenian and the other half Muslim, mostly Kurds. He estimates about 5,000 Turkish soldiers and civil servants also lived in the district. The number of Armenians in Kghi is placed at about 25,000 by Malachia [Maghakia] Ormanian, *The Church of Armenia: Her History, Doctrine, Rule, Discipline, Liturgy, Literature, and Existing Condition*, trans. G. Marcar Gregory (London: A.R. Mowbray, 1910), p. 206. Kévorkian's statistics are based on the Ottoman Census of February 1913-August 1914, which probably did not include emigrants.

[5] Hratch A. Tarbassian, *Erzurum (Garin): Its Armenian History and Traditions*, trans. Nigol Schahgaldian (Boston: Garin Compatriotic Union of the United States, 1975), p. 29, wrote regarding Kghi: "These people's love of learning was reflected in their large network of Armenian schools, which worked in closed cooperation

zartonk or renaissance, major developments changed schooling throughout Anatolia. Armenian educational activity centered primarily in Constantinople under the auspices of the Armenian Apostolic Patriarchate, the American Board of Commissioners for Foreign Missions, charitable foundations, societies, and wealthy benefactors. In a vibrant intellectual and social milieu in the capital city, various groups took it upon themselves to teach working class adults, mainly provincials, to read and write. Driven by debt and unemployment, these migrants, mostly men, had temporarily left their towns and villages in the interior to earn a livelihood in "Bolis" for their families still in the village. They took on manual labor as *hamals* (porters), stevedores, janitors, and street cleaners.

In an effort to reach such people, men like Krisdosdour Ghazarosian and Haroutiune Markarian organized the Andznver (Altruistic) Society in the 1860s to offer free education to adults in the capital city, much in keeping with the tradition of the Mechanics Institutes in the Anglo-American world. For thirty years Ghazarosian lectured every Sunday to the poor and un-educated Armenians in Constantinople. Antranig Bey Gurjikian opened a Sunday School in 1864 to teach physical sciences to the working class.[6] When the men returned to their villages, they took their learning back with them and in this way acted as a conduit of literacy, disseminating knowledge to village young-sters. One of the most important consequences of this movement was to convince a generation of Armenians, who had school-age children that education was crucial to personal advancement and national progress.

Although useful, this method was not as effective as properly organized schools. Toward this end, sojourners in Constantinople, led by more educated compatriots, formed village educational associations with the express purpose of raising funds to sub-sidize a school in the village and to pay a teacher's salary. In the

---

with the education system in Erzurum. This was in keeping with the reputation it had earned in history as a center of education when it bore its ancient name of Khortzean."

[6] Kevork Sarafian, *History of Education in Armenia* (La Verne, CA: La Verne Leader, 1930), p. 205.

1870s, for example, men from the village of Khoups organized the Haikazian Educational Society to improve the education in their village.[7] In this way, they hoped the village children could benefit from the absence of their fathers, uncles, and brothers. Dedicated though such men were in helping their villages, their efforts were often lacking in leadership, direction, and continuity.

In 1880 three major educational societies in Constantinople —the Eastern Educational Association, the Araratian Association, and the Cilician Association—amalgamated to form the Hay Miatsial Enkerutiun (United Armenian Alliance), which took on responsibilities similar to a department of education: course and curriculum design, textbook preparation, teacher training and placement, and school construction and supervision.[8] In addition to the Alliance, societies taking the name Azganver Hayuhiats (Patriotic Armenian Women) and the Dprotsaser Tiknants (Phil-Educational Women) actively promoted the education of women and the training of women teachers. Led primarily by the Armenian intelligentsia, the middle class, and the urban elite, these societies worked indefatigably for almost fifteen years to promote universal education.

Well before the 1890s, rudimentary public schools were beginning to take shape in the district of Kghi. The town of Kghi-Kasaba and the village of Khoups established their schools in 1880 and were the first to work with the Alliance. Several villages, such Darman (Temran), Arek, and Astghapert (Astghaberd), also organized schools in cooperation with the Alliance. By and large, these early schools were for "the children whose parents could afford the tuition." According to an interviewee:

> Whoever could afford to pay the monthly dues at the school would send their children to school. We had 150 households in our village. We could have sent at least 200 children to school

---

[7] *Hushamatian Kghi, Khups giughi* [Memorial Volume of the Village of Khoups in Kghi], publ. of Khoups Compatriotic Union (Fresno, CA: Asbarez Press, 1968), pp. 124-25.

[8] Sarafian, *Education in Armenia*, pp. 216-35. For the Alliance and schooling, see Anahide Ter Minassian, "Sociétés de culture, écoles et presse arméniennes à l'époque d'Abd-ul-Hamid II," *Revue du monde arménien moderne et contemporain* 3 (1997): 7-30.

... in that school, there were hardly twenty-five or thirty boys. Little boys. Like a kindergarten, three to five years of age.[9]

In retaliation for Armenian demonstrations and protests in the 1890s, Sultan Abdul-Hamid dissolved the Alliance and disbanded its schools.[10] School closures coincided with the expulsion of thousands of Armenian sojourners from Constantinople, either to exile in foreign lands or to retreat back to their villages. The villages, in turn, were pillaged and plundered and the Kghi countryside lay in waste. With little or no outside capital and contending with economic ruin, families were obliged to concentrate on providing for their daily bread, reconstructing their houses, and restoring their farms. Left to their own resources at a time of general deprivation, villagers found it difficult to maintain their schools and pay their teachers. In 1899, Khoups villagers reluctantly closed their once highly respected school; instead of attending school, children were out "roaming the streets."[11] School buildings throughout the region deteriorated into "dark and damp places" and local education suffered a major setback. The Hamidian school closures, like the severe limitations on Armenian schools under the Russian tsars, had a debilitating impact on Armenians, especially school-age youngsters.

A villager from Osnag gives a sense of the abject conditions and the informal efforts of villagers to try to educate their children:

In the spring, about April, we no longer attended classes, but attended [sic] our goats, cows, and buffalo while they grazed. We did this all day, until November. In November we continued our education. The period of schooling was only four months a year. We were taught to read and write mainly, and to read some religious works, like the Psalms. . . . At this time, the village

[9] Oral interview with Mr. Arsen Pargamian, Cambridge, Ontario, Feb. 19, 1980.
[10] Sedrak Shahen, "Meroriats Kghien ampop gtserov" [A Brief Sketch of Kghi in Our Day], *Nor Kghi* [*New Kghi*], publ. of Reconstruction Association of Kghi, 1 (1964): 11-13. See also Great Britain, House of Commons, *Sessional Papers*, vol. 79 (1878-79), Reverend C.H. Robinson to Col. Trotter, April 10, 1892, p. 27.
[11] "Azgayin gortser Kghii" [National Endeavors in Kghi], *Hushamatian Kghi*, pp. 190-91.

hired a teacher. The name of our first teacher was Mesrob Der Vartanian, who was elected to this office by the villagers. We also had a small school which was built on the ground with no floor and was very primitive. It was also damp and gloomy. . . . The teacher left after only six months' service and the school continued on the same basis as before—without a teacher but with the help of villagers who could read and write.[12]

Following the Young Turk revolution in 1908, Armenians revived the United Armenian Alliance. Once again, the Alliance endeavored to reform and systematize education among Armenians. To administer to a population dispersed throughout the Ottoman Empire, its leadership divided the country into regions, each under the direction of a superintendent. The Alliance undertook to supervise the construction of schools, to train and to hire competent teachers and teaching assistants, to revise the curriculum to include the sciences, to restructure the grading system, and to prepare new textbooks. The Alliance also encouraged women to enter the teaching profession. Their services came at a crucial time, when large numbers of young men were emigrating either to work or study abroad or to escape conscription.

The United Armenian Alliance and other educational agencies financed their work largely from a tithe levied on Apostolic Armenians by the Patriarchate of Constantinople, from donations by charitable foundations and individuals, from tuition fees, and from funds sent by educational associations abroad. Although universal education was not yet achieved by the Ottoman Armenians, literacy was becoming progressively more accessible to a growing number of Armenian girls and boys.

According to the Alliance's Annual Report for 1911, it supervised fourteen schools in Kghi, with 1,179 students and 31 men and women teachers and teaching assistants.[13] An informant from Astghapert recalled the changes when the Alliance took over the operations of the village school:

[12] Ohannes Torosian, handwritten memoir, translated by his son, Hygus Torosian, St. Catharines, Ontario, in author's possession.

[13] *Miatsial Enkerutiune Hayots* [The United Armenian Alliance] (Constantinople: Matteosian, 1911), p. 42.

The Alliance entered Astghapert in 1910 . . . the [regional] head-quarters [of the Alliance] were in Erzerum. They sent us two men and two women teachers in 1910. Our school left the church building. The number of children increased when the Alliance arrived. Part of the expenses were paid by the Alliance and part by the parents. So with a very small monthly payment, you could send your children to school. Around 1910-11 there were approx-imately 100 to 150 students, both boys and girls, studying in our United Alliance school. . . . Some of the money came [to the Alliance] from America and some from the children's parents.

The Alliance paid the salaries, and the villagers had to cover the remaining expenses. Whoever had the means would pay, while those who were unable might arrange to have the money sent from America.[14] Not every village depended on the United Alliance to supervise its school. The village of Chanaghchi, for instance, was proud of its independence and of its close affilia-tion with Euphrates College in Kharpert. On the other hand, other villages, like Darman, had a school supervised by the Alliance and another run by Armenian Protestants. Regardless of whether they participated in the Alliance or not, almost all village schools depended on funds from abroad.

Founding the Associations

As depressed economic conditions and the need for capital com-pelled more Armenian agrarians to seek employment outside their home regions, as conscription in the Turkish army, especially during the Balkan wars in 1912-13, drove many young men out of the district, and as American industries beckoned immigrant workers, the number of Kghetsi immigrants in North America skyrocketed.[15] In 1911, before the start of the Balkan wars, Simon Vratzian found that 3,000 Armenian men from Kghi between the ages of 20 and 40 had left for work abroad. Many set out with the idea of returning to their village when the state of affairs improved, and as they gathered in different countries

---

[14] Arsen Pargamian interview, Cambridge, Ontario, Feb. 19, 1980.
[15] Vratzian, "Debi Kghi," p. 68.

these émigrés began to focus on the needs of their villages.[16] When he left his home, "the Armenian sojourner did not cut himself off from there. . . . He was anxious about his home country. . . . The comfort and safe life in foreign lands, and the pleasures of living and working in freedom inspired in him dreams of making his homeland like that some day."[17] Pinpointing their allegiance to one small place on the globe nurtured their allegiance to the village and was in turn continually nurtured by it. As men earned the "green dollars of America," their remittances to their families still in Kghi transformed the home scene. Kghetsi sojourners, "pouring out their sweat in the factories of North America" helped their families pay off debts, renovate and reconstruct ruined buildings, and purchase land and property. The *bandukht*s (sojourners) from Kghi revitalized the region. They also breathed new life into village education.

Aware of the educational deficiencies and anxious to improve the schooling of the village children, Armenian migrants in America, like their forefathers in Constantinople a few decades earlier, voluntarily created their own educational associations. Kghetsis first organized a regional association during the Hamidian school closures. Educated Kghetsis in America, such as Markar Baidarian, Mampre Toroian, and Arsen (Damkhajian) Diran, a graduate of Euphrates College and correspondent of *Mshak* (Cultivator), *Tsayn Hayreniats* (Voice of the Fatherland), and *Gotchnag* (Clarion) newspapers, joined forces during the late 1890s to form in Boston the first Kghi Educational Society in America.[18] The society's expressed goal was to mobilize Kghetsis in the United States, Canada, and Mexico to raise funds to develop schooling in all of Kghi.

---

[16] For an account of sojourner mentality, see Robert F. Harney, "Men without Women: Italian Migrants in Canada, 1895-1930," in *The Italian Immigrant Woman in North America*, Betty Coroli, Robert F. Harney, Lydio Tomasi, eds. (Toronto: Multicultural History Society, 1978), p. 84.

[17] Arsen Kitur [Gidour], *Patmutiun S. D. Hnchakian Kusaktsutian, 1887-1962* [History of the S(ocial) D(emocrat) Hnchakian Party, 1887-1962], vol. 1 (Beirut: Social Democrat Hnchakian Party, 1962), p. 220.

[18] See, for example, *Hairenik*, Dec. 9, 1905. See also Levon Srabian, "Kani me ej Levon Srabianen" [A Few Pages from Levon Srabian], in *Hushamatian Kghi*, p. 217.

Eventually, as more migrants arrived in America, the Kghi Educational Society gave way to separate village associations. The Khoups Village Educational Union, one of the first village associations started up in Providence, Rhode Island, in 1900.[19] The Darman society followed in 1902 with headquarters in Troy, New York; Astghapert began in 1903 in Providence; Kghi-Kasaba started in Boston in 1904; and in the same year, Osnag villagers founded their organization in Brantford, Ontario.

Records indicate that emigrants of at least twelve Kghi villages created these independent associations, each with its own constitution, by-laws, accounts, and executive bodies.[20] If the figure of 20,000 Armenians is accepted for the district of Kghi, then twelve associations represents one per 1.666 Armenian inhabitants. Further, if the school-age population is calculated, the number of village educational associations serving the Armenian population of Kghi is quite impressive.

For the people of Kghi, education and emigration were closely linked. Two Protestant schools in Kghi—in Kghi-Kasaba and Darman—played a leading role in education in the district. These and other schools in the region, such as those in Khoups and Chanaghchi, became feeder schools to Euphrates College in Kharpert. Some graduates of the college returned to Kghi to teach, while many more followed their classmates to America. For Kghetsis, Kharpert and Euphrates College became the "gateway" to America.

Settlement in America expanded the newcomer's vision of modernity, of learning, and of potential. Without doubt, the impetus to organize educational associations was affected by the quality and accessibility of education in North America. But the concept and the fundamental initiative did not grow out of the North American or even the diasporan environment. Rather, formation of educational associations in the new world represented continuity with a pre-existing tradition. Reverend Suren

---

[19] See Very Reverand Suren Papaghian, "Khupse ev ir hayrenaktsakan miutiune" [Khoups and Its Compatriotic Society], in *Hushamatian Kghi*, p. 151.

[20] See *Hairenik*, 1900-1910. Almost every issue of the newspaper during these years published appeals for membership by various educational and patriotic societies.

Papaghian, in his account of the Khoups Union in America, asks rhetorically: "Is not the Haikazian Education Society of Khoups, founded in Constantinople in 1870, the forerunner of the Khoups Village Educational Union, founded in Providence, Rhode Island in 1900?"[21] His point is well taken. The commitment to organize educational societies when away from home was rooted in a well-established precedent among Armenians in the Ottoman Empire long before the great migration to North America. The father had sojourned in Constantinople well before the son sojourned in America.

Similarly, the diasporan commitment to promote universal schooling in the homeland was an extension of a legacy that had begun earlier in the Ottoman Empire: the spread of education to the masses, the working classes, and the rural countryside. In short, the drive to raise the general level of learning of the Armenian people in the Ottoman Empire. Three major factors, then, propelled these educational societies: the growing demand for popular education among Armenians in Turkey, the need for outside capital to build and maintain the schools, and the heightened emigration of Armenian villagers to the Balkans, Egypt, England, and especially to North America.

Structure and Function
of the Educational Associations in North America

Émigrés from each town or village, regardless of where they settled, participated in these associations. Before 1915, for instance, the Astghapert Educational Association had branches in Boston, Massachusetts, East St. Louis, Illinois, Providence, Rhode Island, Brantford and St. Catharines, Ontario, Batum on the Black Sea coast of the Russian Empire, Kghi-Kasaba, and, of course, in the village itself. Osnag, a relatively small village, succeeded in setting up branches in Providence, East St. Louis, Brantford, and St. Catharines.

The structure was democratic and egalitarian, since each dues-paying member had one vote. Old country class distinctions soon

---

[21] Papaghian, "Khups ev ir hayrenaktsagan miutiune," p. 153.

vanished in industrial North America—the great leveler—where the son of the rich villager was on par with the son of the poorest peasant, especially if they worked side by side in the same factory. Religion and politics also did not enter the dynamics, at least not critically. Apostolics and Protestants, Dashnakists and Hnchaks, generally cooperated for the benefit of the village, which remained the nucleus of their loyalty.

While membership in the associations was open to both men and women, most of the members were men, and young men at that, reflecting the newcomer society itself. The predominance of Kghi men in America was particularly evident after 1912, when the outbreak of the Balkan wars stepped up conscription in the Ottoman Empire and resulted in a growing exodus of young Armenians. As sojourning and mobility of Kghetsi men intensified, the organizations took on greater fluidity. Members could belong regardless of where they were living and working, and each branch roster could vary from year to year, reflecting the mobility of migrant workers.

Each organization elected a central executive and established a practice of rotating headquarters to different cities. The headquarters changed according to the willingness or numerical strength of the branch prepared to assume additional responsibilities. For example, from 1904 to 1906, the Osnag headquarters were located in Brantford; in 1907, they were transferred to East St. Louis. The establishment of branches and the movement of the executive among them provides a map of village migratory patterns, the availability of jobs, and the high incidence of mobility among Kghetsis. Under such circumstances, the international boundary between Canada and the United States virtually disappeared.

Usually an annual meeting/dinner brought members together from different cities to renew relationships, to discuss fundraising activities, and to negotiate among themselves about sending money to the village. Such an organizational structure gave villagers opportunities for leadership and high-profile status, and their annual gatherings provided a venue for social activities, encounters with potential spouses, and information about job possibilities.

The monthly dues of 25 cents—the price of a good meal in

a restaurant—were augmented by larger sums raised at dinners, raffles, picnics, and the *handes* (program or concert). In 1905, at the Astghapert Association's first *handes* in Canada, M. Zakarian spoke about the value of education and S. Khatchigian started the fundraising. In fifteen minutes, the report proudly noted, the organization collected $222.75. Some members contributed as much as $15 and everyone present, even those who did not have much, made a donation, none less than $5.[22] In 1906 the Brantford chapter of the Osnag Union received $31 in dues from its twenty members; while a year earlier it raised $120 at a concert.[23]

Money was constantly moving from North America to Kghi. In 1908, for instance, the Osnag group sent $1,000 to the village—a very large sum by Anatolian standards.[24] With such donations the members of the associations confirmed their commitment to the village, but they also strengthened the village's dependence on them, a fact that became more controversial as more young men settled in America.

By and large, the money sent to the village was modest compared with the amounts that were banked in North America. From 1902 to 1905 the Darman society built up a treasury of $1,056 but sent only $315 to the village, albeit still a substantial sum in Anatolia and probably enough to pay for the annual school costs.[25] Since its inception in 1900, the Khoups Union sent the Alliance $2,512 (covering the total school expenditures) but kept approximately $20,000 in its treasury in order to build a secondary school in the village. In 1910 the Osnag Union boasted about $1,227 in the regional coffers but sent only $97.57 to the village, despite a general appeal to fund a teacher-training course in Kghi-Kasaba in the summer of 1911.[26]

That the associations kept a tight rein on their funds in North America raises issues about the power of the purse and the collective control over the village school. Undoubtedly tensions

---

[22] Reported in *Hairenik*, Nov. 11, 1905. In Astghapert Association records.

[23] Osnag Village Educational Union records, in the author's possession.

[24] Ibid.

[25] Darman information from *Hairenik*, April 22, 1905.

[26] Osnag Village Educational Union records.

arose between the membership in North America, mostly young men, earning relatively large sums in the factories and mills, and the board of trustees in the village, mostly older men embedded in pre-industrial agrarianism. As the North American membership increased in numbers and as their treasuries swelled with American dollars, members used the power of the purse—at first with hesitation, then with growing confidence—to control school policy in the village. They had something to say about the hiring of teachers and school construction and renovation. They even commented on the curriculum. If a total shift in power did not occur, at least the village hierarchy was forced to consult with members an ocean away before making major decisions.

It is not clear what the operating relationship was among the North American associations, the village school boards, and the United Armenian Alliance. As the educational structure was in a transitional stage, it appears that each village made a separate contract with the association and the sides worked from there. According to an interviewee, a group of sojourners undertook to form a branch of the Astghapert Educational Association in Canada in 1910 in order to bring the Alliance into the village:

> Let's say that annually they [Canadian sojourners] could raise $100 or $150 here. At that time they worked really hard to earn $1 a day [in local factories primarily]. Sometimes they would make $7 or $8 a week. So if there were 50 or 60 Astghapertsi members of the association, they would deduct a bit from their income and they would send that money to the United Alliance headquarters in Erzerum, earmarked for the village school.[27]

Like the Astghapert Association, the Khoups Union sent money via the United Armenian Alliance, whereas the Osnag Union dispatched its contributions directly to the village.

Impact

Essential as these funds were, most villages depended on outside professional guidance, and that came largely from the Alliance.

---

[27] Arsen Pargamian interview, Cambridge, Feb. 19, 1980.

As for the administration of the schools, the educational super-intendent in the region in 1910, M. Minasian, a graduate of Harvard and Yale, emphasized: "The schools were free from encroachments by the local authorities. In the contracts agreed upon between me and the local school boards, I made it specifi-cally clear that they had no right to interfere in the affairs of the school. The principal of the school was the only responsible person in these matters, and he was appointed by me only."[28] The Armenian Apostolic Church continued to maintain control over non-Protestant schooling, but a clear trend was afoot to modernize and secularize the curriculum and to establish a school system and an efficient administration without political inter-ference and nepotism.

In 1910-11 the Alliance reported that in the province of Erzerum, which included Kghi, it was supervising 17 schools, 2 nurseries, 55 teachers, and approximately 2,000 elementary school students. The administration anticipated that in the following year, three more Kghi schools would come under its wing, which, together with the school in Palu, would boost the student enroll-ment to 2,500.[29]

In 1911, Psak Vardapet Ter-Khorenian, the Apostolic head of the region, reported that he had 48 schools in Kghi under his jurisdiction. The priest's report is noteworthy because it gives an idea of the spread of education among the masses in the interior. At the turn of the century, most of the 27 schools in Kghi were closing down. Ten to twelve years later, 48 schools were func-tioning under the jurisdiction of the Apostolic Church, most in conjunction with the United Alliance and at least 2 schools were operating under Protestant auspices. Thus, in 1911-12 no fewer than 50 schools were functioning in the region, that is, one school for every 400 Armenian inhabitants.[30]

In some villages, the number of teachers and the educational

---

[28] Sarafian, *History of Education*, p. 221, quoting from a letter to him by M. Minasian, superintendent of the district of Upper Armenia (Bardzr Hayk) in 1908 and shortly thereafter.

[29] "Hayots Miatsial Enkerutiants Karno shrjanak, 1910-1911" [The United Armenian Alliance's Karin Region, 1910-11], in *Nor Kghi* 1 (1964): 42.

[30] According to Sarafian, *Education in Armenia*, p. 210, the 27 schools operating in Kghi in 1901 had 1,703 students. See also *Nor Kghi* 2 (1965): 34.

budgets doubled and even tripled before 1915. Astghapert, for example, which had paid its one teacher 20 lira before its link with the Alliance, employed three teachers with a budget of 68 lira by 1910-11. Eventually "one school became two and one teacher became four" and enrollment increased to 80 boys and 52 girls, this in a village with only about 450 Armenians in 1914.[31] On a broader scale, progressive Kghetsi leaders, who recognized that the elementary schools were serving as feeder schools to Euphrates College in Kharpert, were planning for the construction of one and perhaps two secondary schools of their own.

Such activity and progress by a minority population aroused alarm and suspicion among the Turkish authorities, for they well understood the meaning of the Armenian conviction that "education is our salvation." In spite of serious constraints imposed by the Turkish government, the educational ferment of the pre-genocide period represented an explosion in rural schooling. Within a period of ten to twelve years, this revolution managed to raise the literacy level of the Kghi countryside. In these sweeping changes, the village educational associations played a critical role by subsidizing the grass roots movement of rural education.[32] In turn, the villages were drawn into the orbit of nascent bureaucracies that provided administrative, pedagogical, and technical assistance.[33] In a deep sense, the establishment of schools with somewhat regular timetables, the selection of teachers by merit whenever possible, and the fostering of an increasingly efficient administration helped to initiate one of the first modern institutions on the Armenian Plateau. This, too, was a profound revolution.

By formalizing and internationalizing their organizations, villagers, scattered about in foreign lands, enlarged the village frame of reference. When Arakel Eghigian traveled to East St. Louis to join his father, the older man took him by the arm and

---

[31] "Hayots Miatsial Enkerutiants Karno shrjanak," pp. 42-44. See also Tigran Paghtoyan [Dikran Baghdoian], "Astghaberdi patmutiune" [History of Astghapert], handwritten account, no date, p. 26, in author's possession.

[32] In 1911, Simon Vratzian noted that every Armenian village in Kghi had a school because of the money sent by her "sojourning sons." See "Debi Kghi," p. 59.

[33] For instance, see Sarafian, *Education in Armenia*, pp. 221-22.

announced, "Kghi is here, my son." In the same vein, Brantford, Ontario, a busy, industrial town, was known as the capital city of the village of Astghapert. By 1914 the village association of Khoups boasted twelve chapters.[34] Strewn like the villagers themselves, from country to country, across mountains and oceans, these contact points inevitably expanded the village's vision of the world. The village social structure with its far-flung kith and kin networks annexed, in a psychological sense, cities in distant lands, and this contact inevitably helped prepare village mentalities for new ideas from a modern, industrial, and urbanized world.

The sojourners were aware of the acculturation they themselves were experiencing in America and of the impact of their American sojourn. In this respect, for example, a young villager was taken by his village friends and relatives to "Galt College," which turned out to be the Galt Malleable Foundries. For him it became the school of hard knocks where he learned about the workers' struggle, strikes, walkouts, and resistance to exploitation. As the villagers came into contact with society in Canada and the United States, as they attended night school, studied English, participated in the struggle for workers' rights, learned about democracy and republicanism, they were invariably transformed. Having experienced the fruits of liberty in North America, having viewed the potentialities of the industrial revolution, and having seen the opportunities of schooling in the new world, the villagers themselves changed. Their metamorphosis shook the home region, as villagers disseminated new ideas to their countrymen still in the native land and those who returned carried back scientific and technological methods and advances.

The elasticity between old world and new had many dimensions. American enlightenment had planted powerful roots in Turkey well before the migration of the Armenian rural popula-

---

[34] Population statistics for Khoups vary. In *Hushamatian Kghi*, p. 178,185 households are shown for 1914. The figure of 300 households and 1,500 people, including sojourners, is given by Hovhannes Pashikian, "Avandakan ev zhamanakagits khoher Khupsi masin" [Traditional and Contemporary Reflections about Khoups], *Nor Kghi* 1 (1964): 33-34. See also "Kghi-Khups giughi hayrenaktsakan miutian 65-amiak gortsuneutian" [Sixty-Five Years of Activity of the Khoups Village Compatriotic Union], written by the Union's executive committee, in *Hushamatian Kghi*, p. 171.

tion to the West. Long before the massacres of 1894-96, the Young Turk revolution in 1908, and the Balkan wars in 1912-13, America had penetrated into the heart of the Armenian Plateau. The American Board of Commissioners for Foreign Missions and its missionaries had imported elements of the American dream, of individualism and reform, and of the Protestant ethic into this backward area. Euphrates College and the city of Kharpert were, for the people of Kghi, the early channel to America, both figuratively and realistically. Once in America, the newcomers encountered a world governed by Protestants. Protestant values and American attitudes inevitably influenced the early settlers, especially young people who attended American schools and colleges and became leaders in the Armenian-American community. While the educational societies tried to maintain and strengthen the link with the old world and while these organizations helped the newcomers retain their identity in America, the interaction between immigrant and environment and the between the old world and new constituted as momentous a factor in the psychology of Kghi as they did of her sons in North America.

One aspect of this link and one of the most imperceptible characteristics of these associations was their secularism. The village educational societies were secular and maintained a separation between religion and civic matters. Education was under public tutelage, and science, rationalism, and the rule of law were eroding faith, revelation, and the Word of the Bible. Had the Genocide not overwhelmed and destroyed the Armenian presence in the Ottoman Empire, associations like the United Armenian Alliance would eventually have brought this secular dimension to a homeland where people still identified themselves primarily in religious terms. The educational associations contributed, then, to a massive reformation of the villages in three ways: they strengthened rural education by providing funds; they prepared the traditional rural mentality for the inflow of new ideas; and they transported elements of modernity and progress back to the countryside. As a result, the home villages did not remain the isolated little hamlets on the Kghi mountainsides but evolved rather as an integral part of a vast and dynamic transoceanic movement of men, money, and ideas.

The village educational associations can be examined in

another context. Men and women from Kghi saw themselves as Kghetsis. Their *erkir* (homeland) was Kghi. No mode of discourse existed in the village whereby they saw themselves primarily as Armenians, except in religious terms. While they may have been identified in America as Armenians, they still identified each other, among themselves, by their clan, their village, and their region. As the educational associations were based on geography—in a specific place on the globe—they differed from political and religious affiliations. The political parties, which upheld the concept of the larger nation, of pan-Armenianism, denounced such regionalism as agents of internal fragmentation and divisiveness. But, by cutting across political lines, the associations mitigated the stridency and eased the partisanship of opposing factions. By affirming loyalty to the home region, they were instruments of cultural maintenance, every bit as effective and profound as the political parties.

The village educational associations also represent a democratizing or at least a proletarianizing of two elitist traditions among Armenians. The first of these was the issue of charity and philanthropy. For centuries, wealthy Armenians had assumed the responsibility of helping their less fortunate compatriots. They had built churches, schools, hospices, and orphanages.[35] During the twentieth century, a democratization of this honored tradition evolved. The indigenous model of philanthropy percolated downwards, as ordinary peasants, unskilled laborers in American factories, imbued with a powerful sense of duty, collectively took up the challenge of communal self-help. Secondly, wealthy Armenians in the vast Armenian Diaspora had for generations donated great sums for schools and churches in the homeland. This Diaspora/homeland relationship was enlarged in the twentieth century when working class villagers, none wealthy or famous, collected funds, penny by penny, dollar by dollar, in North America to remit back to the village to build and enhance their schools.

This emphasis on education attests to the widespread convic-

---

[35] For an account of Armenian philanthropy and capitalism, see Boghos Levon Zekyan, *The Armenian Way to Modernity: Armenian Identity between Tradition and Innovation, Specificity and Universality* (Venice: Supernova, 1997).

tion that education was a vital mechanism not only of social mobility but, more important, of national development. In North America, leaders of the educational associations were progressive men; some were relatively well educated and had themselves benefited from the opportunities offered by the Armenian Apostolic Church, Protestant missionaries, or secular authorities. Now, the rank and file—literate and illiterate, skilled and unskilled—assumed the responsibility, through these associations, of bringing "civilization" and enlightenment to their home regions. For these humble men, the associations symbolized their faith and hope in reforming, uplifting, and freeing an oppressed people.

336

Darman Church Ruins, 1974

Khoups Church Ruins, 1974

338

Astghapert Church Ruins, 1974

❊ 14 ❊

THE DEATH OF ARMENIAN KARIN/ERZERUM

Simon Payaslian

The political situation in Erzerum *vilayet* (province) was relatively calm before the summer of 1914, allowing the Armenians an opportunity for political, economic, and cultural revival after years of persecution and economic decline. The local population expected the region soon to recover its historic role as a center for international trade, linking the Black Sea ports to the eastern vilayets and to Persia, as French engineers had commenced work on the mountainous Trebizond-Erzerum road.[1] The Armenians hoped that the Reform Act of February 8, 1914, signed by Said Halim Pasha, the Ottoman Grand Vizier and Foreign Minister, and Konstantin N. Gulkevich, the Russian Chargé d'Affaires in Constantinople, would further improve conditions. They remained cautiously optimistic that the promised administrative reforms and economic reinvigoration would eventually ease Turko-Armenian tensions and assuage old and new communal grievances.[2] Notwithstanding previous experiences of Ottoman tyranny and massacres, which had left indelible imprints on the collective memory of the nation, the Armenians of Erzerum continued to work toward ameliorating their lot.

---

[1] Ghazar Chareg, *Karinapatum: Hushamatian Bardzr Hayki* [Karin: Memorial Volume of Upper Armenia] (Beirut: Garin Compatriotic Unions of the United States and Lebanon, 1957), p. 460.

[2] Simon Vratzian, *Hayastani Hanrapetutiun* [Republic of Armenia] (Paris: A.R.F. Central Committee of America, 1928; repr., Erevan: Hayastan, 1993), pp. 5-6; Richard G. Hovannisian, "The Armenian Question in the Ottoman Empire, 1876-1914," in Richard G. Hovannisian, ed., *The Armenian People from Ancient to Modern Times*, vol. 2: *Foreign Dominion to Statehood: The Fifteenth Century to the Twentieth Century* (New York: St. Martin's Press, 1997), p. 237.

In February 1914, Rostom (Stepan Zorian), a founder of the Armenian Revolutionary Federation, the Dashnaktsutiun, wrote to a party leader, Simon Vratzian (Vratsian), in Boston to urge the Armenian communities in the United States in general and the Karin compatriotic societies in particular to extend financial support for the New Sanasarian School (*Varzharan*). Rostom pointed to the enthusiasm generated among the Armenian youth toward the school and expressed the hope that once financial difficulties were overcome the Erzerum Armenians would face a much brighter future. If allowed to prosper, he added, they would turn their homeland into a paradise. He remained skeptical on two points, however, doubting that the Turks would allow such advancement and that the European powers and Russia would serve as protectors of the Armenians. Rostom noted prophetically that the current negotiations in Constantinople for Armenian reforms seemed no more than a game, which potentially could lead to a new round of persecutions and massacres.[3]

The Eclipse over the Plain of Erzerum

The outbreak of World War I on July 28, 1914, rapidly altered the political and economic environment in Erzerum. As the Young Turk government under the leadership of the triumvirate of the Ittihad ve Terakki (Committee of Union and Progress; CUP), Mehmed Talaat Pasha, Ismail Enver Pasha, and Ahmed Jemal Pasha, commenced mobilization for the war, repressive measures against Armenians intensified across the empire. On August 1, the prelate of the Apostolic (Gregorian) Church at Karin, Bishop Smbat Saatetian (Smpad Saadetian), reported to the Armenian Patriarchate of Constantinople:

> On Tuesday, the 29th of July [1914], the authorities started to collect from the people carts, oxen, horses, and foodstuffs, without paying anything in return. Also, from the Armenian and

---

[3] Rostom to Simon Vratzian, Feb. 12, 1914, in *Rostom: Namakani* [Rostom: Collection of Letters], ed. and comp. Hrach Tasnapetian [Hratch Dasnabedian] (Beirut: Hamazkayin Press, 1999), pp. 611-12. In another letter to Vratzian on April 2, 1914 (pp. 613-14), Rostom expressed his premonition that 1914 would be a decisive year.

Turkish merchants of the city, all goods at hand—flour, grains, rice, sugar, and cotton worth hundreds of pounds—were taken without their value being paid. There is no doubt that these military preparations are being in anticipation of a war with Russia. . . . We are already receiving news of difficulties from Khnus, Terjan, and the villages on the Plain [of Karin].[4]

During the same period, at its Eighth General Congress held in Erzerum, July 28-August 14, the Dashnaktsutiun party resolved that Armenian subjects of the Ottoman and Russian empires should remain loyal to their respective governments.[5] There were, however, no assurances for the physical protection of the Armenians in either empire. The Armenian population therefore received the Ottoman conscription orders with a sense of extreme anxiety, as military service would remove nearly all men between the ages of 19 and 45 from their communities, leaving their families unprotected against persecution and plunder. And mass arrests and massacres soon followed.

In late August 1914, the local authorities arrested and ordered two Armenian leaders, E. Aknuni (Khachatur Malumian) and Vahan Minakhorian, to leave Erzerum for Constantinople and Samsun, respectively.[6] Petitions to the local government and to Minister of the Interior Talaat to revoke the orders proved futile. Speculations regarding the nature and intention of these orders —whether they would remain limited to a small number of leaders or else signified a broader scheme for mass arrests and

---

[4] Zaven Der Yeghiayan, *My Patriarchal Memoirs*, trans. Ared Misirliyan, and annotated Vatche Ghazarian (Barrington, RI: Mayreni Publishing, 2002), p. 39.

[5] The Ittihadist leaders sought guarantees from the Dashnaktsutiun that if Turkey entered the war the party would mobilize the Armenians in the Caucasus to rebel against Russia and thereby facilitate Turkish advances across the frontier. The Dashnaktsutiun rejected this strategy, instead proposing that Turkey remain neutral. See Vratzian, *Hayastani Hanrapetutiun*, pp. 7-10; Richard G. Hovannisian, *Armenia on the Road to Independence, 1918* (Berkeley, Los Angeles, London: University of California Press, 1967), pp. 41-42; Vahan Minakhorian, *1915 tvakane* [The Year 1915] (Venice: Mekhitarist Press, 1949), pp. 66-71; K. Sasuni, *Trkahayastane A[rajin] ashkharhamarti entatskin (1914-1918)* [Turkish Armenia during the F(irst) World War (1914-1918)] (Beirut: Sevan Press, 1966), pp. 23-24, 26-30.

[6] Minakhorian, *1915 tvakane*, pp. 90-93. See also excerpt of a letter by Bishop Saatetian, in Der Yeghiayan, *My Patriarchal Memoirs*, p. 40.

persecutions—further heightened Armenian apprehension.[7]

Moreover, as the war escalated, the commerce and economy of Erzerum plunged into depression. The Armenian merchants were burdened by discriminatory commercial and exorbitant taxation policies, and Armenian peasants across the great plain came under constant attack by the mounted irregular *chete* and Kurdish bands. Petitions to local, provincial, and central government authorities for remedial measures failed to alleviate the situation.[8] In fact, the Armenians interpreted the solar eclipse on August 21, which for two minutes shrouded the entire region in total darkness, as a bad omen of things to come.[9]

Despite its economic difficulties, the region of Erzerum assumed an enormous geostrategic significance for the Ottoman army when the empire entered the war as an ally of Germany in October 1914.[10] Large military contingents had moved to Kharpert and to Erzerum, while cavalry regiments of between 8,000 and 10,000 men were assembled in Arjesh and the plain of Abagha to the south of Erzerum.[11] Within a few months, the number of Turkish troops stationed in the Erzerum region had risen to nearly 100,000, the burden of service and provisions falling largely on the Armenian peasants.[12] In October, the government commenced search and seizure operations for weapons

---

[7] Rostom to Polso Pat[askhanatu] Marmnin [Constantinople Res(ponsible) Body], Aug. 24, 1914, from Dashnaktsutiun Archives, 103/32, in *Rostom: Namakani*, pp. 617-18; Chareg, *Karinapatum*, p. 458. See also a letter of Sarkis Barseghian to Mikayel Varandian, editor of *Droshak* (Geneva), Sept. 14, 1917, reprinted in Chareg, *Karinapatum*, pp. 461-63; Jean Naslian, *Les mémoires de Mgr. Jean Naslian, Évêque de Trébizonde*, 2 vols. (Vienna: Mekhitarist Press, 1951), vol. 1, p. 150.

[8] Johannes Lepsius, *Rapport secret sur les massacres d'Arménie* (Paris: Payot, 1918; repr. Beirut: Hamazkayin Press, 1980), p. 59; Chareg, *Karinapatum*, p. 463.

[9] Chareg, *Karinapatum*, p. 463.

[10] Levon Chormisian, *Hamapatker arevmtahai mek daru patmutian* [A Panaroma of One Century of Western Armenian History], vol. 3 (Beirut: Sevan, 1975), pp. 442-43.

[11] France, Archives du Ministère des Affaires Étrangères (A.M.A.E.), Guerre 1914-1918, *Turquie*, Barthe de Sandfort, Vice Consul of France at Van, to Bompard, Ambassador of France at Constantinople, Sept. 19, 1914, in Arthur Beylerian, ed. and comp., *Les grandes puissances l'empire ottoman et les arméniens dans les archives françaises (1914-1918)* (Paris: Panthéon-Sorbonne, 1983), p. 4; Haigazn G. Ghazarian, *Tseghaspan turke* [The Genocidal Turk] (Beirut: Hamazkayin Press, 1968), p. 130; Chareg, *Karinapatum*, p. 463; Naslian, *Les mémoires*, p. 151.

[12] Chareg, *Karinapatum*, pp. 463, 465-66.

owned by Armenians, and during the next two months Turkish soldiers pillaged and plundered villages near Erzerum under the pretext of searching for weapons and apprehending draft evaders.[13] In the meantime, under direct orders of Behaeddin Shakir, the Ittihadist chief of the *Teshkilat-i Mahsusa* (Special Organization), hardened criminals were released from prisons for the express purpose of forming them into killer bands to annihilate the Armenians.[14] The conscription of Armenian men into military service seemed planned to coincide with orders to attack Armenian towns in the eastern provinces.

Meanwhile, the German Ambassador to the Sublime Porte in Constantinople, Hans von Wangenheim, who played a central role in advancing German commercial and military interests in the Ottoman Empire, received important instructions from Berlin. He was to communicate to the Turkish authorities his government's assurances for "the rectification of Turkey's eastern borders for the purpose of enabling Turkey to establish direct contact with the Islamic nationalities of Russia."[15] In October, Paul Schwarz, of the German consulate at Erzerum with his own interests in the oilfields of Baku, reported to Berlin on the conditions in Turkish Armenia and noted that while the Turkish population favored Germany, the Armenians in the east preferred closer relations

---

[13] Ibid., p. 463; Ghazarian, *Tseghaspan turke*, p. 130; Naslian, *Les mémoires*, p. 151; Great Britain, Parliament, *The Treatment of Armenians in the Ottoman Empire, 1915-16: Documents Presented to Viscount Grey of Fallodon, Secretary of State for Foreign Affairs*, Miscellaneous no. 31, 1916, comp. and ed. Arnold Toynbee, 3d ed. (Beirut: G. Doniguian and Sons, 1988; London: Sir Joseph Causton and Sons, 1916), p. 637, cited hereafter as *Treatment of Armenians*; Vahakn N. Dadrian, *The History of the Armenian Genocide: Ethnic Conflict from the Balkans to Anatolia to the Caucasus* (Providence: Berghahn Books, 1995), pp. 220-21. On the village of Dzitogh, for example, see Vartiter K. Hovannisian, *Dzitogh Dashti Karno* [Dzitogh in the Plain of Karin] (Beirut: Hamazkayin Press, 1972), pp. 94-95.

[14] On the Special Organization, see Dadrian, *History of the Armenian Genocide*, pp. 236-38. The Ittihad office at Erzerum served as the headquarters for Behaeddin Shakir's operations in the entire region. See Chareg, *Karinapatum*, p. 464; Naslian, *Les mémoires*, p. 152; Christopher J. Walker, "World War I and the Armenian Genocide," in Hovannisian, *The Armenian People from Ancient to Modern Times*, pp. 253-54.

[15] Vahakn N. Dadrian, *German Responsibility in the Armenian Genocide: A Review of the Historical Evidence of German Complicity* (Watertown, MA: Blue Crane Books, 1996), p. 51. See also Otto Liman von Sanders, *Five Years in Turkey* (Baltimore: Williams and Wilkins, 1928), p. 14.

with Russia. Schwarz added that "Russian and British money was being put to good use in Armenia and that Turkish Armenia was an area deserving special attention."[16] The Armenians in Erzerum and in the eastern vilayets in general could hinder and frustrate "the rectification of Turkey's eastern borders" as envisioned in Constantinople and Berlin.

The Russo-Turkish military clashes on the Caucasian front soon engulfed the entire Armenian population across the plain of Erzerum. The Russian military command had estimated that the Ottoman Third Army, composed of the IX, X, and XI Corps and stationed in the Erzerum region under the command of General Hasan Izzet Pasha, would be insufficient for a successful offensive against the key gateway fortress of Kars.[17] For his part, while Izzet Pasha also considered the Third Army inadequate for an offensive, he believed that the Russian forces could not mount a sustainable defense.[18] His assessment appeared deceptively accurate. After an initial advance toward Erzerum in mid-December 1914, the Russian army withdrew from the region. In response, the Turkish army seized the opportunity to assault Armenians in a number of villages and scatter their inhabitants,[19] as in the village of Dzitogh, located about 12 miles north of Erzerum, giving rise to fears of impending massacres.[20]

Preparations for further hostilities on the Russo-Turkish front were underway when the Turkish government issued an Imperial Rescript on December 16, 1914, nullifying the Armenian Reform

---

[16] Germany, Auswärtigen Amtes, Weltkrieg, 11 d secr., vol. 1, Erzberger to Gottlieb von Jagow, Oct. 26, 1914, as cited in Dadrian, *German Responsibility*, p. 57 and note 168.

[17] A.M.A.E., Guerre 1914-1918, *Opérations stratégiques*, Paléologue, Ambassador of France at Petrograd, to Declassé, Minister of Foreign Affairs, Dec. 30, 1914, in Beylerian, *Les grandes puissances*, p. 6; W.E.D. Allen and Paul Muratoff, *Caucasian Battlefields: A History of the Wars on the Turco-Caucasian Border, 1828-1921* (Cambridge: Cambridge University Press, 1953), p. 243.

[18] Allen and Muratoff, *Caucasian Battlefields*, p. 244.

[19] Library of Congress, Division of Manuscripts, The Papers of Henry Morgenthau, Sr., container 7, General Correspondence, Speer, Bible House, to Morgenthau, Dec. 12, 1914.

[20] Dzitogh had become a military garrison in September 1914. See V.K. Hovannisian, *Dzitogh Dashti Karno*, pp. 95-96, 196-98.

Act of February 8.[21] At the same time, as noted by U.S. Ambassador Henry Morgenthau, reports reached Constantinople of massacres of Armenians around Erzerum.[22] Sporadic attacks by soldiers and chete bands, which had increased in frequency since early November 1914 in the Armenian villages near the city of Sivas (Sepastia) and farther north in the region of Shabin-Karahisar, continued well into the month of January 1915 and spread to Erzerum, Van, Bitlis, and Diarbekir.[23]

In the meantime, leading the Third Army of about 95,000 troops, Enver launched his fateful Sarikamish offensive (December 1914-January 1915) in an attempt to capture the fortress of Kars and to advance into the Caucasus. It is beyond the scope of this chapter to present a detailed account of the Sarikamish campaign. Suffice it to note that the poorly organized and poorly supplied operation left the Third Army decimated, with more than two-thirds of the men taken prisoner, wounded, or dead.[24] By the end of December, there were between 5,000 and 7,500 wounded soldiers at Erzerum alone. A typhus epidemic spread throughout the Erzerum region, adding to the miserable conditions.[25] But a misery far greater than ever experienced before was yet to be visited upon the Armenians.

---

[21] Vahakn N. Dadrian, "Genocide as a Problem of National and International Law: The World War I Armenian Case and Its Contemporary Legal Ramifications," *Yale Journal of International Law* 14:2 (1989): 260.

[22] Morgenthau Papers, container 7, Diary, Dec. 12, 1914, cited hereafter as Morgenthau Diary. See also Der Yeghiayan, *My Patriarchal Memoirs*, pp. 53-54.

[23] *Treatment of Armenians*, Doc. 21, "The North-Eastern Vilayets: Statement Communicated by the Refugee Roupen, of Sassun, to the Armenian Community at Moscow; Published in the Russian Press, and Subsequently Reprinted in the 'Gazette de Lausanne,' 13th February, 1916," pp. 80-82.

[24] Hovannisian, *Armenia on the Road to Independence*, pp. 45-48; Sasuni, *Trkahayastane*, pp. 50-53; Allen and Muratoff, *Caucasian Battlefields*, pp. 253, 261-62, 270-71, 283n2, 284; John Keegan, *The First World War* (New York: Vintage Books, 1998), p. 222; "Summary of Armenian History," in *Treatment of Armenians*, p. 637.

[25] Morgenthau Diary, Dec. 24 and 28, 1914. In January 1915, Maria Jacobsen, a Danish missionary nurse serving in Mezre, witnessed Ottoman soldiers returning from the Caucasus front with low morale. She estimated that in Erzerum alone about 2,000 soldiers were dying each day of wounds and famine. Maria Jacobsen, *Oragrutiun 1907-1919: Kharberd* [Diary 1907-1919: Kharpert], trans. Bishop Nerses Bakhtikian and Mihran Simonian (Antelias: Catholicosate of Antelias, 1979), p. 75; Lepsius, *Rapport secret,* p. 50.

Catafalque of the Caucasus

While Enver publicly recognized the loyalty and bravery of the Ottoman Armenian soldiers during the Sarikamish campaign,[26] the Young Turk leadership met on February 14 and, with the excuse that the Armenians were engaged in pro-Russian military and anti-Turkish revolutionary activities and therefore were responsible for the calamitous Turkish military campaign on the Caucasian front, issued a general order to arrest Armenian leaders in Sivas, Bitlis, Erzerum, and Marash, followed by mass deportations from the Cilician towns of Zeitun, Hajin, Sis, Hassan Beyli, and Dort Yol.[27] The subsequent disarmament of the Armenian soldiers and their assignment to labor battalions (*amele taburi*) served only to aggravate Armenian anxieties regarding the intentions of the Ittihadist regime, and fear of massacres caused the flight of thousands of Armenians from across the Erzerum plain to the Caucasus by the spring of 1915.[28]

Neither Armenians nor foreign observers in Erzerum were surprised by the growing hostility toward the Armenians. Referring to the Erzerum vilayet, for example, the prominent German missionary Johannes Lepsius noted that, after the Sarikamish campaign as the political and military situation in the vilayet degenerated into mass attacks on Armenian villages in the months of January and February 1915, the public openly talked of a general massacre of the Armenians.[29] Miss Hansina Marcher,

---

[26] Der Yeghiayan, *My Patriarchal Memoirs*, p. 63; S. Akuni, *Milion me hayeru jardi patmutiune* [The Story of the Massacre of a Million Armenians] (Constantinople: Hayastan, 1921), p. 29; Hovannisian, *Armenia on the Road to Independence,* p. 53; Walker, "World War I and the Armenian Genocide," p. 245.

[27] Akuni, *Milion me hayeru jardi patmutiune*, pp. 26-29; Chormisian, *Hamapatker*, pp. 343-45. See also Nuri Bey to Jemal Bey, Feb. 18, 1915, in Aram Antonian, *Mets vojire* [The Great Crime] (Boston: Bahak, 1921; repr. Erevan: Arevik, 1990), pp. 129-30, 133; Vahakn N. Dadrian, "The Secret Young-Turk Ittihadist Conference and the Decision for the World War I Genocide of the Armenians," *Holocaust and Genocide Studies* 7:2 (1993); reprinted with revisions in "The Armenian Genocide in Official Turkish Records," a special issue of the *Journal of Political and Military Sociology* 22:1 (1994): 173-201.

[28] Henry Barby, *Au pays de l'épouvante: L'Arménie martyre* (Beirut: Hamazkayin Press, 1972; first published, 1917), pp. 20, 185.

[29] Lepsius, *Rapport secret*, p. 225.

a Danish missionary nurse serving in Kharpert at the time, reported that on March 16, 1915, the German Vice Consul at Erzerum, Max Erwin von Scheubner-Richter, paid a visit to the *vali* (governor) of Kharpert province, Erzinjanli Sabit Bey:

> The Vali had declared to him that the Armenians in Turkey must be, and were going to be, exterminated. They had grown, he said, in wealth and numbers until they had become a menace to the ruling Turkish race; extermination was the only remedy.[30]

The vali of Erzerum vilayet, Hasan Tahsin Bey, on the other hand, merely promised to prevent further attacks.[31]

Deportations and Massacres

Conditions across the Erzerum plain continued to deteriorate rapidly, and the districts of Baiburt (Baberd), Terjan (Derjan; Mamakhatun), and Khnus (Hinis) became principal targets of the early deportations and massacres. Beginning in late February and early March 1915, as sanctioned by the Teshkilat-i Mahsusa, the gendarmes attacked several towns and villages, such as Erzinjan (Erznka), under the pretext of searching for weapons and demanded money from their victims. In the village of Mollah near the region of Passin (Basen), they entered the Armenian church during the Easter mass and tortured the local priest. Meanwhile, the Armenian inhabitants of fifteen villages near Erzerum city were forcibly removed to make room for the troops of the Third Army, confirming rumors and reports of their Turkish neighbors about preparations for a massacre of Armenians.[32] Visiting Erzerum in March, Rafael de Nogales, a Venezuelan mercenary serving in the Ottoman army, learned of the impending general

---

[30] *Treatment of Armenians*, Doc. 64, "H[arput]: Statement Made by Miss DA [Hansina Marcher], a Danish Lady in the Service of the German Red Cross at H[arput] to Mr. DB [Zavrieff], at Basle, and Communicated by Mr. DB [Zavrieff] to Lord Bryce," p. 258.

[31] Lepsius, *Rapport secret,* p. 225. Tahsin Bey had been the vali of Van and was transferred to Erzerum in 1914. See Naslian, *Les mémoires,* p. 148.

[32] Lepsius, *Rapport secret,* pp. 60-61, 65-66; Chormisian, *Hamapatker,* pp. 443-44. On the Armenians in Basen, see Sasuni, *Trkahayastane.*

massacres, as Kurds attacked several towns.[33]

On April 18, 1915, following orders from the central govern-ment, the local Muslim religious leaders at Erzerum congregated and, placing the blame of the Sarikamish military disaster squarely on the Armenians, issued exhortations to the Muslim faithful to punish the culprits of their defeat.[34] In late April, mass arrests led to the imprisonment of about 450 Armenian commu-nity leaders, intellectuals, journalists, and merchants in the city, followed by the further escalation of persecution, mass arrests, and killings in early May.[35] On April 28, Ambassador von Wangenheim instructed Scheubner-Richter in Erzerum "to inter-vene against 'massacres' and other excesses which might occur in his area, but cautioned him not to create the impression 'as though we want to exercise a right of protection over the Arme-nians or interfere with the activities of the authorities'."[36]

On May 12, Erzerum deputy to the Ottoman Parliament Vartkes Serengulian (Vardges Serenkulian) reportedly met with Minister of the Interior Talaat Pasha, who insisted that the depor-tations in the eastern provinces were in response to Armenian

---

[33] Rafael de Nogales, *Four Years Beneath the Crescent*, trans. Muna Lee (New York, London: Charles Scribner's Sons, 1926), pp. 44-45.

[34] *Treatment of Armenians*, Doc. 55, "Erzeroum: Abstract of a Report by Mr. B.H. Khounountz, Representative of the 'All-Russian Urban Union,' on a Visit to Erzeroum after the Russian Occupation; Published in the Armenian Journal 'Horizon,' of Tiflis, 25th February, 1916," p. 231; Doc. 56, "Erzeroum: Abstract of a Report by Dr. Y. Minassian, Who Accompanied Mr. Khounountz to Erzeroum as Representative of the Caucasian Section of the 'All-Russian Urban Union'; Published in the Armenian Journal 'Mschak,' of Tiflis, 8th March, 1916," p. 233; Doc. 57, "Erzeroum: Statement by Mr. A.S. Safrastian, Dated Tiflis, 15th March, 1916," p. 237; Jon S. Kirakosyan, *Arajin hamashkharhayin paterazme ev arevmtahayutiune 1914-1916 tt.* [The First World War and the Western Armenians, 1914-1916] (Erevan: Hayastan, 1967), pp. 331-32.

[35] A.M.A.E., Guerre 1914-1918, *Turquie*, Arshak Chobanian, Secretary of the Armenian Committee in Paris, to Jean Gout, Assistant Director of Asia, Ministry of Foreign Affairs, May 13, 1915, in Beylerian, *Les grandes puissances*, pp. 23-24; Chareg, *Karinapatum*, pp. 468-70.

[36] Johannes Lepsius, ed., *Deutschland und Armenien, 1914-1918: Sammlung Diplomatischer Aktenstücke* (Potsdam: Tempelverlag, 1919), Docs. 31, 33, 34, 36, as quoted in Ulrich Trumpener, *Germany and the Ottoman Empire, 1914-1918* (Princeton: Princeton University Press, 1968), p. 207. See also Martin Gilbert, *The First World War: A Complete History* (New York: Henry Holt, 1994), p. 143.

disloyalty and demands for reforms, which, he asserted, were timed to take advantage of the political and military weakness of the regime. When asked if the Young Turk rulers were determined to continue the politics of massacres as pursued during the reign of the deposed Sultan Abdul-Hamid II, Talaat reputedly replied in the affirmative.[37] In a similar vein, during a conference with Enver, when Ambassador Morgenthau mentioned that the government "had threatened to deport all Armenians" in Erzerum, the minister of war replied that "it was due to their [the government's] fear of an uprising."[38] By mid-May, Turkish troops and chete bands had begun the forcible removal of Armenians from their homes across the Erzerum plain.[39]

Local authorities (for example, chief of gendarmes Mehmed Adil Bey), most of whom were virulently hostile to the Armenians, supervised the deportations and massacres.[40] Ahmed Hilmi Pasha, a CUP leader, gained in popularity with his cohorts because of his brutal treatment of the local Armenians. The mayor of Erzerum city, Kamil Pasha, on the other hand, though apparently sympathetic to the Armenians, could not muster sufficient power either to counter or to mitigate the catastrophic consequences of the policies dictated by the central government.[41]

Beginning on May 15, arrests and massacres occurred in Baiburt, and on May 18/19 throughout the province, particularly at Khnus, Erzerum, and Mamakhatun.[42] In Baiburt, the Armenian

---

[37] Lepsius, *Rapport secret,* pp. 235-36.

[38] Morgenthau Diary, May 22, 1915.

[39] Chareg, *Karinapatum,* pp. 469-70.

[40] On the arrest of Adil Bey by the British authorities in 1920 on charges of atrocities and massacres committed against the Armenians of Erzerum, see Vartkes Yeghiayan, ed. and comp., *British Foreign Office Dossiers on Turkish War Criminals* (La Verne, CA: American Armenian International College, 1991), pp. 443-51.

[41] Barby, *Au pays de l'épouvante,* p. 22; *Treatment of Armenians,* Doc. 53, "Erzeroum: Record of an Interview between the Rev. H.J. Buxton and the Rev. Robert Stapleton, a Missionary of the American Board, Resident at Erzeroum from before the Outbreak of War until after the Capture of the City by the Russians," p. 222; Naslian, *Les mémoires,* pp. 151-52.

[42] *Treatment of Armenians,* Doc. 60, "Baibourt: Statement, Reproduced from the Armenian Journal 'Horizon,' of Tiflis, in the Armenian Journal 'Gotchnag' of New York, 18th March, 1916," p. 244; Doc. 53, "Erzeroum," pp. 222-23; Levon Vartan [Vardan], "Karini ev shrjakayki teghahanutiunn u jardere" [The Deportations and Massacres of Karin and Its Environs], in Gersam Aharonian, ed. and comp., *Husha-*

prelate and several other community leaders were murdered.[43] From May 16 to 19, the Kurds, fleeing the areas threatened by a renewed Russian advance, vented their rage on the Armenians as they raided and plundered 38 Armenian towns and villages in the region of Khnus, located in a mountainous terrain about 50 miles south of Erzerum city.[44] Meanwhile, in the city itself, the authorities had arrested 200 Armenians on May 6 and had commenced the deportations of Armenians by May 19, allowing Turkish refugees (*muhajirs*) to occupy their homes.[45] Scheubner-Richter reported: "One cannot rule out that the deportees will be murdered en route."[46]

On May 24, 1915, the Allied Powers issued a public condemnation of the deportations and massacres being committed by the Turkish authorities, declaring that they would "hold personally responsible for these crimes all members of the Ottoman government and those of their agents who are implicated in such massacres."[47] Such strong castigations notwithstanding, on May 26,

---

matian Mets Egherni, 1915-1965 [Memorial Volume of the Great Crime, 1915-1965] (Beirut: Atlas, 1965), pp. 449, 450-51.

[43] *Treatment of Armenians*, Doc. 60, "Baibourt," p. 244.

[44] Ibid., Doc. 53, "Erzeroum," pp. 222-23; Doc. 57, "Erzeroum," p. 237; Chormisian, *Hamapatker*, pp. 444-45; Barby, *Au pays de l'épouvante*, p. 30. See also T.Kh. Hakobyan, S.T. Melik-Bakhshyan, and H.Kh. Barseghyan, *Hayastani ev harakits shrjanneri teghanunneri bararan* [Toponymical Dictionary of Armenia and Neighboring Regions], 5 vols. (Erevan: Erevan State University, 1986-2001), vol. 2, s.v. "Khnus," p. 754.

[45] *Treatment of Armenians*, "Vilayet of Erzeroum," p. 221; Chareg, *Karinapatum*, p. 469; Lepsius, *Rapport secret*, p. 68.

[46] Politisches Archiv des Auswärtigen Amtes, Abteilung IA (German Foreign Ministry Archives), Botschaft Konstantinopel 168, no. 2843, May 9, 1915, quoted by Vahakn N. Dadrian, "Documentation of the Armenian Genocide in German and Austrian Sources," in Israel W. Charny, ed., *Genocide: A Critical Bibliographic Review*, vol. 3: *The Widening Circle of Genocide* (New Brunswick, NJ: Transaction Publishers, 1994), p. 107.

[47] United States, National Archives, Record Group 59, 867.4016/67, Secretary of State Bryan to American Embassy, Constantinople, May 29, 1915; A.M.A.E., Guerre 1914-1918, *Turquie*, "Communication de l'Ambassade de Russie au Département," May 11, 1915, "Communication de l'Ambassade de Grande-Bretagne au Département," May 21, 1915, and "Note du Département à l'Agence Havas," May 24, 1915, in Beylerian, *Les grandes puissances*, pp. 23, 27, 29. In one of its immediate responses to this charge, the Turkish government declared that reports regarding the Armenian massacres were fabrications and that the Armenians of Erzerum, Terjan, Agn, Sasun, Baghesh, Mush, and Cilicia had not been involved in any acts to necessitate such government or public action. See Esat Uras, *Tarihte Ermeniler ve Ermeni Meselesi* [The Armenians in History

another round of mass arrests took place in Erzerum city. Turkish and Kurdish mobs attacked Armenian shops and neighborhoods, while the Armenian population of about 25,000 was being prepared for deportation.[48] On that same day, Talaat Pasha dispatched to the grand vizier a communiqué regarding the deportations:

> Because some of the Armenians who are living near the war zones have obstructed the activities of the Imperial Ottoman Army, which has been entrusted with defending the frontiers against the country's enemies; . . . and because it is necessary that rebellious elements of this kind should be removed from the area of military activities and that the villages which are the bases and shelter for these rebels should be vacated, certain measures are being adopted, among which is deportation of the Armenians from the Van, Bitlis, Erzerum vilayets.[49]

In Constantinople, on May 27, 1915, Enver assured Ambassador Morgenthau that the deportations from Erzerum "had stopped."[50]

By late May, however, the central government, on the pretext that the Armenian "uprising" in Van could spread to other regions, was ready to execute the wholesale deportation of the entire Armenian population from Erzerum.[51] Tahsin Bey had received orders from the Young Turk leaders to implement the deportation and massacre of the Armenians in his vilayet. Ini-

---

and the Armenian Question] (Ankara: Yeni Matbaa, 1950), pp. 617-18; Lepsius, *Rapport secret*, pp. 201-02; Vartan, "Karini ev shrjakayki teghahanutiunn u jardere," p. 453.

[48] Morgenthau Diary, May 22, 1915; Chareg, *Karinapatum*, pp. 469-70; Vartan, "Karini ev shrjakayki teghahanutiunn u jardere," pp. 450-51; Lepsius, *Rapport secret*, p. 68.

[49] Hikmet Yusuf Bayur, *Türk inkılâbı tarihi*, vol. 3: *1914-1918 genel savaşı*, pt. 3, *1915-1917 vuruşmaları ve bunların siyasal tepkileri* [History of the Turkish Revolution, vol. 3: The 1914-1918 World War, pt. 3, The Battles of 1915-1917 and Their Political Effects] (Ankara: Türk Tarih Kurumu, 1957), pp. 37-38, as quoted in Hovannisian, *Armenia on the Road to Independence*, p. 50.

[50] Morgenthau Diary, May 27, 1915.

[51] The Armenian struggle for self-defense at Van began in April 1915. The Russian army occupied the city in May and installed one of the prominent leaders of the Dashnaktsutiun, Aram Manukian, as governor. The Russians withdrew from Van two months later, which led to the evacuation of more than 100,000 Armenians to the Caucasus. See Anahide Ter Minassian, "Van 1915," in Richard G. Hovannisian, ed., *Armenian Van/Vaspurakan* (Costa Mesa, CA: Mazda Publishers, 2000), pp. 210-44.

tially disinclined to engage in atrocities of such magnitude, the
vali eventually acquiesced, although he assured the Armenians
that the deportees would be given protection while still within
his jurisdiction.[52] As a first step, during a meeting with Bishop
Smbat Saatetian, Tahsin Bey informed the local prelate that
nearly 160 Armenian families were to be deported immediately
to Erzinjan.[53]

Receipt of the orders evoked chaos in the city. As the deportations began, Armenian merchants moved their inventories to the
Cathedral of Surb Astvatsatsin. The wealthier families purchased
animals to haul what goods they could take with them. The less
fortunate, stupefied amid the bedlam, with little supplies for their
journey, were forced to march away from home and hearth.
Turks and Kurds looted and plundered the stores and houses
being vacated.[54] Only about 50 Armenian artisans were allowed
to remain in Erzerum city for the purpose of building "a Turkish
club house . . . from grave stones taken from the Armenian
cemetery."[55]

During the first week of June, between 10,000 and 15,000
Armenians from towns and villages in the northern and eastern
parts of the vilayet began their march in long caravans to Mamakhatun and Erzinjan.[56] The initial general deportation from the

---

[52] Naslian, *Les mémoires*, p. 154; *Treatment of Armenians,* Doc. 53, "Erzeroum,"
p. 223; Doc. 54, "Erzeroum: Report, Dated 25th September, 1915, Drawn up by the
American Consul-General at Trebizond, after his Return from a Visit to Erzeroum:
Communicated by the American Committee for Armenian and Syrian Relief," pp.
228-29; Doc. 55, "Erzeroum," p. 231; Barby, *Au pays de l'épouvante*, p. 23. On charges
implicating Tahsin in direct involvement in the atrocities committed during the deportations and the massacres, see Yeghiayan, *British Foreign Office Dossiers on Turkish
War Criminals*, pp. 236-45.

[53] Chareg, *Karinapatum*, p. 471; Naslian, *Les mémoires*, p. 153.

[54] Chareg, *Karinapatum*, p. 472.

[55] During the Russian advance to Erzerum, these artisans were sent to Erzinjan
and imprisoned; subsequently, they were massacred under orders from Kiamil Pasha.
See the account of Ida S. Stapleton (wife of the Reverend Robert S. Stapleton), "Incidents
during the Deportation of Armenians from Erzroom, Turkey, in June and July, 1915,
Known Personally to Dr. Ida S. Stapleton (Mrs. Robert)," dated April 18, 1918, in
James L. Barton, comp., *"Turkish Atrocities": Statements of American Missionaries
on the Destruction of Christian Communities in Ottoman Turkey, 1915-1917* (Ann
Arbor, MI: Gomidas Institute, 1998), pp. 25-26.

[56] *Treatment of Armenians,* Doc. 55, "Erzeroum," p. 231; Chormisian, *Hamapatker,*

cities started on June 7-11 in Erzinjan, home to some 3,000 Armenian families, followed during the next week by three additional caravans, totaling between 20,000 and 25,000 persons from the nearby areas. The first caravan was sent toward Kharpert.[57]

The deportations at Erzinjan were already in progress when, on June 16-18, the first caravan from Erzerum, consisting of 200 families, was marched out of the city, followed on June 19 by a larger caravan composed of about 8,000 people, directed southward toward Kghi, Kharpert, and Diarbekir.[58] Another caravan, consisting of 500 families (about 3,400 individuals) left Erzerum city on June 29, directed westward to Ilija, Mamakhatun, and Erzinjan.[59] By the end of June, the entire Armenian population was being deported from Kiskim (Gisgim), Khotorjur (Khodorchur), Sper (Sber; Ispir), and other towns and villages dotting the banks of the Chorokh River from the northern reaches of Erzerum vilayet to the environs of Baiburt.[60]

In Baiburt and the nearby villages, where several prominent Armenians had been arrested on May 15 and subsequently killed

p. 445.

[57] *Treatment of Armenians*, Doc. 62, "Erzindjan: Statement by Two Red Cross Nurses of Danish Nationality, Formerly in the Service of the German Mission at Erzeroum; Communicated by a Swiss Gentleman of Geneva," p. 246; Lepsius, *Rapport secret*, p. 70; Barby, *Au pays de l'épouvante*, pp. 35, 99; Naslian, *Les mémoires*, p. 164; Chormisian, *Hamapatker*, p. 445; Vartan, "Karini ev shrjakayki teghahanutiunn u jardere," p. 454.

[58] Chareg, *Karinapatum*, pp. 473-74; *Treatment of Armenians*, Doc. 53, "Erzeroum," p. 223; Doc. 57, "Erzeroum," pp. 238-39; Barby, *Au pays de l'épouvante*, pp. 24, 30-31; Hratch A. Tarbassian, *Erzurum (Garin): Its Armenian History and Traditions*, trans. Nigol Schahgaldian ([New York]: Garin Compatriotic Union of the United States, 1975), p. 236. According to Ida Stapleton, the first group leaving Erzerum consisted of 40 families (about 250-300 individuals). They "were allowed to choose the road they should travel. . . . They were not told where they were to go, nothing, simply to go." See Stapleton, "Incidents during the Deportation of Armenians from Erzroom," p. 23.

[59] Tarbassian, *Erzurum*, p. 236; Stapleton, "Incidents during the Deportation of Armenians from Erzroom," p. 24. According to Naslian, the date was June 28. See Naslian, *Les mémoires*, p. 153.

[60] Hakobyan, Melik-Bakhshyan, and Barseghyan, *Hayastani ev harakits shrjanneri teghanunneri bararan*, vol. 2, s.v. "Khotrjur," pp. 789-91; vol. 3, s.v. "Kiskim," p. 143; vol. 4, s.v. "Sper," pp. 673-74.

at Urbaji Oghlu Déré,[61] the deportations occurred in three successive waves during the month of June.[62] As some of the refugees
from other parts of the vilayet arrived in Baiburt, they were
attached to another caravan from that city, bringing the total
number of deportees in the area to 15,000.[63] From there, they
were routed southward to Erzinjan—which by the end of June
had become a major concentration camp for refugees coming
from the north[64]—and to Kemakh (Kamakh) and then into the
vilayet of Kharpert at Agn and Arabkir. Most of the refugees,
however, were murdered by bands of chetes as they marched
southwestward toward Mamakhatun, Erzinjan, and Kemakh, the
treacherous serpentine road along the Kara Su (Upper Euphrates)
from Erzinjan to Kemakh alone being a journey of twelve
hours.[65] At Kemakh, the men were separated from their families
and murdered, while the rest were forced to march on toward
Mosul and Aleppo.

About 5,000 refugees, having passed Mamakhatun, on June
22, 1915, reached the village of Pirich some 10 miles from the
town, and on the following day continued their journey to
Erzinjan, on the way some being robbed and murdered by
Kurdish tribes.[66] As the refugees continued their trek, they were
set upon yet again on June 24 by the local Kurds and Turks, and
the next day chete bands forced them off the road and attacked
the remaining survivors.[67] A large number of them were murdered

---

[61] *Treatment of Armenians*, Doc. 60, "Baibourt," p. 244; Chormisian, *Hamapatker*, pp. 445-46.

[62] According to Lepsius, Baiburt and the nearby villages were home to about 17,000 Armenians. Lepsius, *Rapport secret*, p. 73.

[63] *Treatment of Armenians*, Doc. 53, "Erzeroum," pp. 223-24.

[64] Naslian, *Les mémoires*, p. 164.

[65] *Treatment of Armenians*, Doc. 53, "Erzeroum," pp. 223-24; Doc. 55, "Erzeroum," p. 231; Doc. 56, "Erzeroum," pp. 234-35; Doc. 57, "Erzeroum," p. 238; Morgenthau Papers, container 7, General Correspondence, Morgenthau to Secretary of State, July 31, 1915, reporting that he had been informed by Lepsius of the massacre of Armenian refugees near Kemakh. See also Barby, *Au pays de l'épouvante*, pp. 24-25, 35, 59.

[66] In 1915, prior to the deportations, there were 187 Armenian families (1,484 individuals) in Pirich (Piriz). See Hakobyan, Melik-Bakhshyan, and Barseghyan, *Hayastani ev harakits shrjanneri teghanunneri bararan*, vol. 5, s.v. "Piriz," p. 262.

[67] Barby, *Au pays de l'épouvante*, pp. 36-37, 74-75, 100.

at Kemakh Boghazi, a narrow gorge on the Euphrates.[68] Near Kemakh, about 1,330 refugees were separated from the main caravan and herded by Turkish soldiers and chetes and ordered to cross the Euphrates and march southwestward to a ravine, Duzlu Su, and the nearby hills. After a short walk from there, they reached the gorge of Ghuru Deresi, where, on July 18, nearly all were murdered.[69]

The first caravan of several hundred Erzerum refugees, consisting mostly of women and children, reached the outskirts of Kharpert city on July 2, 1915.[70] It was followed by a second caravan consisting of 8,000 deportees from Erzerum, Erzinjan, and as far away as Ordu and Trebizond on the coast of the Black Sea.[71] One of the main caravans from Erzerum continued from Agn to Arabkir on its way to Malatia, camping for a couple of days at Kirk Göz (Forty Springs) on the Euphrates. There, the escorting soldiers and chetes withdrew, being replaced by the local Kurdish tribesmen under the command of the chieftain Zeinal Bey, overseer of the mass killings on the Firinjilar hills situated in torturous terrain a short distance from Malatia. A few days later, the rapidly diminishing caravan was divided into two groups, one moving toward Urfa, the other toward Suruj.[72] Some of the deportees, particularly those fluent in the Kurdish language, bribed their way to Aleppo. Both caravans, amid plunder and atrocities, were soon forced to march to the Syrian desert.[73]

On June 30, 1915, the U.S. Consul at Trebizond, Oscar Heizer, dispatched a report regarding the situation in Trebizond and the deplorable conditions of Armenian refugees in the re-

---

[68] *Treatment of Armenians*, Doc. 62, "Erzindjan," pp. 246-47; Lepsius, *Rapport secret*, pp. 71-72.

[69] Chareg, *Karinapatum*, p. 477.

[70] Leslie A. Davis, *The Slaughterhouse Province: An American Diplomat's Report on the Armenian Genocide, 1915-1917*, ed. with introduction and notes by Susan K. Blair (New Rochelle, NY: Aristide D. Caratzas , 1989), pp. 59-60; Henry H. Riggs, *Days of Tragedy in Armenia: Personal Experiences in Harpoot, 1915-1917* (Ann Arbor, MI: Gomidas Institute, 1997), p. 120.

[71] "Statement of Dr. Tacy W. Atkinson," dated April 11, 1918, in Barton, *"Turkish Atrocities,"* pp. 42, 44.

[72] Ibid., pp. 478-80, 481.

[73] Ibid., p. 482; Chormisian, *Hamapatker*, p. 447; "Statement by Alpheus N. Andrus," in Barton, *"Turkish Atrocities,"* p. 97.

gions of Baiburt and Erzerum. Heizer had been informed that in Ashkale nearly 150 Armenian women and children were in "wretched condition." The refugees were "wandering about in the forests and on the mountains, some of them naked, having been robbed of their honor and their clothing."[74] Leslie A. Davis, U.S. Consul at Kharpert, relayed to Ambassador Morgenthau numerous reports about the atrocities committed against the Armenians in and surrounding regions of Kharpert. In a report dated July 11, he noted that thousands of refugees were arriving from Erzerum and Erzinjan to the region of Kharpert and Mezre, where government persecutions of Armenians had intensified. The Armenians, he wrote, were being deported not to "somewhere else" but to their certain death. The process of the deportations "seems to be to have bands of Kurds awaiting them on the road to kill the men especially and incidentally some of the others. The entire movement seems to be the most thoroughly organized and effective massacre this country has ever seen." In one instance, Davis spoke with three sisters, whose family of twenty-five was the wealthiest in Erzerum. No more than fourteen had survived, he reported. "When they left Erzeroum they had money, horses and personal effects but they had been robbed of everything, including even their clothing."[75]

Some of the main roads for the deportations converged at Kharpert, as refugees from Trebizond, Erzerum, Baiburt, Erzinjan, Kghi, Agn, Arabkir, and other places marched by Kharpert city. From there, they were forced to continue their journey in different directions: to Diarbekir and Mardin, to Severek and Veranshehir, to Malatia and Urfa. Passing through Kharpert, the refugees were sometimes allowed to stay in a "camp" at the Armenian cemetery located south of Mezre and at another west of Mezre near the Malatia road.[76] Isabelle Harley, a missionary of the American Board of Commissioners for Foreign Missions

[74] US Archives, RG 59, 867.4016/93, Morgenthau to Secretary of State, July 13, 1915, encl. Heizer to Morgenthau, June 30, 1915. Aware of these conditions, the Armenians of Trebizond fearfully expected similar treatment at the hands of the gendarmes.

[75] US Archives, RG 59, 867.4016/122, Morgenthau to Secretary of State, Aug. 10, 1915, encl. Davis to Morgenthau, July 11 [incorrectly dated June 11], 1915.

[76] Riggs, *Days of Tragedy,* p. 146.

stationed in Kharpert since 1911, visited one of these camps:

> There were about three thousand people there, mostly women and children, in a field with nothing to protect them from the hot sun. They told us there were eight thousand when they left Erzroom. The men and big boys had been separated from them on the road and killed. They were not brought by a direct road but had been taken over and through the mountains so that they had been forty-five days on the journey and had been attacked again and again by bands of Kurds.[77]

Those still fit to march continued their journey, while the rest died of illness and starvation or were massacred.

In mid-July, additional caravans of 7,000 Armenians began their journey from the region of Erzerum to Mamakhatun and Malatia. Some of the deportees were massacred in Mamakhatun, while the rest were killed as they approached Malatia.[78] According to the Reverend Robert S. Stapleton, the veteran American missionary in Erzerum city, Bishop Saatetian and the heads of the Armenian Catholics and Protestants in Erzerum left the city with the last caravan on July 28.[79] On the same day, German Vice Consul Scheubner-Richter reported that the goal of the Young Turk extremists was to achieve the "complete extermination" of the Armenian people in Turkey.[80]

By September 1915, the village of Geghvank (Keghvenk), situated near the border of Kharpert province, and the shores of Lake Goljuk had become the burial grounds for thousands of Armenians deported from Erzerum and surrounding regions.[81] Confronted with the specter of the total annihilation of his people across the Ottoman Empire, the supreme patriarch of the Armenian Apostolic Church, Catholicos Gevorg V Sureniants, from his Holy See at Echmiadzin in the Russian Empire, en-

[77] "Statement by Isabelle Harley," dated April 15, 1918, in Barton, "Turkish Atrocities," pp. 67-68.

[78] Levon Vartan [Vardan], Zhamanakagrutiun haikakan tasnhingi, 1915-1923 [Chronology of the Armenian Fifteen, 1915-1923] (Beirut: Atlas, 1975), p. 48.

[79] Barby, Au pays de l'épouvante, p. 31.

[80] See Naslian, Les mémoires, p. 31.

[81] Davis, Slaughterhouse Province, pp. 83, 86.

treated the Allied Powers as Christian states and in the name of humanity to intervene to end the atrocities.[82]

In November, another round of deportations occurred from the Kharpert area. Armenians from the city and its environs, in addition to the remaining refugees from Erzerum, Trebizond, and Ordu camped there, were driven out, although some were offered the option of conversion to Islam to secure survival.[83] By December 1915, the vilayet of Erzerum had been emptied of nearly all of its Armenian population,[84] with the exception of a small number of deportees who had gained refuge with some local Kurds in the Dersim in the northern part of Kharpert vilayet on the Kharpert-Erzerum boundary.[85] By then, thousands of Armenian refugees near the Russian-Turkish border had arrived in the Caucasus,[86] while the rest of the deportees continued their march southward to the Syrian desert.[87]

Although effective in the annihilation of the Armenian people, the Young Turk regime nevertheless did not enjoy the full support of the Ottoman population in this policy. Some Turkish officials and Kurdish tribes refused to comply with the deportation orders, and in some cases the local population assisted their Armenian neighbors or refugees passing through their towns.[88] According to Lepsius, prominent Turks in Erzerum petitioned the central government to end the deportations and persecutions.[89]

---

[82] A.M.A.E., Guerre 1914-1918, *Turquie*, Gevorg V, Catholicos of All Armenians, to Viviani, President of the Council, Minister of Foreign Affairs, Oct. 5/18, 1915, in Beylerian, *Les grandes puissances*, pp. 126-27.

[83] Jacobsen, *Oragrutiun*, p. 139; "Statement by Isabelle Harley," dated April 15, 1918, in Barton, *"Turkish Atrocities,"* p. 70.

[84] A.M.A.E., Guerre 1914-1918, *Turquie*,"Note du Département sur les massacres arméniens," Dec. 1915, in Beylerian, *Les grandes puissances*, p. 151.

[85] Chareg, *Karinapatum*, p. 498.

[86] According to Barby, *Au pays de l'épouvante*, p. 187, there were some 207,000 Armenian refugees in the Caucasus by the summer of 1915.

[87] Lepsius, *Rapport secret*, pp. 170-71.

[88] Richard G. Hovannisian, "Intervention and Shades of Altruism during the Armenian Genocide," in Richard G. Hovannisian, ed., *The Armenian Genocide: History, Politics, Ethics* (New York: St. Martin's, 1992), pp. 173-207.

[89] Lepsius, *Rapport secret*, pp. 194-95. Akuni, on the other hand, contends that the absence of corroborating sources with respect to such local petitions in Erzerum suggests that Lepsius was a victim of fabrications propagated for political purposes. See Akuni, *Milion me hayeru jardi patmutiune*, p. 140.

Nevertheless, while in certain instances local Turks and Kurds saved some Armenian lives, this in no way prevented the wholesale deportations and massacres of the population.

Military Defeat at Erzerum: The Final Phase

The continued Russo-Turkish military clashes across the vilayet of Erzerum and their tragic dénouement removed all hope for the survival of Armenian Erzerum. In late June and early July 1915, the Turkish troops on the Caucasus front resumed their push toward Olti in the province of Kars, and additional army contingents stationed in the northern part of Van province were redeployed to the front across the Alashkert plain in efforts to ensure success. They were pressed back, however, by the Russians, who in January 1916 launched a general offensive and swiftly advanced to the forts of Erzerum, approximately 60 miles west of the Russo-Turkish line. Led by General Nikolai Yudenich, they drove the Turkish army out of the city.[90] The Russians captured Erzerum on February 16, 1916, and in separate columns continued their march to Mamakhatun, Baiburt, Gumushkhane, and Erzinjan, and to Malazkert and Mush.[91]

The Russian advance from Erzerum to Erzinjan gave hope to the few remaining Armenian refugees from Erzerum province scattered in the regions of Kharpert and the Dersim, who with the assistance of local Kurds (for example, the Kizilbash chief Seyid Jemali) had developed an "underground railway," to return to their homeland.[92] Upon their return, however, they found the houses destroyed by the Turkish and Kurdish attacks and the Turko-Russian military campaigns.[93] Yet, in spite of the death

---

[90] Sasuni, *Trkahayastane*, pp. 107-08; Allen and Muratoff, *Caucasian Battlefields*, pp. 355-63; Lepsius, *Rapport secret,* pp. 132-33; *Current History* 3 (1916): 1226.

[91] Allen and Muratoff, *Caucasian Battlefields*, pp. 364-67. See also Peter Hopkirk, *Like Hidden Fire: The Plot to Bring Down the British Empire* (New York: Kodansha, 1994), pp. 195-211.

[92] Chareg, *Karinapatum*, p. 498; Stapleton, "Incidents during the Deportation of Armenians from Erzroom," pp. 23-24; "Statement of Dr. Tacy W. Atkinson," dated April 11, 1918, in Barton, *"Turkish Atrocities,"* p. 47. See also Nazaret Piranian, *Kharberdi egherne* [The Genocide at Kharpert] (Boston: Baikar, 1937), pp. 520-34.

[93] Chareg, *Karinapatum*, p. 498.

and destruction witnessed since late 1914, the future of Armenian Erzerum, from Khnus to Erzinjan, now seemed secured while under Russian control.[94] Writing to Catholicos Gevorg V on March 23, 1916, Boghos Nubar, whom the catholicos had appointed to head the Armenian National Delegation to win European support for the Armenians in the Ottoman Empire, stated: "The capture of Erzerum and the outstanding triumphs of the Russian army, as we hope that it will also save Armenia from Turkish rule, are creating a new phase for the Armenian cause."[95]

The Russians, however, sought to rebuild Erzerum neither for Armenian nor for humanitarian "causes." In late October 1916, referring to the Sykes-Picot agreement signed by the Entente powers earlier that year,[96] Lord James Bryce, the distinguished former British ambassador to the United States (1907-13) who worked closely with Armenophile organizations during the war, informed Boghos Nubar that "Russia plans to turn Erzerum and Bitlis, these two vilayets only, into colonies and deport the Armenians from there; it leaves out Van, where the Armenians are permitted to return."[97]

---

[94] Sasuni, *Trkahayastane*, pp. 112-13, 115-16.

[95] Bibliothèque Nubar (Paris), Doc. 784-791, Boghos Nubar to Catholicos Kevork (Gevorg) V, March 23, 1916, in *Boghos Nubar's Papers and the Armenian Question, 1915-1918: Documents*, ed. and trans. Vatche Ghazarian (Waltham, MA: Mayreni Publishing, 1996), p. 326, cited hereafter as *Boghos Nubar's Papers*. Boghos Nubar (1851-1930) was the son of Nubar Pasha (1825-1899), who had served as prime minister and foreign minister of Egypt. Succinct background information on Boghos Nubar and the Armenian National Delegation is given in the introduction, pp. xvii-xxxiii.

[96] Signed on April 26, 1916, the Sykes-Picot agreement was named after Sir Mark Sykes, senior British diplomat and Near East expert at the British Foreign Office, and François Georges Picot, former French Consul General at Beirut. It provided for the postwar partition of the Ottoman Empire by the Entente powers, whereby most of the Arab-speaking areas of the empire would be divided into French and British zones, while Russia would expand into the eastern Ottoman provinces of Trebizond, Erzerum, Bitlis, and Van. See Harry N. Howard, *The Partition of Turkey: A Diplomatic History, 1913-1923* (Norman: University of Oklahoma Press, 1931); M.S. Anderson, *The Eastern Question, 1774-1923: A Study in International Relations* (London: Macmillan, 1966), pp. 340-41; Hovannisian, *Armenia on the Road to Independence*, pp. 59-60, 62.

[97] *Boghos Nubar's Papers*, Doc. 1754-1756, Meeting of Boghos Nubar with Lord Bryce, Oct. 26, 1916, p. 387. See also, Sasuni, *Trkahayastane*, pp. 116-17. Boghos Nubar was informed of the Anglo-French agreement in early March 1916. Subsequently, he met with René Pinon, Mark Sykes, and François Georges Picot concerning the future of Cilicia in the postwar plans of the Entente powers. See *Boghos Nubar's Papers*,

Nevertheless, by the end of 1916, several humanitarian groups were operating in Erzerum city to accommodate the returning refugees, a policy endorsed by the Russian Provisional Government after the revolution that deposed Tsar Nicholas II in March 1917.[98] These organizations included a locally operated refugee committee, headed by Gabriel Terzian, which provided food and clothing and remained active until February 1918. A branch of the Moscow Armenian Committee, formed by wealthy Armenians, founded a hospital and an orphanage-school in Erzerum under the direction of the German-educated agronomist Mkrtich Ter-Mkrtichian. A branch of the Union of Caucasian Cities functioned in Erzerum under Tigran Aghamalian, and an office of the Brotherly Aid Union (Eghbayrakan Ognutian Miutiun) administered by the prelate, Bishop Zaven Babayan, operated an Armenian school.[99] The Provisional Government also permitted the American missionary Robert Stapleton to return from Tiflis to Erzerum, where he opened an American missionary vocational school. The Armenian homeland appeared to have the potential of recovering from the devastation wrought upon it by the Young Turk regime.[100]

The issues of repatriation of and protection for Western (Turkish) Armenian refugees led to the First Congress of Western Armenians, held at Erevan in May 1917. The conference sought to coordinate the repatriation efforts of various Armenian benevolent and cultural societies, and by the latter part of that year about 150,000 refugees had returned to their native lands in Van, Bitlis, Erzerum, and Trebizond. Armenians hoped that the Russian Provisional Government would continue to facilitate the

---

Doc. 1633-1634, Meeting of Boghos Nubar with Dr. Samné, March 1, 1916, p. 313; Doc. 1652-1654, Meeting of Boghos Nubar with Mr. René Pinon, April 17, 1916, p. 328; Doc. 1745-1748, Meeting of Boghos Nubar with Sir Mark Sykes, Oct. 24, 1916, pp. 382-83; Doc. 1749-1753, Meeting of Boghos Nubar and Mr. Picot, Oct. 24, 1916, pp. 384-86.

[98] Vratzian, *Hayastani Hanrapetutiun*, pp. 26-28; Hovannisian, *Armenia on the Road to Independence*, p. 79.

[99] E.H. Melikian, "Karno hanrayin kianke rusakan gravman shrjanin, 1916-1918" [Community Life in Karin during the Russian Occupation, 1916-1918], in Chareg, *Karinapatum*, pp. 498-501; Vratzian, *Hayastani Hanrapetutiun*, p. 28; Hovannisian, *Armenia on the Road to Independence*, p. 79; Sasuni, *Trkahayastane*, pp. 113, 115.

[100] Chareg, *Karinapatum*, pp. 498-501; Tarbassian, *Erzurum*, p. 247.

repatriation and the establishment of an Armenian administration in the four provinces.[101]

In the meantime, however, demoralization and instability within the ranks of the Russian army caused great consternation for both the Russian Provisional Government and the Armenians. In November 1917, the Bolshevik revolution and the subsequent withdrawal of Russian troops from the front rapidly and radically altered the situation in Erzerum. The disintegration of the Russian army of about 200,000 on the Caucasus front soon thereafter and the desertions already begun months earlier left the Armenians across the Erzerum plain virtually defenseless against Turkish forces.[102]

In desperation, an Armenian army corps was organized in December 1917 under the leadership of the General Tovmas Nazarbekian. The mobilization of Armenian volunteers created an army totaling about 20,000 men, hardly sufficient to protect the vast Erzinjan-Van front and all the Armenian lands to the rear.[103] Although in early January 1918 the Armenian leadership continued to hope that the military corps could save the situation,[104] the Armenian forces were too small in numbers and lacking sufficient military hardware to withstand the superior Turkish forces and to defend the coveted city after the Russian withdrawal, which escalated in January and February 1918.[105] No

---

[101] Vratzian, *Hayastani Hanrapetutiun*, pp. 28-30; Sasuni, *Trkahayastane*, pp. 148-50, 152; Hovannisian, *Armenia on the Road to Independence*, pp. 78-80.

[102] Chareg, *Karinapatum*, p. 501; Sasuni, *Trkahayastane*, pp. 155, 163-65. Hovannisian, *Armenia on the Road to Independence*, p. 113.

[103] Hovannisian, *Armenia on the Road to Independence*, pp. 113-15; Sasuni, *Trkahayastane*, pp. 158-60; Richard G. Hovannisian, *The Republic of Armenia*, vol. 1: *The First Year, 1918-1919* (Berkeley, Los Angeles, London: University of California Press, 1971), p. 22.

[104] Hayastani Hanrapetutiun, Patmutian Kentronakan Petakan Arkhiv (HH PKPA) [Republic of Armenia, Central State Historical Archives], 57/2/513, no. 4, Armenian National Congress to the Council of the Catholicos of All Armenians, Jan. 10, 1918, in *Vaveragrer hai ekeghetsu patmutyan*, girk 5: *Mayr ator S. Echmiatsine arajin hanrapetutyan tarinerin (1918-1920 tt.)* [Documents of the History of the Armenian Church, Bk 5: The Mother See St. Echmiadzin during the Years of the First Republic (1918-1920)], comp. Sandro Behbudyan (Erevan: Voskan Erevantsi, 1999), p. 14.

[105] Aleksandr Khatisian, *Hayastani Hanrapetutian tsagumn u zargatsume* [The Creation and Development of the Republic of Armenia], 2d pr. (Beirut: Hamazkayin Press, 1968), p. 31; Allen and Muratoff, *Caucasian Battlefields*, pp. 457-58; Chareg,

sooner had the Russians evacuated the area than the Ottoman Third Army commenced its movement toward Erzinjan and Erzerum, while Kurdish bands, including those from the Dersim who previously had protected the Armenians from the massacres, attacked the Armenians, weakening what little military capability the Armenian corps possessed.[106] An Armeno-Kurdish conference held at Khnus in late January at the initiative of the Dashnaktsutiun to form a defensive front against the Turkish army failed to generate sufficient support for such an alliance.[107] By February, Turkish troops had advanced toward Kemakh and Erzinjan and on March 12 regained control of Erzerum, as the defenders under the command of General Andranik Ozanian withdrew from the city along with the civilian population.[108]

The Armenians of Karin/Erzerum, having witnessed a brief period of revival of their political and cultural life in their homeland, yet again departed from the city. The Turkish army pressed forward to Kars and Alexandropol, while masses of refugees from Erzerum, Kars, and Van fled toward Erevan and Echmiadzin.[109] The defeat of the Ottoman Empire in October 1918 again stirred Armenian imagination and optimism, but, as it happened, the Armenians of Karin and its plain were never able to return to rekindle their hearths, sow their fields, or reopen their shops.

In early 1919, when teams sent by the American Committee for Relief in the Near East reached the interior of Turkish Armenia, they reported that "there were no refugees" in Van, Bitlis,

---

Karinapatum, pp. 502-03; Hopkirk, *Like Hidden Fire*, p. 258.

[106] Vratzian, *Hayastani Hanrapetutiun*, pp. 67-68, 92-93; Allen and Muratoff, *Caucasian Battlefields*, pp. 458-59.

[107] Sasuni, *Trkahayastane*, pp. 166-67.

[108] Vratzian, *Hayastani Hanrapetutiun*, pp. 93-97; Allen and Muratoff, *Caucasian Battlefields*, pp. 460-63; Hovannisian, *Armenia on the Road to Independence*, pp. 123, 134-35, 137, and *Republic of Armenia*, pp. 24, 27. On the conditions in Erzerum and the difficulties confronted by General Andranik, see Levon Tutunjian, "Karno ankumin voghbergutiune" [The Tragedy of the Fall of Karin], in Aharonian, *Hushamatian*, pp. 811-27; General Andranik [Ozanian], *Haikakan arandzin harvatsogh zoramase* [The Armenian Special Striking Division], transcribed by Eghishe Kajuni (Boston: Azg, 1921).

[109] Vratzian, *Hayastani Hanrapetutiun*, pp. 96-98, 115-16, 119; Hovannisian, *Republic of Armenia*, pp. 27-28; Khatisian, *Hayastani Hanrapetutian tsagumn u zargatsume*, p. 64.

Erzerum, and Trebizond, and that in fact "no Armenians were left in the region."[110] The genocidal policies of the Young Turk regime had been rewarded with the death of Armenian Karin/ Erzerum and all other Armenian-inhabited lands in the Ottoman Empire. The deportations and massacres orchestrated against the Armenians by the tyrannical rule of that government had removed the entire Armenian population from their homeland of three millennia. Armenian Karin, Kamakh, Erznka, Derjan, Baberd, Sper, Basen, Khnus, Kghi, and all the other towns and villages across the province of Erzerum were no more.

---

[110] James L. Barton, *Story of Near East Relief, 1915-1930* (New York: Macmillan, 1930), pp. 110-16.

❋ 15 ❋

THE COMPETITION FOR ERZERUM
1914-1921

Richard G. Hovannisian

The turbulent years of World War I and its immediate aftermath placed the future status of Erzerum in question. As the strategic center and crossroads of the Armenian Plateau, Erzerum—historic Karin—figured in the calculations of all the players of the great game: Ottoman and Turkish rulers, Russian imperial and Soviet strategists, Allied and American policymakers, and, of course, the Armenian leaders themselves.

Erzerum became an integral part of the Armenian Question in the nineteenth century, during which the fortress city was occupied and relinquished twice by the Russian armies. As the Russian military withdrew after each peace treaty, there followed in its train thousands of Armenians who forsook their native towns and villages for the prospect of a more secure existence in a Christian empire. The emergent Armenian resistance movement elicited by the failure of domestic and international plans and promises for reforms found fertile soil in the plain of Karin/Erzerum. In the last in a series of reform measures, in 1895 and again in 1914, the city of Erzerum was designated as the center of a European-supervised administrative region, unofficially an Armenian province. In the first instance, it was Sultan Abdul-Hamid II who acquiesced in European pressure to promulgate the reforms but in fact effectively subverted them by unleashing the massacres of 1895-96. In the second instance, it was the Young Turk (Ittihad ve Terakki) government that had assumed power in 1908 which was constrained in February 1914 to assent to the formation of two administrative regions in the eastern provinces, each with a European inspector-general. Again, Erzerum was selected as the center of one of the inspectorates, encompassing the provinces *(vilayets)* of Trebizond, Erzerum, and Sivas (Sebastia/Sepastia).[1]

These externally-imposed stipulations only served to heighten the anxieties of the Turkish rulers regarding possible loss of the eastern provinces. This fear redoubled with the military fiasco and the further territorial losses in the first Balkan War in 1912-13, as the Young Turk leaders began to view Anatolia and the Armenian Plateau as the last "fall back" position for the empire. It was therefore an area that had to be cleansed of Armenians and any other elements that might someday try to follow the example of the Balkan peoples or provide an excuse for further foreign intervention.[2]

This resolve became all the more emphatic in the summer of 1914 when representatives of the world congress of the Armenian Revolutionary Federation (Dashnaktsutiun) which was meeting in Erzerum gave evasive answers to proposals of a Young Turk delegation, headed by central committee members Behaeddin Shakir, Omer Naji, and Hilmi Bey, to incite the Armenians of the Caucasus against the Russians in the likely event of hostilities between the Ottoman and Russian empires. The Armenian spokesmen urged the Turkish leaders not to be drawn into an imperialistic European conflict, stating that in such an unfortunate eventuality the Ottoman Armenians would do their duty as loyal citizens, just as they had done during the Balkan wars. It was impossible, however, to foment a rebellion in the Caucasus.[3]

---

[1] See Roderic H. Davison, "The Armenian Crisis, 1912-1914," *American Historical Review* 53 (April 1948): 489-505; André Mandelstam, *Le sort de l'empire Ottoman* (Paris and Lausanne: Payot, 1917), pp. 215-45.

[2] See, for example, the paper by Taner Akcam, "Rethinking the Ottoman Archival Material: Debunking Existing Myths," in the conference, "Contextualizing the Armenian Experience in the Ottoman Empire: From the Balkan Wars to the New Turkish Republic," University of Michigan-Ann Arbor, March 7-10, 2002.

[3] Vahan Minakhorian, *1915 tvakane* [The Year 1915] (Venice: Mekhitarist Press, 1949), pp. 66-71; Leo [Arakel Babakhanian], *Tiurkahay heghapokhutian gaghaparabanutiune* [The Ideology of the Turkish Armenian Revolution], vol. 2 (Paris: Bahri, 1935), pp. 76-78; Esat Uras, *Tarihte Ermeniler ve Ermeni Meselesi* [The Armenians in History and the Armenian Question] (Ankara: Yeni Matbaa, 1950), pp. 589-90; Johannes Lepsius, *Der Todesgang des Armenischen Volkes* (Potsdam: Tempelverlag, 1930), pp. 178-79.

Erzerum during World War I

The entry of the Ottoman Empire into World War I as an ally of the German Empire in October 1914 sealed the fate of the final reform program and of the Armenians themselves. A secret German-Turkish treaty in August had committed the Ottoman Empire to war against Russia in return, inter alia, for the annexation of certain territories in the Caucasus. The German alliance fired the imaginations of Young Turk leaders such as Minister of War Enver Pasha. Enver devised a scheme to catch the Russian defenses off-guard by striking across the international frontier in the dead of winter and seizing the fortress of Kars en route to Baku in the eastern Caucasus. He traveled to Erzerum to direct the campaign of the Third Army personally and disregarded the advice of his staff officers and commanders who warned of the dire consequences of a winter operation.

The failure of the Sarikamish campaign at the end of December 1914 and early January 1915 cost Enver Pasha some 80,000 casualties in three army corps and the initiative on the Caucasus front.[4] He returned to Constantinople embittered and in search of scapegoats. The fact that four Armenian volunteer battalions, organized in the Caucasus and composed largely of Ottoman Armenians, assisted the Russian armies could not have escaped his attention. The first battalion under the veteran partisan leader Andranik (Ozanian) was with the Russian forces in northern Persia, while the third and fourth battalions commanded by Hamazasp (Srvandztian) and Keri (Arshak Gavafian) operated on the front facing Erzerum between Sarikamish and Olti. What was more, the Armenian member of the Ottoman Parliament from Erzerum, Garegin Pasdermajian (Armen Garo), had gone over to

---

[4] W.E.D. Allen and Paul Muratoff, *Caucasian Battlefields: A History of the Wars on the Turco-Caucasian Border, 1828-1921* (Cambridge: Cambridge University Press, 1953), pp. 240-41, 251-76, 283-84; Nikolai G. Korsun, *Sarykamyshskaia operatsiia na Kavkazskom fronte mirovoi voiny v 1914-1915 godu* [The Sarikamish Operation on the Caucasus Front during the World War in the Years 1914-1915] (Moscow: Voennoe Izdatel'stvo, 1937), pp. 19-62, 78-93; Maurice Larcher, *La guerre turque dans la guerre mondiale* (Paris: E. Chiron, 1926), pp. 385-89; Felix Guse, *Die Kaukasusfront im Weltkrieg, bis zum Frieden von Brest* (Leipzig: Koehler & Amelang, 1940), pp. 39-52.

the Russians and helped to organize the second battalion of Dro (Drastamat Kanayan), which was poised in Igdir for an advance on Van.[5]

The unfolding of the Armenian Genocide in the city and plain of Erzerum began in May 1915. The villages in particular were subjected to ferocious massacre, whereas the caravans from the city experienced a mixture of outright massacre and deportation toward the Syrian desert. When a Russian offensive in 1916 succeeded in capturing Hasankale in January and then the fortress of Erzerum itself on February 16, there were few Armenians left in the region. The Armenian quarters and villages, completely plundered, stood abandoned. Enver Pasha prepared for a counter-offensive in the spring of 1916 by concentrating ten divisions of the Second and Third Ottoman armies in the Malatia-Kharpert-Diarbekir quadrant, but the campaign was foiled because of the lack of provisions resulting from the deportations and despolia-tion of the land and the successful Russian thrust and capture of the coastline up to Trebizond in April. Then in July, the Russian armed forces, supported by an Armenian battalion, expanded from Erzerum into the western districts of the province—Baiburt (Baberd), Mamakhatun (Derjan), Kghi, and Erzinjan (Erznka).[6]

The Russian foremarch stirred new hopes among the Arme-nians, including the thousands upon thousands of refugees who had fled to Russian territory from Erzerum, Alashkert (Alash-gerd), Bayazit (Bayazed), and Van. But much to their amazement, the tsarist authorities in the Caucasus prevented them from returning home. What was more, orders were soon issued to disband the Armenian volunteer battalions. The motives for these bewildering actions became clear only later, in 1918, when the

[5] For details, see General Gavriil Korganoff, *La participation des Arméniens à la guerre mondiale sur le front du Caucase, 1914-1918* (Paris: n.p., 1927). See also Simon Vratzian [Vratsian], *Kianki ughinerov: Depker, demker, aprumner* [Along Life's Ways: Episodes, Figures, Experiences], 6 vols. (Cairo: Houssaper, and Beirut: Hamazkayin Press, 1955-1966), vol. 3, pp. 21, 27-37.

[6] Allen and Muratoff, *Caucasian Battlefields*, pp. 331-62, 378-83, 400-27; Guse, *Die Kaukasusfront*, pp. 75-88; Larcher, *La guerre mondiale*, pp. 399-402; E.V. Maslovskii, *Mirovaia voina na Kavkazskom fronte, 1914-1917 g.* [The World War on the Caucasus Front, 1914-1917] (Paris: Vozrozhdenie-La Renaissance, 1933), pp. 267-93, 326-30, 362-403.

secret wartime treaties concluded between imperial Russia and its Entente allies, Great Britain and France, were made public by the new Soviet government. By the terms of those agreements, the Ottoman Empire was at last to be dismembered, apportioned for the most part among the three Entente powers. Russia was to expand westward to incorporate the provinces of Trebizond, Erzerum, Bitlis, and Van, while France was to gain direct or indirect control over Sivas, Kharpert, and Diarbekir, together with Cilicia as part of French-dominated "Greater Syria," and Britain, in addition to Egypt, was to take possession of the oil-rich lands of Mesopotamia and other zones of economic exploitation in the Near East.[7] Hence, once the Russian armies had occupied the territories marked for tsarist annexation, there was no further need to foster Armenian national sentiment or aspirations. Rather, the Armenian volunteer battalions were to be dissolved. At the same time, the Viceroy for the Caucasus, Grand Duke Nicholas Romanov, clamped renewed censorship on the Armenian press and circumscribed the activities of Armenian civic organizations.[8] Meanwhile, plans were being drawn up in Petrograd (St. Petersburg) to transfer Cossacks from South Russia to the new expanded borders in "Turkish Armenia."[9]

The heavy concentration of the Russian armed forces in the eastern Ottoman provinces made it clear that when weather and ground conditions permitted, a renewed offensive in the spring

---

[7] See [U.S.S.R.], Ministerstvo Inostrannykh Del, *Razdel Aziatskoi Turtsii po sekretnym dokumentam b. ministerstva inostrannykh del* [Partition of Asiatic Turkey According to the Secret Documents of the F(ormer) Ministry of Foreign Affairs], ed. Evgenii A. Adamov (Moscow: Izdanie Litizdata NKID, 1924).

[8] Karo Sasuni [Garo Sassouni], *Tajkahayastane Rusakan tirapetutian tak (1914-1918)* [Turkish Armenia under Russian Domination (1914-1918)] (Boston: Hairenik, 1927), pp. 108-09; *Hamarot teghekagir H. Azgayin Biuroyi gordsunetian, 1915-1917* [Summary Report on the Activities of the A(rmenian) National Bureau, 1915-1917] (Tiflis, 1917), pp. 8-9; Republic of Armenia, Archives of the Delegation to the Paris Peace Conference, File 1/1, cited hereafter as Rep. of Arm. Del. Archives.

[9] Ashot Hovhannisian, comp., *"Hayastani avtonomian" ev Antantan: Vaveragrer imperialistakan paterazmi shrjanits* ["The Autonomy of Armenia" and the Entente: Documents from the Period of the Imperialistic War] (Erevan: Petakan Hratarakchutyun, 1926), pp. 77-79; Gabriel Lazian, *Hayastan ev Hai Date (Vaveragrer)* [Armenia and the Armenian Question (Documents)] (Cairo, Houssaper, 1946), pp. 199-200; *Razdel Aziatskoi Turtsii*, Appendix III, pp. 360-62.

of 1917 would strike to overwhelm the hard-put Turkish armies. But this action was preempted by the unanticipated Russian revolution in March 1917, which resulted in the abdication of Tsar Nicholas II and the end of the three-century reign of the Romanov dynasty. The near bloodless coup was hailed worldwide by the champions of democracy who placed high hopes on a caretaker administration known as the Provisional Government. Although that government was faced with insurmountable problems, it did lift many of the restrictions that had been imposed on the population and especially the subject nationalities. In the Caucasus, the Viceroy was recalled and the prohibition on repatriation lifted. During the summer of 1917, thousands of Armenian refugees streamed back to their homes in the Russian-occupied territories extending from Erzinjan and Erzerum to Van. The Armenian peasantry enthusiastically hastened to sow their fields, believing that the time of deliverance had finally arrived. The favorable prospect of Armenian self-government under a democratic Russian federative system seemed to be confirmed when Dr. Iakov Zavrieff (Hakob Zavrian), a prominent Armenian public figure, was appointed as assistant in civil affairs to the general in command of the occupied territories, headquartered in Erzerum. Armenian officials were in turn named throughout the region, with Aram Manukian directing the repatriation and administration in Van.[10]

This period of optimism was tinged with growing anxiety, however, as the defeatist propaganda disseminated by Bolshevik agents spread rapidly through the Russian ranks. By the end of summer the Caucasus front, which had been held by more than 200,000 front line and reserve troops, was jeopardized by massive desertion of the Russian peasant-soldiers, who were captivated by the Bolshevik slogan, "peace, land, bread." In an attempt to strengthen the thinning front, Armenian leaders persuaded the Provisional Government under Alexandre Kerensky

---

[10] Simon Vratzian, *Hayastani Hanrapetutiun* [Republic of Armenia] (Paris: Navarre, 1928), pp. 24-25; Sasuni, *Tajkahayastane*, pp. 141-43; Aramayis N. Mnatsakanyan, *V.I. Lenine ev hay zhoghovrdi azatagrakan paikare* [V.I. Lenin and the Armenian People's Struggle for Liberation] (Erevan: Armenian Academy of Sciences, 1963), pp. 224-25.

to authorize the transfer to the Caucasus thousands of Russian Armenian soldiers serving in the European theater. That movement had only just begun, however, when in November the Bolsheviks staged the second revolution of 1917, overthrowing the Provisional Government and giving rise to the bloody four-year Russian Civil War.[11]

The establishment of a Soviet government in Petrograd and Moscow evoked denunciations from the whole of the Caucasus region, except for the proletarian sector of Baku. Georgian, Armenian, and Muslim leaders responded by creating in Tiflis the Transcaucasian Commissariat as a caretaker executive, followed in February 1918 by a provisional legislature, the Seim, to manage affairs pending the liquidation of the Bolshevik "adventure" and restoration of the "democratic" government of all-Russia. The Commissariat worked through the still-loyal Russian army command in the Caucasus to establish a truce with the Ottoman army in December 1917, according to which each side would remain in place along a demarcation line extending from the Black Sea to a point west of Erzinjan and then curving southeastward and passing between Bitlis and Van.[12]

The Russian command, unable any longer to take responsibility for the front, also authorized the formation of the Armenian Army Corps composed of Armenians taken from the regular Russian army and Western Armenian partisan and militia units. General Foma Nazarbekov (Tovmas Nazarbekian) took command, assisted by Dashnakist stalwart Dro as the civilian commissar. The corps was made up of three sub-strength divisions under General Grigorii Areshov (Grigor Areshian), Colonel Moisei Silikov (Movses Silikian), and Western Armenian hero General Andranik Ozanian. Regiments of the first and third divisions were assigned to defend the Erzinjan-Baiburt-Erzerum sector.[13]

---

[11] Garegin Pasdermadjian, *Why Armenia Should Be Free* (Boston: Hairenik, 1918), p. 35; Rep. of Arm. Del. Archives, File 379/1.

[12] [Republic of Georgia], *Dokumenty i materialy po vneshnei politike Zakavkaz'ia i Gruzii* [Documents and Materials on the Foreign Policy of Transcaucasia and Georgia] (Tiflis: Government Press, 1919), pp. 11-23, cited hereafter as *Dokumenty i materialy*.

[13] Korganoff, *La participation des Arméniens*, pp. 77-83; Antoine Poidebard, "Rôle militaire des Arméniens sur le front du Caucase après la défection de l'armée

But the charge to protect a front of more than 250 miles from the Black Sea to Van with only a few thousand replacements for the deserting Russian army was virtually impossible to execute. It was only a matter of time before the Turkish armed forces would move to reclaim the eastern provinces.

The calculation of Lenin to take Russia out of the world war as the only way to preserve the "spark of revolution" so that it might ignite a world revolution necessitated acquiescing in a harsh peace with Germany and its allies, including the Ottoman Empire. In negotiations culminating in the Treaty of Brest-Litovsk on March 3, 1918, Soviet Russia ceded a large part of the European provinces to Germany and Austria-Hungary. And, at Turkish insistence, the new government in Moscow not only agreed to the restoration of all occupied Ottoman territories but, from the prewar Russian side of the boundary, also relinquished the three districts of Kars, Ardahan, and Batum. What was more, in a secret protocol, Russia pledged to disband the Armenian military contingents operating in the entire region.[14] The protests of the Transcaucasian Commissariat and Seim that Soviet Russia was unrecognized and had no jurisdiction in the Caucasus went unheeded as the Turkish armies made preparations to march into the ceded territories.

Already, as the negotiations were proceeding in Brest-Litovsk, Ottoman Third Army commander, General Vehib Pasha, claiming that the Caucasian side had violated the truce and that Armenian bands were victimizing defenseless Muslim civilians, had ordered an advance on Erzinjan. General Kiazim Karabekir's divisions, striking from the direction of Kemakh, had nearly surrounded the town by February 13. The Armenian partisan leader Murad of Sivas (Sepastatsi Murad) attempted to persuade the Russian officers who were still in command to hold the city for a day or

russe (décembre 1917-novémbre 1918)," *Revue des études arméniennes* 1:2 (1920): 150-51; Allen and Muratoff, *Caucasian Battlefields*, pp. 458, 462.

[14] John Wheeler-Bennett, *Brest-Litovsk: The Forgotten Peace* (London: Macmillan, 1938), pp. 256, 405-06; Ministerstvo Inostrannykh Del SSSR, *Dokumenty vneshnei politiki SSSR* [Documents of Foreign Policy of the USSR], vol. 1 (Moscow: Izdatel'stvo politecheskoi literatury, 1957), pp. 199-200; Carl Mühlmann, *Das deutsch-türkische Waffenbündnis im Weltkrieg* (Leipzig: Koehler & Amelang, 1940), pp. 190, 194.

two longer so that the Christian population could be evacuated, but that same evening the order for retreat was issued. The Armenian townsmen, having no time to make preparations, now fled into the freezing night with whatever they could carry. The disorderly throng trudging through deep snowdrifts was repeatedly ambushed by Kurdish bands so that by the time the soldiers and civilians reached Mamakhatun four days later, half of them had been killed or wounded or else had frozen to death or been severely frostbitten. The panic-stricken mass did not stop until it had reached Erzerum behind whose walls scurried thousands of refugees from a 50-mile perimeter.[15] General Karabekir received messages of praise from Vehib Pasha and from Minister of War Enver Pasha, whose imagination once more flew beyond the eastern provinces to unification with the Turkic and Muslim peoples of the Caucasus and beyond.[16]

The fall of Erzinjan created a crisis among Armenian civilian and military circles as only 4,000 troops held the Erzerum line. There was a collective sigh of relief when Andranik arrived on March 3 with reinforcements of about a thousand men. But this was the very same day that far away at Brest-Litovsk these lands were signed away by Soviet Russia. On March 10, Enver Pasha triumphantly issued to the armed forces news of the treaty and instructed General Vehib Pasha to reoccupy all the eastern provinces as well as the districts of Kars, Ardahan, and Batum. Vehib immediately gave notice to the Caucasus army command that it must clear this entire region and that he was marching on Erzerum. By that time, General Karabekir's main force had concentrated to the east of Ashkale, only a short distance from the Armenian front line at Ilija on the western approach to the city.[17]

The offensive began the very next day, on March 11. As the Turkish army advanced from the west, Kurdish mounted partisans

[15] *Dokumenty i materialy*, pp. 41-51, 59-61; Uras, *Tarihte Ermeniler*, pp. 555-66; Sasuni, *Tajkahayastane*, pp. 155-58; Allen and Muratoff, *Caucasian Battlefields*, pp. 461-62; Korganoff, *La participation des Arméniens*, pp. 94-98.

[16] Feridun Kandemir, *Kâzım Karabekir* (Istanbul: Sinan Matbaası ve Neşriyet Fvi, 1948), pp. 153-54.

[17] Joseph Pomiankowski, *Der Zusammenbruch des Ottomanischen Reiches* (Zurich and Leipzig: Amalthea-Verlag, 1928), p. 334; Kandemir, *Karabekir*, pp. 152-54.

attacked from north and south. The Armenian forces were no match, and on March 12 Andranik sounded the order for retreat as the uncontrollable flow of townspeople and refugees passed through the Kars gate leading eastward. As they departed, the Armenians killed many of the Muslim prisoners held in two homes in Erzerum and burned several Turkish villages on their route of retreat. On his entry into the city, Karabekir was overjoyed to find that some 400 canons and large guns and great stockpiles of military equipment, dynamite, and foodstuffs had been left intact.[18]

Armenian abandonment and Turkish reoccupation of Erzerum determined the fate not only of the plain of Karin/Erzerum but also of the whole of Turkish Armenia, which again became the scene of panic and flight. By early April 1918, the Turkish armed forces had retaken all of the Russian-occupied territories and pressed across the prewar frontier to Sarikamish and Novo-Selim on the approaches to the fortress of Kars. Negotiations between the delegations of the Ottoman Empire and the Transcaucasian Seim proved fruitless as the Turkish armies continued to advance. Kars capitulated on April 25, and less than three weeks later, on May 15, Alexandropol (Gumri) in the province of Erevan fell.

It was under these circumstances that the last-ditch Armenian resistance at the approaches to Erevan spared the only remaining Armenian city and may have contributed to Turkish acknowledgment of a rump, landlocked Caucasian Armenian republic that was declared at the end of May. That state, with only about 4,000 square miles of rocky terrain under its jurisdiction, was crammed with countless miserable refugees and led a most precarious existence until the Ottoman Empire surrendered to the Allied Powers on October 30 and Germany capitulated a few days later on November 11, 1918.[19]

---

[18] Allen and Muratoff, *Caucasian Battlefields*, pp. 462-63; Korganoff, *La participation des Arméniens*, p. 108; *Dokumenty i materialy*, p. 93; Rep. of Arm. Del. Archives, File 1/1.

[19] See Richard G. Hovannisian, *Armenia on the Road to Independence, 1918* (Berkeley and Los Angeles: University of California Press, 1967), esp. pp. 157-202.

Erzerum and Armenian Desiderata

The defeat of the Ottoman Empire opened new vistas for the Armenian survivors and the suffocating Armenian republic. The Entente, which had expanded to become the Allied and Associated Powers, including the United States of America, had condemned the perpetrators of the genocide and pledged to punish the guilty parties, individually and collectively, to restore and rehabilitate the survivors, and to guarantee a secure national future for the Armenian people.[20] For a brief time, the Armenian world was buoyed up by euphoric optimism, but those who read carefully the terms of the Turkish surrender in the Mudros Armistice had cause for serious misgivings. The chief British negotiator, in gaining his government's primary objectives regarding waterways, fortifications, and prisoners of war, made concessions to the Ottoman delegation on other points such as the immediate withdrawal of the Turkish armed forces from the Armenian provinces. Thus, while the Turkish divisions in the Caucasus were required to pull back to Kars within six weeks and ultimately to the prewar international frontier, no firm provision was made to remove the Turkish military from Erzerum and the rest of the eastern provinces, which presumably the peace settlement would detach from the Ottoman Empire. In its final form, the Mudros Armistice simply reserved to the Allied Powers the right to occupy all or part of these provinces "in case of disorder."[21] Hence, as many as 20,000 Turkish troops and irregulars were allowed to remain armed in the region of Erzerum. Failure to require immediate withdrawal was to raise major obstacles to Armenian repatriation and territorial expansion when so authorized by the Paris Peace Conference.

---

[20] See Richard G. Hovannisian, "The Allies and Armenia, 1915-18," *Journal of Contemporary History* 3:1 (1968): 145-55.

[21] Minutes of the negotiations are in Great Britain, Public Record Office, Foreign Office Archives, 371/5259, E5732/5732/44, cited hereafter as FO. The terms of the Mudros Armistice are in Parliament, House of Commons, *Sessional Papers (Accounts and Papers)*, 1919, Cmd. 53, and in United States, Department of State, *Papers Relating to the Foreign Relations of the United States, 1918*, Supplement 1: *The World War*, vol. 1 (Washington, DC: Government Printing Office, 1933), pp. 441-43.

These disturbing realities notwithstanding, Armenians were confident that with Allied assistance they would emerge from the nightmare of war and massacres in a strengthened position. Many Armenians, especially the refugees and those living in Diaspora, envisaged a greater Armenia extending from the Caucasus and Black Sea to Cilicia and the Mediterranean Sea. The temporary capital at Erevan would surely be moved westward to the center of the homeland—the *erkir*—at either Erzerum or Van. When the issue of desiderata was put to the first legislative body of the Armenian republic, the Khorhurd, it displayed greater moderation, instructing the delegation departing for Paris to seek the unification of Russian Armenia with the six provinces of Turkish Armenia and secure access to the sea. There were a few voices that considered even this claim to be too ambitious and recommended being content with the Republic's incorporation of the three eastern vilayets of Erzerum, Bitlis, and Van.[22] When the Republic's delegation arrived in Paris, however, Avetis Aharonian was quickly carried away by the sentiments of the diasporan Armenians as expressed by Boghos Nubar's National Delegation.

Aharonian joined Nubar in appearing before the Supreme Council of the Paris Peace Conference in February 1919 to argue the case for a free and separate Armenian state stretching from the Caucasus to the Mediterranean Sea, reparations for the staggering wartime losses, and measures to rescue the thousands of abducted Armenian women and children. But staking claims and making good on them were quite different matters. The decimation of the Armenian menfolk and youth during the genocide heavily taxed the resources of the existing small army and limited its potential for taking by force what might be awarded by the peace conference. This rendered Armenia all the more dependent on external assistance and protection in making its way into the world as a permanent nation-state.[23]

---

[22] Rep. of Arm. Del. Archives, File 74; Al. Khatisian, *Hayastani Hanrapetutian tsagumn u zargatsume* [The Creation and Development of the Republic of Armenia] (Athens: Nor Or, 1930), pp. 97-98; Vratzian, *Kianki ughinerov*, vol. 5, pp. 44-45.

[23] Rep. of Arm. Del. Archives, File 104a/3a; United States, Department of State, *Papers Relating to the Foreign Relations of the United States, 1919: The Paris Peace Conference*, 13 vols. (Washington, DC: Government Printing Office, 1942-1947), vol. 4, pp. 147-56, cited hereafter as *Paris Peace Conference.*

Throughout 1919, both Aharonian and Nubar and the Armenian government led by Alexandre Khatisian appealed for the means to begin the repatriation of the Armenian refugees, both to ease the crush of exposed, starving, disease-ridden exiles in the small existing state and to start the process of reconstruction by preparing the fallow fields before the sowing season had passed. Various plans were put forward for the repatriation in stages to the closest border districts, starting from Igdir to Bayazit and Van, and from Kars to Basen and Alashkert and then extending to the plain of Karin/Erzerum. American physician and relief official Dr. Clarence Ussher, who had witnessed the Armenian defense of Van in 1915, even traveled to Paris to push for a plan to repatriate the Armenians before the peace conference had rendered its decision on the final disposition of these territories. By his plan, which was supported by former U.S. Ambassador to the Ottoman Empire, Henry Morgenthau, and other prominent figures then in Paris, the adult males would return first with seed grain and implements to sow the fields, the older boys and orphans would follow to harvest the first crop, and then after a few more months the women and children would join the men and rekindle their hearths. Ussher suggested that technically the operation could even be conducted under the auspices of the Ottoman government, which after the war would surely be anxious to show that it repudiated the crimes of the Young Turk regime and wished to make amends. While proponents of this and other such plans gained a sympathetic ear in certain American and British official circles, they failed to secure a commitment for Allied officers and a small military force to oversee the repatriation. Rather, the Allied director of worldwide relief, Herbert Hoover, manipulated the situation so as to circumvent any military obligations and instead had one of his staff members appointed merely to supervise relief efforts to aid the Armenians, meaning that the tens of thousands of refugees pressing along the frontiers would be unable to pass beyond the prewar Russo-Turkish boundary to get home.[24]

---

[24] See Richard G. Hovannisian, *The Republic of Armenia*, 4 vols. (Berkeley, Los Angeles, London: University of California Press, 1971-1996), vol. 1, pp. 295-312, vol. 2, pp. 40-61.

Erzerum and the
Turkish Resistance Movement

The Turkish surrender to the Allied Powers created grave fears
and problems for thousands of persons who had participated in
or benefited from the Armenian Genocide. The victorious nations
were on record with the pledge to punish the perpetrators. Moreover, as everywhere else, countless Muslim native inhabitants and
newcomer refugee *muhajirs* in Erzerum had taken possession of
Armenian homes, lands, and goods and now faced the frightful
prospect not only of having to vacate and return these properties
but also of being compelled to leave the region entirely. It was
not surprising, therefore, that local Ittihadist leaders and others
who had the most to lose should initiate efforts to protect the
area from Armenian expansion, insisting that a mere 600,000
Armenians would not be allowed to rule the majority Muslim
population in the eastern provinces. In March 1919, member of
the Ottoman Parliament Jevad Dursunoghlu was instrumental in
summoning the organizational meeting in Erzerum of the Association for the Defense of the Rights of the Eastern Vilayets. The
assembled Turkish and Kurdish notables declared that the eastern
provinces had always been Muslim and Turk. The Armenians
could find no historic identity here, for their claims to culture
and civilization were based on a feudal system in a feudal time.[25]

The Turkish resistance movement gained a strong champion
in General Kiazim Karabekir, who in March 1919 was appointed
commander of the XV Army Corps, with jurisdiction over the
provinces of Trebizond, Erzerum, and Van. Arriving in Erzerum
in May, he immediately took control of the local defense organization, exclaiming: "There is nothing of Armenians here—the
ruins of a few churches and nothing more. . . . There cannot and
there will not be an Armenian government here." Rather, he
boasted, "I shall take Armenia as a pawn. This is the key to

---

[25] Cevat Dursunoğlu, *Milli mücadelede Erzurum* [Erzerum in the National
Struggle] (Ankara: n.p., 1946), pp. 19-20, 33-34, 143-44; M. Tayyib Gökbilgen,
Milli mucadelede başlarken: Mondros mütarkesinden Sivas Kongresine [Beginnings
of the National Struggle: From the Mudros Armistice to the Sivas Congress], vol. 1
(Ankara: Türk Tarih Kurumu, 1959), pp. 74, 114-15.

securing for ourselves the favorable peace settlement that we desire."[26]

In July, Karabekir was joined by General Mustafa Kemal (Ataturk), who had managed to get himself appointed as inspector of the armies in the eastern provinces, including the XV Corps at Erzerum and the III Corps at Sivas, as a way to slip away from the watchful eyes of the Allied authorities in Constantinople. Although he and Karabekir immediately became rivals and competitors, they did collaborate to thwart the looming threat of Armenian expansion into the region. At a gathering convened on July 23 and subsequently memorialized as the "Erzerum congress," Karabekir urged the local notables "to smother the lust of the Armenians and Greeks to our lands and crush their hopes forever." He was miffed that Kemal was able to sway the delegates to be elected chairman but nonetheless joined in the formation of the Association for the Defense of the Rights of Anatolia. The manifesto of the congress declared that the natural frontiers of the nation took in the entire provinces of Trebizond, Erzerum, Sivas, Diarbekir, Kharput (Kharpert), Van, and Bitlis. All attempts to dismember any part of these lands would result in a Holy War—*Jihad*. Neither foreign protectorates nor mandates would be tolerated.[27]

As the Turkish resistance movement began to take shape, General Karabekir played a double role: on the one hand, professing loyalty to the sultan in Constantinople and assuring Allied control officers that he was operating within the terms of the Mudros Armistice, while, on the other hand, circumventing the directives of the central government and British control mission that had arrived to oversee the removal and shipment out of the region of breechblocks from the heavy artillery as well as arms and ammunition in excess of the prescribed limits. He allowed

---

[26] Kâzim Karabekir, *İstiklâl Harbimiz* [Our War of Independence] (Istanbul: Türkiye Yayinevi, 1960), pp. 19-23, 44-45; Enver Behnam Şapolyo, *Kemal Atatürk ve milli mücadele tarihi* [Kemal Ataturk and the History of the National Struggle] (Istanbul: Rafet Zaimler Yayinevi, 1958), pp. 285-87.

[27] Dursunoğlu, *Milli mücadelede Erzurum*, pp. 63-69, 107-20, 151-54, 160-70; Şapolyo, *Kemal Atatürk*, pp. 226-30. See also the collection of articles without publisher or date, *Erzurum Kongresi ve Mustafa Kemâl Atatürk* [The Erzerum Congress and Mustafa Kemal Ataturk].

the first trainload of weapons to depart from Erzerum toward Sarikamish and Kars but secretly arranged for "partisans" to sever the rails near the frontier and help themselves to as much of the arms as they could cart away before he ordered the train back to Erzerum. He explained to the chief of the control mission, Lieutenant Colonel Alfred Rawlinson, that unfortunately the railway was inoperable and the route was impassible.[28]

In June 1919, Brigadier General William H. Beach, chief of British military intelligence in the Caucasus, traveled to Erzerum to admonish Karabekir to cooperate and to caution him that he would be held responsible for the security of all roads in the area under his command. Karabekir professed his readiness to fulfill his obligations although, he claimed, he had received no directives from his government regarding the dismantling and exportation of arms. After Beach's departure, Rawlinson reported that the Turkish officers were no longer complying even ostensibly. A new trainload of munitions reached the border at Zivin in July, but now "rock slides" prevented further passage. Rawlinson's protests to Karabekir were met with the explanation that the local inhabitants were so disturbed by Armenian schemes to seize Turkish lands as far west as Sivas that they would not tolerate the movement of military matériel over Armenian-controlled territory, even if the weaponry was supposedly headed for the port of Batum to be sent to storage depots near Constantinople. He gave assurances that all arms and equipment would be safeguarded by him pending conclusion of the peace treaty. Colonel Rawlinson, expressing personal sympathy for the Turkish position and promising to do his utmost to retain Turkish sovereignty over Erzerum, tried to persuade Karabekir to comply with the stipulated arms limitations, but his coaxing and appeals were unavailing. In view of this impasse, the British senior commander in Constantinople, General George F. Milne, ordered the control mission to withdraw.[29]

---

[28] Alfred Rawlinson, *Adventures in the Near East, 1918-1922* (London and New York: A. Melrose, 1923), pp. 163-234; Karabekir, *İstiklâl Harbimiz*, pp. 359-60; Dursunoğlu, *Milli mücadelede Erzurum*, pp. 61, 73-74.

[29] FO 371/3659, 102537/512/58, FO 371/4158, 1026001/1201900/521/44; Rawlinson, *Adventures*, pp. 184, 190, 225-26, 230-31; Karabekir, *İstiklâl Harbimiz*, pp. 42-43, 46, 87-89.

As Rawlinson prepared to leave at the beginning of August 1919, he was introduced to Mustafa Kemal, who gave notice that "any decision by the Peace Conference to allow Armenian Government any territory beyond the old Turco-Russian frontier would be met by a revolutionary army." In a detailed report submitted to his superiors, Rawlinson drew attention to the fact that many demobilized soldiers remained in the eastern provinces because of the lack of transportation, uncertain conditions in western Anatolia, and a natural desire to resist Armenian aggression: "The *greatest* inducement however has been the deserted state of the Eastern districts from which the pre-war population has absolutely *vanished* or a more correct description would perhaps be 'been exterminated'." Because barely 10 percent of the rural population was left, "the demobilized troops have found free houses and land at their disposal everywhere and the effect has been to produce a population which consists of a unique proportion of trained soldiers who are not only instinctively anti-Armenian, but are at the same time moved by the strongest inducement (i.e. their interest in retaining the properties they have squatted on) to resist any Armenian repatriation or any measure which might result in their losing the advantages they have gained." The entire Muslim population, Rawlinson continued, had been systematically armed, with some 100,000 rifles illegally distributed and the country abounding in concealed military caches. As recently as July, 160 machine guns sent from Erzerum overland to Trebizond by the control mission had "entirely disappeared." Rawlinson concluded that any plan to reduce the territory of Asiatic Turkey and cede any part of it to Armenia would require a sizable Allied military force and entail a "long and arduous undertaking."[30]

Each passing month brought increased hope and encouragement to the Turkish Nationalists. These took a great leap in the summer of 1919 when it was announced that Great Britain would withdraw its armed forces from the Caucasus. British and Indian regiments had occupied strategic sites, especially along the railway and pipeline from Baku to Batum, at the end of 1918 as the Turkish armies evacuated the region and drew back to Kars

---

[30] FO 371/4158, 126001/521/44.

and then beyond the prewar border. The Armenians had attached high hopes to the arrival of these imperial contingents, believing that the enormous Armenian wartime losses and sacrifices would at last be compensated, especially as Turkey was a defeated enemy power and both of Armenia's Caucasian neighbors, Georgia and Azerbaijan, had been established with the support of Germany and Turkey, respectively. These calculations proved illusionary, however, as the primary objective of the British military was to maintain the status quo and a degree of order pending the Paris Peace Conference's rulings on the future of the region. Various proposals by Khatisian's government to have the British assist in the repatriation of Armenian refugees to Erzerum, Bitlis, and Van met with no success. Still, the proximity of the British armed forces to the Armenian republic at Erevan afforded a certain sense of security and reassurance. Now, even that was to be lost and, from the perspective of Karabekir and Kemal, the British will have left without either having disarmed the Turkish armies or repatriated the Armenians. Moreover, throughout the year Karabekir dispatched officers and small military echelons across the prewar frontier into the province of Kars and into the southern districts of Erevan province to encourage, train, and lead Muslim partisans in their struggle to reject the authority of the Armenian government. The Turkish general was careful at all times to list the officers and men on such missions as deserters or absent-without-leave in order to profess compliance with terms of the Mudros Armistice.[31]

The rivalries over the spoils of war among the victorious Allied Powers contributed to repeated delays in completing the treaty of peace with Turkey. Unlike traditional wars when treaties were signed on the field of battle or shortly after surrender, the Turkish treaty was ultimately imposed on the sultan's government almost two years after the end of the world war. This long interval proved critical for the formation and organization of the Turkish resistance movement, whose leaders adroitly exploited the obvious growing cracks among the Allies. In September 1919, Mustafa Kemal took the lead in broadening the resistance to a national movement, at least in name, when the Sivas congress

---

[31] See Hovannisian, *Republic of Armenia*, vol. 2, pp. 68-69, 109-39, 225-26.

created the Association for the Defense of the Rights of Anatolia and Rumelia, superseding the regional organization at Erzerum and dedicated to the preservation of the prewar Turkish boundaries in Europe and the eastern provinces.[32] The immediate postwar gloom and fatalism were now giving way to a spirit of defiance.

The Mandate Question and U.S. Commissions

The fate of Erzerum and the entire Armenian Plateau rested in large measure on the ability of the Armenians to find a power to assist and strengthen the projected Armenian state until it could gather in its dispersed people and stand on its own. It was hoped that the United States, which had been so outspoken in condemnation of the wartime atrocities and which had a sustained record of missionary and educational work among the Armenians, might come forward as the protector or mandatory for the new Armenia. That was the wish of the European powers, too, especially as Russia was in the throes of revolution and civil war and it was undesirable that the eastern Ottoman provinces should come under Russian sway no matter which side won.

At the Paris Peace Conference, President Woodrow Wilson repeatedly indicated his personal sympathy for the Armenians and his hope that the people and Congress of the United States would be persuaded to reach out to Armenia. In fact, in the secret internal U.S. guidelines for the peace settlement, a large Armenian state, with Erzerum at its heart, was projected. But Wilson was an enigmatic leader, frequently changing positions and unwilling to strike hard on the Armenian issue. Hence, throughout 1919, the question of the future of Armenia was left in flux. Meanwhile, the Allied and Associated Powers imposed the harsh Treaty of Versailles on Germany and continued the drafting of the treaties with the other defeated enemy states of Austria, Hungary, and Bulgaria. The Turkish treaty was thus left to the

---

[32] Mahmut Gologlu, *Sivas Kongresi* [The Congress of Sivas] (Ankara: Basnur Matbaası, 1969), pp. 61-112, 219-60; Mustafa Kemal, *A Speech Delivered by Ghazi Mustapha Kemal, President of the Turkish Republic, October 1927* (Leipzig: K.F. Koehler, 1929), pp. 57-133 *passim*.

last.

Armenophile organizations in the United States and Europe repeatedly joined Armenian spokesmen in Paris and London and the Armenian government in Erevan to urge that the Allied Powers take effective measures to resolve the Armenian Question. They protested that thousands of Armenians were dying while waiting to return to their native provinces and that the Turkish authorities were rapidly moving in Muslim settlers from the west and Kurdish tribesmen from the south to alter the demographic composition of the eastern provinces in order to deny the Armenians their rightful patrimony. General Karabekir in Erzerum was violating the Mudros Armistice, yet the Allied Powers, having reserved to themselves the right to occupy the region in case of disorder, remained inactive in face of this blatant defiance.

Instead of completing the draft of the Turkish treaty, for which ample materials had been gathered in Paris, London, and Washington, the peace conference stalled for time in 1919 by approving an American proposal to send a fact-finding mission to the Near East. But, even after that mission, led by Henry C. King, President of Oberlin College, and Charles R. Crane, a prominent industrialist friend of Woodrow Wilson and a trustee of Robert College in Constantinople, had completed its work and drafted its recommendations, President Wilson decided to dispatch a second mission to gather additional information that might be helpful should the United States decide to assume the mandate for Armenia.

The King-Crane commission, June-August 1919, concentrated on Syria and Palestine and did not travel to Erzerum, but it did receive spokesmen of all interested parties, including Armenian Patriarch Zaven Ter-Eghiayan (Der Yeghiayan) and other Armenian leaders in the Ottoman capital as well as in Aleppo and Cilicia.[33] In the portion of their report dealing with the non-Arab provinces, King and Crane confirmed the horrors of the Armenian deportations and massacres, declaring that "these crimes—

---

[33] See Harry N. Howard, *The King-Crane Commission: An American Inquiry in the Middle East* (Beirut: Khayat, 1963); United States, *Paris Peace Conference*, vol. 12, pp. 745-802.

black as anything in human history—cannot be simply forgotten and left out of account in seeking a righteous solution of the Turkish problem." They recommended that, while the total dissolution of the Ottoman Empire should be rejected and Anatolia should be kept inviolable as a Turkish homeland, it was only just that a separate Armenian state be created because of the demonstrated unfitness of the Turks to rule over others, their lack of penitence for the massacres or repudiation of the crime, and their refusal to allow the repatriation and the restoration of goods and properties of the surviving Armenians. It was unreasonable to expect Armenians to live ever again under the oppressive Turkish yoke. Armenia should be awarded some part of the eastern Ottoman provinces but should be made relatively compact in order that the scattered Armenian people might gather in and become a majority in a short time. The new state should encompass the Russian Armenian districts around Erevan and approximately those parts of the Trebizond, Erzerum, Bitlis, and Van vilayets that had been occupied by the Russian armies in 1916. Here, the Armenians could attain a clear majority within five years. Although the state would be modest in size, its territory would be sufficient to ensure economic viability and give the Armenians both a geographic unity and defensible boundaries, thus reducing the responsibilities of a mandatory power and hastening the time for full Armenian self-government.[34]

The King-Crane commission was followed by the second field inquiry, the American Military Mission to Armenia, led by Major General James G. Harbord. This large group included some sixty specialists in government and politics, geography and ethnography, military affairs, public and private finance, commerce and industry, public health and sanitation, agriculture and animal husbandry, the press, and other fields relevant to the responsibilities with which any mandatory power would have to be concerned. The records of the Harbord mission are extensive and, even now after decades, remain an impressive testimony to American organizational skill and thoroughness.[35]

---

[34] *Paris Peace Conference*, vol. 12, pp. 810-48; Howard, *King-Crane Commission*, pp. 232-37.

[35] See the full records in United States, National Archives, Record Group 256,

Arriving in Constantinople from France at the beginning of September 1919, the mission set out on an overland journey of nearly a thousand miles, southeastward by railway through Asia Minor to Cilicia and Aleppo, then eastward to Mardin before turning northwestward by automobile and horseback to Diarbekir, Kharpert, Malatia, and Sivas, and from there eastward to Sushehir, Erzinjan, and Erzerum to beyond the prewar boundary into Kars and Erevan in the Republic of Armenia, and via Tiflis (Tbilisi) and Batum back to Constantinople a month later. All along the way, the mission saw the gruesome evidence of the Armenian Genocide. Harbord later recalled that he and his men "literally dreamed Armenia and Massacres."[36]

Reaching Sivas on September 20, the group was accommodated at the American mission station, where it was learned that fewer than 20,000 of the original 200,000 Armenians of the province still survived and that many Armenian women and children remained confined against their will in Muslim households. General Harbord also met with Mustafa Kemal, who only a week earlier had presided over the Sivas congress. Kemal defined the Nationalist movement in anti-imperialistic Wilsonian terms and denied rumors of renewed persecutions of Armenian survivors, complaining instead about various schemes to dismember the Ottoman Empire and to award parts of Anatolia to Greeks and Armenians. He deplored the wartime massacres of Armenians but ascribed them to "a small committee which had usurped the government." The current Greek outrages at Smyrna, on the other hand, were occurring under the cover of an Allied fleet, and the "Erivan republic" was trying to exterminate the local Muslim population in a "wave of sanguinary savagery." He blamed the British for inciting the Armenians and Turks against each other as a pretext to occupy the entire area.[37]

As the Harbord mission traveled eastward toward the border of the Erzerum vilayet, the telling signs of devastation and

File 184.021, cited hereafter as RG 256. See also Harbord's own account, "Investigating Turkey and Trans-Caucasia," *World's Work* 40 (May, June, July 1920): 35-47, 176-92, 271-80.

[36] Harbord, "Investigating" (May 1920): 36.

[37] RG 256, 184.021/93/96/242/243/247/250/255/257/258/259/263/282/329/342; Harbord, "Investigating" (May 1920): 44-47, and (June 1920): 176-80, 185-90.

depopulation became all the more evident. At Sushehir, two Armenians had the courage to state in the presence of Turkish officials that no Christians had escaped deportation or confinement in Muslim households and that few of the 500 people who had returned since the end of the war had been able to reclaim their goods and properties. In Erzinjan, two Armenians and a Greek priest remained mute as the Turkish authorities reported to Harbord that the prewar and postwar numbers of Armenians for the district were 16,000 and 500 as compared with 97,000 and 61,000 Turks. The American Military Mission was welcomed to Erzerum by local notables and XV Army Corps commander Kiazim Karabekir, who clearly was in charge. He took the party on a tour of the city, pointing to the rubble of two houses where he said the Armenians had burned a thousand Turks before their retreat in 1918. Armenian cruelty, he complained, was continuing, as 40,000 defenseless Muslims had recently been driven from their homes in districts just beyond the frontier. The Armenians had never formed a significant element in the eastern vilayets, in Erzerum city making up scarcely 5,000 of the 45,000 inhabitants and less than 10 percent in the province. The Erevan government had to abandon its imperialistic visions and seek an accord with the patriotic forces of Turkey or else face the consequences. When Harbord left Erzerum toward Sarikamish and Kars in Armenian territory, Karabekir wrote his military comrades that he was now more certain than ever that the Americans would not intervene in any way in Armenian-Turkish affairs.[38]

After meeting Armenian military and government officials and gathering additional information in Kars and in Erevan, the American Military Mission to Armenia returned to Constantinople and then to France and on to the United States. Its records, numbering thousands of pages, were condensed into a primary report and twelve appendices. In the main document, General Harbord reviewed the history of Armenia, the record of persecution and broken promises since the 1870s, the prevailing condi-

---

[38] Harbord, "Investigating" (June 1920): 190-92; Harutiun H. Khachaturian, "Amerikian zinvorakan arakelutiune depi Hayastan" [The American Military Mission to Armenia], *Hairenik Amsagir* 19 (Jan. 1941): 130-32; Karabekir, *İstiklâl Harbimiz*, pp. 302-05.

tions in Anatolia and Armenia, and the feasibility of and requirements for a mandate. A sense of outrage characterized his description of the deportations and massacres that had begun in
1915: "Mutilation, violation, torture, and death have left their
haunting memories in a hundred beautiful Armenian valleys, and
the traveler in that region is seldom free from the evidence of
this most colossal crime of all the ages. . . . Conditions shriek
of misery, ruin, starvation, and all the melancholy aftermath, not
only of honorable warfare, but of beastial brutality unrestrained
by God or man." The Paris Peace Conference, Harbord continued, had decided that Turkish rule over Armenia should end, but
ethnographic and economic considerations complicated the situation. It was recommended, therefore, that the whole area from
Constantinople to Transcaucasia be placed under a single mandatory power, in a federal type of system, with Armenia being one
component until it was able to govern and defend itself. He
concluded by listing reasons both for and against acceptance of
a mandate.[39]

In the report on geography and the boundaries of Armenia,
Major Lawrence Martin proposed a relatively large Armenian
state extending from Van to the Gulf of Alexandretta (Isken-
derun) on the Mediterranean Sea but excluding Diarbekir and
Sivas. If no mandatory power could be found, then the state
should be made smaller so that the western boundary would
extend from Van and Mush to a point on the Black Sea, leaving
Erzerum in but Erzinjan out of the new Armenia.[40] Ironically,
President Wilson did not use either the King-Crane or the Harbord report to advance the Armenian cause. The first was not
made public until 1922, and the second was not released to
Congress until April 1920, by which time the opponents of U.S.
entanglements abroad had grown in strength and simply seized
upon the listed difficulties for the mandatory power to turn them
against Wilson and his belated request for authorization to accept
the mandate for Armenia.

The prospect of an American mandate over Armenia was set
back by the adamancy of Woodrow Wilson in his dealings with

---

[39] RG 256, 184.02101/5.
[40] RG 256, 184.02101/13.

the Republican-dominated Senate and the vindictiveness of the Senate majority spearheaded by Henry Cabot Lodge. In the postwar scheme of things, the assumption of mandates over former colonies or subject peoples of Germany and other defeated powers was to be under the aegis and on behalf of the League of Nations. The statutes (Covenant) of the League were embodied in the Versailles peace treaty with Germany, partly in the belief that the U.S. Senate would not dare reject that critical treaty. But Wilson miscalculated. He lacked the necessary two-thirds majority required for ratification and made no concessions to win over enough votes to carry the treaty and with it American adherence to the League of Nations. Rather, the Senate twice declined to ratify the Versailles treaty, killing any real possibility that the United States would assume the protectorate for Armenia.

Signals of Retreat

So long as there was a realistic possibility of an American mandate for Armenia, the European Allies did not strongly oppose the creation of a larger Armenian state that would include the six eastern Ottoman provinces, an outlet on the Black Sea, and perhaps even a port on the Mediterranean Sea. By late 1919, however, it was clear that the United States would not participate in drafting or become a signatory to the Turkish peace treaty. Hence, it was time for a strategic retreat, which conservative circles both in Great Britain and France had long advocated. As no one was willing to use armed force to remove the Turkish armies from the eastern provinces, certain concessions to the sultan's government, it was suggested, might strengthen its hand against Mustafa Kemal's Nationalists and make possible a reasonable settlement.[41]

Alarmed by these developments, Boghos Nubar and Aharonian appealed anew to the Allied Powers, reminding them of their pledges and promises to free Armenia from "the Turkish yoke." During a brief meeting at the end of November 1919, British Foreign Secretary Lord Curzon bluntly told Boghos Nubar that

---

[41] Hovannisian, *Republic of Armenia*, vol. 2, pp. 404-11, 426-37.

because an American mandate was now highly unlikely, it would not be possible to include Cilicia and a Mediterranean outlet in Armenia. He regretted that the Mudros Armistice had not stipulated the immediate military occupation of the Armenian provinces but maintained that a viable state could still be attained through the unification of the Erevan republic and the three eastern vilayets of Van, Bitlis, and Erzerum.[42]

In a series of meetings between British Prime Minister David Lloyd George and French Premier Georges Clemenceau, December 11-13, 1919, it was decided to proceed with the Turkish treaty without the United States. A French position paper supported a reconstituted Armenian state but noted that, despite their antiquity, high civilization, and intelligence, the Armenians lacked political cadres and like the Jews were widely dispersed. They could not have all the land they were claiming, as this would disadvantage them, especially in view of their great losses since 1895. Hence, in Turkish Armenia they should have the basin of Lake Van, the plains of Bitlis and Mush, and the eastern sector of the province but not the city of Erzerum, with guaranteed rail connections to the sea. A British Foreign Office internal assessment of the French memorandum concurred that an Armenia from the Black Sea to the Mediterranean Sea was no longer feasible but noted that in the eastern provinces the Muslim population, too, had been decimated by invasions, famine, and epidemics and there were sound ethnographic and strategic reasons to include the fortress city of Erzerum in Armenia.[43]

That even the French position was not firm was demonstrated in January 1920 in an additional memorandum that suggested that the Armenian boundary be placed somewhere between Erzerum and Erzinjan to the west, with the new state guaranteed rail access to Batum, which should be made into a free port as had

---

[42] Armenian National Delegation Archives, Minutes of Delegation of Integral Armenia, no. 59, Nov. 29, 1919; Avetis Aharonian, *Sardarapatits minchev Sevr ev Lozan* [From Sardarabad to Sèvres and Lausanne] (Boston: Hairenik, 1943), pp. 31-32.

[43] FO 371/4239, 167432/15167/44; published in Great Britain, Foreign Office, *Documents on British Foreign Policy, 1919-1939*, 1st ser., ed. W.L. Woodward et al., 27 vols. (London: H.M.S.O., 1946-1985), vol. 4, pp. 942-56, cited hereafter as *British Documents*.

been done in the case of Danzig.[44] It was now Lloyd George who had qualms about awarding Erzerum to the Armenians. Circumventing Foreign Secretary Curzon, the prime minister asked the Secretary of State for India, Sir Samuel Montagu, to prepare the British observations on the French memorandum. The resulting document, expressing the views of the India Office and of the War Office under Winston Churchill, recommended easing the restrictions on Turkey further, including allowance for a regular standing army, forgoing reparations, and leaving the sultan in Constantinople. As to the eastern frontier, Montagu stressed that Erzerum should not be detached from Turkey: "Erzerum would be more of a commitment than a source of strength to Armenia. It has always been for the Turks a main defence against their traditional enemy, Russia, and deprivation of it would be a perpetual incentive to the Turks to attack the Armenians for its recovery." Hence, the boundary should run a few miles to the east of the city, thereby leaving the entire Araxes River Valley within Armenia.[45] This and other issues were taken up in formal Anglo-French negotiations in London from February to April 1920.

The London Conference

By the time that the Allied Supreme Council convened in London on February 12, Premier Georges Clemenceau had been voted out of office and succeeded by Alexandre Millerand, who now served both as premier and foreign minister. The London conference reiterated the view that the Allies were committed to the creation of an independent Armenia but that, because of the unwillingness of the United States to share in the responsibilities, there was no longer a question of a greater Armenian state but rather whether or not the smaller Armenian state should include the city and fortress of Erzerum and the port of Trebizond. Foreign Secretary Curzon acknowledged that the British military authorities had advised against the inclusion of Erzerum but insisted that, if that were to be the case, effective measures would be required to dis-

---

[44] FO 371/4239, 170654/15167/44; *British Documents*, vol. 4, pp. 1016-25.
[45] FO 371/4239, 172029/15167/44; *British Documents*, vol. 4, pp. 1036-42.

mantle all fortifications and establish a demilitarized buffer zone between Turkey and Armenia. French Assistant Foreign Minister Philippe Berthelot agreed that the existing Armenian republic around Erevan should serve as the nucleus of the new state, to which the Allies would award additional territories in the eastern Ottoman vilayets. The Allies would honor their obligations to the Armenians, even though so many of them had been massacred or deported that repopulation of the land was a serious problem. The fantasy of a greater Armenia had been encouraged by "the entourage of President Wilson," but fortunately even the Armenians now understood that they could not have Cilicia and much of the other territories originally claimed.[46]

The London conference appointed a commission on February 17 to come up with specific recommendations on the future of the Armenian state inclusive of "the present *de facto* Independent Republic of Erivan and portions of the adjacent Turkish vilayets." Boghos Nubar and Avetis Aharonian appeared before the Armenia commission on February 21 to stress the strategic importance of Erzerum geographically, politically, militarily, and commercially. It was the hub of roads radiating in all directions and was vital for the defense of Armenia. Although the new state would have natural lines of defense in the north, east, and south, the western approach was the traditional avenue of invasion and could be protected only by Armenia's control of the mountainous salient extending beyond Erzinjan and Kemakh. If left in Turkish hands, Erzerum would serve as a base for aggression and become a festering grounds for pan-Islamic and pan-Turkic agitation. Placing the border west of Erzinjan and Kemakh would afford the Armenian army a strategic advantage in the face of a larger Turkish army. During this testimony, it became obvious that British commissioner Robert G. Vansittart was sympathetic to the Armenian arguments whereas French commissioner Albert Kammerer displayed strong skepticism regarding Armenian possession of the city of Erzerum.[47]

In a second meeting with the Armenia commission on Febru-

---

[46] *British Documents*, vol. 7, pp. 42-43, 81-84.

[47] Ibid., pp. 86-87, 97-98; Rep. of Arm. Del. Archives, Files 116/15, 132/31, 133/32, 234/133, and 241/140; Aharonian, *Sardarapatits*, pp. 39-40, 44-46.

ary 26, the Armenian spokesmen were accompanied by Patriarch Zaven, who supported Aharonian's attempt to expose the fallacy of using the terms "Turk" and "Moslem" interchangeably. Kurds, Kizilbashes, Lazes, Zazas, and Yezidis were often lumped together with Turks in misleading statistical tables, whereas these groups were distinct and in many ways alienated from the Turks and lived in general harmony with the Armenians. A memorandum submitted that day showed that some 800,000 Armenians would move into the Ottoman territories to be awarded the Armenian republic. They would migrate from all parts of the former Russian Empire, Georgia and Azerbaijan, the Balkans, the Arab provinces, the United States, and from areas that were to be left within the Turkish state.[48]

The Armenia commission, in its report to the London conference on February 27, ultimately recommended the award of Erzerum to Armenia. Because of the wartime decimation and dispersion of the Armenian people, however, its territory should not be too extensive so that the Armenian element might soon become preponderant. Strategically, it would have been desirable to include Trebizond and Erzinjan, but political and ethnographic considerations precluded this option. Rather, there should be a demilitarized zone between Turkey and Armenia, whose western boundary should run from the juncture of the Erzerum and Trebizond vilayets to the west of Baiburt into the Bitlis vilayet. The coast of Lazistan to the east of Trebizond could be made into an autonomous state under the nominal suzerainty of Armenia in order to allow Armenia to convert the passages from Baiburt into carriage roads to the small Black Sea harbors in that sector. Armenia should also have transit rights over the main road from Erzerum to Trebizond with export-import privileges at that major port. The commission cautioned, however, that nothing would be possible unless effective measures were taken to remove the Turkish armed forces from the area set aside for Armenia.[49]

---

[48] Rep. of Arm. Del. Archives, Files 118/17 and 234/133; Aharonian, *Sardarapatits*, pp. 47-51; FO 371/4952, E708/134/58.

[49] *British Documents*, vol. 7, pp. 268-69, 280-82; FO 371/4932, E1066/1/58, and, for a map of the suggested boundaries, FO 371/4953, E1123/134/58.

On March 24 the Armenia commission submitted a second report, which related to the future of the port of Batum and included the draft articles that would constitute the Armenia Chapter in the Turkish peace treaty. These required the Ottoman government to recognize the independence of Armenia and the cession to it of parts of the Trebizond, Erzerum, Bitlis, and Van vilayets.[50] When the London conference adjourned on April 10, major strides had been made toward completion of the Turkish treaty, yet many details and several policy issues were still outstanding. Although Foreign Secretary Curzon pressed for the summoning of the Turkish envoys at the earliest possible moment to receive the terms of peace, Lloyd George and Millerand wanted a little more time and therefore accepted the invitation of Italian Prime Minister Francesco Nitti to meet a few days later at San Remo on the Italian Riviera to conclude the deliberations.

The San Remo Conference

When the Allied leaders convened at San Remo on April 18, conditions in the Near East were becoming more and more troubling. Christians in Marash and elsewhere had again been massacred, and Armenian survivors and repatriates were again fleeing, this time from the Turkish Nationalist forces that owed their allegiance to Mustafa Kemal Pasha. The underlying problem was that the Allied Powers were unwilling, individually or collectively, to commit the requisite armed forces to implement the treaty they were drafting. They were fully aware that this was the case even as they weighed the merits of whether or not to award Erzerum to Armenia. Prime Minister Nitti, a very small voice in the previous meetings, now declared emphatically that the difficulties facing the Allies would only be compounded if Erzerum were given to Armenia. "It would not be necessary, no doubt, to declare war on Turkey to have the treaty executed, but in effect it would be necessary to wage it. To take Erzerum and to conduct a campaign in the middle of Anatolia would require big forces. The larger Armenia was to be, the greater would be its difficulties; more especially if Erzerum, which was not Arme-

---

[50] *British Documents*, vol. 7, pp. 639-49.

nian, were included." Lord Curzon stood alone at San Remo in reminding the heads of state of the pledges regarding the Armenian people and that "it was not possible to drop the matter entirely and leave Armenia in the lurch."[51]

The Allied divestiture of responsibility continued on April 20 when the military experts explained that it would take twenty-seven divisions to enforce the proposed Turkish treaty as it pertained to the Straits, Thrace, Smyrna, Syria, Mesopotamia, Armenia, and what was left of Turkey. Four divisions would be required to enforce the Armenia Chapter, but at present there were only twenty-two divisions, that is, enough for almost everything except Armenia. Now, Lloyd George exclaimed that the Armenians should be able to fight their own battle, just as the Greeks had done. They should be supplied with arms and equipment and given a fighting chance. "If they were not in a position to defend their own frontiers, then . . . there was no use for a nation of that kind in the world, and not one of the Allied Governments, in those circumstances, would be prepared to assist them to the extent of even a single battalion." Once again, it was Curzon who attempted to draw attention to the fact that the London conference had already decided that the expanse from Erzerum to Lake Van would be awarded to Armenia and that the new state would require external support in order to endure.[52]

Between April 21 and 24 the San Remo conference was occupied with the proposed expansion of Greece to Gallipoli and the outskirts of Constantinople and its control of Smyrna. Nitti used Lloyd George's championing of the Greek cause to raise the need for concessions elsewhere, especially regarding Erzerum, which the Armenians could neither take nor defend; instead all there would be was another massacre. David Lloyd George concurred that it was "an extraordinary proposition" to ask the Armenians to conquer a vast territory when they could barely cling to their existing small state." Curzon could only reiterate that the London conference had considered the Erzerum question in detail and had concluded that leaving the strategic area to the Turks would make the survival of an independent Armenia

---

[51] *British Documents*, vol. 8, pp. 48-49.
[52] Ibid., pp. 54-67.

impossible. Both the League of Nations and the Armenian representatives had already been informed that Erzerum would be included in the future Armenian state. Lloyd George snapped that "the Armenians had really no right to indulge in unjustifiable hopes." Nitti, capitalizing on the split in the British delegation, warned that if the Turks were pressed too hard they would refuse to sign the treaty. The Allies should not give Armenia "something which, in her own interests, she had better not have." Curiously, it was now the French delegation that seemed to support Curzon.[53]

Boghos Nubar and Avetis Aharonian, who were warned in private that the Allies would not assist in taking Erzerum, appeared before the Supreme Council at San Remo to assert that the Armenian army could occupy the area by its own means if given Allied moral, financial, and military support. Aharonian noted that the Armenian republic had defended itself valiantly for two years without receiving a single bullet from the West, so it was certainly capable of taking Erzerum if provided with weapons, uniforms, and instructors.[54] Erzerum was the natural capital of Armenia and dominated the entire plateau. A viable state was inconceivable without that strategic fortress city. After the Armenian delegates had withdrawn, Marshal Ferdinand Foch, as the head of the military experts, expressed grave doubt that the ill-equipped Armenian army could conquer any territory from an enemy force that controlled all the lines of communication. Berthelot, now repeating Curzon's arguments, argued that if the Turks refused to sign the treaty it would not matter whether Erzerum was awarded to Armenia, whereas if they did sign and the treaty became law, only irregular Turkish forces would remain to resist the Armenian army. Right would be on the side of the Armenians, and the Turks eventually would have to accept it. "If the treaty assigned Erzerum to Armenia, Armenia would at least have a legal title to it, and the law had some force of realisation in its very nature." Lloyd George replied that he did not want to seem to be unsympathetic, but the danger was that

[53] Ibid., pp. 89-94, 107-19, 123-26.
[54] Ibid., pp. 116-18, 120-21; Aharonian, *Sardarapatits*, pp. 72-75; Rep. of Arm. Del. Archives, Files 132/31 and 235/134.

conferences lived in a world of illusions. Possession of Erzerum could not be decided in a conference. It would have to be taken by force, and blood would be spilled. If Armenia could not exist without Erzerum, then it should not exist at all.[55]

The Allied leaders were annoyed that the Erzerum question had consumed so much of their time at San Remo. On April 24, Lloyd George suggested breaking the impasse by placing the responsibility for a decision on President Wilson. Unless the United States was willing to step in, the size of the Armenian state would have to be drastically reduced. Supported by Alexandre Millerand, the British prime minister proposed that the United States be asked to accept the mandate for Armenia and in any case to arbitrate whether Erzerum should be included in Armenia or be made into a neutral zone. This move, he explained, would force the Americans "to take a definite interest in Armenia's future." Dismissing Lord Curzon's arguments that the treaty could not be submitted to the Turkish government without definite boundaries, Lloyd George retorted that the boundaries would remain as they were, "that is confined to the Republic of Erivan," until President Wilson rendered a decision.[56]

The next day, April 25, the Allied chiefs of state agreed in the first instance to ask the United States to accept the mandate for Armenia and in the second instance:

> to invite the United States, in case of its unwillingness to assume the mandate, to arbitrate the boundaries, it being stipulated before-hand that Turkey, Armenia, and the other contracting parties would agree to refer to the president on the boundaries within the provinces of Trebizond, Erzerum, Bitlis and Van, and accept in advance any decision as well as any stipulation regarding access to the sea for the independent state of Armenia.[57]

By this decision, not only Erzerum but the entire western frontier of Armenia would be submitted to American arbitration. Such a strategy held the advantage of shifting responsibility for the specific territorial award from the European Allies to the

---

[55] *British Documents*, vol. 8, pp. 121-22, 138-39.
[56] Ibid., pp. 145, 156-58.
[57] Ibid., pp. 177-78. See also RG 59, 180.03801/12.

United States. By allowing Wilson to grant Armenia more territory than either the Allied military or political leaders deemed
prudent and defensible, the Supreme Council was acting, not to
create a viable, united Armenian state, but rather to find excuses
for its failure to do so. By the time the invitation was sent to
Woodrow Wilson on April 26, 1920, the Allied divestiture of
responsibility for Armenia was well advanced.[58] The Allies made
no pretense that they actually expected the United States to
shoulder the mandate or offer military support. They merely
sought an American response in order to make it easier in the
future to explain the nonfulfillment of their pledges regarding the
Armenians. What is perhaps surprising is that Wilson took the
bait. On May 17 he announced his personal acceptance of the
invitation to serve as arbiter of the boundaries between Armenia
and the residual Turkish state, expressing his abiding desire "to
contribute to the welfare of the Armenian people."[59]

With this turn of events, the drafting committee prepared the
following article for inclusion in the Turkish treaty:

> Turkey and Armenia as well as the other High Contracting
> Parties agree to submit to the arbitration of the President of the
> United States of America the question of the frontier to be fixed
> between Turkey and Armenia in the Vilayets of Erzerum,
> Trebizond, Van, and Bitlis, and to accept his decision thereupon,
> as well as any stipulation he may prescribe as to access for
> Armenia to the sea, and as to the demilitarisation of any portion
> of Turkish territory to the said frontier.

The Allied Powers had thus found the perfect escape hatch.

After repeated delays, the Turkish delegation representing the
official government of Sultan Mehmed VI signed the Treaty of
Sèvres on August 10, 1920, thereby recognizing the independence
of Armenia and assuming the obligation to free women and
children abducted or forcibly converted during the war, to coop-

---

[58] For the full communication to President Wilson, see *British Documents*, vol.
8, pp. 217-19, and *Papers Relating to the Foreign Relations of the United States,
1920*, 3 vols. (Washington, DC: Government Printing Office, 1936), pp. 779-83,
cited hereafter as *FRUS, 1920*.

[59] *FRUS, 1920*, p. 783.

erate in the collection of evidence and prosecution of those responsible for the wartime atrocities, and to guarantee full religious and cultural freedom to the minorities remaining in Turkey.[60] Avetis Aharonian signed the treaty on behalf of the Republic of Armenia in what he described as the happiest day of his life. But the delay in completing the treaty for so long had given time for the Mustafa Kemal's resistance movement to consolidate, and the Turkish hero was now prepared to challenge both the sultan's government and the disunited and irresolute Allied Powers. In order to overturn the Treaty of Sèvres, it was essential to destroy the very nucleus of the projected Armenian state, that is, the Armenian republic in the Caucasus. To this end, he sought not only domestic but also foreign support, specifically that of another outcast regime, that of Soviet Russia, which was engaged in its own struggle for survival and hoped to use the prestige of Turkey in the Islamic world to arouse much of the colonial world against the adversarial powers of Great Britain and France.

"Wilsonian Armenia"

Although the Allied Supreme Council invited President Wilson in April 1920 to determine the western and southern boundaries of Armenia within certain limits, it was not until mid-July that the State Department began to assemble a team of experts for the assignment, and it was not until after the Treaty of Sèvres had been signed in August 1920 that the committee began its work. By that time, Woodrow Wilson, against the strong counsel of his closest political allies and even the American Committee for the Independence of Armenia, had on May 24 belatedly submitted to Congress a request for authorization to assume the mandate for Armenia. But it was already a dead issue, and the reasons for

---

[60] The Armenia Chapter became Part III, Section VI, Articles 88-93 of the Treaty of Sèvres. See "Treaty of Peace between the British Empire and Allied Powers (France, Italy, Japan, Armenia, Belgium, Czecho-Slovakia, Greece, the Hedjaz, Poland, Portugal, Roumania and the Serb-Croat-Slovene State) and Turkey—Sevres, August 10, 1920," in *British and Foreign State Papers*, vol. 113, ed. Edward Parkes et al. (London: H.M.S.O, 1923), pp. 672-73. For other relevant provisions, see pp. 681-85, 706-07.

Wilson's action are perplexing. Perhaps, he was so aware of the judgment of history that he wanted to go down on record as having done whatever possible for the Armenian people who were being abandoned, or he may have thought to make this an issue to take to the American people in a presidential election year. Whatever the case, the effect proved more harmful than good, and it took the Senate only a few days to hand the president a stinging rebuke by voting on June 1 to "respectfully decline" his request.[61]

Rejection of the Armenian mandate still left Wilson with the obligation to submit a decision on the borders. This assignment was undertaken by "The Committee upon the Arbitration of the Boundary between Turkey and Armenia," headed by Professor William Linn Westermann, who had been adviser on Near Eastern affairs to the U.S. delegation at the Paris Peace Conference, and including Major (Professor) Lawrence Martin of the Harbord mission and Harrison W. Dwight of the Near Eastern division of the State Department. The committee used as a guideline a combination of ethnic, religious, economic, geographic, and military factors and took advantage of the extensive documentation already gathered as well as direct interviews with General Harbord, missionaries, and others who had personal experience in the region. The primary objective was to draw such boundaries that would allow the Armenian element, when combined with the inhabitants of the small existing Armenian republic, to constitute half the total population at the outset and to become an absolute majority within a few years. As much as it may have wished to do so, the committee was unable to award any part of the Kharpert vilayet to Armenia because of the arbitration limits laid down by the Allied Supreme Council.[62]

The "Full Report of the Committee upon the Arbitration of the Boundary between Turkey and Armenia" explained that less than half the territory claimed by the Armenians was being assigned, but Armenia was receiving as much of the four provinces as was consistent with strategic, economic, and ethno-

---

[61] Hovannisian, *Republic of Armenia*, vol. 4, pp. 1-24.
[62] For the records of the boundary committee, see US Archives, RG 59, File 760J.6715.

graphic considerations. Because the caravan route from Erzerum and Baiburt to Trebizond posed insurmountable difficulties for railroad construction, the Kharshut River Valley ending near the coastal town of Tireboli to the west of Trebizond was being included in order to make possible direct rail access to the sea. The map drawn by the committee followed a series of mountain ridges and water divides, leaving most of Van, Bitlis, Erzerum, and Trebizond in Armenia. In the Erzerum vilayet, the boundary ran along the Kghi (Buyuk) River, a short distance to the east of the town of Kghi, northward to a point 35 kilometers or 22 miles southwest of Erzinjan and 6 kilometers or 4 miles east of Kemakh, and then to the meeting place of the Erzerum and Trebizond vilayets, about 40 kilometers or 25 miles northwest of Erzinjan. Hence, Baiburt, Mamakhatun, and Erzinjan would fall within Armenia, whereas Kghi and Kemakh would remain in Turkey. The boundary continued into the Trebizond vilayet to the Black Sea at a point 9 kilometers or 6 miles east of the small port city of Kerasund (Giresun), thereby leaving the port of Trebizond and the coastline of Lazistan within Armenia. This territorial award would increase the area of the Republic of Armenia to about 155,000 square kilometers or 60,000 square miles. It was anticipated that after the return of the refugees and exiles Armenians would make up about 50 percent of the population and that this percentage would increase rapidly thereafter.[63]

The report was submitted to the State Department at the end of September 1920, five months after the Supreme Council's request to President Wilson, but once again delays followed. It was not until November 22 that Woodrow Wilson signed the final report titled "Decision of the President of the United States of America Respecting the Frontier between Turkey and Armenia, Access for Armenia to the Sea, and the Demilitarization of Turkish Territory Adjacent to the Turkish Frontier." The text of the arbitration decision was cabled to the United States ambassador in Paris on November 24 and delivered to the Allied Supreme Council in early December.[64] By that time, however, the

[63] RG 59, 760J.6715/65.

[64] RG 59, 760J.6715/27/34/40/54/64/65/70/72. The text of Wilson's letter of transmission to the Supreme Council is in *FRUS, 1920*, pp. 790-95.

prospect of a united Armenian state with its southern and western boundaries extending into the provinces of Van, Bitlis, Erzerum, and Trebizond had been wiped away by the realities on the ground. Mustafa Kemal and Kiazim Karabekir effectively nullified the arbitration decision and the Treaty of Sèvres itself by rolling over the Caucasian Armenian republic.

Armenian-Soviet-Turkish Negotiations

As the Allied Supreme Council considered ways to escape from its commitments to the Armenians, Mustafa Kemal continued the process of creating a Turkish counter-government in Angora (Ankara), and Kiazim Karabekir began to prepare for military action against the Caucasian Armenian republic. First, however, it was essential to receive assurances of Soviet financial and military support. One of the earliest actions of Mustafa Kemal as president of the Turkish Grand National Assembly, which convened on April 23, 1920, was to address Lenin and the Soviet government in revolutionary terms with the offer of mutual cooperation. Soon thereafter he dispatched a delegation to Moscow to enter into direct negotiations.[65]

The Armenian government, too, although intensely anti-communist, decided at the end of April 1920 that it could not avoid seeking a modus vivendi with a power that had defied the odds to emerge victorious in the Russian Civil War and was poised to flank the Caucasus Mountains to recover Baku and sovietize Azerbaijan. The three-person Armenian delegation headed by Levon Shant was instructed to gain Soviet recognition of an independent united Armenian state encompassing both the Russian-Armenian and the Turkish-Armenian provinces and permission for the thousands of Armenian refugees scattered throughout Russia to transfer with their movable belongings to the new Armenian state.

---

[65] Türk İnkilâp Tarihi Enstitüsü, *Atatürk'ün tamin, telgraf ve beyannameleri, 1917-1937* [Ataturk's Circulars, Telegraphs, and Declarations, 1917-1937] (Ankara: Ankara Üniversitesi Basimevi, 1961), pp. 304-05; Gotthard Jäschke, "Neues zur russisch-türkischen Freundschaft von 1919-1939," *Die Welt des Islams*, n.s., 6:3-4 (1961): 205-06.

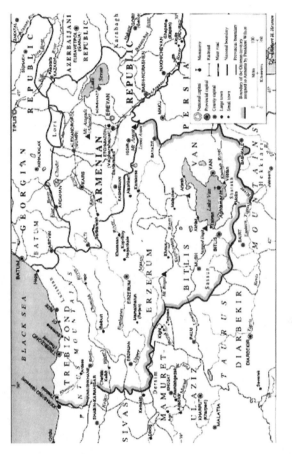

Erzerum and the Boundaries of "Wilsonian Armenia," 1920

In the first meeting between the Armenian delegation and Soviet officials in late May, Foreign Affairs Commissar Grigorii Chicherin stated that the Soviet government wished to reconcile Armenian and Turkish differences. This could be facilitated if Armenia relinquished false hopes founded on Western-imposed imperialistic terms for peace and accepted instead the good offices and mediation of Soviet Russia to reach a just solution. The Armenian spokesmen questioned how such mediation was possible when Mustafa Kemal was claiming not only all of the Turkish-Armenian provinces but also the Russian-Armenian districts of Kars and Ardahan. Chicherin let it be known that he favored the inclusion of Van and Bitlis in Armenia but found it difficult to justify the Armenian bid for Erzerum. Aside from historical and ethnographic considerations, the interests of the tillers of the soil had to be taken into account and, of course, in any mediation the interests of the Armenian workers would also be given their due. The future status of Erzerum was only one of several critical issues discussed in the Armenian-Soviet exchanges, which at first seemed productive but then at the end of June were abruptly interrupted by the Soviet side with the announcement that a Soviet delegation would soon depart for Erevan for direct negotiations with the Armenian government. The apparent real motive was to stall for time because of the impending arrival of Mustafa Kemal's envoys.[66]

General Kiazim Karabekir was often at odds with Mustafa Kemal and chaffed under Kemal's egocentric, overbearing behavior. Still, he concurred with Kemal that the only way to save Turkey was through opening the Caucasus land-bridge between Anatolia and Russia by eliminating the three small independent republics that had emerged there following the collapse of imperial Russia. Azerbaijan had already become a Soviet republic at the end of April 1920, and in June 1920 Karabekir won the consent of the Angora government to deploy his armed forces into the province of Kars from Barduz to Merdenek and from Karaurgan to Sarikamish. The offensive was soon postponed both

---

[66] Hambardzoum Terterian, "The Levon Chanth Mission to Moscow," *Armenian Review* 8:2-3 (1955): 3-22, 94-104; Rep. of Arm. Del. Archives, File 17/17; Hovannisian, *Republic of Armenia*, vol. 4, pp. 46-62.

for technical reasons and because of the receipt by Mustafa Kemal of a Soviet reply to his initial communication. Foreign Affairs Commissar Chicherin expressed praise and support for the heroic Turkish liberation movement but also offered Soviet mediation between Armenia and Turkey to establish "clearly defined frontiers determined on the justice and the right of national self-determination." Because it was necessary to show good faith to the Soviet leaders, the Turkish offensive was postponed pending the results of direct Turkish-Soviet negotiations in Moscow.[67]

The Turkish delegation led by Bekir Sami Bey arrived in Moscow in mid-July and immediately impressed upon Chicherin the need to open the overland Caucasus route for the safe delivery of arms and equipment to Anatolia. During the month-long negotiations, it became clear that the Soviets were prepared to offer Mustafa Kemal military and monetary assistance and to cooperate in other ways. From the Turkish perspective, the only major obstacle was in Chicherin's repeated argument that, in exchange for retaining all other territories of Turkish Armenia and even extending into the Kars district as far as Sarikamish for strategic reasons, the Angora government should be willing to allow the Armenian state to incorporate parts of the Van and Bitlis vilayets. An exchange of populations in these regions would ensure a just and separate existence for both Armenians and Turks. Bekir Sami was adamant in his rejection of the suggestion and in his assertion that he was not authorized to discuss boundaries or territorial matters. In the end, Lenin and Stalin apparently overruled Chicherin. A draft bilateral Soviet-Turkish treaty of friendship was signed on August 24, 1920, with attached military protocols and with no concessions to the Armenians. A member of Bekir Sami's delegation made his way back to Anatolia in September with the good news.[68]

---

[67] *Dokumenty vneshnei politiki SSSR*, vol. 2 (1958), pp. 554-55; Karabekir, *İstiklâl Harbimiz*, pp. 714-18.

[68] Yusuf Kemal Tengirşenk, *Vatan hizmetinde* [In Service of the Fatherland] (Istanbul: Bahar Matbaası, 1967), pp. 149-93; Ali Fuat Cebesoy, *Moskova hâtıraları (21/11/1920—2/6/1922)* [Moscow Memoirs (November 21, 1920-June 2, 1922)] (Istanbul: Vatan Neâriyati, 1955), pp. 61-74, 78-87; *Dokumenty vneshnei politiki SSSR*, vol. 3 (1959), p. 325n8.

Mustafa Kemal now had the assurances he needed and immediately issued the command to General Karabekir to advance into the province of Kars. At that time, the four divisions of the XV Army Corps had an estimated 25,000 officers, enlisted men, and mounted partisans. Karabekir began operations in the Barduz-Olti sector in mid-September and then launched an all-out attack on Sarikamish at the end of the month. By mid-October he had captured half of the province of Kars and driven the Armenians back to the complex of forts at Kars itself. That seemingly impregnable fortress fell at the end of the month amid Armenian confusion and abandonment, and in November the prostrate Armenian government had to sue for peace in the knowledge that not only Erzerum but all other lands of Turkish Armenia and probably much of Russian Armenia, too, would be lost.[69]

At the same time, the Armenian leaders submitted to the inevitable choice between the lesser of two evils, and in negotiations with the Soviet delegation that had arrived in Erevan proclaimed Armenia to be a Soviet republic and relinquished its authority to the Revolutionary Committee of Soviet Armenia. In the agreement on the transfer of power, Soviet Russia pledged to restore the Armenian boundaries as they had been prior to the Turkish offensive, meaning that Soviet Armenia would have to repudiate the Treaty of Sèvres but at least gain back the half of Russian Armenia that had been occupied by the Karabekir's army. But the Soviet authorities soon voided this agreement and reneged on their pledge. Rather, in the Soviet-Turkish Treaty of Moscow in March 1921, repeated in the Treaty of Kars in October between the Soviet republics of Armenia, Azerbaijan, and Georgia and the Turkish government of the Grand National Assembly, nearly all the occupied Armenian territories were left to Turkey, thereby establishing the boundaries between the Republic of Turkey and the Soviet Union and currently between Turkey and the three again-independent Caucasian states. The Western powers, too, recognized these changes when in 1923 they made major concessions to Mustafa Kemal in the Treaty of Lausanne. The Treaty of Sèvres with its Armenia Chapter became

---

[69] Hovannisian, *Republic of Armenia*, vol. 4, pp. 180-202, 237-92.

a dead letter.[70]

Thus ended the contest for Erzerum and the prospect of a united, independent Armenian state with Karin/Erzerum or Van as its capital.[71] Unable to take by force what was given to them on paper, the Armenians once more had sought Western intervention and assistance, but as in the past the Western orientation produced nothing but blood and tears. The prosperous Armenian middle class of Karin and the industrious peasants of its plain would never return. The vivid memories of the exiles and refugees would gradually dim for their progeny, born, educated, and speaking other languages in lands near and far from Erzerum. Yet in strange and unexpected ways, Armenian Karin still reveals itself.

---

[70] Ibid., pp. 373-408.

[71] A final sad page in this saga was the fate of the Armenian prisoners of war, most of whom were captured at Kars and transferred on General Karabekir's orders to Erzerum. There, through the severe winter months of 1920-21, some 2,000 junior officers and enlisted men were subjected to hard labor and harsh living conditions, so that when at last the prisoners were released and sent to Soviet Armenia at the end of 1921 only 98 officers and 531enlisted men still survived. See "Hayaget u hogevorakan gortsich Garegin Hovsepyani dzeragire" [The Manuscript of Armenologist and Spiritual Leader Garegin Hovsepian], ed. and intro. Bagrat A. Ulababyan, *Banber Hayastani Arkhivneri* 30:3 (1989): 125-58; Artashes Babalian, "Karsi ankume" [The Fall of Kars], *Hairenik Amsagir* 2 (April-May 1924): 54-65, 96-112; Karabekir, *İstiklâl Harbimiz*, p. 1024. See also FO 371/4962, E13827/134/58 encl.

❋ 16 ❋

SAROYAN'S ODYSSEY:
JOURNEYS TO ERZERUM

David Stephen Calonne

William Saroyan, in a letter to James Tashjian dated May 14, 1956, thanks him for sending Sarkis Atamian's book, *The Armenian Community* (1955): "I look forward to studying it," he writes, and then requests Sirarpie Der Nersessian's *Armenia and the Byzantine Empire.*[1] Twenty-one years later, on January 6, 1977, Saroyan again writes to Tashjian: "I remember that you mentioned you were sending me some books, when they arrive I shall be most eager to study them. I hope that among them will be *A Journey to Arzrum* by Alexander Pushkin, translated by Birgitta Ingemanson Aridis, $2.50, and *Erzerum (Garin): Its Armenian History and Traditions*, Hratch A. Tarbassian, translated from the Armenian by Nigol Schahgaldian, and published by the Garin Compatriotic Union of the United States."[2] And three years before his death, he writes once more on May 7, 1978: "Somewhere along the line you and I talked or wrote about some books that I was interested in that you said you would send, and while I have forgotten their names, anything you can send will be much appreciated, for as you know I am obsessed by general reading but especially by Armenian stuff."[3]

This, of course, is typical William Saroyan: joyous excitement about books and reading. And it is also typical that Saroyan should be so eager to obtain these specific books concerning Erzerum since throughout his career he was fascinated, as he puts it, with "Armenian stuff." This included historical

---

[1] *Armenian Review* (Saroyan Memorial Issue) 34:3 (1981): 322.
[2] Ibid., p. 339.
[3] Ibid., p. 340.

Armenia and the traditions and culture of the Armenians of Erzerum, Bitlis, Mush, Dikranagerd, Kharpert, Trebizond, and Van, who were thrust into Diaspora and would ultimately become his friends, neighbors, and relatives in Fresno, California, USA.

The epigraph to his great novella "The Assyrian" is taken from Austen Henry Layard's *Nineveh and Its Remains* (1849): "I had traversed Asia Minor and Syria, visiting the ancient seats of civilization, and the spots which religion has made holy. I now felt an irresistible desire to penetrate to the regions beyond the Euphrates, to which history and tradition point as the birthplace of the wisdom of the West."[4] Saroyan read, knew, and remembered a huge amount of Armenian lore, and this desire to move back and into Armenian space and time, even to Urartu and ultimately to Mesopotamia, to the "birthplace of the wisdom of the West," grew increasingly strong as he was nearly pulverized by the pain of his divorce, remarriage, second divorce, and the disintegration of his family during the late 1940s and early 1950s.

Beethoven's string quartets composed near the end of his life illustrate the composer's deepening interiority, just as Saroyan later in life moved ever closer to Armenian earth, descending inwardly toward Armenia for supplies of primal imaginative power. His actual journeys to Armenia multiplied as he grew older, traveling there in 1960, 1964, 1976, and 1978. The city of Erzerum was on his itinerary, and here I want to trace Saroyan's exploration of Erzerum in the autobiographical memoirs, *The Bicycle Rider in Beverly Hills*; *Here Comes, There Goes, You Know Who*; and *Letters from 74 rue Taitbout*, and, in his late plays, *Armenians*; *Bitlis*; and *Haratch*, as well as his depiction of his brother Henry (named "Krikor" in the stories), who was born in Erzerum.

William Saroyan was an extoller of cities. Paris, New York, London, Moscow, Vienna, Warsaw, San Francisco, Fresno, all became mythologized through the alchemy of his art, became part of his imaginative world, became "places where I've done

---

[4] William Saroyan, *The Assyrian and Other Stories* (New York: Harcourt, Brace, 1949), p. 2.

time," and ultimately became central characters in his stories, novels, memoirs, and plays. Like D.H. Lawrence, he had a genius for discovering what Lawrence called "the spirit of place." Throughout his life, Saroyan would eagerly ask new people he met about their names, genealogies, and origins and from which Armenian towns their families came. In his writing he hymned the names of Armenian places as lovingly as John Milton sang Oreb, Sinai, and Sion hill in *Paradise Lost*. So Saroyan's intense questioning of Armenian acquaintances was part of his urge toward a kind of recovery: after all, he had lost his father Armenak at the age of three, lost his family during his stay at the Fred Finch Orphanage in Oakland, lost his wife and children. And the Armenians had lost a hallowed home-land—*Hayastan, erkir drakhtavayr* (Armenia, Land of Paradise), as Hovhan Vanandetsi (1772-1841) memorably and lyrically sang.

In "The Grapes," the second chapter from his autobiography *Here Comes, There Goes, You Know Who*, Saroyan describes his childhood and the Armenian population of Fresno: "And there, all through the town, were the Armenians, from Bitlis, Van, Mush, Harpoot, Erzeroum, Trebizone, Diarbekir."[5] This list is significant, for Erzerum will reappear obsessively in similar litanies of Armenian cities which Saroyan composed throughout his career.

William Saroyan repeatedly invokes Erzerum as he tells the story of the Saroyan family odyssey of wandering, which began in Bitlis, as Takoohi Saroyan gives birth to daughters Zabel in 1899 and Cosette in 1902. Armenak, Saroyan's father, reached New York alone in 1905, while in that same year, the Saroyans, presided over by grandmother Lucy Garoghlanian, stayed for about four months in Erzerum where Saroyan's brother Henry was born. William Saroyan was born on August 31, 1908, in Fresno.

The telling and retelling of the story of the Saroyan family's exodus from Bitlis through Erzerum to Trebizond becomes a kind of epic in which Saroyan sings, as Homer sings the terrible

[5] William Saroyan, *Here Comes, There Goes, You Know Who* (New York: Simon and Schuster, 1961), p. 6.

and wonderful tale of wandering and harried Odysseus, his family's mythic journey of exile in search of home. He was, after all, the only Saroyan born in America, and his relatives became his way of knowing about Armenia, his link to his own partially buried identity, his family's history, and the cataclysm of the genocide.

Erzerum's role in that terrible history was significant. According to Robert Mirak in *Torn Between Two Lands,* there was an incredible "rush" to leave Turkey after 1890: "In 1892-1893, 3,500 Armenians obtained visas from the Russian consulate in Erzerum to flee to Russia, and an equal number crossed the Russian frontier without passports; in all, an estimated 20,000 men, women and children sought the protection of the Romanov Empire. In 1894 the Armenian archbishop of Erzerum and the Russian authorities both cut the flow of Armenians to Russia by granting permits only to those crossing for temporary visits."[6] Thus, Erzerum, like Bitlis, was central in the Saroyan family's history and was equally an area of cataclysmic conflict.

Erzerum was also the stage upon which one of Saroyan's heroes, General Antranig (Andranik Ozanian), enacted valiant deeds. Richard Hovannisian points out that, after the Russian armies had abandoned the Caucasus front in 1917-18, Antranig, who "arrived in Erzerum at the beginning of March [1918] to organize the defense, found it impossible to control the panic or stem the stream of civilians and soldiers fleeing through deep snowdrifts toward Kars. On March 12 a Turkish division, commanded by General Kiazim Karabekir, entered Erzerum and took possession of 400 large fortress guns, great stockpiles of military matériel, and, most important, the strategic center of the Armenian plateau."[7] When Saroyan visited Père Lachaise cemetery in Paris, it was Antranig's tomb he hurried first to visit, rather than those of Balzac, Wilde, Modigliani, Proust, or the other great artists. Erzerum was doubtless for him the place of

[6] Robert Mirak, *Torn Between Two Lands: Armenians in America 1890 to World War I* (Cambridge, MA: Harvard University Press, 1983), p. 46.

[7] Richard G. Hovannisian, "Armenia's Road to Independence," in Richard G. Hovannisian, ed., *The Armenian People from Ancient to Modern Times,* vol. 2: *Foreign Dominion to Statehood: The Fifteenth Century to the Twentieth Century* (New York: St. Martin's Press, 1997), p. 292.

General Antranig and Armenian suffering as well as the place of the Saroyans.

Saroyan describes the family's exodus through Erzerum in "Hovagim Saroyan" from *Letters from 74 Rue Taitbout, or Don't Go but if You Must, Say Hello to Everybody*—an account repeated in his 1951 novel *Rock Wagram* (Arak Vagramian). Saroyan writes in his "letter" to Hovagim Saroyan:

> Your father and my mother's father were brothers, and I knew my mother's father (Minas) has died in Bitlis, and, dying, had said to my mother's mother, "Get the family out of here, leave this place, go anywhere else, but do not stay here any longer, go to America if you can manage." And of course she *did* manage, although it wasn't easy: the people who control the papers and the rubber stamps had to be bribed with gold one by one, and then transportation had to be paid for, first by donkey train over high mountains along narrow roads from Bitlis to Erzeroum, where my brother Henry was born in 1905, and from Erzeroum to Trabizon, where a ship carried them to Constantinople, and then to Marseilles, where they all had to work to raise money for the train ride across France to Le Havre, where again they had to work until there was enough money to put everybody on the ship that sailed to New York—a long crossing, far below in the ship, in steerage, where hundreds of families prepared their own meals and made sleeping places on the floor, followed at last by the terror of Ellis Island.[8]

In *The Bicycle Rider of Beverly Hills*, Saroyan again tells the tale of the journey through Erzerum:

> My father reached New York alone in 1905. After two years he was reunited there with his wife, his daughters Cosette and Zabel, which appears to be a variant of Isabelle. He saw for the first time his son Henry, born in Erzeroum, en route to America. This journey from Bitlis to New York took almost two years, for it was necessary for my grandmother Lucy who was in charge of the journey to halt several times while she and daughters Takoohi and Verkine and her son Aram worked to

---

[8] William Saroyan, *Letters from 74 rue Taitbout, or Don't Go but if You Must, Say Hello to Everybody* (Cleveland: World Publishing, 1969), pp. 24-25.

earn money for further passage.

They spent three or four months in Erzeroum, a month or two in Marseille, and almost six months in Havre. My uncle Aram, then eleven or so, learned French and acted as interpreter for many Armenians on their way to America. The women knitted stockings which Aram sold to small shopkeepers.[9]

In *Here Comes, There Goes, You Know Who,* there is a picture, marked "Erzeroum" in the text and "Le Havre" on the photograph itself, with the date 1906. In the photograph are uncle Aram Saroyan, Lucy with Henry on her lap, aunt Verkine with Zabel standing before her, Takoohi, and Cosette.

The fact that his brother Henry was born in Erzerum, of course, made the city personally significant to Saroyan. The sensitive nature of his relation to his brother Henry, who was three years older, is apparent in many of Saroyan's early stories. What is noteworthy in these masterpieces is the way Saroyan combines the theme of Erzerum with the question of loss, the homeland, and his family's epic-making journey. Saroyan confronts in Erzerum and in his relation to his older brother Henry his own submerged Armenian identity.

Perhaps the most revealing story about Erzerum and Henry is "Around the World with General Grant," from *Little Children* (1937), in which Saroyan substitutes Trebizond for Erzerum as Henry's birthplace. It is a story about two boys who look at a travel book and yearn to make journeys of their own. Saroyan writes:

My father had been dead for eight years. My brother Krikor was fourteen years old. I was eleven. My father had entered the world in a mountain city in Armenia, a city now destroyed. My brother Krikor was born in Trebizond, on the Black Sea. He was born on the way to America, between travel by donkey and horse over the earth of the Old World and travel by ship over the seas of the Old World to the New World. As an infant he was never long in one place. From the city in the mountains to Trebizond, from Trebizond to Marseilles, from Marseilles to

[9] William Saroyan, *The Bicycle Rider in Beverly Hills* (New York: Scribner, 1952), pp. 117-18.

Havre, from Havre to New York, and from New York to
California. He wept a good deal, naturally.[10]

As fiction writers do, Saroyan preserves some aspects of
reality and alters others: his brother Henry was in fact three
years older than Saroyan, born in 1905, while William was born
in 1908. Armenak Saroyan died in 1911 when Saroyan was
three years old, so the story takes place in 1919. Saroyan
disguises his brother's birth in Erzerum, and he does not reveal
the place of his father's birth in Bitlis. Henry is named Krikor
in the stories after Krikor (Grigor) Lusavorich or Gregory the
Illuminator.

As we have seen, Saroyan journeyed frequently to Armenia.
In June 1935, following the success of his first book, *The
Daring Young Man on the Flying Trapeze* (1934), he met
Eghishe Charents in Erevan. And he went again to Armenia in
1960, 1976, and 1978. In 1964 he visited the great towns of
historic Armenia, among others, Trebizond, Van, Mush, Diar-
bekir, Kharpert, Bitlis, and Erzerum, which resulted in the plays
Armenians (1971), *Bitlis* (1975), and *Haratch* (1979). During his
visit to Erzerum, Saroyan decided to write a new play, *The
Istanbul Comedy,* which is presently in the William Saroyan
Collection at Stanford.[11]

In *Bitlis*, the play in which Saroyan recounts his visit to his
father's town, the author comments on the positive treatment he
received in Erzerum: "Surely you must have noticed by now
that wherever we have gone—Ankara, Merzifon [Marsovan],
Samsun, Trabizond, Erzeroum, Van, Tatvan, and now Bitlis—we
have met with nothing but warmth and high respect."[12] Thus,
when Saroyan finally actually arrived in Erzerum, he was hap-
pily surprised, although also clearly nostalgic as he sensed the
totality of the loss of historical Armenia.

In *Haratch*, which takes place at the Paris headquarters of a
noted Armenian newspaper, Arpik Missakian, the editor tells

[10] William Saroyan, *Little Children* (New York: Harcourt, Brace, 1937), pp. 123-
24.
[11] William Saroyan, *An Armenian Trilogy*, ed. Dickran Kouymjian (Fresno:
California State University Press, Fresno, 1986), p. 27.
[12] Ibid., p. 103.

Saroyan that she is weary of the elderly Armenian men who
come to her to print their memoirs, which she finds boring. But
in Act 2, her attitude softens and she declares:

> I want your memoirs. *Haratch* needs your memoirs. There are
> not many more of you older boys with memoirs of Van, Mush,
> Sassoun, Kars, Ardahan, Erzeroum, Dikranagerd, and all of the
> other great cities of our country. I made a mistake in not letting
> you know that your memoirs are the very thing *Haratch* needs,
> for that is the simple truth, as I am sure our other friends here
> will agree, will you not?[13]

It is natural that Arpik should include Erzerum among "the
great cities of our country."

Erzerum also enters the debate over the fate of Armenian
territory and what the Turkish people have done with it.
Hrachia, the editor from Soviet Armenia, declares in Act 2:

> What is it that the Turks have done with their ownership of our
> lands and cities, and with the banishment of our people, and
> with the continuing animosity toward all Armenian institutions
> and peoples—the few that remain in Istanbul and Ankara, Izmir
> and Erzeroum. I have heard of nothing. Certainly nothing of any
> interest to the world, to people everywhere. We have sent out
> through Aram Khatchatourian our music. Through Martiros
> Sarian our painting. Through Victor Hampartzoumian our
> science. And many many others. What about the Turks? Do
> they like being Turks?[14]

Noteworthy here is that Erzerum is seen to be as significant as
Istanbul, Ankara, and Izmir, in Saroyan's mind.

And yet another reference to Erzerum occurs when the
character named Bitlis, asked by Arpik Missakian whether he
will include his visit to the editorial office of *Haratch* in his
memoirs, replies: "When? Who can live long enough to remember all of his great experiences. I am still in Bitlis. I have not
even reached Erzeroum on the way to Trabizond and Samsun

---

[13] Ibid., p. 149.
[14] Ibid., p. 159.

and Bolis and Athens and Genoa and Marseilles and I have so much to remember, but nothing more exciting more pleasant than this gathering together of great Armenians."[15]

Thus, we can study as in a laboratory the ways writers transform the facts of their experience into art. Here again we have the itinerary of the Saroyan family, spoken by a character named Bitlis. Erzerum becomes a place on the road to the new world: what might have been for the Saroyan family a march of death becomes an enumeration of the cities through which they passed to new life—Bitlis, Erzerum, Trebizond, Constantinople, Marseilles.

In the play *Armenians* (1971), Saroyan creates a character named Erzeroum. While the characters, Bitlis, Moush, Knadjian, Jevelikian, and the rug merchant from Harpoot (Kharpert), quarrel over the proper destiny for modern Armenia, Erzeroum steps in:

> In a family there are many children. Each child has a character of his own. One may be swift in nature, another may be slow. A third may be melancholic, a fourth may be entirely blithe, and so on and so forth. It would be foolish if we imagined that in our family all of the children are alike. Let us not be surprised by any of our children. There is nothing wrong in a man who sells rugs for a living.
> *Knadjian.* Yes, that was nicely put. Are you perhaps a Presbyterian preacher?
> *Erzeroum.* No, but I don't consider it a poor profession. I am a farmer.
> *Jivelikian.* You don't speak like a farmer.
> *Erzeroum.* Nobody speaks like a farmer or a rug merchant or anything else of that kind. Every man is who he is before he is what he does for a living.[16]

It is significant that Knadjian asks Erzeroum if he is a Presbyterian preacher, for that was the calling of Saroyan's father. The character Erzeroum is highly thoughtful and philosophical, as are the other representatives of Armenian cities in the play.

---

[15] Ibid., p. 160.
[16] Ibid., pp. 83-84.

They are each identified from their city of origin: he *is* Erzeroum. As noted, Saroyan would typically quiz Armenians concerning their place of birth, and in this play each character symbolizes and represents his Armenian town with great verve and passion.

Loss, memory, art, recovery: for Saroyan writing is an act of transformation, of taking the raw materials of his life and the terrible truths of Armenian history and creating new possibilities of perception. Erzerum, the city of his brother Henry, one of the way stations of the Saroyan family's odyssey, came to have symbolic meaning to him as a great Armenian city—a city he frequently returned to in his work and finally in his life as well. In a letter to Harry Keyishian dated October 30, 1970, Saroyan, discussing future plans to come to New York and visit Keyishian's father, invokes Erzerum in connection with Mount Ararat and the Turkish occupation of his beloved Armenian towns: "I expect that someday when I am in New York again I will visit your father's place apparently very near the restaurant I sometimes go to: Ararat. We [Armenians] have that name everywhere: grocery stores, restaurants, coffee houses, tailors' shops, shoemakers, and so on and so forth, but Turkey has the mountain, and Kars, Ardahan, Ani, Van, Bitlis, Mush, Erzeroum and our proper country—time will do it, though, if it really matters, and one day Bitlis will be Armenian again."[17]

And I am sure that William Saroyan, who celebrated the glory of *being* above all else, lamenting the fact that "Turkey has the mountain" also would have wished Kars, Ardahan, Ani, Van, Mush, and his brother Henry/Krikor Saroyan's Erzerum might once again be places where Armenians could *be*.

[17] William Saroyan, "Letter to Harry Keyishian," in *Ararat: A Special Issue on William Saroyan* 25 (Spring 1984): 112.

INDEX

Association for the Defense of the Rights of Anatolia and Rumelia, 383

Association for the Defense of the Rights of the Eastern Vilayets, 378

Assyrians, 154, 180

Astghapert (Asdghapert; Astghaberd), 30, 58, 320, 322, 323, 331, 332

Astghapert Educational Association, 318, 325, 326, 328, 329

Astghberd. *See* Astghapert.

Asturian, Hovhannes, 202

Atamian, Sarkis, 409

Atatürk University, 61

Athens, 206n42, 417

Atticus, Greek Patriarch, 68

Austria, 216

Austria-Hungary, 372

Avag Vank, 59

Avetis (Garegin Vemian), 203, 204, 214

Avril, Philippe, 129

Ayvazian, Eghishe Vardapet, 193

Azatutiun Hayrenasirakan Miutiun (Liberty Patriotic Society), 193n13

Azerbaijan, 183, 184n86, 382, 393, 402, 404, 406

Azganver Hayuhiats (Patriotric Armenian Women), 320

Azgayin Miutiun (National Union), 277n39

Azgayin Sahmanadrutiun. *See* Armenian National Constitution.

Azgayin Usumnakan Khorhurd (National Educational Council), 263

Babayan, Bishop Zaven, 361

Babayan, Khosrov, 273n32, 277

Baberd (Papert), 2, 100, 136, 137, 138, 143, 145, 364. *See also* Baiburt.

Babylonian, 39

Bachmann, Walter, 101

Bagarich, 136

Bagayarich, 37, 38n13

Bagrat, *Eristav*, 93

Bagratid/Bagratuni, 1, 37, 64, 88, 97, 304

Bagrat *magistros*, 93

Bagratuni, Ashot, 97

Bagrevand, 51

Baiburt (Bayburt), 37, 46, 51, 57, 60, 156, 180, 213, 214, 226, 263n3, 274n34, 347, 349, 353-54, 356, 359, 368, 371, 393, 401; *sanjak*, 46. *See also* Baberd.

Baidarian, Markar, 324

Baku, 343, 367, 371, 381, 402

Balkan/Balkans, 135, 326, 336, 393

Balkan War (1912-13), 309, 323, 326, 332, 366

Banak (Bana; Penek), 27, 90, 96; Church of, 90-92

Barduz, 404, 406

Bardzr Hayk, 1, 3, 4, 26, 27, 31, 33, 41, 42, 61, 65, 136, 138, 144, 190, 192. *See also* Upper Armenia.

Bardzr Hayots Society, 199

Baronian, Hagop (Hakob Paronian), 276

Barsamian, Mgrdich (Mkrtich Parsamian), 277

Barshamina, 38, 39

Basen (Basean; Passin), 46, 74, 137, 138, 141, 143, 145, 263n3, 274n34, 347, 364, 377

Basil II, Emperor, 81

Batak, 184n86

Batnots, 138

Batum, 166, 326, 372, 373, 380, 381, 386, 390, 394

Plutarch, 82
Poghsoyian, Hovhannes, 277
Pontic, 63, 178, 181, 183n85,
184n86
Pontus Mountains, 1, 33, 138
Porter, Robert Ker, 132
Procopius, 66, 67, 69, 71, 72
Protectors of the Fatherland. *See*
Pashtpan Hayreniats.
Protestant, 4, 54, 265n12, 305, 330;
boys' school, 266, 306; girls'
school, 266; missionaries, 185,
306 335; population, 50; schools,
325. *See also* Armenian Prot-
estant.
Providence, Rhode Island, 324,
325, 326
Ptarij, 57
Ptghni, 97n30
Ptolemy, 40
Pushkin, Alexander, 409

Qaya, 177

Raffi (Hakob Melik-Hakobian),
205
Raouf Pasha, 242, 245
Rawlinson, Lieutenant Colonel
Alfred, 380, 381
Redcliffe (Canning), Stratford de,
British Ambassador, 164
Refayie (Refayet), 46
Reid, James, 28
Robert College, 384
Rock Wagram, 413
Rohkrämer, Thomas, 151
Roman/Byzantine, 26, 36; Empire,
1, 40, 41, 81
Roman Catholic, 50, 52
Romanov, Grand Duke Nicholas,
Viceroy for the Caucasus, 369
Romanov Empire, 370, 412
Romanus, Emperor, 78, 82

Rome/Roman, 1, 26, 34, 36, 38, 39,
40, 42, 54, 57, 69, 70, 71, 81, 82,
86, 137, 139
Rostom (Stepan Zorian), 206n42,
213, 214, 215, 217-18, 340
Russian Armenia/Armenian, 31,
180, 197, 200, 201, 365, 371,
376, 385, 402, 404, 406
Russian Empire, 3, 4, 48, 141, 142,
268, 293, 326, 341, 358, 366,
393
Russian Provisional Government,
31, 361, 362, 370, 371
Russia/Russian, 2, 46, 56, 133,
155, 160, 174, 177, 178, 181,
191, 205, 207, 212, 213, 216,
231, 235, 240, 250n49, 272n31,
279, 293, 299, 308, 309, 321,
336, 339, 340, 343, 344, 350,
358, 365, 383, 391, 402, 412;
army, 30, 53, 60, 193, 196, 197,
198, 199, 201, 220, 344, 351n51,
358, 359, 360, 362, 363, 367,
368, 369, 370, 371, 372, 385;
Bolshevik revolution, 31, 362,
371, 372; Civil War, 371, 402;
March revolution, 31, 361, 370
Russo-Turkish War (1828-29), 48,
53, 141, 296
Russo-Turkish War (1877-78), 28,
48, 53, 143, 166, 190n2, 192,
193, 195, 197, 205, 239, 244,
296
Russo-Turkish wars, 3, 46, 48, 53,
60, 147-87, 232, 344-47, 350,
359-60, 362-63, 365-83 *passim*
Rycaut, Paul, 128, 131

Saatetian, Bishop Smbat (Smpad
Saadetian), 60, 340, 352, 357
Saban, Bishop, 93
Sachtleben, William L., 29, 224-51
passim